GOT A REVOLUTION!

GOT A REVOLUTION!

The Turbulent Flight of Jefferson Airplane

JEFF TAMARKIN

ATRIA BOOKS
New York London

For Caroline and Max

"With you standing here I could tell the world what it means to love."
—Marty Balin and Paul Kantner, "Today"

ACKNOWLEDGMENTS

THIS BOOK REALLY BEGAN IN 1967 when, as a 14-year-old rock and roll kid living on Long Island, I heard "Somebody to Love," "White Rabbit" and then the *Surrealistic Pillow* album for the first time. The music of Jefferson Airplane suggested a more stimulating way of life and transported me to another place.

Nine years later, ensconced in a tiny Haight-Ashbury apartment in San Francisco, I began writing about music professionally, and as soon as I could swing the assignments I interviewed members of what had by then split off into Jefferson Starship and Hot Tuna. They were all intelligent, outspoken, creative, fascinating people and I wanted to communicate that. Within the next few years I nabbed most of the key figures, writing about them for several publications. Throughout the '80s I kept up with the musicians and tried to speak with them whenever I could.

Then, in 1992, when I learned that RCA Records was planning to release a Jefferson Airplane boxed set, I lobbied for the job of writing the liner notes and the label went for it. Since then, I've annotated more than 25 Airplane-related CDs, and for each new project I've interviewed the musicians again.

With those conversations as a basis, and having established working relationships with all of the major parties involved, I decided it was high time the world had a book on Jefferson Airplane. I've long felt they were one of the most important American rock bands, one that truly represented the exhilaration, experimentalism and chaos of the 1960s, and one whose gripping, sometimes unbelievable story needed to be told.

They were also one of the most successful organizations in rock, selling more than 50 million records worldwide throughout their long, convoluted history, increasing the size of their audience after each of two name changes. More than 20 albums and singles released as Jefferson Airplane, Jefferson Starship or Starship have received gold or platinum awards by the Recording Industry Association of America, indicating more than a million dollars in sales per title. In 2001, *Billboard* still ranked Jefferson Airplane/Starship among the all-time 50 leading sellers of albums and 65th on the singles chart. And in 1996, the Airplane was inducted into the Rock and Roll Hall of Fame, affirming their status among the elite.

Oddly, however, although hundreds of rock biographies have been published over the years, there had never been one about these talented artists and their complex relationships. The esteemed San Francisco journalist Ralph J. Gleason published a series of interviews in paperback form way back in 1969, and Grace Slick has been the subject of one biography and one autobiography, but no one had yet tackled the entire Airplane tale comprehensively, despite the group's undeniable impact on its generation. So I elected myself to do the job.

Without the cooperation of the artists, this book would not and could not have happened the way it did. As nearly all of the major individuals who took part in this saga were still alive and well, and at a point in their lives where they were able to reflect with some degree of perspective, I felt there was no excuse to tell the story without their involvement—they were, after all, the ones who lived it. Fortunately, virtually all of the main players in the story agreed readily to participate, and were extremely helpful, patiently answering, as best they could, my ceaseless questions about events and minutiae that in many cases took place more than 30 years earlier.

Hundreds of hours of interviews for this book were conducted between 1998 and 2001, and I used some quotes from my earlier interviews as well. All of the stand-alone, blocked quotes in the book are from interviews I conducted personally. Where other sources are used, they are woven into the narrative and attributed.

So, first I would like to thank the six extraordinary musicians who comprised the prime-era Jefferson Airplane lineup: Marty Balin, Jack Casady, Spencer Dryden, Paul Kantner, Jorma Kaukonen and Grace Slick. They all donated a great deal of their valuable time to help this project come to fruition, never attempting to influence what was said about them in the book and never once screaming, "Enough, already! How am I supposed to remember which shirt I wore on June 3, 1967?!"

Other former members of the Airplane also gave me their time and recollections: John Barbata, Joey Covington, Signe (Toly Anderson) Ettlin, David Freiberg, Bob Harvey and Jerry Peloquin all came up with great stories.

Bill Thompson, the former manager of Jefferson Airplane, Jefferson Starship, Starship and Hot Tuna, has a photographic memory and, when that wasn't enough, he made available to me his original calendars from 1968 onward, annotated with concert and recording session dates, meetings, etc. He was extremely supportive, enthusiastic and helpful throughout the project. His contribution was nothing less than vital.

From the various incarnations of Jefferson Starship, Slick Aguilar, Craig Chaquico, Pete Sears and Mickey Thomas were all graciously accommodating, as were Hot Tuna's Michael Falzarano, Sammy Piazza, Will Scarlett and Bob Steeler. Kenny Aronoff shared his remembrances of the 1989 Airplane reunion, and Peter Kaukonen had plenty to say about a number of topics of interest.

Pat Ieraci, known affectionately as Maurice, was a wellspring of information on the recording process, studio hijinks and the Grunt Records experiment, plus he and his family have gotta be the nicest people in the whole world. Thanks for the delicious baked ziti, Pat and Cecelia!

Cynthia Bowman, Toni Brown, Chick Casady, Michael Casady, Nadine Condon, Pat Dugan, Skip Johnson, Les Kippel, Bill Laudner, Glenn McKay, Jacky (Watts Kaukonen) Sarti and Todd Schiffman all worked closely with some or all of the musicians at one time or another, and their anecdotes and viewpoints were all priceless.

Producers/engineers Stephen Barncard, Larry Cox, Dave Hassinger, Rick Jarrard, Ron Nevison, Al Schmitt and Peter Wolf enlightened me on what took place within the studio walls.

Other musicians, both from the Bay Area community and outside of it, offered valuable insights: Sam Andrew, Jesse Barish, Bill Collins, David Crosby, Donovan, John Hammond, Mickey Hart, the late Nicky Hopkins, Al Kooper, Ray Manzarek, Country Joe McDonald, Barry Melton, Jerry Miller, David Nelson, Darby Slick and Peter van Gelder.

The San Francisco scene was always about more than just the music. Paul Baratta, Kim Fowley, Wavy Gravy, Chet Helms, Alton Kelley, Elliot Sazer and John Van Hamersveld each provided another point of view.

Members of the Airplane's families offered yet another look at who these people are and where they came from: thanks to Joan (Buchwald) Benton, Julia (Girl Freiberg) Brigden, Jean and Joe Buchwald, Alexander Kantner, China Kantner and Sally (Mann) Romano. Thanks also to Airplane friends and associates Halimah Collingwood (Sherry Snow), Barbara Langer, Trish Robbins, Ginger (Jackson) Schuster, Steve Schuster and Janet Trice Swinburne.

Various members of the media and/or the music industry added a piece or two to the puzzle: Special thanks to Dick Clark, and to Les Garland, Nicholas Johnson, Howie Klein, Michael Klenfner, D. A. Pennebaker, Tom Smothers, Joe Viglione and Howard Wolf, who cleared up some myths.

Matthew Katz, the Airplane's first manager, turned down my requests for a formal interview but answered some questions via e-mail, for which I am thankful. Thanks also to Ray Andersen, Jimmie Haskell, Tommy Oliver, the late Neely Plumb, Tom Rounds, Howard Solomon (owner, Café Au Go Go), Omar Spence, Owsley "Bear" Stanley and Martha Wax, all of whom provided information.

In addition to those who were interviewed for the book, I had the good fortune to receive encouragement and assistance from many others.

First, special thanks to Dawn Eden for hooking me up with my book agent, Sheree Bykofsky. And thank you, Sheree, for handholding and sage advice! Thanks also to Janet Rosen at the agency.

Kimberly Meisner, my patient editor, did a commendable job knocking some sense into my head and helping transform a sprawling epic into a readable book. Paul Schnee nurtured the project at Atria Books and helped guide it along during the initial writing process. Thanks also to Demond Jarrett, Steve Lee, Lisa Keim, John Paul Jones, and everyone else at Atria who worked on the book in one capacity or another.

My brother, Dave Tamarkin, is a walking encyclopedia of concert dates, band personnel, set lists and concert recordings. Fortunately for both of us, he loves this music as much as I do. Thanks for everything, bro. Thanks also to Dave's wife, Maria Tamarkin.

Bonni Miller, who worked with me for years in the editorial division at *Goldmine* magazine, transcribed each and every interview tape and read the raw manuscript. When I say I couldn't have done this without her, I mean that, literally.

Steve Bedney also read an early draft and offered valuable editing tips.

Rochelle Rabin sifted through tons of legal paperwork regarding the lawsuits involving the Airplane and Matthew Katz and managed to both make sense out of it all and help greatly in crafting the sections of the book dealing with those cases. Thanks also to Jeff Webb, who acquired most of those court papers for us.

Joel Selvin of the *San Francisco Chronicle* made available to me his entire thick file on the Airplane. What a vital treasure trove that was! Thanks also to Nick Meriwether.

Ben Fong-Torres, David Gans, Blair Jackson, Dennis McNally, James Olness, Alec Palao, Ed Perlstein (Center to Preserve Music Culture), Bob Sarles (Ravin' Films) and Steve Silberman, all of them San Francisco's finest, supplied inspiration and useful information. Jo Johnson of the Moby Grape family provided some invaluable background on a couple of the book's most colorful characters.

Thanks also to writers and researchers Johnny Angel, Robert Christgau, Scott Cooper, Bill Dahl, Fred Dellar, Peter Doggett, Colin Escott, Pete Frame, Michael Heatley, David Hinckley, the late Cub Koda, Harvey Kubernik, Colin Larkin, Mark Lewisohn, Bill Parry, Mark Paytress, Barbara Bladen-Porter, Domenic Priore, Todd Prusin, Robert Pruter, Steve Roeser, Steve Rowland, William Ruhlmann, Stan Soocher, Bruce Sylvester, Dave Thompson, Neal Umphred, Richie Unterberger, Robert Weiner, Allen Wiener, Paul Williams (*Crawdaddy!*) and Carlo Wolff. They all contributed to my knowledge and understanding of the subject matter.

The folks at BMG Music made their Airplane archives available to me over the years and were supportive of the project. Thanks go to Dalita Keumurian, Glenn Korman, Randall McMillan, Alex Miller, Michael Omansky, Mike Panico, Frankie Pezzella, Rob Santos,

Bruce Scavuzzo, Tom Tierney and to Paul Williams of the House of Hits.

Michael Gaiman at Mission Control was instrumental in setting up some interviews and helping me find some missing persons. Thanks also to Ron Rainey Management and to Scott Harrison.

Both the New York Public Library and the San Francisco Public Library's San Francisco History Center provided a wealth of information on genealogical and historical issues. Thanks also to Leslie Czechowski of the Grinnell College Archives in Iowa.

In New York, Don Paulsen, John Platt and Bob Strano besieged me with Airplane videos, tapes and photos. Also helping with photo leads were Jonathan Kane, Linda Matlow, Roger Ressmeyer and Sue Schneider. Thanks to Mike Frankel for the slide show. And thanks also to Mira Tamarkin.

Karen Deal Balin, Kimberly Chaquico, Linda Imperial, Vanessa Lillian Kaukonen, Annie Piazza, Diana Balfour Quine, Jeannette Sears and Lauren Taines displayed great restraint as I grilled their soul mates about their sordid pasts.

On the Internet, there is a "listserv" mailing list for fans of the "Jefferson Family," 2400 Fulton Street (in honor of the address of the Airplane's former headquarters in San Francisco), and the folks who post messages on the list are the most knowledgeable and incisive Airplane fans on the planet. There must be a hundred or more Fultonites on the list who took the time to offer information and/or materials during the course of my research, and I know I'd miss a lot of them if I tried to make a comprehensive list, so I'd just like to thank everyone on the mailing list but specifically mention Jeff Zahnen, who maintains it. For more information about 2400 Fulton, see the Sources and Resources section at the back of the book.

On a personal level, thanks to Sherry Max, Kenny Tamankin, Larry Rossman, Mike Bauch, and especially Lydia Sherwood for support and encouragement throughout the project.

My father, Nat Tamarkin, passed away shortly after the project got under way, but was pleased that his boy done good, and my mother, Gert Tamarkin, also let me know often that she was proud, even if she still thinks it's all too loud. It was in August 1967 that I went on a family vacation with my parents and brother to the Expo '67 World's Fair in

Montréal. On our way out one day we passed a pavilion whose marquee read "Free Concert Today—Jefferson Airplane." I begged and they said okay, but only 15 minutes. Dave and I went in, heard some intense, crazy music, saw lots of wild-eyed people gyrating madly and I snapped a picture from afar. Only years later when I found the photo in an album did I realize I had not seen my first Airplane gig at all, but rather their opening act, the Grateful Dead. Hey, whatever it was, I liked it. It felt right. I wanted more. I soon got it.

Finally, the loves of my life, my wife and most trusted editor, Caroline Leavitt, and our precious, perfect son, Max Tamarkin, who learned the words "Jefferson Airplane" around the same time he learned the word "cookie," didn't always get to see a lot of me while I was working on this, but they never once complained. And they always greeted me with smiles when I emerged bleary-eyed from my cocoon. There's a lot of talk about love in this book, but I never have to go beyond my own walls to find it.

Go ride the music . . .

Jeff Tamarkin
May 2003
JeffAirplane@aol.com

CONTENTS

FOREWORD

by Jann Wenner, editor and publisher of *Rolling Stone*

IN 1967, THE GREATEST ROCK AND ROLL CITY in America was San Francisco. And the most exciting and successful rock and roll band in San Francisco and the country was Jefferson Airplane. With their electrifying live shows and two great anthems of that euphoric summer, "Somebody to Love" and "White Rabbit," Marty Balin, Grace Slick, Paul Kantner, Jorma Kaukonen, Jack Casady and Spencer Dryden—the classic Airplane lineup—were both architects and messengers of the psychedelic age, a liberation of mind and body that profoundly changed American art, politics and spirituality. It was a renaissance that could only have been born in San Francisco, and the Airplane, more than any other band in town, spread the good news nationwide.

The Airplane were the perfect missionaries. Casady's opening bass lick in "White Rabbit," Kaukonen's searing guitar solo in "Somebody to Love" and the breathtaking voices of Balin, Slick and Kantner evoked everything that was magical about San Francisco—the poster art and light shows; the hallucinatory joy of a night on the Fillmore dance floor; the spirit of camaraderie and radiant change. In their musical influences and personal histories, the band members also embodied the roots and contradictions of their birthplace. Balin was the working-class romantic with the heartbreaking voice, Kantner was a refugee of Jesuit schooling, rescued by folk music and Beat culture; Kaukonen and Casady came from serious educations in blues and R&B. And Slick was an icon of cool and fight, a product of prep school and upper-class privilege who brought style, biting wit and incomparable singing to the revolution.

Together they were unbeatable. In a city full of amazing bands, the

Airplane were Stars, outshining the Charlatans, Quicksilver Messenger Service and, for a long while, the Grateful Dead. The Airplane house at 2400 Fulton Street was the big hang, the local capital of hippie luxury. But for the Airplane, success was also a soapbox, and the *Billboard* charts were the front lines. Inside the commercial thrust of the band's records was a rebellious heart, a frank running commentary on drugs, sex and democracy unlike anything else on Top 40 or even underground FM radio. And in the midst of the hits and indulgence, the Airplane scored the most important victory of all: They survived, first as Jefferson Starship in the 1970s, today as legends, one of the most important and inspiring bands in rock.

The Airplane were also *Rolling Stone's* flagship band: We emerged together in San Francisco and built our work and art on similar dreams. The band's manager, Bill Thompson, came from the world of journalism, and it was Bill who first got Ralph J. Gleason to see the Airplane at the Matrix and write about them in the *San Francisco Chronicle*. At the same time Ralph and I conceived and founded *Rolling Stone*, I saw the band in every club and dance hall in the city, in Golden Gate Park and at people's houses. The Airplane appeared on the front page of *Rolling Stone's* debut issue, November 9, 1967, in a news flash on the making of *After Bathing at Baxter's*. They were featured on the cover four times—twice as the Airplane, twice as the Starship—and we reviewed and reported on their music and lives the entire way: the albums, the drug busts, the censorship battles with RCA Records.

To this day, when I hear "Somebody to Love" and "White Rabbit," I go back to the ecstasy and energy of 1967, when the whole world was about to change and San Francisco was the nexus of hope. We at *Rolling Stone* were proud to be the Airplane's voice in print, because they were our voice to America. This is their story.

INTRODUCTION

by Paul Kantner

Forward
. . . as always
Paul Kantner here
San Francisco calling

So what are you lookin' at?
What are you lookin' for?

The secrets
The reasons
The joy of the path?

Nearly most anyone can learn *how* to play music
Fewer can discern the *why*
It helps to have Pete Seeger and the Weavers in your (my) distant
    past
as Reverend Gary Davis was in Jorma's
or as Betty Grable was in Grace's

Why San Francisco?
Why Jefferson Airplane?

divine guidance
destiny
fortuitous circumstance
or just another bozo on the bus???

Beyond all that, I just call it random factors
seeming events, unplanned, unexpected and, most importantly,
    unprepared for
can't predict them, plan for them, or even know how to deal with
    them
beyond your capabilities
a vortex

In our time 'twas things like (in no particular order):
Rock & Roll
Little Richard—*THE* King!—and Jerry Lee, Chuck Berry, Bill
    Haley, James Dean. Brando's *Wild One*
And then, the Beatles and Stones, et al., in music
the advent and escape of LSD into the culture
marijuana for white children
peyote, mescaline, et al.

the birth control pill . . . leading directly to:
the sexual revolution (there goes the neighborhood)
the civil rights movement (ditto)
the atomic bomb
the ban the bomb movement . . . leading to
the peace movement
the Beats
modern jazz (Miles, Coltrane, Roland Kirk . . .)
good Communists—Pete Seeger, et al.
JFK
The JFK murder and the aftermath
Martin Luther King
RFK
(that dulled the sheen of America and only served to define the
    path—Nixon, Hoover, early Goldwater, blah blah blah)
. . . getting my drift?

All that swirl of events and factors led to one fuckingly cool
    decade, didn't it, my brothers and oh my sisters?
Random factors!!!

For me, it was the Kennedy aftermath that really shut the door on
    that world that had existed before. There was no further
    reason to hold hope in those people, those values, that plan.
An entire alternate quantum was necessary.
And all the rules died.

And into this world was born
Jefferson Airplane
Thank god
for me, anyway . . .

Don't get me wrong. Our new parallel universe in San Francisco
    in nineteen-sixty-something did not become a world couched
    in hate, or rejection or soapbox ranting, but a world involved
    in creating a new and different realm for ourselves . . . naive,
    hopeful, a children's crusade, if you will . . .
and a world in which we were *for* things, not necessarily against
    things. We succeeded in creating a place that, for a brief,
    shining moment, embodied all that we had been taught to hold
    dear.

Built on the truths of the lessons we were taught, and learned (!),
    in those god-awful civics classes:
truth, beauty, justice (!) and the American way
equality before all the sky

And dedicated to the proposition that *all* men were created equal,
    and were destined for a place where life, liberty and,
    particularly, the pursuit of fucking happiness were definable
    and achievable goals.

And fuck all the rest of you and your terribly outdated, illogical
    and, most importantly, untruthful ways.

And it worked for a while, didn't it?
showed that it was possible?
And some of those thought patterns continue today
ripples felt well into this next century
The Sierra Club mentalities

Amnesty International
the ACLU thought streams

Jefferson Airplane was a mirror of its time
madmen in a time that demanded madmen
a catalog of the highs and lows
a reflection of the quantum

Shining, I like to think, in its own peculiar way

And that's what they rarely see or write about or televise or film
    effectively in their endless analyses of "the sixties," San
    Francisco and those particular years. Mostly they will focus on
    the drug overdoses, the chaos and anarchy, the "breakdown."
    Nobody concentrates on the uplift, the freedom, the passion,
    the unbridled joy and ecstasies of the era, well beyond the
    mere sex, drugs and rock and roll.

San Francisco
49 square miles surrounded entirely
by reality

Know what I mean?

And now, we live
we go on
we still explore
the *why* of making music

The future is about nerve
Those who have it
Those who don't.

Over & out
Battle Stations! . . .
con amor

Paul
San Francisco

"Music is the weapon of the future."
—*Fela Kuti*

HALFWAY DOWN THE STAIRS IS A STAIR

IN AKIRA KUROSAWA'S 1950 JAPANESE FILM CLASSIC *Rashomon*, four strangers are discussing a rape and murder. Each agrees that brutal crimes have been committed, but that's about all they can agree on. The seductive film's strength is that it presents each side of the story in a completely plausible way, so that the viewer comes away unsure which of the versions presented is the truth—if any.

Like *Rashomon*, the story of Jefferson Airplane, the band's Paul Kantner has astutely postulated, is also one of many truths. There's a cliché these days, "If you can remember the '60s, you weren't there." It's a wisecrack intended to imply that denizens of that era were so zonked-out that their craniums have been reduced to space dust. But that's not the case here; the former members of Jefferson Airplane were there all right, and they do remember the '60s. Yet each has such a distinctive personality and outlook on life, and the '60s was such a kaleidoscopic whirl, that, despite being in the same band, no two of them experienced the Airplane years the same way.

As in *Rashomon*, reality here is a composite—or a close approximation of one—that materializes when all of the jagged pieces of the jigsaw puzzle are locked into place. Through interviews, extensive research, common sense and process of elimination, an epic tale slowly—and incredibly—emerges.

Jefferson Airplane was comprised of highly creative, forward-thinking individuals who, by happenstance, found themselves involved in one another's lives at the vortex of the '60s. Breaking down barriers, challenging authority and oneself, walking on the edge of society's rules—it was a way of life not only for the Airplane but for a generation. A genuine youth movement was unfolding, something that had never before occurred. Whether the young—led by the cutting-edge rock bands of the day—were going to change the world was never the question in the '60s, only how.

Today we may snicker at the naivete of such sentiments, an honest belief that rock musicians who sometimes had trouble finding their own feet could somehow make a serious dent on global politics and basic human consciousness. But perhaps the notion isn't as nutty as it seems in this revisionist, jaded age. More was accomplished than some care to admit. A revolution did occur, even if most of its skirmishes involved ideas and words rather than weapons and bloodshed.

For San Francisco's Jefferson Airplane, music was the vehicle toward change. They celebrated freedom, growth, searching, risk taking, adventure, independence, open-mindedness, love and good ol' fun. Their music promoted strength in the face of adversity and staring mortality in the eye. It rejected phoniness and fear, especially of the unknown and the hostile. It proclaimed that it was okay, even recommended, to believe in the impossible, to trust oneself, to surrender to fate and encourage chaos. The Airplane, in a manner of speaking, even said it was okay to be a jerk, as long as being a jerk was what you really wanted to be.

Just as there are few definitives in the Jefferson Airplane story, there is no single, accepted way of experiencing their music. For some, the Airplane was at its core a collective of superb musicians honing their craft as they went along, engaging in brain-bending improvisational safaris into rugged sonic terrains previously uncharted. The band's instrumentalists, particularly lead guitarist Jorma Kaukonen, bassist Jack Casady and drummer Spencer Dryden, were widely praised for their aptitude as innovative players.

Others gravitated mainly toward the distinctive voices of Grace Slick, Marty Balin and Paul Kantner, and to their words, which any two listeners—including, quite often, those in the band—might interpret differently. Or might choose not to interpret at all.

Some perceived the Airplane, from around 1968 on anyway, as a politically oriented band, while others preferred the love songs or their impressionistic works. Some thought of them just as a dance band and, for sure, they were that too—music to take large quantities of drugs and go berserk to.

The Airplane fits all of those descriptions, and more; that's what kept them alive for seven years. When all of those components came together, a force beyond the members' control took over and transformed Jefferson Airplane into a mind-altering substance. That they attained greatness on many occasions goes without saying; that they had their bad nights does too.

The Airplane was a constantly mutating organism—no two albums were alike and personnel changed several times. Concerts were unpredictable. One never knew where they would head next, and neither did they. Kantner describes the Airplane as an "orchestra without rules." That's how they—and their faithful—liked it.

That it couldn't last forever was virtually written into the script.

1 IF ONLY YOU BELIEVE LIKE I BELIEVE

MARTY BALIN WAS a single-minded creature from the day he was born. All he ever wanted was to express himself artistically—his way. Some called him a loner, moody, weird, an egotist, but he had no time to waste with that. Marty didn't suffer fools gladly.

> MARTY BALIN: I've always had the same mind, the same consciousness. I just couldn't wait till my body grew up to my mind. I was totally aware of who I am, what I wanted to do and what I was going to do.

By high school, he was accomplished enough as a painter to earn a scholarship, talented enough as a dancer and actor to handle both Shakespeare and musicals. But more than anything, the kid could sing. Marty, his mother once said, could whistle a tune before he could even speak.

Marty's father, Joseph Buchwald, had also been an iconoclast, ambitious and determined. Joe's parents, Samuel and Celia, had, like hundreds of thousands of persecuted eastern European Jews during the early part of the 1900s, shipped out to America with little more than a promise in hand. They settled eventually in Cincinnati, where Samuel found work within the family trade of tailoring. Joe was born there in 1917 and married an Episcopalian orphan girl born Catherine Eugenia Talbot. Jean, as she was called, also hailed from Cincinnati, where a couple named Charles and Magdalene Edmonds had adopted her.

Joe and Jean remained in Cincinnati, where their two children were born, first a girl, Marilyn Joan, in 1938 and, on January 30, 1942, a boy, Martyn Jerel Buchwald.

If the Buchwalds' interfaith marriage was a problem for others, Joe didn't lose any sleep over it. Although Joe's parents had instilled in him the traditions and beliefs of Judaism, he couldn't stand the discipline religion demanded. Religion divided people, and he believed in bringing them together. The Buchwalds judged others by who they were, not by the God they worshipped—or didn't worship.

When Marty was young, his father took him to jazz concerts, where he witnessed Louis Armstrong and, on another occasion, a fierce drum battle between Gene Krupa and Buddy Rich. Sitting up front, Marty stared bug-eyed as the spotlights darted from one musician to the next. He was transfixed by the effect the music and the lights had upon the audience. As soon as he was old enough, he told himself, he would be up there too.

It didn't take long. Both of the Buchwald kids loved to express themselves, but Marty was unstoppable. When Joan, as Marty's sister preferred to be called, took tap dancing lessons, her kid brother watched like a hawk and quickly picked up the moves. Soon he was adept enough to join his sister in shows, often the only boy dancer in the troupe.

Marty also painted and was crazy about the movies and the theater. He performed whenever and wherever someone would listen—acting, singing, dancing—especially after the family relocated to California in the late '40s. They hadn't planned on living in San Francisco, but Marty had been a sickly child, suffering from a heart murmur and a bronchial condition, and the Buchwalds hoped that the fresh, dry air of Phoenix would cure him. But there was no work for Joe in Arizona so the Buchwalds pushed westward, first to Los Angeles and then north. Living in a predominantly black neighborhood in the city of Richmond, across the bay from San Francisco, Marty was drawn to gospel, the earthy sounds of early rhythm and blues and the street-corner vocal harmony style later known as doo-wop.

In the 1950s Joe found work in San Francisco as a lithographer. The family settled in the Haight-Ashbury district, years before the arrival of the flower children.

JOAN (BUCHWALD) BENTON: It was just a little neighborhood, kind of pleasant, with not a whole hell of a lot going on.

All the while, Marty performed, whether in a church choir or a local production of *The Nutcracker Suite*. His infatuation with the world of the arts expanded as he reached his teens, and he took his first steps toward becoming a professional, landing jobs as a dancer and playing the role of Action when a touring company of *West Side Story* came to town. In the audience one night was Bill Thompson, who later became Marty's roommate and eventually Jefferson Airplane's manager.

> **BILL THOMPSON:** Marty was considered kind of unusual at that time. He was in a gang, the Lairds. He tried to act tough, but he wasn't; he was the kind of guy that, when he'd get mad at someone, would say something like, "You knucklehead!"

By 1962, Marty, now 20, was bored and restless. He'd been granted a scholarship to the Art Institute in San Francisco and had taken college preparatory classes at San Francisco State College while still in high school, but any desire to complete his formal education was quickly supplanted by his interest in the arts, including the new sounds that were sucking in the nation's youth. Rock and roll was his generation's private language, and Marty spoke it well. He'd become hooked one evening when his sister threw a party, playing the same three rock and roll records—by Elvis Presley, Little Richard and Jerry Lee Lewis— over and over again. Marty also loved the raw rhythm and blues sounds of the day: Ray Charles, Bobby "Blue" Bland.

> **MARTY BALIN:** But I never wanted to be like [the black artists]. I wish I could, but I'm not. I remember at high school they had this thing etched in stone: "Of all the good things in the world a man can learn, is to learn himself." And all I ever wanted to do was to learn what music was inside me.

By the early '60s, most of the trailblazing rock and roll stars were already fading from view: Elvis was in the army, Chuck Berry in trouble with the law, Little Richard in the ministry and Buddy Holly dead in a plane crash. While rock certainly didn't die during this era, as one popular song later suggested, its public face, encouraged by governmental pressure and several other factors, did temporarily soften. Well-scrubbed, nonthreatening pinup boys—Frankie Avalon, Fabian and a bunch of guys named Bobby—replaced the wild boys.

Marty fell somewhere in between. He was too soulful and sexy to throw his lot in with the whitewashed camp, but his solid education, city street smarts and artistic background didn't allow him to engage in the sort of unfettered country-boy abandon that had marked the first wave of rockers.

Still, with his brooding demeanor, dark good looks and natural ability with a song, Marty saw no reason why he too couldn't be a singing star, and when an opportunity to record presented itself, he took it. While in L.A. accompanying a female acquaintance to a music publishing house, he found himself invited to sing background vocals on a session. There, at Gold Star Studios, Marty came to the attention of Jimmie Haskell, a young arranger who had made his name working on Ricky Nelson's hit records. Haskell took Marty under his wing, but nothing came for free. Marty's father first had to pay for the session, hiring the musicians, singers and recording crew, and *then* Haskell would record the aspiring performer.

Marty learned the three songs Haskell had asked him to learn and brought in one that he cowrote, "I Specialize in Love." When Marty arrived at the studio, he found a full orchestra and several of the top session musicians in Los Angeles there to accompany him, among them guitarists Glen Campbell and Barney Kessell, drummer Earl Palmer, keyboardist Jack Nitzsche, Milt Jackson on vibes and bassist Red Callender. The Blossoms added background vocals.

After the sessions were completed, Joe Buchwald, along with Marty's new manager, Renny T. LaMarre, worked out a deal with Challenge Records, a label owned by cowboy singer/actor Gene Autry, to release the four songs on two 45 rpm singles. But when the records were sent out from the pressing plant, the singer's name on the record label did not read Marty Buchwald but, rather, Marty Balin.

MARTY BALIN: They didn't like my name. Renny LaMarre had a bunch of theaters and one was called the Bal. One day he said, "How about Balin?" I couldn't think of anything named Balin, so I said okay.

The Challenge recordings never made the charts, but they reveal the neophyte Balin to be a well-developed vocalist already. Although the music is consistent with the frothy pop of the era—post-Elvis, pre-Beatles romantic, teen idol puffery—with more than a trace of Gene Pitney and the young Paul Anka in Balin's style, all of the hallmarks of

Marty's later approach with the Airplane are present and accounted for. The voice glides easily, swoops and swirls fluidly, playing with the lyric in a nonlinear, often surprising manner. It's a smooth, flexible voice, unabashedly alluring without being schmaltzy. Balin's mastery of dynamics is fully formed; the honey in his voice is as sweet as it would ever be. Yet there is a toughness behind it too, as if the singer has been around the block a few times more than he's letting on.

Despite the failure of the Challenge records, Marty Balin enjoyed his first taste of the rock and roll life. But he was soon drawn into folk music, which had become pervasive throughout the Bay Area over the past several years, ever since the Kingston Trio had broken out of San Francisco in the late '50s. With a preponderance of colleges in the Bay Area, and a student population that tended to lean left politically, folk had become the music of choice for the post-high school set. By 1963, artists like Bob Dylan and Peter, Paul and Mary had reached the mainstream with songs that carried a message. With a young president in the White House, the civil rights movement dominating the news and the dual threat of nuclear annihilation and the escalating Cold War, the puppy love–obsessed rock and roll of the day could no longer speak to an increasingly disaffected college-aged youth.

Marty Balin got by on his nylon-string Martin guitar, and his voice adapted easily to the high-spirited lead and tight harmony singing preferred by the folk groups. He began hanging out at the Drinking Gourd, a folk club at 1898 Union Street in San Francisco. One night in April 1963, he met three other singers looking to form a group.

Led by multi-instrumentalist Larry Vargo, the Town Criers also featured tenor and baritone singer Bill Collins, who played 12-string guitar and five-string long-neck banjo, and Jan Ellickson, a female soprano whose vocal style was similar to that of Joan Baez. Marty became their featured male vocalist, singing tenor and playing guitar and string bass. Having dabbled in songwriting for several years (his first composition, written around 1959, was called "Wish I Were"), Marty also teamed with Vargo to come up with original material.

Also in 1963, Marty married his girlfriend, a Las Vegas dancer named Victoria Martin. They took an apartment on 16th Avenue, and their daughter, Jennifer Ann, was born later that year. The group played regularly at the Drinking Gourd through 1964, and was also booked at college campuses and the hottest local folk clubs: Coffee & Confusion, the Coffee Gallery, the Hungry i and Barney Gould's Gold Rush.

Reviews were encouraging. The *San Francisco Chronicle* covered the Town Criers on three occasions, calling them first a "great find" and then a "beautifully harmonizing folk-singing group." By January of 1964, the paper was raving: "The upsurging folk group pours out three-part harmony, then doubles back with counter melody . . . strong, unusual balanced sounds that have been exciting audiences since they first joined forces."

The Town Criers' repertoire was fairly typical of young folk groups of the time, a mix of the traditional and new, of political and social commentary tempered with humor, songs like Hoyt Axton's "Greenback Dollar," the spiritual "Oh Mary, Oh Martha" and the Jimmy Dean hit "Big Bad John" (done as a parody of the right-wing John Birch Society). "Wayfaring Stranger," a song recorded by dozens of folk acts, provided opportunities for the Town Criers to show off their individual vocal skills, and Marty took a solo turn on "900 Miles," an Odetta tune. The group recorded its gigs on several occasions, but never released an album or single.

By the middle of 1964, the Town Criers' run, as was true for many of the folk revival groups and soloists during this period, was coming to an end. Dylan had sounded the clarion bell: the times they were a-changin'. President Kennedy had been assassinated, domestic unrest and America's involvement in the Vietnam conflict were escalating and young people were starting to band together in their own communities, with their own rules.

The '60s was beginning in earnest, but folk music was not to be the sound of the decade. Once the Beatles arrived on American soil in February 1964, nothing would be the same again. Collins was the first to exit the Town Criers, in the spring of 1964. By June the group had packed it in. Marty went to work with his father in the lithography trade, hoping to put together enough money to go to Europe and study sculpture.

At the same time, Marty's brief marriage was on the rocks. While still legally attached to Victoria, he started seeing Janet Trice, a registered nurse from Brooklyn.

For several months during this interim period Marty performed as a solo artist. Jacky Watts, an English girl who'd just arrived in the Bay Area, happened upon one of Marty's shows in June 1964. That evening marked the beginning of a long professional and personal relationship between Jacky and what was to become Jefferson Airplane.

JACKY (WATTS KAUKONEN) SARTI: My first night in San Francisco I went to the Drinking Gourd, which was a spit-in-the-sawdust type of place. Marty Balin was playing there, doing a Rod McKuen song. There was this really rowdy drunk and Marty stopped almost in midword, removed the drunk from the bar and then went right back into his word, and carried on singing. I thought this was astonishing.

Jacky soon moved into an apartment on Frederick Street with Janet Trice and Judy Barry, the future wife of Bill Thompson. Marty, meanwhile, had it all figured out by March of '65. A new musical hybrid called folk-rock, exemplified by San Francisco's own Beau Brummels and soon to become a national craze via groups like the Byrds in L.A. and the Lovin' Spoonful in New York, was beginning to bubble under on both coasts. Marty decided to form a band, one that mixed folk-rock's pointed songwriting and electrified rock and roll with the musical freedom of jazz. He'd incorporate the other arts that had always captivated him: graphics, dance, whatever was available. He'd be its leader, its guiding force and spirit.

MARTY BALIN: I had seen Trini Lopez do a folk song with an electric guitar. I said, "That's the direction it's going." But the folk people were prejudiced; nobody wanted drums in those clubs in the folk era. So I was really an outsider at the time.

Marty also decided to open a nightclub, similar to the folk rooms he'd played with the Town Criers, but catering to the fans of this new sound. He'd decorate it, help publicize it and provide the music. It would be a sensation, and his band would make history.

Now, if only he had the backing capital—and others to share his vision. He approached Bill Collins about joining him in his new venture, but Collins had a steady gig as a solo performer. Marty sat in the Drinking Gourd wondering who among the singers there might go for his idea.

MARTY BALIN: One night they had a hootenanny. This guy came in and he had two [instrument] cases. He was a weird-looking guy. I said, "Hey, give him my spot. Let me see what he does."

And it was the funniest thing. He started to play, and then just stopped. He said, "I can't do this."

And for some reason I said, "That's the guy. That's the guy, right there."

His name was Paul Kantner.

2
ALTERNATE QUANTUM UNIVERSES

ONCE DESCRIBED AS being "resistant to authority and control," San Francisco has, since its inception, served as a final refuge for those whose ideas and lifestyles are too unacceptable, or just too bizarre, to survive in the mainstream. For the most part, San Franciscans have always co-existed peacefully, not only tolerating aberrant behavior, but often celebrating and encouraging it. The city has long been a mecca for artists, radicals and eccentrics, an intellectual stronghold.

For a musician, San Francisco provides the ideal climate in which to create. Seiji Ozawa, a former conductor of the San Francisco Symphony, once said, "There is a very free feeling in this city. People who live here have very free minds, which is very important for me to make music."

Paul Kantner is a San Francisco original: unconventional, colorful, bright, self-assured, cerebral, cosmopolitan and fiery. He has also been called strong-willed, arrogant, self-righteous, pushy, impertinent, oblivious, autocratic and confrontational to a fault, but his obstinacy and steadfastness are primary reasons he has been able to maintain a committed following. Kantner has confessed that his greatest talent isn't singing or playing the guitar, but rather his ability to keep the thing going at all. For one so fond of chaos, his organizational skills are laudable.

It's part of the Kantner mystique that he often speaks in inscrutable riddles, skirts an issue only to return to it after innumerable detours, generalizes when specifics are required and pinpoints when he can get away with simplifying. Unlike so many who proselytize for a living, Paul Kantner usually comes armed with facts to support his outbursts— or enough bluster to fake it—and understands the responsibilities that come with his power as a celebrity musician. He subscribes to the old countercultural maxim: Think globally, act locally.

Friends and associates often say that Paul is really a shy, private man, reluctant to open up, difficult to get close to, that he's blocked out much of his past. He has been known to carry long-term grudges, harass, cajole and taunt, and to throw tantrums. His legendary stubbornness can be infuriating, his unwillingness to compromise unreasonable. Others have found him intolerable and worse.

But once that wall is penetrated, many who've known him say, there is no one who is kinder, more generous, more fun, more down to earth, more stimulating or more loyal.

Born March 17, 1941, Paul Lorin Kantner has, for the better part of his life, served as a one-man chamber of commerce for the city of San Francisco, touting the city's incommensurable charms and open-armed hospitality. San Francisco, by its very nature, makes it easy for him to flourish.

The only native San Franciscan in Jefferson Airplane, Kantner is an enigmatic individual whose core being is wrapped up in the city's laissez-faire, raffish nature.

PAUL KANTNER: If I'd been born in any other city I probably would have been executed by now.

Paul's adult life has, in effect, largely been a reaction against an early childhood that saw him experience abuse, tragedy and abandonment and subsequently he spent his precious youth in the most rigid and trying of environments: religious and military schools. The situation in which he found himself was utterly antithetical to his natural free-spiritedness and left a permanent mark on his soul. Yet history must applaud his miserable predicament, for Paul Kantner—and by extension Jefferson Airplane—could not have turned out the way he did had he led a so-called normal '50s childhood.

His father, Paul Schell Kantner, born in 1889 to Charles and Belle Harnet Kantner, was a white-collar sales worker of German extraction. Originally from Bruceton, West Virginia, the senior Paul Kantner was a considerably older man of 51 when his namesake was born—he had already sired two grown children with a previous wife by the time he married 39-year-old Cora Lee Fortier.

PAUL KANTNER: I have a half sister, Mona, almost 30 years older than me, and I had an older half brother, Bob, who flew Corsairs off aircraft carriers in the Mediterranean during World War II. He had one of the Kantner distinctions of clumsiness, dropping his aircraft into the Mediterranean about seven times—and living.

Cora Kantner, Paul's mother, came from mixed German and French stock. Her own mother, Grace, had performed in vaudeville, and was on her second marriage, to a man named Harry Johnson, when Cora was born. Paul's few memories of his mother are not all pleasant—one prominent recollection is of her threatening to throw him in the oven when he misbehaved. When Paul was only eight, Cora died of polio, and instead of attending the funeral, young Paul was packed off to the circus.

Now hitting 60 and left alone with a young son, the elder Paul knew he could not raise the boy himself. He enrolled him in St. Joseph's Military Academy, a Catholic boarding school in Belmont, California. Young Paul Kantner, future rock and roll firebrand, was, essentially, raised by the Catholic Church.

PAUL KANTNER: I was an abandoned little child. The school was out of necessity, but still rather drastic. Nuns and guns. As a result, I now fear nothing.

After St. Joseph's, Paul transferred to St. Mary's College High School in Berkeley, run by the progressive-minded Christian Brothers. It was Kantner's only positive experience with formal education.

Paul's innate lust for learning, and something of a loner's personality, had earlier led him to indulge heavily in science fiction, fostering a life-long obsession with the mysteries of the unknown and the possibilities of exploration: he would rarely feel earthbound again. He read voraciously, losing himself in what he calls "alternate quantum universes." Later his visits to these imagined foreign shores would provide fodder for much of his songwriting.

In 1959, Paul began attending Santa Clara University, another Catholic institution. Having graduated from a high school that encouraged self-discovery, this no-nonsense Jesuit college was destined to be a bust for Kantner—it was too late to turn back now. Next came San Jose State.

PAUL KANTNER: I was beginning my senior year there when circumstances of society pulled me away into another quantum and I just went with it. School became irrelevant.

Those circumstances, in no particular order, included sex, drugs and—not yet rock and roll, but folk music. All three, Paul surmised, were preferable to going to class. Playing guitar and banjo, which he'd begun doing in 1959, was infinitely more enjoyable than sitting through lectures.

During his last semester at San Jose, Paul fell into a relationship with Ginger Jackson, a good-looking, black-haired girl with a big smile. Ginger had, at 18, married and almost immediately divorced a Santa Cruz surfer and folk singer named Bill Laudner, who would later resurface as a key component of the Airplane's road crew. Paul and Ginger lived together for about two years, and worked at the same Santa Cruz cannery. Or, to put the situation into proper perspective, she worked at the cannery while Paul hung around, providing moral support.

GINGER (JACKSON) SCHUSTER: Sorting out rotten vegetables made me vomit. Paul would come by and cheer me up, and clown around. He was funny and smart, fairly ambitious and driven, all the things you'd want in a guy. He was already practicing all the time. And there was a lot of pot smoking and drinking going on.

Paul had been introduced to marijuana through future Jefferson Airplane lead guitarist Jorma Kaukonen (pronounced YOR-ma COW-ka-nen), who, at the time, went by the nickname Jerry. A new transfer student at Santa Clara around the same time that Paul was dropping out, and a year older than Kantner, Jorma was already an accomplished fingerpicking-style guitarist, well-traveled, intelligent and steeped in the blues. Although the two were only acquaintances at the time, they traveled in the same orbit, playing clubs like the Cabale in Berkeley and the Tangent and Offstage on the Peninsula, the chunk of land south of San Francisco encompassing the cities of San Jose, Santa Clara and Palo Alto, as well as their numerous suburbs.

The fact that Jorma had turned Paul on to marijuana made them members of the same semisecret society. Although the drug would become ubiquitous later in the decade, in the early '60s it was still something of an underground phenomenon, considered dangerous and addictive by the mainstream of society, something only crazed jazz musicians and hipster comedians ever went near.

But despite the warnings that it would lead to harder stuff, the folk crowd on the Peninsula had made pot a staple of its diet, and Paul Kantner discovered quickly that alternate states were a place in which he was happy to reside—marijuana became a lifelong companion.

In short time, Paul dumped the cannery job, quit school and concentrated on playing music. Paul and Ginger's place became one of several way stations for the clique of musicians and dopers that was developing on the Peninsula and in Santa Cruz, a quick hop to the southwest. Many of the people who surface in this tale—Kantner, Bill Laudner, David Crosby, David Freiberg, Jerry Garcia, Jorma Kaukonen and Janis Joplin among them—put in appearances on the Peninsula during these pre-rock years.

For Kantner, there could be nothing better than this life. Only a few years ago he was a prisoner of nuns. Now he was a dope-fiend folk singer with good friends who were willing to try almost anything. He was primed for the future.

PAUL KANTNER: The '60s made up for my school years. I was like a child in a candy store. We were educated to pursue beyond the boundaries of the known. I was taught that you're supposed to take what you know and build on it.

Folk music was a step up from the John Philip Sousa marches that had been the music of choice at military school. Kantner's entree into folk had been the Weavers. Comprised of Pete Seeger, Lee Hays, Fred Hellerman and the female singer Ronnie Gilbert, the leftist harmony quartet had, in the staid early 1950s, turned politically potent folk songs into popular music. They had barely survived the McCarthy witchhunts of the era, but ultimately emerged intact and more popular and influential than ever.

For the young Paul Kantner, the Weavers were an inspiration. He devoured their music, along with that of other folk stars of the era. Paul found himself greatly affected by the open exchange of ideas that took place among those who played and listened to folk music. They were an intellectual crowd, a literary bunch, and no topic was taboo—he was at home in their world.

Having amassed a repertoire, Paul began performing in folk clubs while still attending college, both as a solo performer and as part of a trio. Alternating on Gibson six-string guitar, Vega banjo and a hand-made twelve-string guitar, Paul played venues like the Folk Music Theater in San Jose. He became increasingly involved in other aspects of the local folk scene as well, for example, teaching guitar and banjo at Norm Benner's San Jose music store, where Jorma also taught. After the Folk Theatre was transformed into the Offstage, Kantner and some of the other folkies set up the Folklore Center in a corner of the club, selling guitar picks, strings and marijuana.

Paul also helped book artists to play at the club, bringing in a diverse grouping of performers both nationally popular and locally renowned, among them Mother McCree's Uptown Jug Champions, a lively, irreverent group that included future members of the Grateful Dead. Paul rubbed elbows with all of the folkies that passed through the area, among them a young David Crosby, who Paul had first met in San Jose in 1963. Crosby was a rebellious loner whose chief pleasure was found in singing.

> **DAVID CROSBY:** We got into this thing because we couldn't do anything else. It's what we were born to do. When we started playing, there wasn't any money to be made, but we were happy campers.

For a brief while, Kantner moved south to Venice Beach near L.A.—the only time Paul lived away from northern California. He shared a house with Ginger Jackson, their friend Steve Schuster and Sherry Snow, a blonde folk singer who had also met Kantner and David Freiberg in San Jose. Crosby was also in Venice at the time.

> **DAVID CROSBY:** We were trying to make a living being folkies. We'd all read *Stranger in a Strange Land* and we kept all our money in a bowl, on the mantelpiece—if you got some you put it in there and if you needed some you took it out.

In Venice, the living was cheap and easy. Getting by, and having a good time, involved little if any effort. But occasionally the real world poked its head in the door, as it did when President Kennedy was assassinated on November 22, 1963.

PAUL KANTNER: For me the Kennedy assassination proved the linchpin point of our generation, which almost switched the universe—what R. Crumb calls the Space-Time Motherfucking Continuum—over 180 degrees. Everything that was before was not after that.

The unfolding of events throughout the remainder of the '60s, Kantner has said, will never be—cannot be—properly analyzed or explained. There have been a few times during the course of history when—like all of the planets aligning—certain elements of history, culture, politics, science, art and human consciousness all coalesce simultaneously into a new totality. The '60s—which brought into focus the Beatles, LSD, Vietnam, the assassinations, the sexual revolution, space exploration and the civil rights and peace movements—was one such time.

In 1964, Paul and Ginger returned north from Venice and, along with some of the others in their crowd, got a place in Holy City, halfway along the mountain road that connects San Jose to Santa Cruz. The gang eventually ran out of money and skipped town for San Francisco, renting a five-bedroom place on Turk Street. But not before they had tasted the delights of lysergic acid diethylamide, LSD-25, an event that would alter their lives in a most profound manner.

Paul Kantner didn't have to be coerced into taking LSD. After becoming an avid fan of the leaf of the *cannabis sativa* plant—marijuana—he was primed for the next step up the hallucinogenic ladder. Acid opened him up to a whole other plane of existence.

PAUL KANTNER: Acid came in about a year after marijuana. I remember one night at the Offstage, a guy brought a Fender amplifier and a Fender guitar, with reverb and vibrato, and LSD, all in one fell swoop. Went off into the cosmos.

Acid was hardly a new creation when this posse of young California musicians got hold of it. It had been around since 1938, when Albert Hofmann, a Swiss chemist, accidentally synthesized the substance. By the 1960s, LSD had found its way to celebrities who helped spread the word about its miraculous properties: novelist Aldous Huxley *(Brave New World)* was one of the first major proponents of the drug's use, and actor Cary Grant was an avid experimenter. Poet Allen Ginsberg, Harvard psychologist Dr. Timothy Leary and Ken Kesey, a Stanford graduate student and aspiring writer, were other high-profile advocates. Eventually, so too were the Beatles.

There is no overstating the enormous impact that Hofmann's cocktail had on life during the era of the Airplane. But it was not the beginning or end of the story.

PAUL KANTNER: Acid for us was just a tool rather than a religion, like a good dessert after a fine eight-course meal. It was as good as several other tools.

At the Turk Street apartment, there was always music. Crosby's friend Jim McGuinn, a guitarist who'd become enamored of the Beatles of late—and had dared to play their songs folk-style in L.A. clubs—was one houseguest. Crosby, Kantner and Snow also liked to pack their guitars and head down to the Coffee Gallery, where they too would play Beatles songs. They also worked up interpretations of songs by Bob Dylan, who had, for a couple of years now, been the most significant folk singer in America.

So Kantner wasn't overly surprised when, a few months later in early 1965, Crosby and McGuinn turned up in a rock and roll band, the Byrds, or when their interpretation of a Dylan song, "Mr. Tambourine Man," became the number one single in America. Nor was he shocked when, in the early spring of 1965, Dylan himself committed folk blasphemy by releasing *Bringing It All Back Home*, an album that consisted of both electric rock and acoustic folk. The folk purists raised hell, but the album went to the Top 10.

Kantner had crossed the line toward rock and roll himself after seeing the Beatles' film *A Hard Day's Night*. He'd been a sideline fan of the early rock and rollers—Little Richard, Chuck Berry, Dion and the Belmonts—but when the softer, prefabricated singers took over from the rebels in the late '50s, Paul had stopped listening to pop radio and tuned in to folk. The Beatles lured him back.

Paul was stoked for the change. Like so many other events that now seem so monumental, there wasn't much thought behind the move, it just happened when it did. He hadn't forgotten how otherworldly that electric guitar had sounded through that Fender amp the first time he'd taken acid. The Weavers were cool, but the Beatles were the future.

So maybe Paul had electricity on his mind that night in March of '65 when he stepped onto the stage of the Drinking Gourd on Union Street, then decided not to go through with it.

PAUL KANTNER: It was a noisy, drinking kind of crowd. So I said, "This sucks. I've had enough, good-bye."

As I was leaving Marty said, "Hey, you want to start a band?"

3

LET'S GET TOGETHER

SAN FRANCISCO, PRIOR to the mid-'60s, had not been much of a rock and roll town. The city hosted its fair share of homegrown combos, but no one in the music industry looked to San Francisco for signs of the next big thing. During the era when Top 40 and AM radio reigned, only a handful of hit singles came out of the city. There were few recording studios in town or places for rock and roll bands to play.

San Francisco prided itself on being an intellectual center. Jazz and folk music were popular, but those styles didn't sell to kids, and the money in the record biz was, increasingly as rock and roll took a bigger slice of the pie, about appealing to the youth market.

Beatlemania gave San Francisco rock the kick-start it needed. The rush by young Bay Area rock and roll fans to buy electric guitars and comb their hair over their foreheads was as swift as it was anywhere else. The first San Francisco rock band to make an impact nationally was the Beau Brummels, who took a mix of haunting folk harmonies and Beatlesque electricity to the charts in early 1965 with "Laugh, Laugh" and "Just a Little."

The Charlatans were closer to the mark. Attired like acid-addled exaggerations of Old West characters, they played an electrified, often warped variation on old-timey jug band music and blues. They had style and vision: The rudiments of the San Francisco rock scene— the light shows, the psychedelic posters, the frenzied dancing to am- plified music and the bucketloads of LSD—were all in place when the Charlatans began their brief moment of glory in the early summer of '65.

However, the Charlatans were headquartered not in San Francisco but hours away at the Red Dog Saloon in Virginia City, Nevada. And although some intrepid Bay Area hipsters made the pilgrimage, the

Charlatans had mostly an implied, indirect effect on the growing community of disenfranchised young rock and roll–bred artists, students, musicians, activists, post-Beat poets, dopers and unclassifiable oddballs mushrooming in San Francisco.

If a true San Francisco rock environment was going to rise, it would have to be up to Marty Balin and Paul Kantner to create one.

MARTY'S BAND was going to require a rhythm section if it was going to rock for real. To play the standup bass guitar, Marty recruited 30-year-old Bob Harvey, an acquaintance who had performed bluegrass music on the Peninsula in a group called the Slippery Rock String Band. One night at the Drinking Gourd in March of 1965, Harvey had overheard Kantner and Balin discussing forming a folk-rock group. Harvey asked if he might join too, was invited to rehearse and was in.

Marty already had a drummer in mind. Jerry Peloquin was the boyfriend of Jacky Watts, the young British woman who was now rooming with Marty's girlfriend Janet. Peloquin had played drums in the United States Marine Band and had held a job with the Capitol police force in Washington. Upon moving to San Francisco, he became an optician and soon fell into a relationship with Jacky, facilitating the meeting with Marty.

Marty and Paul also wanted to bring a female singer into their nascent, nameless group. They had heard a woman named Signe (SIG-nee) Toly at the Drinking Gourd hootenannies and remembered her having a powerhouse of a voice—she could belt out the blues with the best of them but also worked wonders in a more traditional folk harmony setting.

Born in Seattle and raised in Portland, Oregon, Signe Ann Toly had sung in a group imaginatively dubbed Two Guys and a Girl, which once performed at a rally for presidential candidate John F. Kennedy. A series of accidents sidelined her for a couple of years, but by the end of 1964, she'd begun singing in San Francisco's folk clubs. Signe joined Marty and Paul's new band, but kept her day job as a secretary for several months, until she was sure this thing was going someplace.

With the vocal team and the rhythm section in place, the group was quickly taking shape. Now they needed a place to call home.

• • •

THE MATRIX WAS the ideal name for the nightclub at which this new band was going to give birth to the San Francisco rock scene. A matrix is a point from which something originates, takes form or develops; it's also another word for womb.

But that's not where the club's name came from. Elliot Sazer, one of the three engineers who financed and, along with Marty, founded the club, coined it.

> **ELLIOT SAZER:** It's also a mathematical term. We used to have a wall at the Matrix that had a collage on it. About half of the wall was pages from matrix algebra books. People used to stand, stoned, in front of the wall and try to figure out what this stuff meant.

Marty had hooked up with Sazer and his two friends, Ted Saunders and Paul Sedlewicz, after the trio heard him singing one night at the Drinking Gourd. When Marty told them his idea of opening a club and showcasing his new band there, they listened.

> **ELLIOT SAZER:** He said he'd round up musicians, and we would own a piece of them. In return, we would put up the money and buy them their instruments and give him a piece of the bar. It wasn't planned. Paul [Sedlewicz] and I did not get together one night and say, "We're very unhappy with the sound of music and we're going to change it."

Sazer walked around San Francisco until he stumbled upon a failing pizza restaurant called the Syndicate, at 3138 Fillmore, near Lombard, in the Marina district. The trio bought the site from U.S. Pizza for $12,000, free and clear of debt. The engineers received 1,200 shares of stock from the owner as part of the deal, and Marty was given a 25 percent ownership in the club in the form of stock options. In return, it was agreed, the other three board members—Sazer, Saunders and Sedlewicz—would get 12 percent of the group's future earnings. The engineers renovated the pizza joint, turning it into the club of their dreams. Marty began painting a mural, hung a large model airplane from the ceiling and added other decorative touches. Other band members and their friends pitched in, painting and carpentering. By the beginning of the summer of '65, the group was in rehearsals. They agreed to give 105 performances at the Matrix over the next seven years and the engineers fronted the band $1,300 for instruments.

It was time to make music. They worked up a handful of blues, folk, and rock and roll standards, and adapted some songs by local writers.

BOB HARVEY: Nobody was writing original stuff yet. David Crosby had one song that he wanted us to do called "Flower Bomb": "I'm gonna build a flower bomb and drop it on your mind. I'm gonna build a flower bomb . . ."

DAVID CROSBY: I refuse to answer on the grounds that it may incriminate me. It's not a real song. Never happened. This conversation never took place. Apocryphal.

SIGNE (TOLY ANDERSON) ETTLIN: No, that's honestly one we did. He wrote that and gave it to us.

SOMETHING WAS STILL missing, though. None of the lead guitarists they'd auditioned were quite right for what the band had in mind. Paul and Marty could play decent rhythm guitar, but they needed someone with a distinctive lead sound, a guitarist who could truly drive them, give them an edge and an identity. All of the great new bands had strong lead guitarists: Eric Clapton in the Yardbirds, Keith Richards of the Rolling Stones and George Harrison with the Beatles. The Byrds had Jim McGuinn, who had made the switch from acoustic guitar to the electric Rickenbacker 12-string seamlessly. And down on the Peninsula, Jerry Garcia, a talented bluegrass player who'd frequented the folk clubs, had recently morphed into an inventive, risk-taking electric rock guitarist with some locals called the Warlocks.

Marty was sitting around with Kantner in Paul's apartment, working on tunes, wondering where he could find a guitar player that knew how to rock and roll. Then his instincts kicked in again, just as they'd done not so long ago when he'd approached Paul at the Drinking Gourd.

MARTY BALIN: Jorma was teaching guitar to some guy upstairs. He came walking down and he looked perfect. He had the guitar in his hand and he looked like Mr. Style. I said, "Who's that?"
Paul said, "Oh, that's Jorma Kaukonen."
"What's he do?"
"Oh, he plays great guitar but he's much too good for us."

4 BLUES TRAVELER

THE LAST THING that Jorma Kaukonen ever expected was to play rock and roll again. He'd done it before, in the late '50s, but Jorma was a kid then; that was just for kicks. That was before he'd given his soul to the blues. Blues was music to be taken seriously; rock and roll was play stuff. But even a purist can be persuaded by technology.

> **JORMA KAUKONEN:** I had just graduated from college and I was thinking about going to Europe. My wife, Margareta, was Swedish so we had family over there. So when Paul asked me to play in the band I said no at first. But I went up to San Francisco anyway, to audition at the Matrix, and Ken Kesey was with them; he had a tape delay unit with him, an Echoplex. They plugged my guitar into it and I just flipped. They sucked me in with gadgets.

Jorma Ludwik Kaukonen—older of the two sons of Jorma Ludwig Kaukonen and the former Beatrice Love Levine—was worldlier than the others in Jefferson Airplane. Although born in Washington, D.C., Jorma had spent considerable time during his youth on foreign soil, absorbing the native cultures. His wanderlust—both literal and musical—has remained unabated throughout his adulthood.

Jorma's paternal grandfather, Jaakov (later changed to Jacob), had come over from Finland early in the twentieth century, settling in Ironwood, Michigan. He married Ida Palmquist, also Finnish, and worked in the iron and copper mines before settling into his chosen profession as a custom tailor. The couple sired Jorma Sr. and two brothers, the family eventually moving to Los Angeles.

Despite harboring radical political views, most of Jorma Sr.'s professional life was spent serving his country. His first government job was with the FBI, where he worked as a fingerprint clerk. His leftist leanings soon led him to the like-minded, Connecticut-born Beatrice

Love Levine. Beatrice's father, Dr. Benjamin Samuel Levine, was the son of a Russian rabbinical scholar, but Ben's wife, the former Vera Faith Haskevitch, had been the family's true powder keg—an anarchist, she had once been imprisoned in Siberia.

Jorma Sr. and Beatrice married on Christmas Day in 1936, and Jorma Jr. arrived on December 23, 1940. Due to the nature of Jorma Sr.'s work, the Kaukonen family rarely stayed in one place for long during the '40s and '50s, making stops in several states before settling down in the D.C. area. It was during that transient period that the elder Kaukonen's colleagues took to calling him Jerry. The name Jorma was difficult for them to relate to, and at a time when anything remotely Germanic-sounding was suspected to be un-American, he accepted the nickname without complaint. Little Jorma, tired of being constantly tormented over his appellation as well, also became Jerry after some kids threatened to string him up as a Nazi spy. He didn't return to his given name until shortly before joining Jefferson Airplane some two decades later.

During one of his trips home, Jorma Sr. and Beatrice produced a little brother for Jorma Jr., Benson Lee Kaukonen, who came to be called Peter. By 1952, the expanded family was on the move again, living in Pakistan, where Mr. Kaukonen had become the director of the Asia Foundation—possibly a front for the CIA. They returned to D.C. for one year and then, in 1956, headed for Manila, in the Philippines. Kaukonen next graduated to the State Department, for which he worked until his retirement around 1970. Jorma Jr., after years of being shuttled around the world, finished his senior year at Woodrow Wilson High School in D.C. in 1959.

Washington had a bustling music scene in the late '50s, and the teenage Jorma Kaukonen imbibed it all eagerly. Rock and roll, country and western, rhythm and blues and black gospel all moved him, and he was taken in by bluegrass, which had a strong foothold in D.C. But the music that went straight to his heart was the blues.

Jorma had befriended a boy named Charles Casady, known to his friends as Chick. A year older than Jorma, Chick had two younger brothers, Jack and Michael. Both Chick and Jack had contracted rheumatic fever as children, and it was during the many hours Chick spent confined to bed, listening to far-off radio stations, that he discovered the music called the blues. Chick took to buying records on independent labels like Vee-Jay and Chess, and Jorma shared his enthusiasm.

Like a couple of the other future members of the Airplane, Jorma took piano lessons as a child, attempting to play classical music, but neither the instrument nor the form excited him. He dabbled in the violin and the recorder, learning enough on the latter to play some duets with his father, but he couldn't commit to any of those instruments either—they didn't have the magic. The guitar, though, that had potential. He could visualize himself coaxing some sounds out of one of those. Soon, he began to see how he might want to do little *except* play guitar.

JORMA KAUKONEN: A guy named Michael Oliveri taught me to play "Down in the Willow Garden" and "Jimmy Brown the Newsboy." My dad bought me a Gibson guitar and I started to take classical lessons from a guy named Sophocles Papas, a Greek-American who was a protégé on some level with Andrés Segovia. I learned three or four chords and a couple of different keys, and I thought, That's it! I'm ready to go.

Just as he was getting ready to go, though, the Kaukonen family again went, leaving for their year in the Philippines. Jorma continued to play guitar while there, but it wasn't until he returned to D.C. that he put the instrument to good use, forming a rock and roll band with Jack Casady called the Triumphs. Their first paying job was on New Year's Eve 1958–59 at the Chestnut Lodge in Rockville, Maryland, a hospital for the mentally ill, after which they played the usual teen gigs: dances, parties, local clubs. The Triumphs got as far as making a record, waxing two original songs, "Magic Key" and "Symbol of Our Love." One copy of the 78 rpm acetate, owned by Jorma, is known to survive, but it has never been released to the public.

The group's days were numbered anyway: In 1959, before the Triumphs could take over the rock and roll world, Jorma was off to Antioch College in Ohio, leaving rock and roll behind for the next six years.

At Antioch, Jorma admittedly didn't spend as much time studying as he could have. Instead, he indulged heavily in the guitar, learning from an advanced player he met at the school, an older student named Ian Buchanan. Buchanan became a mentor not only to Jorma but to another aspiring blues guitarist who attended Antioch, John Hammond Jr., the son of the legendary record scout who'd discovered jazz giants Billie

Holiday, Count Basie and Charlie Christian (and would later sign both Dylan and Bruce Springsteen).

JOHN HAMMOND JR.: Jorma and I hit it off because we loved blues. I was too intimidated to ask him to show me any stuff, but I would watch. Ian and Jorma hung out together, and every now and then Jorma would invite me up to the guy's place to watch him play.

Jorma was taken by Buchanan's "finger-style" guitar playing, in which the strings are played with the fingers rather than a pick. A basic finger-picker usually uses the thumb to keep an independent rhythm going on the lower-toned strings, while two or three of the other fingers provide the melody. Fingerpicking is applied to numerous styles of music, from ragtime and jazz to Celtic and varieties of world music, but traditionally it has been used most often in blues, country and folk. Fingerpicking is usually associated with the acoustic guitar, although Jorma later managed to become quite adept at adapting the style to the electric guitar.

Buchanan, who would later commit suicide, introduced Jorma Kaukonen to the blues of the Reverend Gary Davis, setting the young musician on one of the most meaningful journeys of his well-traveled life. Already in his sixties, the blind Davis, steeped in the Piedmont style of blues, was undergoing a career renaissance when Jorma first heard him, as were many other blues musicians who had labored in obscurity for decades before being taken to heart mostly by white college students during the folk revival of the '50s and '60s. Davis's songs have remained in Jorma's repertoire since those college days.

Jorma stayed at Antioch for two years. Then, at the recommendation of Hammond, he took a work-study job at a physical rehabilitation institute in New York. At night, he'd spend his time frequenting the clubs of Greenwich Village, taking in a number of performances by his blues heroes as they came through town.

When the New York lark was finished in 1961, Jorma returned to Ohio. But his mind was no longer on his studies and Antioch was happy to see him go. He headed back to the Philippines for a while, attending a Jesuit college and studying anthropology. Then, in 1962, Jorma enrolled at Santa Clara, the same school that had briefly provided a roof over Paul Kantner's head.

JORMA KAUKONEN: Santa Clara was a very conservative school. I was not a freak by any stretch of the imagination, but by their standards I was. There was one other freak in the school, named Bob Kinzie. Bob said, "You know, there's a guy you really ought to meet." So we went to Santa Cruz, and I met Paul Kantner. He was living in a shack with a bunch of surfers and had a charming folk act.

While attending Santa Clara, Jorma met many other musicians who would impact his life. He played often at the Folk Theater/Offstage, where he ran into Jerry Garcia, Dino Valente and Billy Roberts, later the author of "Hey Joe," one of the most often covered songs of the '60s.

Some of the most rewarding experiences for Kaukonen during this period were his frequent collaborations with a singer from Port Arthur, Texas. Janis Joplin was, like Jorma, a blues purist, with a bawdy style modeled after the likes of early twentieth-century singers Bessie Smith and Memphis Minnie.

JORMA KAUKONEN: She knocked everybody's socks off. We played together and I remember thinking, Man, it truly doesn't get any better than this. And I still feel that way. I think that she was one of the greatest blues singers that I've ever heard.

Jorma befriended two other guitar players during this time that would have an impact on his musical development. The first was the Maryland-born Steve Talbot, a regular at the Cabale, a Berkeley club where Jorma also played. The other was Steve Mann, from San Leandro, California, who had left college in the early '60s to try his luck in the music business. A song Jorma later wrote, "Mann's Fate," was composed in deliberate emulation of Mann's style.

JORMA KAUKONEN: I remember when Janis was alive we used to say, "How long do we have to do this before we'll be real?" Steve Mann was real to me—I was a college student and he worked on the railroad.

By mid-1965, a degree in sociology from Santa Clara firmly secured, Jorma left academics behind to pursue his true vocation, the guitar. Before that, though, at the beginning of 1964, he had taken his parents up on an offer to tour the Soviet Union. Jorma saw the tour as an adventure not to be passed up.

But any notions of gaining something culturally from the voyage were quickly supplanted by romance. On the way to Leningrad, Jorma met the tall, striking Margareta Lena Pettersson, a 20-year-old from the south of Sweden. After Jorma returned home, they wrote letters back and forth and it was agreed she would come to live with him. With a little coaxing from his father, Jorma quickly proposed to Margareta. They were married in California just weeks later, on January 29, 1964.

She was an intelligent woman who spoke five languages and had a talent for art. But from all accounts, not the least of them from Jorma, Margareta could be a difficult woman, prone to extreme behavior and violent mood swings. Their tempestuous relationship was troubled from the start and stayed that way—for more than two decades.

> **JORMA KAUKONEN:** The marriage was classic impulse stuff, but I don't think we were a very good couple together. She was really bright, but incredibly self-destructive. She was a ball-buster, no question about it. Some people liked her, some people hated her; you couldn't ignore her, there's no question about that. But she kept me focused on a lot of traditional stuff that I might not have done otherwise.

Jorma continued playing the folk circuit and teaching guitar, virtually oblivious to the arrival of the British rock and roll hordes. He began to develop a following, including Bob Weir, a teenager from the Peninsula who reportedly tape-recorded Jorma's performances in order to study his technique.

Jorma also continued to collaborate with Joplin whenever possible. Prior to one of their engagements at the Coffee Gallery, Jorma set up a tape recorder at his apartment to capture their rehearsal. Those tapes later made the rounds among collectors, notorious as much for the surreal clickety-clack of Margareta's unrelenting, oddly percussive typing in the background as for the glorious music Janis and Jorma made together. Two songs from the so-called typewriter tape, "Trouble in Mind" and "Hesitation Blues," later appeared on a Janis Joplin boxed set.

Had Margareta been home typing one early summer afternoon in 1965, instead of waiting on the streets of San Francisco's North Beach for her husband to return from his teaching job in San Jose, there's no telling how the story of Jefferson Airplane might have unraveled.

JORMA KAUKONEN: We were living in a $13-a-week hotel. There was a cop who was a real badass. He thought my wife was a hooker. They got one handcuff on her and before they could get the other one on she beat the piss out of him; she damaged the policeman severely. When I got home from work there were seven cops dragging her into the paddy wagon. My father had some highly placed political connections and they wound up intervening on our behalf. But we had to sign something saying we would stay in San Francisco.

The result of the couple's detainment was that Jorma auditioned for the new band being assembled by Marty Balin and Paul Kantner, and by June, the lineup was finalized. Marty Balin, Paul Kantner, Signe Anderson, Bob Harvey and Jerry Peloquin were joined by the last piece of the puzzle, Jorma Kaukonen. They practiced daily at the Matrix and tightened their presentation in their first few months together. They were confident that they had something original, even something special.

But what they didn't have was a name.

There have been many dubious tales of how the moniker Jefferson Airplane (never *the* Jefferson Airplane, just Jefferson Airplane) came about. One rumor is that it was the name of someone's dog, or perhaps a cat. Another is it was a slang term for a roach clip used to hold the tip of a burning joint.

But, simply, it was an in-joke that got carried away. A tribute to the bluesman Blind Lemon Jefferson and an inexplicable nod to the miracle of flight united to give rise to one of the great band names of the '60s.

JORMA KAUKONEN: Steve Talbot had named me Blind Thomas Jefferson Airplane. Steve Mann was Little Sun Goldfarb and Tom Hobson, another guitar player friend of mine, was Blind Outrage. The band was coming up with all these really stupid names and I said, "If you want something really silly, try Jefferson Airplane."

5
IT'S NO SECRET

MATTHEW KATZ—HE PRONOUNCED IT "CATES"—wanted so badly to manage this new group that called itself Jefferson Airplane. It wasn't that he knew anything about rock and roll, but he knew the power that music held and he believed that this group could make a difference, a positive one, in the world.

He'd been around. Born in Massachusetts in 1929, Katz had been to college and in the Air Force. He'd worked in vaudeville, had studied ballet and assisted his identical twin brother Bernard at the latter's company, which manufactured plastic coffee can lids and shrink wrap for record albums. He'd performed a bit as a folk singer-guitarist himself, and had managed a radio disc jockey, Fred Goerner, who was writing a book, *The Search for Amelia Earhart.*

Then, in mid-'65 came the flash: Matthew should put together a group of musicians, something to steer these troubled youths away from violence. This was important; this was going to be his life's purpose. He'd done some social work and had seen things that made his heart ache and his skin crawl: kids playing Russian roulette, kids jumping into sex before they were ready. Matthew knew that music, not preaching, was the diversion they needed.

Katz began to put out the word. At a music shop near the Matrix, he met Jerry Peloquin, who told Matthew about the new group that was forming. Within days Matthew Katz and Marty Balin were discussing their collective future.

Matthew had actually met Marty once before, when Marty was with the Town Criers. Impressed with Marty's singing, Matthew had offered right then and there to manage the folk group, but Larry Vargo hadn't agreed to Katz's terms, and that was that.

Now here was this same kid, Marty Balin, and this time they were on the same wavelength. During their initial conversations, Matthew mentioned that he had access to an unrecorded Bob Dylan song, "Lay Down Your Weary Tune," which Marty desperately wanted for the new group.

It was late June, early July. The band was just starting to coalesce into something worth paying attention to. Matthew told Marty he had to return to Los Angeles, where he had a second home, and that the musicians should not speak with anyone else who claimed they could do something for his group—he was their man. Still, there was some hesitation among some band members, who didn't quite trust the would-be entrepreneur.

MARTY BALIN: We wouldn't sign with the guy. He was a little weird for us, a little slick.

Jefferson Airplane would ultimately decide to sign with Matthew Katz though, and some would regret that decision for the next two decades, others for the rest of their lives. The protracted, wearying court battles over the terms of the Katz-Airplane contracts became legendary in legal circles, where Marty's given name of Martyn Buchwald is better known as one of the parties in a precedent-setting artist-management case than as a singer for Jefferson Airplane.

When he arrived in San Francisco, Matthew told the band his ideas. Everyone drinks coffee, he said, so he would place records inside coffee can lids (no doubt the ones manufactured by his brother's company). They would just play their music and have no worries, he assured them.

It didn't take long for the Airplane to agree that Matthew Katz should be their manager. Although some of the band members were still apprehensive, the majority now was convinced that Katz could put them on the musical map. Admittedly, the guy was odd—he wore ruffled shirts, flowing, red-lined capes, Spanish hats and a goatee, liked to drive fancy cars; he was flamboyant—but then, who were they to decide what was and wasn't strange? Maybe strange was what they needed in a manager—they certainly didn't want one of those old, cigar-chomping showbiz types.

JERRY PELOQUIN: Matthew was articulate, he had a lot of charisma, he was imperious, sort of a Rasputin-like guy. He was a dashing character. But he was also obdurate, free with giving commands and saying how things were going to be. He fashioned himself [as] a kind of impresario.

Matthew began working with the band on its presentation and appearance—he somehow managed to convince the men they needed to wear suits—and he bought them new equipment. They in turn agreed to show up for gigs on time and behave professionally. Matthew agreed to give them advice on lighting, staging, setup, even the music selection. He would attend their shows and try to get the media to do the same— he would act as their spokesman. What he would not do, at least not officially, was serve as their booking agent. That had to be someone else's job, the law said.

Marty, acting on his father's advice, suggested that Matthew, for his efforts, should receive 20 percent of the band's net income. That triggered the first disagreement. No way, said Katz. He would draw up a sliding scale: he'd take 10, 15 or 20 percent of the gross, depending on the amount of income brought in, the higher figure applying to any payment totaling more than $300. Their contract would carry a term of five years, and Matthew would have an option to renew it. The band would be paid a weekly salary, whether the musicians worked or not. It sounded like a good deal to the Airplane—at the time.*

Matthew also promised to put his publicity smarts into high gear. After the band finally settled on a name, Paul Kantner coined a slogan, "Jefferson Airplane Loves You." Matthew liked it: He would have buttons and bumper stickers plastered all over the city, he'd fly the phrase on a banner from the back of a plane and every time he or anyone involved with the group answered the phone, they would no longer say "Hello," but rather, "Jefferson Airplane loves you."

And, he said, they wouldn't call this music folk-rock, like everyone

---

* Matthew Katz declined several offers to be interviewed for this book. All of the information regarding Katz and his relationship with Jefferson Airplane in this book was gleaned from other interviews he's given over the years, interviews with people who have worked with him (including the Airplane) and from the volumes of court decisions and depositions taken during the two-decades-long series of trials involving Katz and the group.

else was doing. The music of Jefferson Airplane, declared Matthew Katz, was more like jazz-rock or, better yet, folk-jazz. That's what it should be called, he said, "fo-jazz."

Matthew Katz would make sure that everyone in San Francisco—and eventually the world—knew the name Jefferson Airplane. There would soon be a "San Francisco sound," he promised, and it would revolve around Jefferson Airplane.

Although Matthew began acting as their manager, the musicians still hadn't found a convenient time to sign a contract with Katz. They were too busy rehearsing for their opening, too tired from working on their show and getting the Matrix ready, too busy arguing amongst themselves over the terms of the contract. They insisted to Matthew that they did want to sign, but first they had more questions about what exactly Katz would do for them, what practical tasks he would perform to get them work, get them a recording deal. When Katz returned to Los Angeles to tidy up some of his affairs before the group's, and the club's, opening, he still didn't have a contract in hand.

IN LATE 1964, Marty Balin's wife left him and took their baby with her. Marty kept their apartment and took in a roommate two years his junior, Bill Thompson. Although Thompson and Balin had known of each other before—Bill had attended Washington High, the same school from which Marty had graduated—they had not become friends until after a mutual friend, Gary Blackman, provided a more formal introduction.

William Carl Thompson was a southerner, born in Oklahoma City in 1944. His parents, Blanche Seaton and Carl William Thompson, divorced when he was two, and Bill never knew his father—Bill didn't find out until many years later that he had three half-brothers via his father's remarriage. After high school, Thompson enrolled at City College of San Francisco, while simultaneously working as a copy boy at the *San Francisco Chronicle*. He was living in a hotel when Marty asked if Thompson wanted to move in with him. They got a place at 22 Belvedere in the heart of the city's colorful new youth mecca, the Haight-Ashbury district. Freed from the constraints of his marriage, Marty was in the mood to try new things.

BILL THOMPSON: He took LSD at Gary Blackman's house and we went outside, and he's looking at everything. A guy comes up and takes a knife out and goes, "Hey, man, give me your money."

Marty looks at me and goes, "Is this part of the trip?"

MARTY BALIN: Thompson's all nervous, and I'm just as loose as a goose. I'm looking at this guy and he's sparkling. I'm going, "Man, you are beautiful." And then I put my arm around the guy.

Finally the guy gave up and said to Thompson, "Hey, man, you better take this guy to a hospital."

It wasn't all play, though, in the summer of '65. As the projected opening date for the Matrix loomed ever closer, the band rehearsed constantly. The musicians also took their first tentative steps toward writing original material. "It's No Secret," Marty's first composition for the band, was a praiseworthy start, rhythmically forceful, with plenty of room for the rapidly developing Jorma and the rhythm section to show off.

The lyrics in the chorus were far removed from anything riding the top of the charts—they were almost depressing: "As I get older the years they get heavy for you/Is it any wonder I feel like my whole life is through?" Marty sang. Although the Beatles, Dylan, the Byrds, the Stones and other top artists had begun dabbling in more mature subject matter in 1965, pop was still basically music for teenagers, and although the San Franciscans had every intention of being successful, they let it be known from the outset that they would not pander to get there.

Most of the band's other early writings—Marty and Paul's collaborations "Let Me In," "Come Up the Years," "Runnin' 'Round This World" and "Bringing Me Down"—also boasted a sophisticated lyrical outlook and progressive instrumental arrangements that belied the musicians' brief time together. They'd learned what they needed to learn from their folk apprenticeship—that music could carry a message and still appeal to large numbers of people—and they understood from their rock and roll contemporaries that the music could be innovative and outreaching while maintaining an inherent excitement at its very core.

But most of the songs performed by the first incarnation of Jefferson Airplane were still borrowed from outside sources. For Signe, Jorma brought in "Chauffeur Blues," popularized by Memphis Minnie. Signe, Paul and Marty each took a verse of "High Flyin' Bird," a gorgeously melodic, melancholic folk song, written by West Virginian Billy Edd Wheeler, which they'd picked off of a Judy Henske album. From Dino Valente, writing under his given name of Chester Powers, they adapted "Let's Get Together." "Tobacco Road," written in 1960 by John D. Loudermilk, was another early staple of the Airplane's sets. So was "The Other Side of This Life," by one of Paul's heroes, Fred Neil, the southern singer-songwriter whose composition "Everybody's Talkin' " would later become a huge hit for Harry Nilsson.

There were also songs that were tried out for a while and then dumped. Marty did his best guttural Wilson Pickett soulman shouting on "In the Midnight Hour," a requisite tune for every mid-'60s garage-rock combo, and Jorma returned to the blues to give Jimmy Reed's "Baby, What You Want Me to Do" the Airplane treatment. The guitarist also worked up Jerry Leiber and Mike Stoller's rock/R&B staple "Kansas City" with the band. They took on "I'll Feel a Whole Lot Better" by the Byrds, and of course there was "Lay Down Your Weary Tune," the Dylan song that Matthew had procured. The arrangements came easily.

> **PAUL KANTNER:** It was real natural, electrifying folk, just plugging yourself in. All we were doing was playing the stuff we were playing before, through an amplifier. It was rather crude at first.

But before they ever played a note in front of an audience, several weeks before they finally signed Matthew's contract, it started becoming obvious to the band that Katz was not their kind. This was a man who, according to a 1977 article by Al Goodman and Regan McMahon in *BAM* magazine, had once given an interview in which he admitted, "I am an egomaniac, but you see, I think I am a giant." The Airplane disagreed.

> **BOB HARVEY:** He didn't speak the same language that the group spoke. He didn't talk the talk and walk the walk.

> **MARTY BALIN:** He became a megalomaniac. Over the bar in the Matrix we had a straitjacket from the insane asylum, with his name on it. He hated it.

Why they aligned with Katz, then, is anyone's guess. Perhaps they should have sensed the trouble that lay in their future, but they didn't. They weren't paying attention to boring details like contractual riders and percentage points. All they knew was that they had a band and they were starting to make some fine music together, and that this go-getter said he'd help them.

The momentum was so great that all anyone in the band could think about was the August debut show. It was set for Friday the thirteenth to bring them luck, and both the Matrix and Jefferson Airplane had to be ready. First, however, there was trouble to ward off. The city of San Francisco had begun sniffing around the club, not thrilled about having such a questionable establishment sprouting up in a conservative part of town. Building inspectors were dispatched on a regular basis, but the owners played by the rules, and finally, the Matrix was ready for business. Posters began appearing around San Francisco: COMING TO THE BAY AREA! THE MATRIX. SAN FRANCISCO'S FIRST FOLK NIGHT CLUB. OPENING AUGUST 13. PERFORMANCES START AT 9:00. 3138 FILLMORE IN THE MARINA.

The poster, in stark contrast to the graphics-rich works of art that had been drawn to promote recent events like Ken Kesey's Acid Tests and the Red Dog Saloon performances by the Charlatans, was marked by simple black lettering on a white background, printed by Marty's lithographer father.

The poster did not mention Jefferson Airplane. They were not intended to be the main attraction: This was to be a new kind of club for a new kind of community, a lively gathering place for the city's enlightened young, not another dive that served entertainment and liquor to customers who never interacted with one another except for the purpose of finding a sexual partner for the evening. Although the Matrix was designed so that the performers—folk, rock and blues would be featured, as well as comedy—could be seen and heard from anyplace within, and sound good, the music was to be secondary to the atmosphere. The stage was almost level to the ground and the musicians were not hyped as stars—when they weren't playing, they mingled. They were no different than anybody else. This was a place to meet other friendly, hip people, not to stare at a band.

However, due to an archaic San Francisco ordinance, patrons at the Matrix often had little to do *but* stare at the band. Much to the chagrin and bewilderment of club owners and musicians, the city had placed an ordinance on the books prohibiting dancing in an establishment unless food was served (were people supposed to eat while they danced?). The

Matrix, which had removed the pizza ovens to make space for a dressing room, was refused a dance permit, and was forced to set up tables and chairs and operate as a listening room.

Still, the Matrix was the talk of the town. Despite the lack of a featured band on the poster, it did the job it set out to do: word of mouth was so strong that, on opening night, the Matrix was sold out, the line snaking down the block. Unfortunately, the band and the owners had been so tied up with putting the final touches on the club that they'd neglected minor details—like hiring employees.

> **ELLIOT SAZER:** People would just stumble into the club and say, "Can I work for you?"
> We'd say, "We can't afford any more help right now."
> And they'd go, "No, we just want to hang around here. You don't have to pay us."

Still, despite the inviting and exciting atmosphere of the Matrix, the buzz afterward was not so much about the room itself, but the band that had played. Some might say the applause even went to their heads.

> **JORMA KAUKONEN:** Success did come quickly, and I think we had a real sense of entitlement. We were big stars all of a sudden.

Bill Thompson was there that first night. As Jefferson Airplane's newly appointed press agent, it was his responsibility to secure notices about the group and the club. With his connections at the *Chronicle*, Thompson was in an ideal position. He was friendly with the paper's music writers, the highly influential jazz critic Ralph J. Gleason—who had alienated some of his loyal readers recently by championing the new rock—and the younger, but also well-respected John L. Wasserman. Thompson called the writers, and convinced both men to come to the Matrix and check out the Airplane.

On August 29, 1965, in the widely circulated Datebook section of the Sunday edition of the *Chronicle*, Wasserman devoted the better part of a page to the Matrix and the Airplane, his piece accompanied by a large photo of the Beatle-banged 23-year-old Marty Balin strumming an acoustic guitar. The article was titled "The Matrix: Social Blues Via the Jefferson Airplane."

Wasserman praised the Airplane's singing and instrumental work, and their "musical approach and style." The group, wrote the critic, did not play "folk music, nor blues, nor rock and roll, yet there is something of all these forms in the Airplane's sound." Wasserman noted with foresight, "Although there are but hints at this time, it is entirely possible that this will be the new direction of contemporary pop music."

As much of a boost as Wasserman's profile was, what Thompson and Katz really wanted was a positive nod from Gleason. They got it two weeks later, on September 13, when the venerable critic headlined his "On the Town" column, "Jefferson Airplane—Sound and Style." Predicted Gleason, "I don't know who they will record for, but they will obviously record for someone."

That was the tip-off. In the following weeks, virtually every record label of significance—and some of little import—sent scouts to hover inside the Matrix. Katz arranged it so that at least two would be in the club simultaneously on any given night, each thinking he'd better make a move before the other. Gleason had given the band a legitimacy it couldn't have bought with a million buttons and bumper stickers. It had been exactly one month since their first public performance.

BOB HARVEY: After Ralph Gleason did that column there was pandemonium. I never believed that a newspaper column could have that kind of effect until I actually saw it happen.

Gleason, in the column, did note that the band was "just getting started and has problems and difficulties which are obvious." That wasn't news to some of the band members, but to them, the problems were named Jerry Peloquin and Bob Harvey.

Although several reasons have been suggested for Peloquin's ouster, one being that Jorma refused to play in a band with someone who'd worked as a cop, what's probably closest to the truth was that Jerry had complained once too often about the band's pot smoking. Being a military-trained drummer who also had some jazz background, Peloquin became frustrated with the meandering of the rhythm.

According to Peloquin, the situation came to a head one day when Paul's eyeglasses broke. Jerry went to the optical shop where he worked and made Kantner a new pair. When he returned to give Paul the glasses, he found out that Kantner had been interviewing drummers.

JERRY PELOQUIN: I came back with a head full of steam and beat the shit out of him. And Marty essentially said to me, "Paul is more important to me than you are."

It fell to Marty to find a new drummer. There were plenty of them around, but Marty needed magic to work for him again. Talent was only part of the requirement.

Balin cast his eyes around the Matrix one day and they froze on Alexander Spence, who everyone called Skip. Marty had no idea if the kid even played an instrument, but it hardly mattered.

MARTY BALIN: Skippy was this beautiful kid, all gold and shining, like a little Buddha. I always go by people's vibrations, my first intuition. I just saw him and said, "Hey, man, you're my drummer."

And he said, "No, I'm a guitar player."

I said, "No, no, no, you're my drummer." I gave him some sticks and said, "Go home and practice and I'll call you in a week."

He said, "Well, I'll give it a try." And he was great. His hands would bleed he would give so much. The girls would hang around the back of the stage just to get a look at him.

Legend to the contrary, though, when Skip Spence told Marty that he was not a drummer, that was not entirely true: He had played the snare drum in his high school marching band and did a bit of drumming in junior high school rock and roll bands. But Spence had also been playing the guitar since age 10, and he had every intention of pursuing that instrument before Balin decided he should do otherwise.

Alexander Lee Spence Jr. was a Canadian, born in Ontario in 1946. By the time Marty found him, Spence was married with the first of four kids on the way, had already been in and out of the navy, had performed as a folk singer, taught guitar and played with a San Jose rock band called the Topsiders.

Spence had gone to the Matrix with several local musicians he'd befriended. David Freiberg, John Cipollina and Jim Murray—soon to comprise three-fifths of Quicksilver Messenger Service, another of the original San Francisco giants—were planning on rehearsing at the club that afternoon on equipment borrowed from the Airplane. They invited Skip, with whom they had jammed that day in a Sausalito park, to come along for the ride.

What attracted Balin to Spence wasn't solely his rock star looks but a boundless energy that Marty wanted to see behind the drum kit. Spence was an avid rock and roll fan who had once phoned Little Richard personally to protest the rock and roll pioneer's exit from show business to join the ministry. Marty sensed that Skip had what it took to morph into a drummer, and he was right: When he opened at the Matrix in September, no one in the club could have suspected he had only just met the band days before and, especially, that he was relatively new to his instrument.

> **SIGNE (TOLY ANDERSON) ETTLIN:** All he wanted to do was be a part of that band. He didn't know how to play drums; he played from his heart. If you listen to every album he's on, that boy's just beating his heart out.

Just days after Skip Spence joined Jefferson Airplane, he was a guest at Signe's wedding to the Matrix's lighting man, Jerry Anderson. She had known Anderson for years already, had had a crush on him in Portland when she was 14. Signe hooked up with him again when he turned up in the Bay Area and was a month pregnant by him when they decided to tie the knot.

Jerry Anderson more than made up for Signe's lack of interest in drugs. Not surprisingly, LSD was present at the affair, and Signe's wedding doubled as the occasion for an event that must surely go down as a rock and roll red letter date: Skip Spence's first acid trip. Signe still vividly recalls Spence spending most of the night in a corner, babbling incoherently, off in his own world, a place where he would spend a great deal of time for the remainder of his troubled life.

TWO DAYS AFTER HER WEDDING, when most newlyweds would be on their honeymoon, Signe Anderson was in Los Angeles, auditioning for one of the legends of rock and roll.

It had been arranged for the band to play for Phil Spector, whose sister had heard the commotion about the group and called them. Spector, in 1965, was considered by many to be the finest pop record producer in America. His string of successful records with the Ronettes, the Crystals and, more recently, the Righteous Brothers, was lauded as monumental, and his trademark "Wall of Sound" technique was emulated by dozens of competitors. To be taken under Spector's wing would be a major coup for the young band. The Airplane, accompanied by Katz, flew to L.A.

But Spector was also known to be something of an oddball, a reclusive character, notoriously difficult to deal with.

JORMA KAUKONEN: I remember he had bodyguards and a pellet pistol, which he was shooting. He made me uncomfortable.

BOB HARVEY: I've never seen a more paranoid bastard in my life [than Spector]. He didn't want us in the room where he was, so he had us play out in the hall.

While they were in L.A., Matthew also arranged for the band to meet with Capitol Records, the Beatles' and Beach Boys' label. They were heard by Voyle Gilmore, producer of the Kingston Trio, who offered the band a then-standard deal: a $5,000 advance and 5 percent artists' royalties over a five-year period, with one-year options to follow. But Matthew wanted to hold out for more, so the Airplane blew off the offer, as they had done earlier when Barry DeVorzon of Valiant Records, which would hit paydirt the following year with the Association, came up to the Matrix dangling a contract. The Airplane also said no to Colgems Records, a year away from major success with the made-for-TV group the Monkees, to jazz label Fantasy, which would score in a few years with Creedence Clearwater Revival, to Elektra, soon to sign the Doors, and to London, then the Rolling Stones' label in America.

They at least considered Columbia Records, then hot with both the Byrds and Bob Dylan on their roster, and got as far as recording a demo for the label. The band taped a number of its best-received songs for staff producer Allen Stanton, both originals and covers, but this time it was the label that turned them down.

PAUL KANTNER: Columbia didn't like us, because we weren't in their model. The Byrds were much more orderly and the Byrds also didn't record their early music themselves. We were a little anarchic musically. I mean, if you're looking for normal music, that wasn't us.

With the addition of Skip Spence to the band, the drummer problem had been solved. But now it was Bob Harvey's turn to get the pink slip. Jorma, in particular, felt Harvey was dragging the band down. They were an electric band now, getting louder and more complex in their arrangements. Harvey played an acoustic bass and thought like a blue-grass musician. Even after Harvey made the switch to an electric bass the band agreed that he wasn't cutting it. Jorma wanted a bassist who could give the band some solid backbone, a player he could really trade off with.

The first person Jorma called as a possible replacement was his brother, Peter, who was attending Stanford University in Palo Alto. Peter was interested, but Mom and Dad Kaukonen put a quick kibosh on that idea—one musician in the family was enough, they said. Jorma had someone else in mind for the job, and recalled that his D.C. buddy Jack Casady had fooled around with the bass a bit. Jorma had never ac-tually heard Jack play the bass, only the guitar, he explained to the oth-ers in the band, so inviting him in might be risky. But Jorma felt that Jack was a good enough musician that he could pick it up.

When Jorma first informed Jack that he was playing in a rock and roll band, Casady's initial reaction was to laugh. He thought Jorma, the folk-blues traditionalist, was joking. Once Jack was convinced that Jorma re-ally was in a rock band, Jorma spelled out the situation. Casady said he'd have to think this over—he was going to college, had steady work—but he'd surely entertain the thought.

They left it hanging, with Jorma telling Jack he had to discuss the matter further with his bandmates, and that he'd get back to him soon. Both played hard to get.

A few days later, when Jorma Kaukonen told Jack Casady that he def-initely wanted him to come to San Francisco and try out for the band, and that if he was accepted he'd get paid whether the band worked or not, there was no hesitation: Jack made his mind up in the next breath.

Send him a plane ticket, Jack said, and he'd be there as soon as he could.

6

BASS IS LOADED

AS JACK CASADY DISEMBARKED at San Francisco International Airport, Jorma Kaukonen said to him, "I sure hope you can play."

Bob Harvey never knew what hit him. He should have read the signs more closely.

> **BOB HARVEY:** The first hint was David Crosby coming into the Matrix and listening to us. When we got done with the song he said, "Good song, but get rid of the fucking bass player." That was clue number one.

> **DAVID CROSBY:** Nah, I would never do that. Good story. Wrong.

The photo of Jefferson Airplane on the poster promoting the group's October 30, 1965, concert at the Harmon Gymnasium in Berkeley still depicts Bob Harvey. But by the night of the show, he was already gone. In his place was Jack Casady, one of the most extraordinary musicians the rock world has ever known.

John William Casady was born to William Robert Casady and Mary Virginia Quimby Casady, of Washington, D.C. Jack, as he's been called since childhood, arrived on April 13, 1944, in between brothers Charles Warren "Chick" Casady and Robert Michael, known by his middle name.

Jack, like most of the Airplane members, was descended from European stock and, like both Marty and Jorma, had both Jews and gentiles in his family tree: Jack's paternal grandfather, John Casady, an Irish Protestant known as Pop, had married Rose Koletsky, a Polish Jew. The couple settled in D.C., where Pop did plaster relief work, and they bore two sons, John Warren and Jack's father. Both entered the medical profession, William becoming a dentist and John a doctor.

JACK CASADY: My father really wanted to go into electronics but his mother said, "Feh! Fly-by-night business. It'll never amount to a thing." That was one of the sad elements in my father's life.

Jack's mother was originally a New York City girl, the daughter of Charles Henry Quimby Sr. and the former Mary Louise Pryor. The Quimbys' history in America can be traced back to the 1600s, with one notable entry in the genealogy being Harriet Quimby, the first female aviator in the world to receive a pilot's license and the first woman to fly across the English Channel. Unfortunately, in 1912 the flamboyant Harriet also became one of the first women to die in a plane mishap, when she and her copilot fell from their two-seater into Boston Bay during an exhibition flight.

Airplanes, it seems, run through the Casady bloodline. Jack's 39-year-old father was drafted into the Air Force in 1953, to take part in the Korean conflict. The experience caused him to close his practice and nearly ruined him—when he returned, at age 42, he had to start nearly from scratch.

Jack went to grammar school, junior high and high school all within blocks of his home, finally graduating from Woodrow Wilson, the same school Jorma had attended. Unlike the other members of the Airplane, Jack's family didn't move around—he spent his entire youth living at 4727 Reno Road in D.C.

Music, particularly the classics and jazz, was a presence in the Casady household, and the boys were encouraged to take an interest. Jack learned to pick out the roles of the various instruments of the orchestra, how the sections melded their separate functions into one whole. He pieced together the places that melody and harmony held, and the rhythm. He listened to music for its emotional qualities but also to understand its construction. Jack also had access to his father's considerable jazz record collection.

One day in 1956, Jack took a peek in the attic of his house and found his dad's old Washburn guitar. He started to pluck around with the instrument, becoming increasingly infatuated with the guitar, and took lessons briefly, but became discouraged and decided to study on his own. He soon earned enough money to purchase a Fender Telecaster electric guitar and, needing an amplifier, bought one from a schoolmate.

When Jack's mechanically minded father took one look at the contraption, he knew Jack had been bamboozled. Together they built a new amp and speakers, instilling in Jack the notion that a piece of electronic equipment could always be customized to suit his requirements.

As he became more immersed in all things musical—he even played trombone for a while—Jack began to avail himself of Chick's collection of vintage blues records, and to listen to the distant radio stations that broadcast rhythm and blues and rock and roll. He also began going out to hear live music. By 15, Jack was playing in nightclubs, his parents believing he was off doing something less sinister than mingling with unsavory characters in less savory places. But Jack had long ago learned to live his life to the fullest, to believe in himself, work hard and follow his dream, and he wasn't going to let anyone or anything keep him from it. At seven, Jack had been hospitalized with rheumatic fever.

> **JACK CASADY:** The program I was in—I was accepted into it because of my father's and my uncle's medical connections—was basically an experiment in the use of penicillin and how it's connected to heart disease. Half the kids died and half didn't, it was that easy. It certainly gave me an insight into life and death.

During his teen years Jack began spending time with Chick's friend Jorma Kaukonen, trading guitar licks and turning each other on to favorite records. Although the two boys were a few years apart in age, they now had some things in common—guitar, blues and rock and roll. The band they formed, the Triumphs, with Jack playing Fender lead guitar, continued until Jorma left for college. After Jorma's departure, the standard six-string guitar remained Jack's primary instrument, but he also fooled around a bit with the electric bass, an instrument he'd first encountered during one wild night out with Jorma.

> **JACK CASADY:** We went into this black club and got shit-faced and played there. They had a Fender Precision bass onstage, and I remember we flipped to see who would play the guitar. I figured I'd let him play the rhythm and I'd try the bass out. That started my career.

By the early '60s Jack, now the proud owner of a Fender Jazz model bass, was versatile enough that he never lacked for work, and a typical week might find him playing with a bluegrass band one night, a concert band the next and then a blues band or an organ trio, alternating between guitar and bass and working anyplace from military bases to roadhouses. There was a two-week stint with the doo-wop group Little Anthony and the Imperials, and a show with one of James Brown's drummers. He played with local teenage rock combos, one of which, the Offbeats, sometimes included future cult guitar hero Danny Gatton.

As the folk music boom began to peak in the early '60s, Casady found himself drawn to the blues revival side of the movement. And although he didn't play jazz, he listened to it, particularly awed by bassist/keyboardist Charles Mingus, bassist Scotty LaFaro and multi-instrumentalist Eric Dolphy.

At 18, Jack moved out of his parents' house and supported himself by teaching guitar and bass. He had about 40 students and a two-room apartment in Bethesda, Maryland. The following year, he entered Montgomery Junior College, where he stayed for two years. Occasionally he'd meet up with Jorma in New York City, but once Jorma made the move to California they lost touch—until Jorma made the fateful call asking Jack if he wanted to join a band. By that time, Jack had lost interest in rock and roll.

JACK CASADY: I was aware of the British bands but all I heard was the Stones copying tunes that I had grown up with, and I wasn't impressed with the Beatles. I had actually stopped playing for about a year.

When Jorma called to inquire if Jack might want to join this oddly named aggregation, Jefferson Airplane, it took a while for him to decide whether he wanted to give up school and his teaching gig.

JACK CASADY: If you dropped out of college you went to Vietnam. But I said okay and went out there in October 1965, when the band was three months old. I had a mustache at the time.

Jack Casady's mustache is nearly legendary in Jefferson Airplane lore. Jorma's friend, the other members agreed, was not the hippest-looking fellow when he first arrived. He resembled a particularly nerdish chemistry student: short, slick hair swooped over to the side, starchy white shirts and that godawful handlebar mustache. Marty called him "Joe Okie" and Paul almost sent him back home.

JACK CASADY: Paul hated the mustache and hated me; he didn't like my style of playing or my attitude. He asked me to cut the mustache and I cut half of it. If I looked one way to give a profile picture I had no mustache and if I looked the other way I had one. I actually played like that onstage one night. Then I shaved it off.

UNTIL JACK'S ARRIVAL, the Airplane had confined their performances almost exclusively to the Matrix. The club had been designed with them in mind, they were able to fill the room to capacity each time they played (which wasn't that difficult as it didn't hold much more than a hundred bodies) and they liked the place. But as the Airplane's reputation spread, there was more of a demand for their services and, like any new band, they needed all the work they could get. The most pivotal of the first outside gigs was undoubtedly the one dubbed by its comic book–loving promoters "A Tribute to Dr. Strange." It took place October 16, 1965, at Longshoreman's Hall in San Francisco's Fisherman's Wharf, and also featured the Charlatans, the Marbles and a brand-new band called the Great Society, with their beautiful singer Grace Slick. The event was presented by a four-person collective calling itself the Family Dog, who lived together in a communal house on Pine Street, and was billed as a "Rock and Roll Dance and Concert."

That hit home with the Airplane—their music was meant to be danced to. Ralph Gleason agreed, and had pointed out the frustrating ban on dancing at the Matrix in his very first *Chronicle* column on the band. So when the Family Dog came to see him about putting on a dance concert, Gleason listened with interest as Luria Castell, one of the founders, outlined the plan of this decidedly unbusinesslike troupe. One group of young renegades from straight society was not always aware of the others, she explained. Rock groups were forming every day. Students and other concerned citizens were protesting social conditions and our nation's policies abroad. Artists were experimenting with new graphic forms and unexplored media. But for the most part, these endeavors took place in separate worlds. Castell, along with fellow Dogs Ellen Harmon and Alton Kelley, ran all this down for Gleason, how they wanted to bring it all together. They told him about the dance they were putting together.

Permits were secured, bands were enlisted, handbills were drawn by

Kelley and printed by Joe Buchwald, and the word went out. But when Ralph Gleason arrived at the hall, he couldn't believe what he was seeing. This was like no other dance he'd ever witnessed. Everyone approaching the hall, Gleason later wrote in his 1969 book, *The Jefferson Airplane and the San Francisco Sound,* appeared to be going to a costume party. Men dressed as characters out of the Old West, long-haired girls wore long dresses. There were "riverboat gamblers" and "mining camp desperados," black leather and brown buckskin. Inside, the action was intense. The crowd, Gleason reported, danced wildly all night as the bands played. A light show, although primitive by later standards, pulsated to the beat of the music. "It was orgiastic and spontaneous and completely free-form," Gleason wrote.

> **BILL THOMPSON:** People were holding hands, dancing to the music, 20, 30 people going around in a circle. They'd get caught up in the energy and excitement. There was so much freedom.

> **PAUL KANTNER:** Before the dances, we were just the band at a party, because we weren't connecting with an audience, even at the Matrix. There was the structure there of a stage and an audience. The party was often much more interesting. But that wall broke down almost instantaneously.

JACK CASADY WAS ON AN AIRPLANE to join the Airplane a few days after the October dance concert. When he arrived, he was introduced to their manager. Almost immediately, Matthew Katz descended upon Jack, contract in hand. But Jack, after talking to the others, held off on signing.

For weeks, before Jack's arrival, there had been arguments galore between the band and Katz over the contractual issue. Marty at first said he wanted only to work with Matthew on a "handshake agreement." Katz, however, nixed that idea and continued to demand a five-year written pact. Marty agreed to a single year but soon flip-flopped again, telling Matthew he didn't understand contracts anyway, that none of them did, and they weren't going to sign something they didn't understand.

Once RCA Records began to show interest in the band, however, offering a significantly higher monetary advance than the other labels had, things began to change, and some of the band members agreed it was time to give Matthew what he wanted. They hadn't necessarily had a change of heart about him but, according to court testimony given by Marty in 1977, Matthew had told the Airplane that RCA would not record the band unless the company had a valid, signed management contract (they would later find out that such a contract was not necessary).

So, on September 23, Matthew—who later denied in court that he had ever told the band they couldn't get a record deal without signing with him first, calling the charge "absurd"—presented his management contract to the band one more time. They volleyed back with a list of demands. Matthew said no to all of them, but promised that the contract would just be temporary anyway—he'd be happy to change the terms after the record deal was finalized, to redraw the contract so that everyone was happy with it. Balin, Kaukonen, Kantner, Harvey and Spence all signed Matthew Katz's artists' management contract.

Matthew remembered it as a happy day when he recalled the event in a deposition nearly three years later. "The group came in, surrounded me, embraced me warmly. One of them—two of them, actually—put their arms around me and kidded around with me a bit. They said they had all decided they wanted to sign the contracts for management with me, and they requested to sign, and they signed them. I was very touched and happy about it."

But Signe would not sign. She still did not feel the contract was fair. The others were furious. How dare she hold out? Her refusal to sign the contract could jeopardize their record deal (although none had been formally offered yet). Signe's husband was adamant though: no way was she putting her autograph on that paper. Marty and Jorma erupted, arguing with the Andersons. Later, in a court deposition, Jorma remarked, "I remember yelling at her husband, that he was an asshole. . . . He was making it difficult to talk to Signe or anyone else."

Signe, however, didn't budge, not until the very day Jefferson Airplane entered RCA's studio to cut the first track for their album.

SIGNE (TOLY ANDERSON) ETTLIN: I held out for a long time, because I read the contract. The boys didn't. They wanted so bad to have that money that they signed and never read it. I'm the only one who said, "Wait a minute, you're not gonna get away with this crap." That put a bad bond in between the boys and me.

• • •

WHATEVER RELUCTANCE JORMA and the others had to making the commitment had dissolved by the end of 1965. The opening of the Fillmore Auditorium as the premier rock venue in San Francisco was the catalyst that truly convinced them that the new universe they'd envisioned was beginning to materialize.

The man behind the Fillmore was a gruff character named Bill Graham who, it seemed to many who'd met him, was a most unlikely candidate to become the foremost promoter of rock concerts for the next quarter century. He had no experience or interest in rock music and didn't understand the mind-sets or lifestyles of those who made or listened to it. He was coarse and belligerent, short-fused and petulant. Graham was not a man to be crossed and he made as many enemies as friends, if not more. But when he liked you, he could be the best pal you'd ever had.

PAUL KANTNER: The Family Dog were hippies and Bill Graham was Bill Graham. One was a family cooperative and the other was a capitalist-led business. But both were of equal value and I don't think you could disparage one at the cost of the other.

Bill Graham's story plays out like a Cecil B. DeMille epic.

Born Wolodia "Wolfgang" Grajonca in Berlin on January 8, 1931, the boy who would become Bill Graham lost his father when he was just two days old and was sent, along with one of his five sisters, to live in an orphanage. When Wolfgang was eight, the siblings were in Paris on what was supposed to be an exchange program and were stranded in the strange city as the Nazis kept them from returning to Germany, putting a halt to further Jewish immigration. As the war heated up, Wolfgang witnessed all of its horrors, including the death of his sister from pneumonia. Finally, in 1941, the 10-year-old was shipped off to America.

In the Bronx, Wolfgang, now known as Billy, was taken in by a family but still experienced hardship due to his German past. He fought back not with his fists but by learning to speak fluent English and working hard to assimilate. He took in American culture, sneaking off to the movies, playing ball—a street kid. He took whatever jobs he could find, making his way in 1948 to the Catskills, the upstate New York mountain resort area favored by Jewish vacationers from New York City. The following year, he changed his name legally to William Graham.

Bill Graham loved music, particularly the Latin sounds he went to hear in Harlem, but he didn't get the chance to enjoy much entertainment thanks to the government of his adopted country, which drafted him to fight in the Korean War. By 1954, discharged from the military and now a U.S. citizen, Graham pursued his own American dream, acting on Broadway in *Guys and Dolls* and in a cameo in the film *Breakfast at Tiffany's*.

In 1963, he settled in San Francisco and fell into a job as business manager for the radical theater company the San Francisco Mime Troupe. Graham was not particularly interested in the Mime Troupe's politics, but it didn't take long for the brash newcomer to assert himself, leading to a falling out with the Troupe's founder, Ronny "R. G." Davis. Among other points of contention, Graham had brashly suggested that each Mime Troupe gig be billed under the rubric "Bill Graham Presents."

By the summer of 1965, the Troupe's future was suddenly jeopardized when the San Francisco Parks Commission cracked down on the provocative content of its presentations, leading to a showdown and the city revoking the Mime Troupe's permits. During a confrontation in Lafayette Park, with the Mime Troupe fully intending to incite an arrest in order to spark debate on the issue, Graham proved a star organizer. He was then chosen to arrange a benefit performance to raise funds for the Troupe's legal fees, and was met with support by the movers and shakers of the city's underground arts community, concerned about the censorship implications of the bust. The Family Dog agreed to help Graham organize the benefit and a number of performers volunteered to donate their services, among them poets Allen Ginsberg and Lawrence Ferlinghetti, New York political/satirical folk-rock group the Fugs, guitarist Sandy Bull, jazz group the John Handy Quintet, radical comedy group the Committee and Jefferson Airplane.

The first San Francisco Mime Troupe benefit was held November 6 at the Troupe's Howard Street loft. It was a tremendous success, with $4,200 raised. More important than the money, everyone seemed to agree, was the sense of solidarity among dissimilar factions. When Graham presented a second benefit, on December 10, this time at the underutilized venue the Fillmore Auditorium, in a black section of town at 1805 Geary, he did more than help the Mime Troupe: He set himself up as one of the most successful entertainment impresarios of the era and helped launch the counterculture into orbit.

After his first visit to the venue, Graham became convinced that the Fillmore was an ideal site for dances. It had ambience, style and history—and great acoustics. Built in 1910, it first served as the Majestic Hall and the Majestic Academy of Dancing. It became a roller-skating rink in the 1940s and then, in 1952, when promoter Charles Sullivan renamed it the Fillmore Auditorium, after the district in which it sat, it began hosting the greatest names in rhythm and blues music.

Although Graham's own recollection was that he had heard about the Fillmore via Ralph Gleason, and the Mime Troupe's Davis claimed that he'd found the building, the generally accepted version is that Graham learned of it through the Family Dog. Before the hippie dance promoters had even thought to negotiate a lease with the owner, the story goes, Graham had already written out a check.

Luria Castell had a vicious exchange with Graham during that first Fillmore event. Before long she left San Francisco and headed off to Mexico. Graham, meanwhile, said good-bye to the Mime Troupe. That left two competing organizations—polar opposite in terms of methods and demeanor—promoting rock dances in San Francisco: the Family Dog, now operating under the guidance of Texan hippie Chet Helms, and Bill Graham Presents, run by the Holocaust escapee.

That second benefit, featuring the Airplane and other acts, was an even greater success than the first, but the true winner was Bill Graham, the tough-talking, hard-nosed expatriate New Yorker who carried a clipboard and got things done amidst the chaos. Not everyone loved him—Graham was prone to venomous eruptions when someone annoyed him with even the slightest infraction—and even those who did love him sometimes hated him. But they all had to admit that he could put on a show.

When Ken Kesey wanted to put together a larger, better organized Acid Test than the ones that had taken place before, he knew who to call: Bill Graham. When the three-day multimedia Trips Festival was scheduled for January 21 to 23, 1966, at Longshoreman's Hall, following the staging of the third and final Mime Troupe benefit, it was Graham who kept it from disintegrating into pandemonium.

At the Trips Festival, both the Grateful Dead (who had recently changed their name from the Warlocks) and the recently formed, still Janis Joplin-less, Big Brother and the Holding Company played. But Jefferson Airplane did not. They were out of town, spreading the San Francisco gospel. Having completed the initial recording sessions for their first album before the new year, it was high time for Jefferson Airplane to take off.

7
AFTER YOU

RCA RECORDS HAD NEVER HAD a real rock and roll band to speak of. What RCA had was Elvis.

That was not too shabby, but though he was and would forever be the King, Elvis Presley was in something of a slump in 1965. The Beatles and their British Invasion buddies had succeeded in accomplishing what had been unthinkable only a few years earlier, making Elvis yesterday's news.

RCA knew that it needed to update its image—badly. For nearly four decades, RCA Victor and its associated labels had been a giant. From Enrico Caruso to Tommy Dorsey, Hank Snow to Perry Como, the company boasted an untouchable track record in every area of music. From the time that the Radio Corporation of America acquired the Victor Talking Machine Company in 1929, RCA's labels had been among the major producers of recorded music. After Colonel Tom Parker, Presley's manager, had finagled Elvis's contract away from Sam Phillips and Sun Records and gotten his boy signed to RCA, the company's profile zoomed higher than Sputnik.

But the 1960s hadn't been as sweet. RCA had nothing that qualified as a hot name in rock and roll. All of the other major labels had grabbed up the key English groups, and now they were doing the same with the American contenders. RCA knew that it needed a Jefferson Airplane. Whatever that was.

Oddly enough, it was the raspy-voiced poet/troubadour Rod McKuen, according to Matthew Katz, who led RCA and the Airplane to each other. Once called by *Newsweek* "the king of kitsch," McKuen was performing at the Hungry i in San Francisco and heard the scuttlebutt about the Airplane. Recently signed to RCA, McKuen had written some songs he thought might work for the Airplane—perhaps he was aware that Marty had occasionally performed some McKuen material during his solo days—and he contacted Katz, inviting him to one of his recording sessions in L.A.

There the poet introduced Katz to Neely Plumb, manager of the label's A&R (artists and repertoire) department. Plumb, a one-time big band musician who'd played with greats like Artie Shaw before going into the business end to oversee product releases for RCA, dispatched Al Schmitt, one of RCA's staff producers, to San Francisco to hear the Airplane. When Schmitt returned, reporting that he was quite pleased with the group, Plumb made Matthew an offer. Katz and his attorney played around with the contract, penciling in some changes that Matthew later said he felt benefited the group, and finally, on November 15, RCA Records signed two contracts: one with Matthew Katz Productions, and one with Jefferson Airplane, the latter for a precedent-setting $25,000 advance plus "good production money." The last point was what caused Matthew to prick up his ears and what sold the band on RCA.

The Airplane never laid eyes on the final recording contract until the moment they signed it. They had found the bidding war tedious and were happy to finally be with a label. But perhaps they should have looked over the papers, if only to see Matthew's addenda.

MATTHEW KATZ'S FINANCIAL DEALINGS with Jefferson Airplane and RCA Records are still something of a labyrinthine mystery decades after the fact. Even a 21-year court battle to sort out the shenanigans that transpired in 1965 and 1966 never got to the bottom of it all. With memories frayed and much evidence evaporated with time, it ultimately became impossible for either side to prove its case definitively. Based on depositions and trial testimony given during the late '60s and '70s by most of the major players in the saga, however, a picture emerges, and it's not a pretty one: By the time the courts finally closed the book on the convoluted case in 1987, the prize at stake—contested royalties plus interest accrued—had swelled to more than a million dollars.

The evolution of the Katz versus Jefferson Airplane saga can be traced back to February 1965, months before Matthew met Marty Balin. At that time, formulating his plan to manage a group, Matthew applied for an artists' manager's license but it was denied. Matthew was advised, correctly, by the California State Labor Commission that if he was only managing one artist and not acting as a booking agency, he need not procure such a license. But Katz was further informed that if he did choose to act as an unlicensed manager, he could negotiate jobs only if promoters called him first, that he could not initiate calls regarding potential jobs.

Katz began acting in an official capacity as the Airplane's manager in September 1965. According to later court testimony by Airplane members, he told the band privately that, despite his legal obligation to stay out of the booking business, he would take care of them, including procuring work.

Nothing came for free, though. When the RCA contract was offered, Matthew (according to his own trial testimony) added a clause that would give him a cut of the band's production money. According to the arrangement Katz set up, he would receive a percent of sales, providing he supplied a suitable independent producer, while that producer would be paid a flat fee. Matthew is listed on the first Airplane album as a co-producer but, according to group members, the sum total of Matthew Katz's production work on the record was to offer opinions as to how he thought the recording should sound.

Despite the band's numerous complaints about him, though, Matthew did, without a doubt, assist the Airplane in getting off the ground. When, for example, Paul went to the musicians' union to apply for membership and, after a confrontation supposedly provoked by his long hair, was shown the door, Matthew marched down to the union office. He informed an official there that these rock musicians were going to be important to the union in the future, and before the day was out Kantner had his card.

In terms of publicity, Matthew was obsessive. He paid girls to hand out "Jefferson Airplane Loves You" buttons and bumper stickers at concerts, not even necessarily concerts where the Airplane was performing. He also paid the girls to scream and shout out band members' names when the Airplane served as opening act for a more popular band, in order to drum up enthusiasm among the uninitiated.

Matthew convinced the hip San Francisco clothing shop the Town Squire that it was in the store's best interest to give the group members a discount, as they'd be sure to tell everyone where they got the cool threads, and he arranged for local music shops to give the group a break on equipment.

JORMA KAUKONEN: Matthew was very responsible for getting us our first recording contract, for getting people in the industry to take us seriously and listen to us and for opening some doors. Matthew, of course, had his own agenda, but so did we.

The group's agenda on December 16, 1965, was to record the first track for its debut album. Leaving San Francisco behind, the Airplane arrived several days prior to the session for an extended stay in Los Angeles. Once the band settled in, the first item on the menu was to resolve their issues with Matthew over his personal management contract, which the musicians still believed they were required to sign before they could record. Matthew had made no effort to amend the contract, as he'd promised he would and, according to Marty's later court testimony, would not even give Marty a copy of the contract.

"I used to ask him [Katz]," Marty told the court, " 'why can't we see accounts and papers and have copies of contracts we put our names to?' Matthew . . . wouldn't talk about it."

Finally, on the eve of the December recording sessions, eager to put an end to the standoff and get on with making their record, the band cornered Matthew and told him they wanted to draw up an agreeable contract immediately. Marty told the court in 1977, "We were tired of talk, talk, talk. We wanted to see him put it in writing. We basically forced him to do it right there at that moment."

Marty produced a typewriter and Signe, still holding onto her job as a legal secretary in case the band fell apart, drafted a letter to Katz. The reworked contract proffered by the Airplane detailed the percentages that Katz would receive for his services, still adhering to the sliding scale that Matthew had proposed at the outset. The group presented its offer to Katz and, as Marty recalled at the 1977 trial, "We watched him sign it. . . . It was like a little victory for us."

Even after the changes were drawn up, however, Signe was still hesitant to commit. She informed Matthew again that she was happy to sign a contract with RCA, but not with him. She didn't like Matthew's agreement because it specified, she believed, that Katz would have a stake in "any and all artistic endeavors," including any work she might engage in if she left the band.

By that time, the others had become so disgusted with the ongoing battle that they'd begun to consider kicking Signe out of the group. As a last resort, they suggested that she see an attorney of her own choosing to have the contract evaluated independently. Signe did and, according to one of Matthew's later depositions, that attorney advised Signe that it was indeed in her best interest to sign the contract. Finally, on December 16, Signe gave in, just hours before the tapes began rolling in Hollywood.

Jack, meanwhile, had also held out on signing, until he was certain that he was going to be accepted permanently into the group. By the day of the first session, confident that he was staying and not wanting to be the lone dissenter, Jack Casady shrugged, didn't even bother reading the thing and added his signature to the papers handed him. But, in a bizarre postscript, during the trial years it was discovered that the Jack Casady signature on Matthew's contract was not in Jack's hand. To this day Jack has no idea what it was that he signed, but it wasn't Matthew's contract, and whoever did sign Matthew's contract wasn't Jack Casady.

In any case, by the end of 1965, Jefferson Airplane belonged to Matthew Katz, a man they neither liked nor trusted.

BILL THOMPSON: Matthew was a snake oil salesman, a real slippery kind of a guy.

With the contracts tucked away, Jefferson Airplane was finally ready to record. When the group arrived at the studio they were met by their new producer, Tommy Oliver, and an engineer, Dave Hassinger. Oliver was an old Air Force buddy of Matthew's and had logged plenty of arranging and production experience, with more than 30 albums to his credit—only none of it with rock and roll. Oliver was also a musician (he was briefly in a band with future Airplane drummer Spencer Dryden), and had worked with mainstream pop singers, among them Doris Day. Oliver assured the Airplane over several meetings that despite his non-rock credentials he could handle the job.

Hassinger, a one-time communications engineer for the Atomic Energy Commission, was brought in at the group's request. In his late thirties at the time, Hassinger had been around recording studios for years—he'd worked with jazz greats Duke Ellington and Harry James and had been employed at RCA since 1959. But he'd also recently worked with soul music giant Sam Cooke and had engineered *Out of Our Heads* and *December's Children*, the most recent albums by the Rolling Stones. The Stones' breakthrough record, "Satisfaction," had been Hassinger's handiwork.

Jefferson Airplane finally entered the recording studio the week before Christmas 1965, emerging with an album that many consider to be among the finest of rock debuts. Although not wholly original—they were still making the transition from derivative folk-rock to their own sound—and somewhat rudimental, all of the basic elements were in place: Jorma and Jack's inventive, intuitive approach to guitar and bass interplay, Skip's sympathetic and playful drumming and the trademark vocal blend that would characterize Jefferson Airplane throughout their career.

The sessions began with "Runnin' 'Round This World," one of Paul and Marty's first collaborations, and "It's Alright," one of Jorma's first stabs at an original composition. "It's No Secret" and "High Flyin' Bird" were taped on December 18, after which the band returned to San Francisco to see in the new year.

Although some Airplane members have maintained that the first album was recorded in a matter of days, RCA paperwork tells a different story, one of an album pieced together over a period of three months, a few songs at a time. The next set of sessions took place from February 19 to 28, 1966, producing the largest group of finished takes: Marty and Jorma's "And I Like It," Marty and Paul's "Bringing Me Down," Signe's bold and boisterous lead vocal on "Chauffeur Blues," the band's covers of "Tobacco Road" and "Let's Get Together," and "Don't Slip Away," written by Marty with Skip Spence.

A third and final batch of songs was cut between March 16 and 21: Paul and Marty's "Let Me In," "Come Up the Years" and "Run Around" and, finally, "Blues from an Airplane," another team effort by Marty and Skippy. All told, the Airplane recorded 14 songs, but if they thought they were done with the album and that it would soon be on its way up the charts, they were in for yet another surprise.

• • •

VANCOUVER IS A BEAUTIFUL CITY, although in January it can be bitter. Yet that was where the Airplane found themselves for two weeks during the first month of 1966. Although they had played the club It's Boss while in L.A., the band was still little more than a rumor outside of the Bay Area, and Matthew thought that the Canadian gig would be an ideal way to introduce them.

At the invitation of two young promoters calling themselves Captain Consciousness Productions, the Airplane was booked into the Kitsilano Theatre for a three-night weekend stay. But upon their arrival in Vancouver, disappointment set in. As soon as the Airplane took a look at the accommodations that had been arranged for them, they were horrified. Accustomed though they were to less than luxury living conditions, this was appalling. The hotel was a dump: freezing, dirty, a fleabag in the middle of nowhere. This was too disgusting even for a rock band. For the pregnant Signe, especially, the minitour was a nightmare—she and her husband were so cold in their room they had to use a window curtain as an extra blanket.

To make things even worse, the band lost money. The Kitsilano shows were to pay a thousand dollars, a university gig also scheduled would bring in an additional couple of hundred. By the time Matthew paid all the bills, including $900 in "transportation costs," and deducted his cut, there was nothing left.

On top of that, Bill Graham had called them in Vancouver to inquire whether Jefferson Airplane might be interested in a paying gig at the Fillmore the following month, three nights as headliner. Too upset with their present predicament to make any decisions, they told Graham they'd let him know when they returned. Graham hung up the phone screaming about how he didn't like to be kept waiting.

When they did return home, Matthew, they soon discovered, was nowhere to be found. He had taken off unannounced on vacation, leaving them without any money.

In Matthew's absence, Bill Thompson became the band's de facto representative. He arranged the February 4 to 6 Fillmore dates, and got the band's fee doubled in the process. When Matthew returned, he made Thompson the Airplane's assistant manager.

The Airplane knew the Fillmore weekend could be vital for them. Although they hadn't been out of town long, in their absence they'd missed the Trips Festival, a monumental event, and already some locals were accusing the Airplane of selling out because they'd gone to L.A. to make a record. If they hoped to maintain their local credibility they would have to be more visible in San Francisco.

The Trips Festival had, however, advanced Graham's standing within the San Francisco "head" community, even if he was its token straight. His role, as he saw it, was to be the responsible party. And if his caustic attitude rubbed some people the wrong way, that was their hang-up. At least they'd be able to count on him.

Now, with the Mime Troupe benefits and the Trips Festival behind him, it was time for Bill Graham to work for Bill Graham. The formula was obvious and simple: strip down the essence of the Trips Festival to the basics. Present two or three hot acts (and feel free to mix rock with blues, jazz or even a poet or a comic), send the music through a good sound system, bring in a light show for something visually stimulating, provide some refreshments (bushels of free apples were a Fillmore trademark) and allow the audience to, as the local saying went, freak freely. And try to keep the cops and the city at bay.

Graham booked Jefferson Airplane for the three-night dance concert at the Fillmore in February, along with "the Sights and Sounds of the Trips Festival." The run was ultimately a success, and Graham continued to book the Airplane on a regular basis, usually for one weekend a month. But when they returned for the weekend of April 1 and 2, there was a run-in. Graham had been instructed by Matthew not to give the Airplane any money, that he would be away on another out-of-town trip, ostensibly to New York to promote them, and would pick it up on his return.

Told this by Graham before the weekend of shows, Marty was livid—the band was broke, he said, and they wouldn't play unless Graham paid them in advance. Graham reluctantly forked over the money. With the cash in hand, Marty approached each band member and asked how much they owed on their bills, how much they needed for equipment and food. He then doled the requested sum to each musician and noted, in a ledger, the transaction, to the penny.

When Matthew finally returned and inquired as to what had become of the Fillmore payment, Marty handed him the itemized payout records, along with the leftover cash. "Here, this is how you keep a record," Marty told the shocked manager.

Money issues continued to exasperate the band throughout that winter and spring—they knew it was coming in, but they were unable to get their hands on any of it. Some time early in the year, the band proposed that Matthew set up bank accounts for each of them, and Katz obliged. He was to deposit $50 a week into each account so that the musicians would have some spending money but, according to Marty's later depositions, he never did this with any regularity, and each member bounced several checks.

There were also questions concerning payments that were to have been made by RCA—the band claimed it had yet to receive anything. They later learned, according to trial testimony, that Matthew had been endorsing checks made out to the Airplane with "Matthew Katz, Power of Attorney," a right they may or may not have granted him. In fact, Katz was the only person who could sign checks on the Airplane's account.

By the time Matthew finally got around to depositing the Airplane's RCA money, in September 1966—a month after they fired him—there was little more than $3,500 left in the account, according to the court records.

Complicating the situation further was the issue of the group's song publishing. Without informing the musicians, who knew less about publishing law than they did about management, that they could allocate their original songs to any music publisher that would accept them, or set up their own publishing concern, Matthew, according to court records, told the Airplane that they had to make him their publisher. For this purpose he set up a company, After You Publishing, which, like Matthew Katz Productions, he owned wholly. The agreement he set forth would assign publishing rights for individual compositions to After You. But by the spring of 1966 Katz was insisting adamantly that the band assign him the publishing for all of its original material. A great deal of arguing ensued but a solution was finally reached—in theory: Katz agreed to give the band a 20 percent kickback on publishing royalties earned, offering them, in essence, one-fifth of the proceeds from their own music when, legally, they could easily have owned it outright if they'd bothered to look into the law.

The problem with the 20 percent return, the Airplane later learned, was that the agreement they signed never specified After You Publishing, only Matthew Katz Publishing—a company that never existed. Katz admitted in his own 1977 testimony that he wrote and signed the agreement this way knowing it was bogus.

But the Airplane had other problems beside money. Just days after he signed the publishing agreement with Matthew, Skip Spence skipped off to Mexico. He forgot to mention this to the band, and left no indication if or when he might return.

For the third time in their brief existence, Jefferson Airplane went looking for a drummer.

8 JUST A DREAM

JEFFERSON AIRPLANE TOOK PRIDE in being from San Francisco. And by the spring of 1966, they had every reason to be proud. The music scene that they had helped to foment, along with all of its artistic and social trimmings, was in full flower, and the city was quickly becoming a magnet for young adventurers from all over the country.

The hippies, as the media came to call them, were, by an overwhelming majority, white, middle-class kids. They did not come from poverty, yet many of them chose to live in squalor, forsaking the comfort they'd grown up with to search for deeper meaning in their lives. They came to San Francisco, often with only the clothes on their backs, because it was a place where living took precedence over making a living.

For many, it wasn't just about running away from the familiar, the tired and the repressive, but about running toward something, finding a new lifestyle, the adrenalinelike rush of constant experience, another way of thinking altogether. It was about metamorphosis.

Although the city on the whole, with its live-and-let-live attitude, was considerably hospitable to young people, the Haight-Ashbury section—its heart the intersection from which it takes its name—was emerging by the first half of 1966 as the center of the action. Once inhabited by the affluent, the Haight had deteriorated into something of a ghost town by the 1940s and '50s.

By the end of the '50s, though, the Haight was being rediscovered. Its cheap rents and fascinating Victorian architecture were welcomed by students from San Francisco State College, as well as artists and other creative people. By 1965–66, the Haight had supplanted North Beach as San Francisco's most happening district.

"Haight Street," Marty Balin said in a 1966 interview with Los Angeles radio station KFWB's *Hitline* magazine, "is just like Carnaby Street [in London]. Long hair, boutiques, ice-cream parlors, band sessions and plays in the park, pie fights—it's just great."

Shortly thereafter, for a brief while, the corner of Haight and Ashbury became the most famous in the city, maybe even the world.

SPENCER DRYDEN HAD NEVER HEARD of Haight-Ashbury before he came to San Francisco to audition for Jefferson Airplane. He'd been to the city before, and had moved among the Beats and hipsters in their natural habitat, but this was something different. Spencer had ventured to San Francisco from his L.A. home at the invitation of Matthew Katz after the band informed its manager that it was letting Skip Spence go. Although he didn't stay long in Mexico, Skip, the others in the Airplane had determined, was not reliable, not committed to being a member of Jefferson Airplane.

The Airplane had begun noticing Skip's erratic behavior fairly early—he had practically been living on LSD since he'd first tasted it, and was prone to bursts of sudden and inconsolable paranoia. Kantner recalled one time when he, Skip and Marty took acid and headed up to Mt. Tamalpais in Marin County, one of the most breathtakingly scenic spots in the state. As Paul navigated the snakelike uphill road, Skip became increasingly nervous, finally demanding to be let out of the car. When Paul returned hours later, he found Skip exactly where he'd left him, as if he'd been waiting for a bus.

Although Skip had become workmanlike as a drummer, he had made it clear that he was still first and foremost a guitarist and songwriter. The Airplane retorted that they had enough of those already. When the band dismissed him, Skip accepted his fate resolutely and even volunteered to stick around long enough to help break in his replacement.

The Airplane gave Matthew the okay to put out the word to his L.A. friends that there was a job opening up north. Popular legend has it that studio drummer Earl Palmer recommended Spencer Dryden to Matthew, but Dryden himself remains unsure to this day who exactly did.

Spencer may have been the newest recruit in Jefferson Airplane in the spring of 1966, but he'd already logged more playing time than the rest of them, and more hands-on experience with show business. He was born in New York City, on April 7, 1938, and given the name Spencer Dryden Wheeler. Both of Spencer's parents were show people, and Spencer was the nephew of one of the most acclaimed personalities in the history of Hollywood, the brilliant silent film actor and director Charlie Chaplin, whose own middle name was Spencer.

Spencer's father, Leo George Dryden Wheeler—who later took the stage name Wheeler Dryden—was an Englishman, the product of an affair between Hannah Chaplin, the mother of Charlie, and George Wheeler, an actor who went by the name Leo Dryden. By 1938, the year of Spencer's birth, Wheeler Dryden was living in New York and appearing on Broadway. He was married to a girl named Alice, close to 20 years his junior and working in the ballet company of Radio City Music Hall. Like Wheeler Dryden, Alice's people were originally from Europe, but her parents called Toledo, Ohio, home and Alice herself hailed from upstate New York.

Spencer's birth effectively killed Alice's show business career, and when Spencer was one year old, the family moved to Los Angeles, where Wheeler went to work for Chaplin as an assistant director. In the Chaplin biography *Tramp*, author Joyce Milton describes an "idyllic picture of domesticity" at the family Christmas party in 1943, when "five-year-old Spencer Dryden, the son of Charlie's half-brother Wheeler, read 'The Night Before Christmas.' "

When Spencer was six, his parents separated, and his mother remarried. Spencer split his time between both parents' homes, living with his mother during the week and, on Friday nights, taking the bus to stay with his character actor father.

Spencer, who spoke with a British accent into his teens, met the likes of Abbott and Costello, Boris Karloff and Stan Laurel while growing up, and once auditioned for a Howard Hughes movie. But despite his showbiz pedigree, acting was not to be his calling: Spencer's future life began taking shape when he was 11 years old.

SPENCER DRYDEN: Every Halloween they had a parade at my grammar school. I remember I looked out the window and there was this long line of kids in costume, and the guy leading the parade was playing a snare drum. I thought, That's what I want to do. I want to be the first guy in line.

By 12, Spencer was playing drums in a Dixieland jazz band. While attending Woodrow Wilson Junior High School, he met a banjoist for Dixieland pioneer Kid Ory, who allowed him to tag along to jazz concerts, and Spencer once sat in with Shelly Manne, the jazz drummer. He also discovered rhythm and blues and rock and roll during this period, and although his jazz cronies disdained the new sound, Spencer liked what he heard, particularly Elvis Presley. While attending Glendale High School, Dryden picked up some rock and roll attitude, spending his time with what some might call "the wrong element."

> **SPENCER DRYDEN:** I was hanging out with some hard-ass people, the guys that got into fights and smoked and listened to that Negro music, people that drove hot rods and made loud noises with mufflers, driving around with nothing better to do than tip over trash cans.

Spencer's parents, who shared joint custody of the boy, reacted the way many concerned parents might, especially in the '50s: First, they sent their son to a psychiatrist and then, at 16, shipped him off to the Army and Navy Academy in Carlsbad, California, "the West Point of the West." Like Paul Kantner, Spencer used his military school experience as an excuse to veer even further from mainstream society.

After graduating in 1955, Spencer took a few classes at Occidental College but, deciding he wasn't cut out for higher education, he left after two weeks, working odd jobs. He joined a club called the Flying Coffins, a gang that raced cars and engaged in other teenage mayhem. During one rumble, Spencer was beat up fairly seriously, enough of a warning signal to send him scampering back to Hollywood, where he went to live with his father.

Out of school, out of work, Spencer went for a drive. Somewhere near Sunset and La Brea, he saw a group of cool-looking guys sitting on the porch of a house. Investigating further, he learned that it was the Westlake College of Modern Music. Spencer convinced his parents to send him there and "they decided it was better than getting beaten up." That was followed by courses at Valley Junior College and he considered going on to UCLA, but when it turned out that his Westlake education had produced no transferable credits, Spencer decided to skip the formalities and finally do what he really wanted to do all along, play the drums.

While he was going to music school in 1956, Spencer joined his first rock and roll band, the Heartbeats, a group of local hotshots that included future guitar legend Roy Buchanan and Tommy Oliver, who would later produce the first Airplane album. During this same hectic time, the late '50s, Spencer's father died, and Spencer got married for the first time, to a woman named Carole Crawford. He was also given his first taste of marijuana, still very much an underground phenomenon.

SPENCER DRYDEN: All of a sudden I met a more interesting set of friends, people that knew something that other people didn't.

Following his brief rock and roll sojourn, Dryden returned to his first love, playing jazz, working with a young Charles Lloyd. Spencer was soon gigging regularly, mostly in the L.A. strip clubs.

SPENCER DRYDEN: All the jazz guys on the West Coast made their living—because you couldn't make a living playing jazz—by working burlesque. It was a place where you could be free with your playing, be around a lot of chicks and get paid a decent salary.

By 1965, Spencer was employed at one such joint, the Interlude, upstairs from the Crescendo (later the Trip). During his breaks, he often walked downstairs to check out the rock bands. One night, he saw a particularly innovative band, the Mothers, the first he'd experienced that was trying to do something truly different with rock. Sporting a spiffy little mustache and completely in control of his band's every move was a fellow named Frank Zappa.

Having accepted rock and roll as a viable musical direction, Spencer joined an L.A.-based folk-rock band, the Ashes. Originally called the Young Swingers, the Ashes recorded one single with Spencer, "Is There Anything I Can Do," which was released on the Vault label. Ironically, the recording date was December 16, 1965, the same day that found the Airplane at RCA Studios cutting their first tracks for the label.

The Ashes gained a reputation as a fairly formidable outfit, but after a year things began falling apart. Between singer Barbara "Sandi"

Robinson becoming pregnant and Spencer receiving the phone call that would change his life, the Ashes decided to pack it in (although they reemerged later as Peanut Butter Conspiracy, recording three post-Dryden albums).

When Matthew Katz rang, Spencer was ready for a drastic lifestyle upheaval. He had divorced Carole and was living with his second wife, Jeannie Davis, and the couple's infant son, Jeffrey. Jeannie and Spencer had met on the club circuit, where she was a dancer going under the name Athena, "the Golden Grecian Goddess."

> **SPENCER DRYDEN:** In between the two marriages I went with a girl called Debbie Ray, "the Girl with the Million-Dollar Legs." Everybody had these names. There was one girl called Just a Dream and my friend said, "What would happen if you invited her for Thanksgiving? 'Would you please pass the butter, Just a Dream?' "

After his initial meeting with Matthew in May 1966, it was agreed that Spencer would fly up to San Francisco to meet the Airplane and audition. Two days later he was there.

> **SPENCER DRYDEN:** I put on my cool clothes, my cowboy hat and my saloon jacket, and my string tie and my boots. The only thing I carried on the plane with me was my cymbal. I met everybody, including Skip, the guy I was going to replace. We talked a little bit, I listened for a while and they took a break. Skip pulled out a joint. I said, "Far out, I'm home."

THE LATE SPRING OF 1966 was a rather eventful stretch for Jefferson Airplane. In May, the group finally signed the publishing contract that Matthew Katz had been after them for months to endorse. Later that month, Signe Anderson gave birth to Lilith, her first daughter.

Signe, who met Spencer for the first time while she was lying on her back in the hospital, barely missed any work—she was back onstage with the band in three weeks. But she did miss one of the more unusual engagements Jefferson Airplane ever played. On June 6, Spencer Dryden played his first gig as the band's new drummer—at a private party for the Republican Alliance. Held at the Sheraton Palace Hotel in San Francisco, the date had been booked by Matthew in spite of the band's fervent protestations.

It wasn't just that the Airplane disliked the Republican Party. More to the point was that they had made a group decision to avoid supporting politicians of *any* party. Any statement they wanted to make, any position they wanted to take, could be expressed through their songs and by their example, by the way they lived their lives—not by lending their name to a political horse race. Politics just wasn't high on their priority list—the group shied away from lyrics that pointed fingers at the government, the military or other specific targets. The Airplane's music, Marty Balin would later say, was about "love power."

That didn't mean the Airplane was unaware or unconcerned about what was going on in the country and the world—they were all intelligent, well-schooled and well-read people, were plugged in to the news and had opinions on the issues, which they understood affected them and their peers directly. And they thought nothing of forgoing an evening's paycheck to perform for a cause they believed in.

Like an increasing number of Americans, the band was frightened and angered by what had become two of the most divisive issues in the nation since Lyndon B. Johnson had become president: the escalating war in Vietnam and the draft. LBJ had already committed thousands of U.S. troops to the conflict in Southeast Asia, and a growing percentage of the American public was having difficulty understanding any purpose at all for America's involvement. Some of the male members of the Airplane had plenty at stake: they were still within draft age, and their immediate plans did not include putting on a uniform and marching off to a war they did not understand or support.

The same month that Jack arrived in San Francisco, October 1965, news of the war was becoming more startling each day: as U.S. planes bombed North Vietnam and rebel Viet Cong positions, some 150,000 reservists at home were being trained for imminent duty. The number of draftees being summoned was also increased; at the same time, draft cards were being burned in public by those who simply were not going to go, whatever the consequences. All of this activity, both foreign and domestic, was broadcast into American homes night after night: the first televised war.

As antiwar sentiment became more widespread throughout the United States, prowar forces stepped up their own offensive, leading to clashes between the two sides: peaceniks versus patriots. Battle lines were drawn on several fronts.

The Bay Area had long been a hotbed of political activism—the Free Speech Movement, the first major student revolt of the era, was headquartered at the University of California at Berkeley—and this was certainly truer than ever in the fall of 1965. On October 15, an estimated 15,000 antiwar demonstrators marched down Telegraph Avenue in Berkeley, heading for the Oakland Army Terminal, the nearest local departure point for soldiers heading off to the war. The day did not go peacefully. While Berkeley is the ultimate college town, Oakland is a more conservative working-class city, and the forces in power were not about to allow antiwar marchers to stop their city from functioning. The demonstrators, among them Ken Kesey, Allen Ginsberg and other counterculture figureheads, were met by a huge phalanx of Oakland police officers, who made it clear that the insurgents were not going beyond the city limits.

The marchers reassembled the following day to try again, just hours before the Dr. Strange dance starring Jefferson Airplane was about to get under way in San Francisco. What the dissidents had not counted on this time was the presence of a large number of Hell's Angels—the outlaw bikers who had recently befriended Kesey, Ginsberg and company, gulping down copious quantities of acid with them—alongside the cops, ready to bust "Commie" heads. In the complex sociopolitical structure of the day, the antiwar protesters did not yet fully understand that simply because the Hell's Angels sported long hair and beards, rode noisy motorcycles, dressed funky, got stoned and broke laws, that did not mean that they were political radicals or even liberals. They considered themselves staunch defenders of America, looked down upon the marchers and were, they had written to President Johnson, even willing to volunteer their own forces for service in 'Nam if it would help America win. The marchers were turned back, bruised and confused but not defeated. For the duration of the volatile '60s, nothing in the arena of politics would ever be in plain black and white again.

The political undercurrent to the new rock in 1965–66—not just in San Francisco, but everywhere—was undeniable. Topical songs lamenting the state of the world were in vogue. Indeed, "Eve of Destruction," a doom-and-gloom anthem written by 19-year-old P. F. Sloan and recorded by Barry McGuire, entered the *Billboard* singles chart just days after the Airplane opened at the Matrix—despite being banned on many radio stations across the country. And, of course, everyone under the age of 30 within earshot of a radio or phonograph was familiar with Bob Dylan's politically oriented anthems.

But the other side was selling records too. In February 1966, the same month that RCA released "It's No Secret" as the first Jefferson Airplane single, the label charted with the prowar "The Ballad of the Green Berets," by Staff Sgt. Barry Sadler, a Vietnam vet. It ultimately rose to number 1 across the nation.

The Airplane, however, shied away from protest. In their cover of Dino Valente's "Let's Get Together," they asked not that anger be directed outward, but rather that the community look in on itself and learn to live in harmony. When the Airplane did get tough in those early days, it was usually to address a romantic conflict, a dispute with a potential soul mate. Like the Beatles, who had broken out a new, more mature lyrical stance on their late 1965 *Rubber Soul* album, the Airplane was frank and often bitter in their early writing. They were not in the business of sugarcoating, but their primary lyrical concern at that time was still the tricky intricacies of interpersonal relationships, not the state of the nation. The Airplane's politics was one of Haight, not hate.

SIGNE (TOLY ANDERSON) ETTLIN: There was no fucking message. No matter how much somebody wants to make out now that we were saying something, we weren't saying anything; we were singing. We were making *music, good* music, and making the world a nicer place for people.

SPENCER DRYDEN WAS STILL ADJUSTING to the culture shock that was San Francisco and its attendant chaos when he was called upon to face the final hurdle: the Marty test. As the founder of Jefferson Airplane, Marty was the final arbiter: if he didn't like the drummer from Los Angeles, Spencer would be heading south. Dryden met with Balin in North Beach and they talked music, talked San Francisco. Marty gave the thumbs-up.

But before Spencer would make a firm commitment and pull up roots from the city he had called home nearly his entire life, he first needed to discuss money with Matthew. Spencer told the manager that he had a wife and child to support, that he'd be giving up a steady gig teaching music, that the move north would cost him. Spencer asked for a hundred dollars a week, double what the others were getting. Matthew relented, but not before lecturing the new recruit on loyalty.

SPENCER DRYDEN: He told me, "There may be some things that you're going to see and not understand. I've been straight with you, and I feel like you trust me. You're older, you've been around the block, played with a lot of people. I'm looking at you to come in and be the glue. Stick by me. I won't steer you wrong."

Spencer called his wife and told her the plan: He'd move to San Francisco by himself for a little while, and she and the baby would follow after Spencer found them a place to live. He moved into Skip's old room in Paul's place. Then he got busy learning the ways of Jefferson Airplane.

SPENCER DRYDEN: I'd never cheated on my wife. But now they were saying, "Let's get the guy laid." I didn't realize how loose and free everything was so I started forming an attachment to this woman, who had other attachments as well, and that wasn't the way the game was played in San Francisco. It was basically musical beds.

Then one day, "You mean, he's never done acid? Oh, fuck! We've got to change that. Now!" I really had no idea what I was getting into. They're lighting candles, I drop this little pill. "How do you feel? Okay, we're going to go out now, you don't have to drive." They took me to the Fillmore. My feet never touched the floor.

9
A MULE TEAM KNOCKING DOWN A PICKET FENCE

JEFFERSON AIRPLANE WAS THINKING OPTIMISTICALLY. Skip Spence had developed impressively during his brief tenure; his uniquely chaotic drumming style had given the band an edge. But Spencer Dryden added another dimension, his jazz-informed licks and subtle percussive tricks bringing to the songs new shadings—Spencer was an experienced, dedicated drummer, not a guitar player moonlighting as one. The instrumental team of Spencer, Jack and Jorma was slaying audiences every time they played.

Spencer was thinking that his relationship with Jefferson Airplane might just work out better than the one to Athena, "the Golden Grecian Goddess," who'd been waiting to join him up north, unaware that her husband had begun tasting the local flesh almost as soon as he'd touched down in San Francisco. Spencer did eventually move his family to San Francisco, but the marriage didn't survive the new freedoms he was discovering. Although they did not divorce legally for another four years, Spencer and Jeannie went their separate ways.

Spencer enjoyed playing this new kind of rock music more than a jazzman ought to, and he was touched by the kindness the San Franciscans had shown him. One of his first gigs was particularly notable, a show at Daly City's Cow Palace where, on June 24, the Airplane bagged a spot on a multi-act show sponsored by one of the top San Francisco AM rock and roll radio stations, KFRC: the all-star bill also featured the Beach Boys, the Lovin' Spoonful, the Byrds, the Sir Douglas Quintet and others.

Spencer quickly discovered that all was not blissful in the land of Jefferson, however. Matthew Katz may have thought his little pep talk would win the new employee's allegiance, but it didn't take long for Spencer to realize why Matthew had even felt it necessary to make that speech—or why the band had taken Spencer aside and cautioned him not to get too attached to the manager. By late June, tensions between Matthew and the band began to reach a boiling point and Spencer found himself caught in the tug-of-war.

While Matthew was vacationing, Marty had received a call from Barry Olivier, who promoted the prestigious Berkeley Folk Festival. Olivier wanted to give the Airplane the honor of being the first rock band to play the festival. Arrangements were made for the July 4 date, but the band subsequently learned that Matthew—who, according to the state, was not even supposed to be booking gigs for them—had contracted with a powerful disc jockey in Seattle for the Airplane to do a weeklong run of shows there, starting on June 27. The series would conflict directly with the Berkeley job.

Olivier was understandably upset, and pressured the Airplane to keep the Berkeley appointment. It was ultimately worked out so that the festival would pay for their transportation back from Seattle and both parties would feel satisfied, even if this meant cutting the Northwest stay short by a few days. It was just as well: the band was happy to see the NOW LEAVING SEATTLE sign. The first hint of trouble came when they arrived at the venue and a security guard refused to allow Signe to bring her newborn daughter inside. No sooner was that problem ironed out than the band was told that, due to an archaic Seattle union rule, no more than five musicians could occupy the stage simultaneously—the Airplane, of course, were six. The promoter suggested that Signe not sing with the band, but the Airplane was having none of that either, and again they won out.

There was also the hovering threat of a drug bust; the Airplane believed they had been specifically targeted and everyone spent their time in Seattle looking over their shoulders. No one got popped, but the gigs turned out to be a bust of another kind, with sparse attendance at all of the shows. The band returned happily to the Bay Area.

As a warmup, they first played two nights at a club called Losers North—part of a complex that also included a Losers South—in San Jose. There they shared the bill with the hot singer-songwriter Jackie DeShannon. Following one of the shows, a few of the band members engaged in conversation for several hours with DeShannon, whose music business experience far exceeded their own, and they received a crash course in the ethics of management and the importance of proper bookkeeping. The gist of what DeShannon told them: fire Matthew Katz.

Matthew was giving them few reasons not to. The next giant conflagration came on July 26, when the Airplane played another show at the Cow Palace, this time with the Rolling Stones. Originally, the Airplane was scheduled to perform following intermission, immediately before the Stones. On the night of the show, however, they were informed that the Stones were traveling with their own opening act. Accordingly, the Airplane would have to appear before the intermission.

Matthew refused to give up the band's spot and loudly threatened to pull the Airplane from the show altogether. He would sue the Rolling Stones, he told the promoter, KFRC program director Tom Rounds, and generate loads of publicity for his client by making a stink.

> **BILL THOMPSON:** Matthew goes, "We're out of here, we're leaving." There are 13,000 kids out there. So the band defied Matthew and he created a big scene.
> Tom Rounds later called me and said, "As long as Matthew Katz is the manager, we will never play a Jefferson Airplane record."

This was not the type of publicity Jefferson Airplane desired—Rounds was an extremely powerful man in San Francisco radio. At that stage of their career, with their second single, "Come Up the Years," just starting to get air time on the station, alienating Rounds was something the Airplane didn't want to do. They played before intermission while Matthew sulked.

Matthew was collecting enemies. Rounds, Graham and Olivier were all people who could help the group, yet none of them wanted to work with Katz. Neither did Ralph Gleason, or Ted Saunders of the Matrix.

> **BILL THOMPSON:** Bill Graham hated Matthew. Matthew came to the Fillmore Auditorium and he had a clicker [to count the number of patrons entering the hall]. He's standing up at the top of the stairs and wearing a top hat and cape. The next thing I know, Bill is punching Matthew and they're rolling down the stairs. And these were older men, compared to us.

Some time early that summer, Marty confronted Matthew about his tactics, and asked to see the bookkeeping records that would show him how much the band had earned. Matthew's reaction, according to a later deposition by Marty: "He blew a tantrum. He threw his stuff off his desk and told me he didn't have to tell me anything and I was nothing, that *he* was Jefferson Airplane . . . he got very purple in the face, and finally looked at me and said, in fact, 'You're fired.' I went back to the band and said, 'I think it's time that we fired Matthew because he just fired *me*.' "

The band didn't act on the termination immediately. First, following a series of shows at Losers South in early August, where they shared the bill with Big Brother and the Holding Company, now featuring Janis Joplin as their singer, Spencer and Paul discussed the situation further. They decided it was their turn to confront Matthew. "What haven't I done for you?!" Spencer recalled Matthew shouting. "If it wasn't for me you wouldn't even have this band, you wouldn't have these gigs. I'm going to run this thing. You don't need to see the books." The band decided to hold an emergency meeting at the communal space Marty was now sharing with Jack.

At the meeting, which was also attended by Graham and Saunders, the Airplane agreed to fire Matthew. They had their attorney, Maxwell Keith, draw up two letters—one signed by Keith and the other by the Airplane—informing Katz that his services were no longer required.

Until they could find a new manager, the Airplane asked Bill Thompson, Marty's ex-roommate, to pinch-hit, to "talk to the straights." He would have his work cut out for him immediately.

BEFORE HIS DISMISSAL, Matthew Katz had arranged for the band to play a series of shows at Mother Blues, a folk/blues-turned-rock club in Chicago. These were to be the first gigs for the Airplane away from the West Coast, just in time to celebrate the August 15 release of the band's album. But when they arrived, once again the Airplane met up with one calamity after another. For starters, due to an airline strike, the trip to Chicago took hours longer than it should have, and half of the band's luggage failed to turn up at the airport.

Adding to the drama was Signe—stuck in a room with a hungry infant, no money to buy her food, no air-conditioning and an outside temperature pushing into triple digits—announcing that she was quitting the band. She'd come to the decision soon after arriving in Chicago: she couldn't be a new mother and a singer in a rock band at the same time.

There was just too much pressure—from her husband, from the others in the band, from within herself—and too much discomfort. It was time to give up this life.

Thompson spent a good part of that first afternoon trying to mollify Signe—he even went out and bought her diapers—but in the middle of the night, Signe called his room, saying she was leaving. Thompson calmed her down as best he could and offered Signe a raise if she would stay on. With an important booking and media event planned for Los Angeles directly following the Chicago stay, Signe's departure at that time would have been disastrous. Signe promised she would "finish business" before making any rash moves. But the band knew that she wouldn't last much longer. And even if she didn't quit right away, her husband had become so irascible, so insufferable to the others, that they would have to kick her out just to be rid of him.

From Chicago, the Airplane flew to Los Angeles, where they hosted a press party and played several nights at the Whisky-A-Go-Go, beginning August 24. The band had performed in L.A. before, but this was to be their first major engagement there. The Whisky was the most important showcase club in town, and the gigs were taking place at a crucial time, on the heels of the album's release.

Immediately, though, the territorial L.A. crowd's well-entrenched skepticism toward San Francisco reared its head. The morning after the opening show, Pete Johnson wrote in the *Los Angeles Times* that the Airplane was "hard to classify and difficult to enjoy." The writer complained that the band's set was "not properly coordinated," with too many fast songs bunched together and too many ballads in a row. Marty Balin's voice, he wrote, was "pitched too high for comfortable listening."

A few weeks later, on September 17, the Airplane again headed south from San Francisco. They'd been invited to perform at the Monterey Jazz Festival, another prestigious if controversial booking. Just as they had recently broken new ground by becoming the first rock band to play the Berkeley Folk Festival, now—perhaps as a tribute to the very fact that, as the L.A. critic had noted, they were "hard to classify"—Jefferson Airplane was being asked to do the same at a jazz gathering.

The Airplane was scheduled for a Saturday afternoon set, sharing a bill not only with established jazz and blues artists Jimmy Rushing,

Willie Mae "Big Mama" Thornton and Muddy Waters, but with the Paul Butterfield Blues Band, the astounding combo out of Chicago that included the "three B's of the blues," Butterfield on harmonica and vocals, and Michael Bloomfield and Elvin Bishop on guitars.

Monterey promoter Jimmy Lyons, like the Berkeley festival's Olivier, had made a decision—at the behest of Ralph Gleason—to expand the event's horizons by incorporating the new rock, leaving many jazzbos grumbling. Despite the noble intentions of the writer and the promoter to give an endorsement to the cultural upheaval that rock was proclaiming, the jazz crowd wasn't ready for the invasion—or intrusion.

Leonard Feather, an esteemed if somewhat curmudgeonly jazz critic, stridently condemned the Airplane's inclusion at Monterey in his review. Asking hypothetically whether such a group should be allowed there, he answered his own question with "a resounding, roaring, amplified, hyperthyroid no." Feather laid into the Airplane, singling out the "raunchy voices and reverberating guitars . . . the sledgehammer rhythm, monotonous melodious concepts and almost nonexistent harmony."

He ended his review with a description that Paul Kantner still cites as one of his all-time favorite putdowns of the group, stating that the Airplane has "all the delicacy and finesse of a mule team knocking down a picket fence."

That, Kantner believed, was exactly what Jefferson Airplane was trying to be.

AFTER ALL THE MONTHS OF PROBLEMS, arguments, hard work and anticipation, *Jefferson Airplane Takes Off* was selling briskly—even if virtually all of those sales were taking place in and around San Francisco. Exact figures are difficult to come by, but reports from the time indicate that anywhere from 10,000 to 20,000 copies of the album were sold in California during its first couple of months in circulation. On the basis of those sales alone, *Takes Off* entered the all-important *Billboard* albums chart with the September 17, 1966 issue of the magazine, ultimately peaking at number 128 and staying on the chart for a total of 11 weeks.

In the rest of the country, where the Airplane was still largely unknown, sales of the record were negligible, with perhaps as few as 1,000 copies finding their way to consumers. Still, RCA continued to push the album and ordered new pressings, hoping for a breakthrough.

But what exactly did RCA order its plants to manufacture? That is a question record collectors have been pondering for decades.

RCA didn't realize it at the time, but somewhere, at some unknown point during the manufacturing process, at least one of the three RCA pressing plants in the U.S. goofed, resulting in as many as five known variations of the debut Jefferson Airplane LP.

Officially, there was to be one stereo and one monaural—or mono—pressing of the record. (Until stereo became the industry standard in the late '60s, many albums were released in both formats.) According to experts in the rare records business, first pressings of *Takes Off* consisted of 12 tracks—both mono and stereo copies were manufactured, but only a tiny handful of either ever made it outside of the pressing plant. The second pressing, apparently manufactured only in mono, dropped one song. Finally, there was a third pressing, in both mono and stereo, also consisting of 11 tracks, two of which contained altered lyrics. Those were the albums that nearly all buyers received in 1966 and henceforth.

How and why, and even when and where, the mutant variations of *Takes Off* were created remains a mystery. What caused the confusing situation in the first place, however, has never been in question.

RCA executives, it seems, were concerned that some of the lyrics on the album might be more than America could handle. Some time shortly before the album's August release, Neely Plumb, the 53-year-old A&R man who had signed the group, ordered the Airplane back into the studio to change specific words in two songs, "Let Me In" and "Run Around." These revised versions were intended to replace the originals that the Airplane had recorded in December and March, which Plumb found offensive.

RCA also decreed that a third song, "Runnin' 'Round This World"—despite its appearance months earlier as the B-side of the "It's No Secret" single—was to be yanked from the album entirely, reducing *Takes Off* to 11 cuts. Although some record buyers had already heard the song, the label didn't want to take any chance that the track would get the album banned in certain parts of the country, so the company opted to delete it.

What were the scandalous lyrics? The words that RCA found objectionable in the three songs, all credited to Balin and Kantner (but mostly written by Paul), were, even by the standards of a few years later, laughably mild. In "Let Me In," a song about spurned sexual advances, Paul sang, in the original rendition, "Oh, let me in, I wanna be there/I gotta get in, you know where." RCA knew where too, and had Paul record a substitute line, changing it to, "Oh, let me in, I wanna be there/You shut your door, now it ain't fair." In the original version of the same song, Paul also sang, "Don't tell me you want money," perhaps inferring that the woman being pursued was a prostitute. In the revised take, at RCA's demand, that became the innocuous and context-free "Don't tell me it's so funny."

Similarly, in the original "Run Around," another song of troubled love, Paul, Marty and Signe harmonized on the words, "Blinded by colors come flashing from flowers that sway as you lay under me." No good, said RCA—no swaying while laying allowed. The new words: "That sway as you stay here by me."

"Runnin' 'Round This World" was ultimately deemed unsalvageable altogether. Here the group really went over the line, the record company insisted, by declaring, "The nights I've spent with you have been fantastic trips." Not only was the singer admitting to having a good time with this person after dark, but he was suggesting that their fun-filled evenings were the equivalent of LSD experiences—or perhaps that the couple had even taken the stuff.

> **MARTY BALIN:** They'd find all this meaning and give it a great deal of importance, but "trips" was just a slang word to us, part of the language. They'd sit us down with their censors and talk to us and we'd say, "You guys are crazy."

An attempt by the band to rework the song by replacing the word "trips" with a guitar arpeggio by Jorma didn't pass muster with RCA and "Runnin' 'Round This World" was relegated to the cutting room floor after the initial pressing, not to find its way to a Jefferson Airplane record for another eight years.

For many years, few Airplane fans were aware that lyrics had been changed and a song expunged from the group's debut album. But eventually, record collectors began to unearth the scarce mono pressings that included not only the different words to "Run Around" and "Let Me In," but the unexpurgated "Runnin' 'Round This World" as well. These rarities became highly sought after in the collecting world, and by the mid-1990s copies in near-mint condition were changing hands for as much as $3,000; two ultrarare stereo copies of the first pressing, the only ones known to survive, later went for more than $10,000.

There have been other mysteries regarding *Takes Off* as well, including some album covers that showed "Runnin' 'Round This World" on the track list while the records inside those particular jackets did not actually include the song.

As for why RCA would find fault with these lyrics, particularly the word "trips," the highly charged social atmosphere of the mid-'60s must again be considered. For a few years, it had been fashionable among those who disdained the music preferred by the young to find insidious prodrug meaning in virtually every song with allegorical lyrics. The hysteria became a parlor game, peaking in 1966 around the time that the Airplane's first album was ready for release. Some of the songs in question were, without a doubt, about drugs: The Rolling Stones left nothing to the imagination in their "Mother's Little Helper" when they sang about "little yellow pills," and Bob Dylan's "Rainy Day Women #12 & 35," with its "everybody must get stoned" chorus, was most assuredly not suggesting that people throw rocks at one another. But was his "Mr. Tambourine Man" really a dope dealer? Was Mary, the subject of the Association's "Along Comes Mary," marijuana itself? When the Byrds sang "Eight miles high, and when you touch down, you'll find that it's stranger than known," were they describing a drug experience or, as the group insisted, an unpleasant plane trip to London?

All of this is somewhat amusing in retrospect, but at the time the censorship or outright banning of any song accused of having drug connotations was a serious concern. Artists were hurt by the allegations when radio stations refused to play the pinpointed songs and cautious retailers pulled the records from the shelves. Songwriters worried about how their words might be misconstrued.

The Airplane, like all of the trend-setting groups, was caught in a world in flux. Rock music was evolving at a lightning pace, and exponential artistic growth was not only accepted but expected. The Beatles and the Beach Boys, who only a few years earlier had been turning out clever but simple pop records like "I Want to Hold Your Hand" and "Fun, Fun, Fun," were, by 1966, producing masterful, mature and complex works of art, *Revolver* and *Pet Sounds*, respectively, using the studio itself as their palette. But the media and the distributors of the music were still operating under the old rules—they wanted three-minute love songs that played well on Top 40 radio, not music that ruffled feathers.

Jefferson Airplane Takes Off failed to establish the group as a national phenomenon, but it stands as a fine testament to the Airplane's natural songwriting abilities and sophisticated musicianship, even at this early stage. Many more have come to appreciate it in later years than bought it when it was new. The music on *Takes Off* was conceived with an older listener in mind, someone who understood that life's relationships were far more complex than one would surmise from the hit songs of the day. The album opened with "Blues from an Airplane," a brooding, bass-dominated ballad written by Skip Spence with words from Marty. Its confessional lyrics gave notice that the people playing this music were beyond fantasizing about perfect love and eternal happiness, that their emotions ran deep.

A bluesy undercurrent runs through much of the material, more overtly in some spots than others. Jorma, for his part, is still finding his way as a player of an electric instrument, yet his deft fingerpicking is versatile and his solos are concise, well-crafted and exciting; occasionally, he is dazzling in his balance of dexterity and chasteness. He is experimenting with technique and technology, devising different ways to coerce his instrument into doing things it doesn't ordinarily do.

Casady, however, is fully formed, his trademark melodic approach well suited for the relatively uncomplicated song frameworks. Jack anchors the album and gives it an undeviating rhythmic drive, drawing on the experience of those countless long nights as a player for hire. From the thundering funk lines that underpin "Blues from an Airplane" and "And I Like It" to the walking boogie in "Bringing Me Down" and the descending scale of "Let Me In," Casady is always in the forefront, never relegated to the backseat that most bassists routinely took at the time. Although the original album notes falsely claimed that Jack had played with James Brown, he proves the equal of any musician the taskmaster Godfather of Soul might have hired.

The vocals too are formidable. Signe is a knockout when she takes a lead (as on "Chauffeur Blues" and "Let's Get Together") and Marty is alternately smooth and raving, a frontman whose delivery drips with sex and sweat. Paul, who never pretended to be a technically virtuosic singer, and who somehow knew how to make sounding off-key a virtue, is compelling in an honest folkie sort of way. Together, in harmony, they were beautiful.

These were succinct, traditionally structured pop songs. But already the Airplane was reaching in every direction, exploring possible avenues of growth, defining what the back cover of the album trumpets as "A Jet Age Sound." Like the band depicted on the album cover, the music was young. It's a relic of its age yet, as Ralph Gleason said in his liner notes, "music [that] speaks for all time."

THE ALBUM RECEIVED LITTLE PRESS ATTENTION, if only because there was very little real rock press to speak of. Most mainstream newspapers and magazines didn't cover rock music at all—it wasn't considered a newsworthy art form. If they did, it was to report on screaming girls mobbing the Beatles or something one of them said or did.

In 1966, though, two new publications surfaced that treated the new rock as something to be taken seriously. The first was *Crawdaddy!*, edited by rock fan Paul Williams, who was tired of the giddy teenybopper hyperbole of the other popular music magazines of the day. The Airplane first received major coverage in a cover story in issue number 7, which appeared in January 1967. In a three-page review of *Takes Off*, assistant editor Tim Jurgens praised Casady's work and some specific tracks but felt, overall, that *Takes Off*, while "the most important album of American rock issued this year," was nonetheless "faulted." Jurgens wrote, "This is still a very good record, but we might have had a great one."

In early August, a couple of San Francisco rock fans, David Harris and Greg Shaw, published the first issue of a mimeographed newsletter, *Mojo-Navigator R&R News*, which offered up-to-the-minute news, gossip, opinions, interviews and reviews of the latest in rock, particularly the local music. They sold it for 10 cents on the streets of San Francisco.

In the publication's third issue, dated August 23, Harris offered his mixed thoughts on *Jefferson Airplane Takes Off*: "I don't mean to say that it comes off poorly . . . because it doesn't. Marty Balin and Signe Anderson's vocal harmonies are impeccable and the instrumental parts (especially the bass) are well arranged. The lead guitar, Jorma Kaukonene [*sic*], has been a whole lot better recently than he is on this LP, but his playing here is at a respectable level."

Harris went on to note that Balin had, since the recording of the album, begun implementing a new "crying" vocal approach, "not unlike that used by some Chicago R&B singers." And, making one wonder if perhaps Harris was fortunate enough to own one of the uncensored original pressings of the album, the reviewer commented that, "Paul Kantner's voice is turned down for an obvious and stupid reason on 'Let Me In,'" to which the writer presciently added, "When the hell are record companies going to grow up?"

10

FREE MINDS, FREE BODIES, FREE DOPE, FREE MUSIC

JEFFERSON AIRPLANE MISSED THE THRILL of hearing their record blaring from apartment windows and storefront speakers all over the Haight. During the first couple of weeks that *Takes Off* was in the stores, they were out of town on tour. The band was beginning to recruit fans in other parts of the country, but the Airplane's popularity was, undeniably, still greatest at home, and it was there that they felt most comfortable. Several of their out-of-town travels had been nightmarish, but an evening in San Francisco almost always went well.

At the Fillmore, the band was in its element and the audience was open-minded. When the Airplane had played in San Jose in March, the evening's headliner, jazz keyboard star Ramsey Lewis, refused at first even to play on the same bill as the hairy upstart rock group. But a week later, when the Airplane shared the Fillmore stage with Russian poet Andrei Voznesensky and his San Francisco counterpart Lawrence Ferlinghetti, there was no dissent from performers or fans—everyone involved thought that the match was inspired. It was understood that such diversity in the cultural menu was a good thing.

A year after the opening of the Matrix, San Francisco music was flourishing; dozens of fine new bands were working steadily at a number of local venues, and established acts, both nationally and internationally known, included the city in their itineraries. Donovan, the rising Scottish folk-rocker, was so impressed by the Airplane that he placed a reference to them—"Fly Jefferson Airplane, gets you there on time"—in a new song, "Fat Angel." The Airplane began covering the tune themselves, with Kantner singing, shortly after Donovan released it.

DONOVAN: We in the scene in Europe knew all about San Francisco. I heard about the Airplane when I first came to California in

1965. I did not go to San Francisco until 1966 but for me, they were *the* band there at the time. I saw them live but didn't meet them. I heard their records first and I loved them from the start. I wrote the song "Fat Angel" before I met them. The artists of the scene communicated through the vibes.

Ironically, one of the casualties of the San Francisco music explosion was the Matrix. Although it actually remained open until 1971 (under a series of managers), its importance diminished as the larger ballrooms grew in popularity. With its small capacity and lack of dancing facilities, the Matrix couldn't compete with the roomier, multimedia-equipped dance halls. Once they could fill larger rooms, the Airplane rarely played the Matrix.

BY 1966, THE POPULAR NEW MUSIC, eruptions in art, film and literature, stirrings of a sexual revolution, LSD and an overall attitudinal shift among young people were converging to transform the Haight into a joyful bohemian village. The Haight became a tiny nation-state whose citizens rejected much of what those outside of its borders considered the norm. They banished the vestiges of '50s America and developed their own language, their own way of thinking, their own utopian dreams.

Acid heads—and seemingly everyone in the Haight was one—found themselves lusting after the answers to life's more daunting questions, both temporal and spiritual. Interest in Eastern philosophies, yoga and meditation, natural, environment-friendly lifestyles and what LSD proselytizer Dr. Timothy Leary called "countless realities" all mushroomed. Crawl through that window and you couldn't go back. Who'd want to?

Conformity, of course, was to be avoided, and thus clothing was another means of asserting independence. The greasy pompadours, tight chinos and circle skirts of the previous youth generation gave way to florid Edwardian and Victorian-style finery, Wild West gear, the so-called Mod look. As if to say gloom was out and ecstasy was in, the dark shades and black duds of the Beats were replaced by color and long hair, wild stripes and swirls, paisley and polka dots, bell-bottoms, miniskirts, fringe vests, Indian gauze, sandals and boots, ponchos, granny dresses and granny glasses. Anything went as long as it wasn't something Dad would wear to work or Mom to lunch with the ladies.

Mismatched castaways salvaged from thrift shops and army-navy stores were transformed into an artistic statement.

The mass media delighted in focusing on the fashion element of the youth movement, as well as the Haight's rapidly expanding population—alarmist feature articles in both the *San Francisco Chronicle* and the *Examiner* raised local hackles—but the media largely eschewed reportage on the euphoric nature of the Haight experience in favor of jumping on the anti-LSD bandwagon. By August 1965, both usage and the associated outcry had escalated, and Sandoz, the Swiss company that had first synthesized LSD, ceased production of the drug. Up to that time, recognizing the potential importance of LSD to the medical community, the lab had distributed samples free of charge to experimental and clinical investigators, but when it became apparent that Sandoz could no longer guarantee who ended up with the stuff and what they did with it—or who copied the recipe—the company decided it was best to get out of the acid business altogether.

Their decision was a moot point by then. With amateur home brewers like Augustus Owsley "Bear" Stanley III (better known simply as Owsley and a close friend of the Airplane and the Grateful Dead) turning out potent LSD doses by the thousands, and playing Johnny Acidseed by giving away more than they sold, there was no stopping this runaway psychedelic train. The Airplane, on a number of occasions, tossed doses of acid to their audiences.

MARTY BALIN: I remember one time when we were throwing it out like M&M's. I'd say, "Look, it's the FBI," and you'd see guys with binoculars watching this whole scene.

By the time LSD was finally made illegal, on October 6, 1966, an occasion marked in San Francisco by a stoned-out party in Golden Gate Park featuring a number of the top bands, there was enough of it in circulation already to keep the populace afloat for years.

Not all of the Bay Area acid gobblers took it solely for recreational or spiritual purposes, though. For the Diggers, a streetwise group of radicals, the lesson of LSD was that there was a whole world of people out there who needed to be clothed, fed and sheltered before they could even think about being free. The Diggers did their part by giving away food—collected through various methods from local merchants—on a daily basis in the Panhandle. Anyone, hippie or straight, black or white, who wanted something to eat, could come to the park and the Diggers would feed them. The Airplane and the other San Francisco bands also practiced altruism, performing numerous concerts for groups and causes of all kinds and waiving their fees.

> **PAUL KANTNER:** There was a great romantic ideal of taking care of "the people." We had that naive hope that we were champions of the poor and dispossessed, being somewhat poor and dispossessed ourselves. There was a Robin Hood–like capacity there. All you had to do was go out and play and make a large amount of money for somebody who really needed it.

Many of the benefits and free concerts that abounded in San Francisco were produced with the assistance and blessing of Bill Graham, but the promoter never pretended to be anything but a business entrepreneur. The Family Dog's Chet Helms, on the other hand, filled the role of the anti-Graham, paying scant attention to traditional business models. Helms was a long, tall Texan, but he sure wasn't a cowboy. With his horn-rimmed glasses, dark blond hair streaming past his shoulders and a scraggly beard to match, he looked like a media-concocted caricature of a hippie.

Helms, accompanied by traveling companion Janis Joplin, had initially hitchhiked from Austin to San Francisco in 1963. Three years later, during which time Joplin had returned to Texas, they repeated the journey and Helms united the singer with Big Brother and the Holding Company, which he managed. After taking the reins of the Family Dog operation, Helms formed an alliance with John Carpenter, the original manager of the Great Society, and Howard Wolf, a talent buyer from L.A. who'd taken over that band's management from Carpenter.

In early 1966, Helms and Carpenter met with Graham about the possibility of using the Fillmore on evenings when Graham had nothing going on. It was arranged that Graham would put up the finances, while Helms, Carpenter and Wolf would book the acts and stage the shows.

> **CHET HELMS:** It was just a handshake agreement that we would do shows on alternate weekends. [Graham's] concern was just being able to produce that many events. Part of it was that other than the

Airplane he really didn't know the bands. He wasn't part of the street and social and party scene, and John and I were fairly central to that. We did about four shows over a three-month period there.

Graham went first, presenting the February 4 to 6 "Sights and Sounds of the Trips Festival" show with the Airplane. To promote the event, Graham hired an artist, Peter Bailey, to design an eye-catching two-color poster listing all of the pertinent information. With a horse-drawn biplane at its center, the yellow and red piece of artwork became the first of some 287 posters that would ultimately be commissioned to promote Graham's San Francisco concerts through the summer of 1971.

In time, the increasingly elaborate, intricate and thoroughly psychedelic San Francisco concert posters—created by such then-unknown artists as Wes Wilson, Rick Griffin, Stanley Mouse, Alton Kelley and Victor Moscoso—came to be viewed as a major art movement and a significant symbol of the era. Along with the series of 147 posters created for the Family Dog's shows, the Fillmore posters have provided some of the most enduring artistic images of the '60s. Today, the posters, as well as the smaller handbills and tickets that duplicated the poster art, are highly collectible, often commanding hundreds or even thousands of dollars, and have been the subject of museum and gallery exhibitions.

Even the bottom line–minded Graham understood that the value served by the posters went beyond filling the room on a given night: they helped to promote an image of the Fillmore as *the* place to be.

ALTON KELLEY: We'd go to San Francisco State, drive across the bridge to Berkeley, put up posters in the Haight, North Beach. We'd go down the block, put them in windows and on poles and turn around and go back the other way and 90 percent of them would be gone.

Clear from the onset of their collaboration was that Bill Graham and the Family Dog practiced radically different business styles. Wolf tried his best to act as peacemaker, but Helms was no match for Graham, who ended the short-lived union once he was confident he could bring in the popular bands without outside help. After one final show together, Helms and crew set up shop at the Avalon Ballroom, located at 1268 Sutter. The Avalon, built in 1911, was, like the Fillmore, a grand old dance hall, with an L-shaped balcony, mirrors, columns and red wallpaper. Helms leased the venue for $800 a month and the Family Dog sponsored their first show there on April 22 and 23, 1966, starring the Blues Project, the New York counterpart to the Butterfield Band, and the Great Society.

Things went smoothly for a few months, with Graham booking the Airplane into the Fillmore on a regular basis. But the rivalry between the two promoters finally came to a head in July, when the Family Dog presented the Airplane and the Great Society at the Avalon. Graham felt he'd been robbed. He called Matthew Katz, still the band's manager at the time, and told him he didn't want the Airplane playing for anyone else in San Francisco but Bill Graham. Helms took the snub personally, but to Graham it was just good business.

> **HOWARD WOLF:** The difference between the Fillmore and the Avalon was attitude. At the Avalon, at the end of the evening, everyone wanted to just hang. No one wanted to go home. At the Fillmore, after the show was over they'd get up and they'd leave.

But to the folks who simply liked dancing to rock and roll, it often mattered little, in the end, where the money went, who put on a show or what the promoter believed in.

> **PAUL KANTNER:** Nobody came to the Fillmore to see a band. There wasn't adulation of performers to any great degree, and the people in the audience were often far more interesting than the people on the stage.

In any case, Jefferson Airplane never played the Avalon for Chet Helms again. And once Bill Graham began serving as their new manager, he made sure of it.

11
WONDER WOMAN

GRACE SLICK LEAFED through the Sunday newspaper halfheartedly, and her future stared her in the face. On a sizzling-hot afternoon in August 1965, she came upon John Wasserman's article about Jefferson Airplane. Grace's gaze lingered on the photo. Marty Balin, the caption said. He looked interesting, Grace thought—dark and brooding, turning away from the camera, unsmiling. He didn't look like any rock and roll singer she'd ever seen. He was sexy. He looked like someone with a brain. Grace convinced her husband, Jerry Slick, that it might be fun to check out this group with the bizarre name. If nothing else, it would be a night out.

> **GRACE SLICK:** I went to see Jefferson Airplane at the Matrix, and they were making more money in a day than I made in a week. They only worked for two or three hours a night and they got to hang out. I thought, This looks a lot better than what I'm doing. I knew I could more or less carry a tune and I figured if they could do it, I could.

Grace and Jerry had already created some music together, for films he'd made in college—he could play the drums and she not only had a decent voice but could get by on piano, recorder, guitar and a few other instruments. Jerry's brother, Darby Slick, was developing into an accomplished guitarist. They had a couple of other friends who could also contribute.

The Slick trio pieced together a band, named it the Great Society (officially the Great! Society), wrote some songs, practiced a bunch and, not much more than a month later, were playing their first gigs and making records. A year later, nearly to the day, Grace was singing in Jefferson Airplane.

• • •

GRACE SLICK NEVER WANTED TO BE A ROCK STAR. She hadn't even paid much attention to rock music until she started making it herself. She found most of it silly. Grace had harbored no childhood dreams of becoming a singer or a musician. That took dedication, which she admittedly didn't have. The best thing about being onstage, she later said, was that it was the least crowded place at the party.

Although she ultimately became one of the most recognized names and faces of the 1960s, Grace Slick never strove to become an icon of her generation, or the symbol of San Francisco's hippies. She wasn't really much of a hippie at all, when it came down to it. She liked wearing makeup and nice clothes, and the idea of communal living mortified her—she treasured her privacy, even insisting on her own room when she was involved with one of the band members. Grace Slick didn't like dirt, especially other people's dirt.

Nor did Grace Slick ever aspire to be a spokeswoman for the women's movement. There was no radical feminist dogma governing her every move—she just did what she wanted to do, offending women and men alike. Grace saw no need to pit the sexes against each other—most of the people in her inner circle were male, and quite often she just went along with whatever they wanted.

That she was often called the "Acid Queen," or the "Voice That Launched a Thousand Trips," was ironic too. Acid was far from her favorite drug. Although Grace took LSD quite willingly for a while and it affected her consciousness, her music and her life, she much preferred good old-fashioned booze.

So Grace Slick was an unlikely candidate for rock stardom—until the 1960s got in the way of her privileged upbringing, until risk and excess and change became something to embrace rather than avoid. Grace was the product of high society, a rich kid from the 'burbs, groomed for the good life. She could have had it all, it was hers for the asking. And she tried, she really did. She played by the rules, and came so close to grabbing the golden ring: the marriage to the boy next door, the proper finishing school education, a respectable career.

But once having it all became a goal within reach, Grace discovered that she didn't really want it all. She realized she had never wanted any of it. Now she couldn't wait to get rid of it.

• • •

GRACE BARNETT WING SLICK JOHNSON was born October 30, 1939. According to her FBI file, she made her first appearance in Highland Park, Illinois, although most bios say Evanston and Grace simply tells people Chicago because it's easier. Such is the enigma of Grace Slick, where truth, fiction and mystery often entwine seamlessly and—confused even further by her own self-professed flawed memory—any variation therein might be equally credible or farfetched.

Her ability to spin yarns about herself, to re-create her reality, may have been genetic. Grace's mother, Virginia Elizabeth Barnett Wing, was originally from Idaho, born in 1909 to Marcus Whitman Barnett and Annie Mary Sue Neill Barnett. When Grace was growing up, she bonded in special ways with her maternal grandmother, who she called Lady Sue. The older woman regaled young Grace with tales of being a champion skater in her youth, dazzling onlookers with her special skates festooned with tiny electric lights, a blurry rainbow on ice. Only when Grace was older did she realize that in Sue Barnett's day, the ability to attach electric lights to skates was years away from being executable.

But not all of the stories Grace heard of her family's past were the product of fertile imaginations: Grace's heritage on her mother's side is dotted with fascinating historical connections going back generations. Although Grace describes her mother's family as "a mishmash of Celtic-Irish-Scottish," mostly Protestants, their arrival on these shores can be traced back four hundred years to England. The clan that eventually produced Grace Slick began its reign in the New World when John Whitman, one of the original Puritans, arrived in Weymouth, Massachusetts, early in the seventeenth century. Following the family tree through its countless branches and leaves, one finds lines to Walt Whitman, the revered poet, and to Marcus Whitman, a well-known missionary who died spreading the word of God to the Native Americans of the Northwest.

Grace loved to hear about her great-grandmother Lizzie, Elizabeth Auzella Whitman. In *Grace Slick: The Biography*, the 1980 book written by Barbara Rowes with Grace, Lizzie is described as "an Annie Oakley type, the first pioneer to carry violin and guitar on the wagon trains into the Northwest Territory, a one-woman orchestra on the new frontier."

Lizzie was a maverick, an independent woman before there was a polite term for such a person. Married at 18 to Harry Kelso Barnett of

Belfast, Ireland, a merchant living in Lewiston, Lizzie did the unimaginable, leaving her husband behind and taking young Marcus Barnett with her. Mother and son lived well on their own, surrounding themselves with culture, and Marcus became quite a singer.

But his fine voice wasn't enough to keep Marcus's own wife singing his praises. According to the Rowes book, in 1917 Sue Barnett picked up and left Marcus. She put down roots in Seattle—another single mother—and carved out a nice living as a bootlegger, home-brewing beer in her basement during Prohibition.

Grace's mother was more conventional than either Lady Sue or Lizzie had been, but in her youth she exhibited an independent streak. Virginia Barnett inherited the family's proclivity for performing, and she entertained high hopes of making it as a singer and actress in Hollywood. She got as far as working as an understudy to Marion Davies, the lover of newspaper baron William Randolph Hearst, and she sang in a few nightclubs, as well as the prestigious Pantages Theater on Sunset Boulevard. But a proper education, still a luxury for women at the time, was not to be passed up, and it was in a music class at the University of Washington that Virginia met Ivan Wing. With that, a promising showbiz career was tossed away and soon enough, Virginia Barnett became Virginia Wing, wife and mother.

> **GRACE SLICK:** It wasn't considered right to be the wife of a banker and be a saloon singer. She sang around the house, the way people do when they're happy. She had a good voice, for pop music, "Stardust" and songs like that.

Ivan Wilford Wing was born in Seattle in 1907, to Arthur Wilford Wing and Grace Josephine Dow Wing, after whom the future Ms. Slick was named. Although little is known about the Wings' background in comparison to the Barnetts' and Whitmans', Ivan conducted some genealogical research and discovered that the Wings had Norwegian roots, possibly with some Swedish ancestry mixed in. The family name was originally Vinje (pronounced VEEN-ya), anglicized to Wing upon arrival in America.

The Wings were not a wealthy family when Grace was born, but it didn't take long for them to advance their status to upper middle class. After graduating college, Ivan Wing found work as an investment banker, first in San Francisco, next Chicago (during which time Grace was born) and then Los Angeles. Grace enjoyed her brief stay in L.A., but in 1945 the Wing family was uprooted again, back to San Francisco. Grace loved this city as well, especially taken by the beauty of Golden Gate Park, where she would often sit with her drawing materials and sketch the placid Japanese Tea Garden.

By September 1949, just before Grace's tenth birthday, a brother named Chris was born in San Francisco. Shortly thereafter, when Ivan received a raise, the Wings were able to move south to Palo Alto, an affluent suburb on the Peninsula, where Grace attended public schools.

Formal education was not something Grace took too seriously, however. Although quite bright, she had an innate disdain for the rigid teaching methods and the mandated curriculum. She managed to squeak by and get decent grades, but clearly she was more interested in applying herself to what might later be termed acting out—in her case literally. She put on little plays, made her own costumes and told stories, concocting her own fantasy world. She would become Alice in Wonderland or Maid Marian or Wonder Woman or characters from Grimm's fairy tales or *Little Women*. If there was an audience—even just her parents—Grace performed for them. If there wasn't, she performed for herself.

As a child, Grace spent an inordinate amount of time in museums and learned how to draw rather well. She read voraciously and she wrote, but even then her creations were often oblique, her poems and stories' meanings known only to herself. Grace also took piano lessons as a child, but she did not have the fortitude at the time to pursue the instrument.

GRACE SLICK: I played it because it was there. I also eat food if it's there.

None of this intellectual behavior endeared Grace to her doll-playing, rope-jumping, approval-seeking peers, and Grace's response to their snubs was to grow a suit of armor. She became a clown, wising off in class, hurling insults and sarcastic cracks. Grace Wing was an outcast, a classic outsider who was misunderstood and ostracized for being different. Set against the backdrop of budding postwar white-bread suburbia, Grace's behavior was viewed as antisocial. This was not someone whose fecund imagination was considered worth nurturing, but rather an odd-ball best avoided. Her extroverted personality was not proper for young women of means.

But still, Grace was able to display decorum, to keep herself in check. She could play their game even if they didn't appreciate hers.

GRACE SLICK: I didn't yell. It was okay to be loud when you're happy, but you kept your anger to yourself.

When Grace began attending David Starr Jordan Junior High School, she was still a self-described nerd: overweight, bad hair (which puberty had caused to change from blonde to dark brown), uncool clothes. She came to realize that if she was ever going to be noticed by the other kids in school—which is all that most teenagers want—she would have to make an impression. In her own mind, Grace didn't believe she had what it took to become one of the popular girls, but a quick look around and she understood what needed to be done: She began to dress tougher, took up smoking and drinking, suppressed her interest in classical music and art and took up comic books and the raw sound of early rhythm and blues. She increased the wisecracking, lost weight and joined the basketball cheerleading squad.

But when Grace invited all of her new "friends" to her fourteenth birthday party and, one by one, they called to cancel because they all had something else to do, she realized the ploy hadn't worked. She would never be one of that crowd. They hated her.

Grace had another chance to start over when she moved up to Palo Alto High School and yet another when she transferred again, in the fall of 1955, to Castilleja School for Girls, a private finishing school, also in Palo Alto, which she attended for two years. She continued to cheerlead, this time for the football team at a local boys' school, and soon she had boyfriends. One of them took Grace back to his parents' place in Carmel when they weren't home and introduced the underage girl, fortified by liquor, to the world of sex. Once the hangover cleared the next day, Grace had few recollections of the momentous event.

In truth, the most lasting relationship to come out of this period was the one with alcoholic beverages. Grace was already an experienced drinker by the time she turned 16. She swigged gin straight from the bottles in her parents' liquor cabinet and no one thought of it as more than a passing phase.

She was as happy to see graduation day as Castilleja was to be rid of her. Although Grace had no burning desire to attend college, she decided that if she were going to go, she would get as far away from Palo Alto as possible. At the recommendation of a classmate, Grace enrolled in Finch College, a hoity-toity school on Park Avenue in New York. She stayed there from September 1957 until the following June.

> **GRACE SLICK:** I just wanted to hang out in New York but you can't say to your parents, "Why don't you give me $20,000 so I can hang out in New York?"

Grace adored New York. She loved walking the streets, going to Central Park. On weekends she took the train to Princeton, New Jersey, where she had a new boyfriend who could drink as much as she could.

During her New York period, Grace investigated the folk music craze and learned how to play some of the popular folk tunes on guitar. One night she went to see Odetta perform at a Greenwich Village nightclub and snuck into the singer's dressing room, where Grace sang for the star, accompanying herself on guitar. Odetta told Grace that she had a nice voice, and encouraged her, although she warned Grace that the music business could be a tough career choice.

For her sophomore year, Grace transferred to the University of Miami to study art, not because of the school's academic reputation but because she'd heard it was a top party school. During her tenure there, her grades didn't improve much, but she discovered the bawdy topical comedy of Lenny Bruce, all the rage among the hip. It was also during her stay in Miami that Grace first smoked marijuana.

The educational system finally lost its weak grip on Grace in 1959. She returned to Palo Alto and made one spiritless stab at entering the world of show business by auditioning for a record label, but the black owners of the company were uninterested in a white girl singing Gershwin show tunes, and Grace went back to the workaday world, toiling at jobs she loathed.

In the summer of 1960, Grace received a call from her best friend, Celeste "Cece" Shane, inviting her down to Beverly Hills to join her in promoting the presidential campaign of John F. Kennedy. Although she was largely apolitical, Grace was happy to have finally found others who didn't prejudge her or expect her to conform and, like many optimistic young Americans, she believed in JFK. Cece's friend Jill St. John, a promising Hollywood starlet, was another member of their small clique. Grace attended political parties and even shook the hand of the young senator from Massachusetts, but the experience did nothing to endear her to the political system itself. She moved back into her parents' home in Palo Alto and began supporting herself by modeling.

Although her friends had told her she was the wrong body type, Grace persisted, and she found work at a posh department store.

> **GRACE SLICK:** Modeling is something you can do if you don't know how to do anything else. I was a couturier model for I. Magnin's. I'd wear two- or three-thousand-dollar outfits and show them to all these old ladies, and then go home and wear a denim dress and sandals.

Grace had no idea what she was going to do with the rest of her life; she just knew it wasn't going to be this. But neither could she have predicted her next move: marriage.

Bob and Betty Slick and their three sons, Gerald, Darby and Danny, had once been next-door neighbors of the Wings in Palo Alto. Even after the two families moved apart, they remained close. Grace had never paid much attention to the boys, but after she returned from school, she was reintroduced to the oldest one, known as Jerry. He was hardly Grace's type at all, yet she found in herself a desire to impress him and he saw in her a strength that he admired. Their romance was swift, if passionless—a month after they began seeing each other, they were engaged.

Grace really just wanted to live with Jerry, not marry him. But children of society did not shack up, and a wedding was planned. Grace had decided when she was a little girl that if she ever did tie the knot, it would be at San Francisco's Grace Cathedral (she liked the name), and on August 26, 1961, the ornate church became the site of the union of Jerry Slick and the woman to be known forevermore as Grace Slick. Darby, the middle brother, served as Jerry's best man, and the newlyweds honeymooned in Hawaii.

When they returned, Jerry enrolled at San Diego State University and Grace worked in the accounting office at a department store. While they enjoyed the beauty of the city, Grace was unhappy there. After one semester they headed back north and Jerry transferred to San Francisco State College. They rented a house in the Potrero Hill section, Jerry taking film courses while Grace read and reinvented herself as a bohemian.

The Slicks gradually shifted into the intellectual postbeatnik class, becoming increasingly aware politically, listening to folk records by Bob Dylan and Joan Baez and taking up a bit of organic gardening.

GRACE SLICK: We'd grow dope in the backyard, for our own entertainment. And we had a fabulous situation because the landlord was an Italian lady who, like me, lost her mind when she saw anybody in a uniform. She took a shotgun to the door—you couldn't come anywhere near those buildings.

Although Grace remained faithful to her husband in the early stage of the marriage, she wasn't surprised or upset to occasionally find him on the couch with another woman—Grace simply went off to bed by herself. If messing around with another woman made him happy, she thought, why should she interfere? But by 1964, as Jerry became more involved in filmmaking, the couple drifted further apart. They still shared some mutual friends, but that list dwindled as Grace's devotion to alcohol made her an unwelcome guest at social events.

DARBY SLICK: We had a friend named Roy Baxter, who used to have parties, and that's where I first started to see Grace get really outrageous. There was a German guy that used to come to these parties and she used to regularly attack him.

It was at one of Baxter's bashes that the Slicks met a British chemist who told them of the wonders of hallucinogens. At his apartment, he served Grace and Jerry a vile-tasting brew consisting mainly of the essence of peyote buttons. The drug intrigued Grace, and she soon graduated to LSD and other psychedelics. They showed her that there were many levels of consciousness, and that there was no finality. Acid allowed her to see that there was much more than meets the eye, and it showed her how to apply those lessons to a personality that already operated under the assumption that life was ludicrous.

During that spring of 1965, Grace and Baxter engaged often in lengthy conversations. Baxter tried to interest Grace in the new rock and roll music that was sweeping the country, but she couldn't warm up to it. Even in her adolescence, she'd preferred Bartok, Prokofiev and the musical *South Pacific*. The phenomenon of Elvis Presley had passed her by completely, and she found the Beatles' early songs childish.

GRACE SLICK: But then the Rolling Stones came along and I thought, Yes, this is it! Attitude and snide and don't take yourself too seriously.

Grace also developed an interest in jazz. The music had always been on the fringes, but Grace had never really made the effort to study it or understand it. Then a friend of Jerry's, Bill Piersol, introduced her to the greats. She was particularly enthralled with the landmark Miles Davis album *Sketches of Spain*. All things Spanish had long fascinated Grace, and here was an exquisite piece of thinking person's music built around Spanish imagery. She played it over and over, and soon her hunger for other styles of music blossomed.

Grace had an opportunity to put her own expanding musical talents to use when Jerry began working on his final project at San Francisco State, an independent film called *Everybody Hits Their Brother Once*. The film had developed out of Jerry's senior thesis, with a script by Piersol. A 45-minute meditation on the absurdities of life, it featured soundtrack music by Grace Slick, who also appeared in the film.

Grace entered a recording studio for the first time at the college, laying down a pretty Spanish guitar melody. She was intrigued by the three-track recording technology, which allowed her to overdub—to record on one track and then, on another track, play along to what she'd recorded—and then do it all over again, creating a virtual group of Graces.

Grace and Jerry were living in Marin County by the summer of 1965. They'd become card-carrying members of the artistic community, experienced dopers and rock fans. But the Slicks were only peripherally aware of the scene that was developing nearby. They hadn't made any moves to check it out firsthand until Grace's eyes came to rest upon the newspaper photo of Marty Balin that August.

12

THE GREAT! SOCIETY REALLY DOESN'T LIKE YOU MUCH AT ALL

SIGNE ANDERSON WAS THROUGH. She knew it, they knew it, there was no sense prolonging it. They'd tried to make it work, but there were too many obstacles. Everyone was ready to face the future.

She'd had a good run. Although her tenure with the Airplane lasted barely more than a year, Signe had earned her part of the rave reviews. She'd been there for the band's first album, and all of those landmark gigs. She had a strong fan following. She'd even been immortalized, along with the rest, on a *Bell Telephone Hour* TV special on the San Francisco sound. By the time that program aired, though, the Airplane had a new female lead vocalist.

> **MARTY BALIN:** We asked Signe to leave. Her husband was an idiot; it was embarrassing us. At one party with RCA people, he's going around with "Jefferson Airplane Loves You" pins, *sticking* them into guys' chests, like you see marines do.

> **BILL THOMPSON:** The band had me fire Signe after the Monterey Jazz Festival. I was political about it: "The guys don't think it's a good idea for you to be in the band, and it just doesn't seem to be working out."
>
> Then she got it out of me who was gonna replace her. She started crying, "They think she's better than me, don't they?"

For Signe, who says she was not fired but departed on her own, leaving the band was practical, and necessary.

> **SIGNE (TOLY ANDERSON) ETTLIN:** I never wanted to leave, but I had another priority, my husband and my child. People always think that sounds really corny and dumb. They say, "But you were finally making it."
>
> And I say, "If you have nothing left when you've gotten there, then why bother to take the journey?"

The precise dates of Signe's last gig and Grace's first show remain another Airplane mystery. Almost certainly Signe wrapped it up some time during a three-show run at the Fillmore the weekend of October 14 to 16, 1966. Whether she played all three concerts and then left, or whether she cut out before the third gig, is a matter of confusion. Thompson is certain that Signe played the first two nights and that Grace stepped in for the third, a recollection shared by others and repeated, whether true or false, as history throughout the years. Signe swears she stayed for all three, and was even given a warm sendoff by Bill Graham, flowers and all.

She may be right. It wasn't until October 17, the day after the Fillmore run ended, that Ralph Gleason wrote: "Grace Slick from the Great Society replaces Signe Anderson with Jefferson Airplane this week and her debut will be at the Opera Fol De Rol Wednesday," referring to a benefit at the San Francisco Civic Auditorium on October 19.

Whenever she actually left, for the most part, Signe Anderson remains the answer to a rock trivia question: What was the name of Jefferson Airplane's first female vocalist? Every so often, someone gets it right, and that's enough for her.

There was never really any doubt who was going to be Jefferson Airplane's second female singer. Grace Slick had long been friendly with the band and was familiar with their repertoire. The Great Society had often opened shows for the Airplane, and Grace always stuck around to watch them perform. And the Airplane couldn't help but notice Grace. With her long, straight, dark hair and piercing blue eyes, she was a stunning, radiant figure. Onstage, her charisma was palpable. She drew her audience in without even trying.

The Great Society, formed in the summer of '65, was not unlike the Airplane in their personnel and approach, yet they'd quickly developed their own musical identity, more experimental and exotic, less pop-oriented or bluesy than the early Airplane. Darby Slick, the Great Society's lead guitarist, brought to the band a wide range of sophisticated musical influences, including the improvisational language of jazz. He was also in love with the sound of the Indian sitar, having discovered it long before George Harrison and the Beatles introduced the instrument to most Western ears.

Prior to the band's formation, while Jerry Slick worked on his student films, Darby often met privately with Grace to get high and make music. She tinkered with the flutelike recorder and Darby the acoustic guitar, not playing structured songs so much as improvising freely. What neither Grace nor Jerry realized was that Darby concealed an obsessive crush on his sister-in-law. Finally, one night, Grace volunteered herself to him, much to Darby's shock. They drove down to the Slicks' Santa Cruz beach house and made love.

DARBY SLICK: Jerry and Grace had told me that they had an open marriage, and they were both making it with other people. Jerry was out with somebody else at the time and we were both drinking a lot. Grace doesn't remember that this even happened.

In the spring of 1964, a frustrated Darby, deciding he needed to be far away from Grace and Jerry, hitchhiked to New York, taking an apartment in Brooklyn and spending day after day attending Lenny Bruce's obscenity trial. When winter set in, though, New York became inhospitable and Darby returned to the Bay Area. He continued to visit his brother and Grace, and one evening arrived to find the couple engaged in impromptu music making with Jean Piersol, the new wife of Jerry's screenwriter friend Bill. Darby picked up an electric guitar and joined in. Before long they were rehearsing daily, Jean and Grace sharing lead vocals. Grace played guitar, along with Darby, and Jerry hit the drums.

At first the group had no name, and no bass. But it did have songs— Grace, Darby and Jerry had all begun composing, and they also learned an array of eclectic, well-chosen covers, including "Sally, Go 'Round the Roses," a 1963 hit for the girl group the Jaynetts. But no sooner had they gotten off the ground than Bill and Jean Piersol announced they were moving to San Jose and leaving the group. To replace the missing musicians, the Slicks brought in Bard Dupont, a disgruntled postal worker, and his friend David Minor, on bass and guitar, respectively. The band's name, the Great Society, came via Bard's friend David Freiberg, who chose it in mock honor of the domestic program of then-U.S. President Lyndon Johnson—despised by the band members and many other young people—which would supposedly improve the quality of life for all Americans.

DARBY SLICK: It was a joke: We hippie scum are your Great Society.

Early on, the Great Society hooked up with John Carpenter as their manager. They auditioned for Tom Donahue and Bobby Mitchell, high-profile DJs for San Francisco AM station KYA, who also ran the local Autumn Records label and the club Mother's. Donahue was sufficiently impressed with the Great Society and, in October 1965, took them to Golden State Recorders on Harrison Street. With Donahue rolling the tapes and local photographer Ray Andersen shooting the proceedings, the band performed a "demo album," running through about a dozen of their songs—nearly all of the recordings remained unreleased for decades.

They were also rewarded with a two-week engagement at Mother's, but before they went to work for Donahue, the Great Society played their first public gig, on October 15, at the Coffee Gallery on Grant Avenue. The very next evening they were sharing a bill with Jefferson Airplane at the first Family Dog dance at Longshoreman's Hall. But Darby, for one, didn't share Grace's enthusiasm for the headliner. Perhaps, then, Darby was the culprit behind one of the Great Society's most memorable publicity efforts, countering the ubiquitous "Jefferson Airplane Loves You" buttons with a fittingly sarcastic one of their own. It read: "The Great! Society Really Doesn't Like You Much At All."

Attendance was sparse at the Mother's gigs, mostly tourists, topless dancers, drunks and sailors (and drunken sailors), but the extended stint gave the band a good opportunity to polish its material. Gleason gave them their first review, a short *Chronicle* piece. He singled out "Father Bruce," Grace's song about Lenny Bruce, as a highlight and remarked, "I have a strong feeling they will make a reputation for themselves."

As had happened to the Airplane, once Gleason gave the Great Society his blessing, record scouts, including one from the large Decca label, lined up to check out the band. Grace blew off one producer who didn't impress her—perhaps she would have been more cordial (or perhaps not) had she known that he was Bob Crewe, a record industry giant who'd cowritten and produced most of the chart-topping records by the Four Seasons, one of the most popular American groups of the '60s.

Concurrent with the Mother's run, the Great Society returned to Golden State for the first of several recording sessions that would take place over the next couple of months. There they were introduced to their new producer, a young, ambitious rhythm and blues disc jockey named Sylvester Stewart who would, a couple of years later, do just fine for himself under his nickname, Sly Stone.

Sly was a workhorse who thought nothing of running the group through a song dozens of times in an effort to hone it to perfection. Unfortunately, he found himself working with musicians who did not believe in accepting outside opinions.

DARBY SLICK: We weren't happy to work with any producer, so there was kind of an adversarial relationship right from the beginning, which was unfortunate because he was just trying to do a nice job.

GRACE SLICK: Sly could play any instrument known to man. He could have just made the record himself, except for the singers. It was kind of degrading in a way.

Autumn wanted to release David Minor's song "That's How It Is" as the band's first single, but the Great Society vetoed the choice. Instead, they picked a composition that Darby had dashed off one morning while coming down from an acid trip, alone and depressed because his girl-friend had spent the night with another man.

Darby wrote, and Grace sang:

When the truth is found to be lies
And all the joy within you dies
Don't you want somebody to love?

The Great Society first recorded the song, originally titled "Someone to Love," on November 30, 1965. It would be another year and a half before most of the world heard it. But it wasn't the Great Society's version that they'd hear.

DARBY SLICK: Our version was sadder. I'm not saying it was better, but there was a sharper contrast between the verse and the chorus. Everybody who heard it said, "This is a hit." And as soon as the Airplane heard it, those guys were also saying, "This is a hit."

For the flip side of the single they chose "Free Advice," another of Darby's compositions. It took several weeks of misfires in the studio before the band came up with a usable version, and even then, on December 4, the Great Society played no fewer than 54 takes of the song before an exasperated Sly threw in the towel, telling Donahue he could do nothing more with them.

"Free Advice," with its Eastern-influenced melody, was finally completed in January 1966. Northbeach Records, a subsidiary of Autumn, sent out some promotional copies but the single was never sold at retail. Few copies survived, making the Great Society's "Someone to Love"/"Free Advice" a valuable record, commanding hundreds of dollars on the collector market.

Inspired, Grace sat down to write a new song of her own. Drawing on her love of all things Spanish, she fashioned a snaky bolero rhythm. Then, thinking back on her childhood fantasies, she suggested a correlation between the mystical worlds of those timeless tales and the quests that she and her fellow seekers were undertaking as young adults:

> *One pill makes you larger and one pill makes you small*
> *And the ones that Mother gives you don't do anything at all*
> *Go ask Alice when she's ten feet tall.*

There had never been another song like "White Rabbit." Originally called "White Rabbit Blues," it was Lewis Carroll meets Ravel meets *Sketches of Spain*. Electric guitars and snare drums piled atop one another, blatant drug allusions crossed paths with bedtime stories, all climaxing in a smashing crescendo, a bellowing Grace inventing a catch phrase for her generation, "Feed your head! Feed your head!"

GRACE SLICK: "White Rabbit" came fast, probably half an hour one day and finish it up the next. It's an interesting song, but it didn't do what I wanted it to. What I was trying to say was that between the ages of zero and five the information and the input you get is almost indelible. In other words, once a Catholic, always a Catholic. And the parents read us these books, like *Alice in Wonderland*, where she gets high, tall, and she takes mushrooms, a hookah, pills, alcohol. And then there's *The Wizard of Oz*, where they fall into a field of poppies and when they wake up they see Oz. And then there's *Peter Pan*, where if you sprinkle white dust on you, you could fly. And then you wonder why we do it? Well, what did you read to me?

The Great Society, like the Airplane, quickly recognized that their manager was incapable of managing them. Darby was put in the unwanted but imperative position of firing John Carpenter, who went on to write about music for a couple of years and was later murdered while hitchhiking. Howard Wolf, who had often advised Carpenter on matters relating to the band, assumed managerial duties, working at getting them a record deal and otherwise attempting to guide their career.

Also like the early Airplane, the band quickly realized that its bass player wasn't cutting it. In March, just before the release of the single, Bard Dupont was dismissed from the group. His replacement was a friend of Darby's, Peter van Gelder, who could also play saxophone.

Between Darby's Indian music leanings and Peter's jazz influences, the Great Society began to stretch the songs out onstage, pushing their jams into fascinating exploratory realms. Grace played a number of instruments, including guitar, bass, recorder, piano and organ, and was quickly devising a noteworthy stage persona, conversing with the audience between songs yet standing stock still while singing, her eyes trained on the others in the band.

Grace must have been aware of her popularity by the spring, because she was already thinking about her next move. When the Great Society opened for the Blues Project at the Avalon in late April, Grace was riveted. She made a mental note and tucked it away in the back of her mind: If this thing didn't go someplace soon she would either join the Blues Project or find another band as strong as they were.

The Great Society did grow that summer. They reworked several of their older songs into more dynamic, captivating pieces, and their new ones were more fully realized, not just formless jams. Grace was becoming a dynamo, developing her own take on scat singing, a jazz-associated freeform technique that turned her voice into another lead instrument while giving the group a unique approach to vocal harmony. Grace didn't so much try to blend with the other voices as provide a counterpoint to them, going off on her own ride, encircling them, somewhat divorced from the main goings-on, yet never so far away that she didn't make sense within the framework of the song.

In the summer of '66, the Great Society's deal with Donahue was declared null and void when the label failed to release any music by the band, and then Autumn Records went bankrupt, freeing the group to go label shopping. Wolf arranged a deal with Mercury Records, but just as the contracts were about to be issued, Darby and Peter decided to go off to India for an indefinite period, to study North Indian classical music. The Great Society was on the verge of a possible breakthrough, but there was nothing anyone could say to change Darby and Peter's minds. And no one really tried.

Even if their departure hadn't been enough to kill the band, the Great Society would have self-destructed before long. Grace's marriage to Jerry Slick was in shambles, and it was getting more difficult for them to be around each other day and night. Besides, Darby still had a thing for Grace, creating a rift between the two brothers.

In the early fall, David Minor left the band. It wasn't long until the Great Society was pronounced dead. For Grace, the new developments provided the opening she needed. She had nothing specific in mind, but when Jack Casady asked her nonchalantly in September if she'd consider joining Jefferson Airplane, it didn't take more than a minute for her to answer.

13 TRYING TO REVOLUTIONIZE TOMORROW

BILL THOMPSON REMEMBERS THE MOMENT when he knew for sure that Jefferson Airplane really had the power to transform people. It happened not in San Francisco, but in Iowa, Grace Slick's first show with the band away from California.

> **BILL THOMPSON:** It was the Grinnell College homecoming dance. All of the girls wore these long, frilly dresses down to their ankles, and corsages, the guys had suits and ties and their parents were with them, sitting in the bleachers watching. The band did three sets. We brought a light show with us. The first set, they're looking at us like we're Martians: "What the hell is this?" The band had pretty long hair at the time, even compared to the Beatles. The second set, they started to dance. Then the parents all went home, and by the third set, the kids went nuts.

Thompson had taken over Grace Slick's management contract from Howard Wolf, paying him $750, "like buying Manhattan from the Indians for beads," Thompson later said. Then Jefferson Airplane truly took off.

> **DAVID CROSBY:** When they got Grace in the band, that was just beyond belief. She was stunning. She had a power and intensity onstage that Stevie Nicks should only ever dream she could get. With Marty she was like a bullfighter with a bull. She would circle him and dart at him and pull from him and electrify him and touch him with bare wire. And Marty rose to the occasion.

> **MARTY BALIN:** She was just like we were: drugged-out, drinking, free and ballsy and outrageous. She just fit in great.

Not all of the Airplane's fans accepted Grace readily, however.

> **PAUL KANTNER:** She was coming into a pretty well-gelled situation. A lot of people were angry. There was a whole Signe contin-

gent, among RCA as well, who were really fond of her. I was too; I thought Signe was a great singer. And Grace always stood in awe of her. So when Signe left there were a lot of people saying, "Oh, my God, the Airplane is dead."

After a few weeks of rehearsals, Grace made her maiden appearance with the Airplane in San Francisco. Then came a gig in Santa Barbara, followed immediately by Iowa. The Airplane had no idea that their reputation had penetrated so deeply into the Midwest.

PAUL KANTNER: All the kids came in prom gowns and tuxedos. Then we came back to Iowa a year later and they were having nude mud love-ins and everybody had their faces painted.

At first, Grace was tentative onstage. She learned the parts that Signe had sung in tunes like "Go to Her," "Runnin' 'Round This World" and "High Flyin' Bird," but performed no lead vocals and none of her own material. The forceful personality and the improvised vocals were initially kept in check. But it didn't take long for Grace to find her place, and to learn how to apply her technique to the Airplane's repertoire.

JACK CASADY: Grace would lead us in different directions. I could play a lot more aggressive bass lines than I could to some of the things that Signe would do, which were much more folk-oriented. Here was something I could put my teeth into.

GRACE SLICK: Our voices together were a tag team kind of thing. Marty would be singing and I'd do something else off the top of that and Paul would be somewhere else underneath. It was a little sloppy, actually, it wasn't precise, but it was fun because you could do anything you wanted to. It wasn't like, how come you didn't sing that flatted fourth?

JEFFERSON AIRPLANE TAKES OFF had been in the shops for barely two months when the Airplane returned to Los Angeles at the end of October to begin work on their sophomore album. Their new singer, having had only a few weeks to rehearse the new material, was with them, full of ideas and vigor.

For the engineering duties, RCA recalled Dave Hassinger, who had done such a commendable job on the debut. But *Takes Off* had sold only moderately, and the label wanted this next release to be the band's breakthrough, so a more commercial approach was needed. The band hadn't gotten along with Tommy Oliver, the producer of the first album, and it was decided that someone younger and more in tune with the Airplane's music was needed. The label felt that Rick Jarrard would be perfect for the job.

Like Oliver, Jarrard was a musician himself, and he knew rock and roll. He had played with a rock band, the Wellingtons, that had appeared on (and recorded the theme song for) the TV sitcom *Gilligan's Island*. As a staff producer for RCA, Jarrard would later produce albums by José Feliciano, Harry Nilsson and others, as well as the first demos by the Carpenters. But to many rock fans he is best known for the one and only album he produced for Jefferson Airplane, *Surrealistic Pillow*.

On October 31, 1966, Halloween, Jefferson Airplane recorded the first two songs of 11 that would comprise the new album: "She Has Funny Cars," a collaboration between Marty (words) and Jorma (music), and "My Best Friend," written by Skip Spence, their former drummer.

"She Has Funny Cars"—the title, Marty says, is nothing more than "surreal nonsense"—was chosen to open the album, and is emblematic of just how far the band had grown artistically over the previous several months. The song gets off to a crashing start with Spencer Dryden—who, like Grace, was making his first appearance on an Airplane album—walloping the tom-toms and cymbals to a quasi-Bo Diddley beat. Jack and Jorma enter simultaneously, doubling up on the signature riff, both attacking their instruments with more ferocity and volume than could be found anywhere on the debut. Marty takes the lead vocal: "Every day I try so hard to know your mind and find out what's inside you."

Grace and Paul join on the next line, in perfect three-part harmony: "Time goes on and I don't know just where you are or how I'm gonna find you."

A few solitary bass notes, and the tempo shifts to a light swing. Marty and Paul engage in a call-and-response with Grace, but instead of echoing them she sings a contrapuntal lyric dissociated from the main storyline. Soon she zooms up and away, no longer singing words at all but expounding on a pure note, increasingly intense, cutting through everything in its path. Occasionally, she meets them on common ground:

"And I know, and I know, and I know, your mind's guaranteed, it's all you'll ever need, so what do you want with me?"

"Some have it nice," Marty suggests, slyly. "Fat and round," retorts Grace, a classic Slick non sequitur. Then all three: "Flash! Paradise!"

Jack Casady, meanwhile, wrings unworldly fuzz out of his bass. "Trying to revolutionize tomorrow," Marty contributes. The song fades, Jack's bass groaning like a dinosaur dying in agony. In just over three minutes, Jefferson Airplane has defined psychedelic music.

"My Best Friend" is the polar opposite in temperament. Set to a lazy hop-along rhythm, the mostly acoustic ballad is the embodiment of the love-power ethic, sung in uplifting tandem harmonies. They were off to an auspicious start, but the Airplane had felt, even before leaving for L.A., that they might need a pair of sympathetic ears, a *compadre* with no ties to RCA who could aid them in making decisions in the studio. On the second day of sessions, Jerry Garcia of the Grateful Dead joined them. Credited as "Musical and Spiritual Adviser" on the back of the album cover, Garcia offered valuable arranging advice, helping to shape songs. He also contributed guitar to three tracks on the album and two that didn't make the final cut.

Or did he? Oddly, despite confirmation of Garcia's involvement by all of the band members, Rick Jarrard claims that Garcia had nothing to do with the album.

> **RICK JARRARD:** Jerry Garcia was never present on any of those sessions. Jerry Garcia played no guitar on that album. I never met Jerry Garcia. I produced that album from start to finish, never heard from Jerry Garcia, never talked to Jerry Garcia. He was not involved creatively on that album at all. That's really gotten to me all these years, because I sweated blood on that album. If Jerry Garcia was there, he was in his spirit form.

Is it feasible that Garcia could have come and gone from the studio, added his guitar parts and helped the band devise arrangements without RCA knowing about it? And if the Airplane was sneaking him in and out, why is he listed on RCA's label copy—the paperwork submitted to the company by the band to account for all musicians who performed on the record—as a guitar contributor? By listing him, Garcia would have to be paid, and why would the band pay him for guitar work that never happened?

Garcia does not receive credit on the album jacket for any specific musical input, but that could have been due to the fact that he was signed to Warner Bros. Records with the Dead and it was just easier to skip the formalities. But one thing no one disputes is that Garcia came up with the album's title: "That's as surrealistic as a pillow!" he exclaimed after hearing one take played back. It stuck.

Despite friction between the Airplane and Jarrard, the sessions continued, work was completed and a classic rock album was pieced together in just three weeks.

The next day, the band cut "Plastic Fantastic Lover," a pounding rant inspired by the most pervasive American addiction of all, television. Marty had written the song during the band's trip to Chicago, after looking at a plastics factory. His vocal is deliberately cool yet full of urgency, matched in its fury by Jorma, Jack and Spencer. The song was used to close out the album when Jarrard assembled the final sequence.

Garcia is credited on the RCA label copy for playing guitar on that one, as he is again on the next day's session for Marty and Paul's "Today." Marty's pleading vocal is emotionally stirring, the band building to a grand climax behind him. It's one of the great love songs of the era, an unabashed romantic paean devoid of both irony and gushiness.

Like most of the album, "Today" is double-dipped in reverb, a sonic characteristic of the album that received mixed reactions from the Airplane but which the producer felt added texture to the recording.

RICK JARRARD: That's one of the tools that you use. You're painting a picture. A lot of artists think, I just want my voice up there, raw. They forget that when you're onstage, you've got a lot of visual things going for you, but when you're creating a record you have to replace those visuals and embellish.

"White Rabbit" was recorded on November 3. In the hands of the Great Society, Grace's showpiece had been a gypsy trance dance. An extended instrumental section reminiscent of the Butterfield Band's "East-West" preceded the body of the song. It had an insistent tempo, marked by rocking drums and a repetitive guitar line. The Airplane slowed it down and stripped the ornamentation away, kept the core melody and restored to the song the bolero rhythm that Grace had envisioned. Jack wrote a new, funky bass part, Spencer stayed close to his snare and Jorma played a bold, seductive, yet simple guitar line that transforms smoothly into chunky, aggressive chords at the choruses.

Grace, of course, was the focus, and she delivered a commanding, no-nonsense vocal performance devoid of her trademark improvisations. What had begun as an allegory became an anthem for a generation.

MARTY BALIN: It was a masterpiece, really. Perfectly written for the perfect time.

Marty's "3/5 of a Mile in 10 Seconds" was cut next. Like "Plastic Fantastic Lover," it's a throbbing rocker, a protest song:

Do away with people blowing my mind
Do away with people wasting my precious time
Take me to a circus tent where I can easily pay my rent
And all the other freaks will share my cares.

Jorma's economical, well-framed guitar solo cuts the rave-up in half, after which Marty returns to complain about "things that come on obscene" and the inflated price of dope, "'specially when it's sold by a kid who's only 15." As for the title, it has no cryptic hidden meaning—Marty lifted it from the sports pages.

The Airplane took a short break after the "3/5" session, playing the Fillmore and traveling to Vancouver. When they returned to L.A. on November 14, the band recorded "J.P.P. McStep Blues," another song by Skip Spence. The departed drummer joined them on the session, as did Garcia. The track never made it to the *Pillow* album, but it was dusted off in 1974 for the *Early Flight* album, a collection of outtakes.

Also recorded that day was "How Do You Feel," with lead vocal by Paul, and Grace tootling on the recorder. Another sweet ballad, its style is highly reminiscent of the Mamas and the Papas, the hit L.A. folk-rock group. Authored by Tom Mastin, a songwriter Kantner knew from his Peninsula folkie days, as well as a friend of Rick Jarrard's, it's the only song on the album penned by someone not directly associated with the Airplane.

The following day two songs were committed to tape. Encouraged by Marty to write more, Paul came up with "D.C.B.A.-25," the *Pillow* song closest in feel to the folk-rock of *Takes Off.* A straightforward duet with Grace, its title refers simply to the song's chord progression and, Paul being Paul, the batch of acid—LSD-25—that put old Albert Hofmann's name into the history books.

The next session that day was for the other song Grace imported from the Great Society, "Somebody to Love." With that group, Darby Slick's composition was played almost as a midtempo shuffle. The first change the Airplane made was to virtually double the tempo, cranking it out at a breakneck pace that remains nearly static from verse to chorus. The Airplane version is tightly reined, placing Grace front and center and leaving no slack. Garcia was reportedly responsible for the new arrangement.

The second change was lyrical, a reference to "in bed" being softened to the more radio-friendly "in your head."

All told, it's a tour de force performance and, upon its release in early 1967, it would become, along with "White Rabbit," one of the defining recordings of the era.

Marty's "Comin' Back to Me" was the album's other breathtakingly beautiful ballad, alongside "Today." Marty had written the song in one sitting, after smoking some potent marijuana. He headed to the studio immediately to record it, using whichever musicians were present at the time: Jack, Garcia and Grace, who played the mournful recorder behind Marty's acoustic guitar. Marty's words are pure poetry:

The summer had inhaled and held its breath too long
The winter looked the same as if it had never gone
And through an open window where no curtain hung
I saw you, I saw you
Comin' back to me.

Two more *Pillow* sessions yielded outtakes that turned up later on *Early Flight:* Grace put her stamp on "Go to Her," a song that Signe had sung, and Jorma—joined by his old Ohio schoolmate John Hammond on harmonica, Garcia and pianist Goldy McJohn (later of Steppenwolf)—cut the bluesy "In the Morning," a song he authored.

Jorma had one other song that he'd been goofing around with in the studio. He had no intention of recording it for the album—after all, it was a solo acoustic piece that he had written while giving a guitar workshop in Santa Clara in 1962, an instrumental fingerpicking workout whose John Fahey-like style was completely out of character with the electric rock of the Airplane.

But Rick Jarrard was so impressed with it he insisted it had to be included on the album. He convinced Jorma to come into the RCA studio one day by himself.

JORMA KAUKONEN: "Embryonic Journey" was the first song that I ever wrote. I was just fooling around, fingerpicking, and I fell into doing that song. There's a descending line on it; I got the idea from Pete Seeger's "Bells of Rhymney." I didn't think it was gonna fit in, but of course it did fit in and I'm really glad that he made me do it. For me, it bridged the gap between rock and roll and folk. It happened absolutely organically.

With *Surrealistic Pillow* completed, the Airplane went home to play Thanksgiving weekend at the Fillmore. The following weekend, they returned to L.A. for a week of shows at the Whisky, missing the opportunity to witness Moby Grape, the band that Skip Spence had cofounded after his return from Mexico. Everyone who caught them agreed that this was one outstanding band, some of the greatest rock and roll to emerge yet from San Francisco. But to the Airplane, the most astonishing thing of all was that, although Skip Spence was well aware of the turmoil the Airplane had been through, Moby Grape's manager was Matthew Katz. Katz had, in fact, helped engineer the band's formation.

Moby Grape was a record company's dream band. Their complementary three-guitar lineup could produce a thunderous noise or the smoothest ballad, not unlike what Buffalo Springfield was doing down in L.A. Their songs were expertly composed and had both commercial possibilities and the integrity demanded by San Francisco audiences.

But the Grape was doomed. Its saga is one of squandered potential, ill-advised promotional schemes and other absurdly misguided business decisions, bad luck, blunders and excruciating heartbreak. Moby Grape could have had it all, but ended up with nothing. There were busts and a second album generally considered inferior to their superb debut. Then, in 1968, began the downfall of Skip Spence. He became increasingly unreliable and unpredictable, disappearing into a drug-induced psychosis. A diagnosed paranoid schizophrenic, he lived out much of his life during the next few decades in institutions as a ward of the state.

Moby Grape chugged along only for a couple of years before circumstances did the band in, and the former members subsequently spent decades in litigation with Katz over the ownership of the band's recorded legacy and their right to use the name Moby Grape.

JEFFERSON AIRPLANE'S OWN LEGAL PROBLEMS with Matthew Katz began shortly after they fired him, when the band's attorney, Maxwell Keith, rescinded their management contracts with Katz and Matthew filed for arbitration to enforce the contracts.

The dispute went first to the California Labor Commission, which had the power to void noncomplying talent agents' contracts, but the commission handed the mess over to San Francisco Superior Court. In January 1967, that court sided with Katz, sending everyone to arbitration. But the Airplane, not ready to give up, appealed to the Supreme Court of California in the matter cited as *Buchwald v. Superior Court.*

The Supreme Court created a new legal precedent by deciding the appeal in the band's favor, reasoning that since Katz was definitely booking the band and otherwise acting as its manager, the contracts could be voided. The court sent the case back to the Labor Commission, which ruled that the management and publishing contracts between Katz and the group were void, that the Airplane owed Katz nothing and that he in fact owed them nearly $50,000, which he'd received as commissions from the band.

An unhappy Katz then appealed that decision to the Superior Court of San Francisco, which requested that he post a bond in the amount of the judgment. But by 1970 Katz had not put up the bond, and the Superior Court dismissed his appeal. Katz then appealed that dismissal to the Supreme Court, in a new case cited as *Buchwald v. Katz.* Once again, the court made new law, this time regarding the consequences of failing to post bond in an appeal from the Labor Commission's award. But the Supreme Court partly agreed with Katz: they ruled that his failure to post a bond shouldn't prevent him from proceeding with the appeal itself, and the case was reinstated.

Eventually the Airplane's original lawsuit, a second suit, and Katz's appeal from the Labor Commission were consolidated into one large case and the litigation continued. In 1973, Katz sought an accounting of publishing royalties on the Airplane's songs and brought RCA Records in as a defendant. In response, RCA froze all royalty payments due the copyright owners of each song, as well as freezing producer royalties to Katz.

The case finally went to jury trial in January of 1977. The jury upheld Katz's management contracts with Buchwald [Balin], Kantner and Kaukonen but found that Katz had obtained contracts with Jack Casady and Signe Anderson through fraud, and that the contracts had been validly rescinded by the two of them. They also found that Katz obtained all of the publishing agreements "in violation of his fiduciary responsibilities to all of the plaintiffs," and they too were rescinded.

However, the second phase of the trial, during which monetary awards were to be decided, never occurred. The case ultimately dragged on into the '80s, but no settlement was ever reached. Further, Katz still claimed that he had exclusive copyright ownership of certain Airplane tunes, a claim the band flatly rejected.

By the late '80s, BMG Music, which by then owned RCA Records, was holding on to 20 years' worth of accumulated royalties that they could not distribute. BMG's lawyers ultimately took the initiative and asked the court to dismiss the entire group of cases, on the condition that the court order the royalties to be paid out to the proper parties. The band members joined BMG in that motion, hoping this would put an end to the years of litigation.

Finally, in June 1987, a new judge, Ollie Marie-Victoire, dismissed the suits, for the reason of "delay of prosecution." In his order, the judge reprimanded Katz, saying that he had "sabotaged the settlement negotiations." By that time the royalties being held had reportedly grown to around $1.3 million plus more than $700,000 in interest. Most of the money was awarded to the band, with Katz receiving about $130,000.

Katz then filed two more appeals, both of which were decided against Katz in September of 1987, the judge calling Matthew's motion for reconsideration "frivolous and totally without merit." He ordered the royalties to finally be distributed. Only then, some 22 years after the original band members first met him, was the Airplane finally able to put Matthew Katz behind them.

BILL THOMPSON: This lawsuit lasted so long it could have voted.

Ironically, the band left an unintended legacy. To this day, the legal precedents created in the cases of *Buchwald v. Superior Court* and *Buchwald v. Katz* are still the law in California, and both cases are cited in the annotations under the provisions of the California Talent Agencies Act that they helped define. So the names Buchwald and Katz are still inextricably bound, if only in the law books.

14
ACID, INCENSE AND BALLOONS

"This summer, it should be madness, because all the publicity has gotten out. There's one street called Haight . . . H-A-I-G-H-T. Haight Street is full of love, see?"

—*Marty Balin, February 1967, speaking to* Hit Parader *editor Don Paulsen*

THE SUMMER OF LOVE began in January.

The official title of the momentous occasion that ushered it in, if there was anything official about it, was "Pow-Wow—A Gathering of the Tribes: Human Be-In," although most denizens refer to it simply as the Be-In. It was the first event that brought together a mass of young people—for no real purpose other than celebrating their own existence—who had chosen alternative lifestyles. For many of them, it was an awakening; they had no idea that their numbers had grown so vast.

Over 20,000 revelers came to the Polo Grounds in Golden Gate Park that sunny winter afternoon of January 14, ostensibly to listen to gurus and poets and bands, but mostly just to be. Counterculture celebrities Dick Gregory, Richard Alpert, Jerry Rubin and Lawrence Ferlinghetti spoke to the crowd. The assembled multitude heard Quicksilver, Big Brother, the Airplane and other bands. Buddhists meditated, Allen Ginsberg chanted and Timothy Leary exhorted the crowd to "turn on, tune in, drop out."

Out of the sky, a parachutist fell, landing right on target as the Grateful Dead finished a song. The politicos met the acid heads met the Hell's Angels met the swirling rock and roll dervishes and all coexisted peacefully. It was all over in four or five hours but it heralded the arrival of what the media would come to call the love generation.

As he often did, *Chronicle* music critic Ralph Gleason wrote eloquently about the event: It was, he said, "a statement of life, not of death, and a promise of good, not of evil."

Paul Kantner, after reading Gleason's piece on the Be-In, began appropriating and embellishing upon some of the writer's words and concepts, crafting a new song:

Saturday afternoon, yellow clouds rising in the noon
Acid, incense and balloons.

THE BE-IN RECEIVED MEDIA COVERAGE throughout the United States and abroad, further broadcasting the word that San Francisco was a groovy place to be if your own hometown was boring—and compared to San Francisco, what town wasn't? The Airplane's own profile, meanwhile, had been raised considerably when they received their first taste of major national publicity just weeks prior to the Be-In, in a December 1966 *Newsweek* story on the new San Francisco music. The article deemed the Airplane "the most popular of the groups."

This new notoriety outside of their own community created occupational hazards, however: The first dope bust involving an Airplane member had occurred during the band's stay in Los Angeles, when Jack was nabbed in his hotel room for possession of hashish and the hookah he used to smoke it. Nothing ultimately came of the arrest, and the incident was mercifully kept out of the papers, but it was becoming obvious not only to the Airplane but to many high-profile rock musicians that their highly publicized high times were becoming of greater interest to ambitious law enforcement officials—members of the Beatles, the Rolling Stones and the Grateful Dead would all see the inside of a jail cell before long. Jack Casady was soon nabbed a second time when, serving as a human guinea pig for an especially potent new hallucinogenic called STP, he was picked up near Monterey, sitting stark naked in a mud puddle, contemplating something or other, a large grin plastered across his face.

If they were to become media darlings and attract more attention, the Airplane was going to need someone well organized who could handle their business affairs and help orchestrate their rise. In late 1966, the band asked Bill Graham to become its manager. Unlike Matthew Katz, Graham was someone with whom the band had a positive rapport. Although his lifestyle and modus operandi were radically different from their own, the group realized that Graham, with his business acumen and connections, could give their career the guidance it required.

Right at the start, however, there was a standoff with Graham regarding contracts. After the Katz calamity, the band members were understandably reluctant to commit their signatures to another binding management agreement, whereas Graham wanted some guarantees that he wouldn't get burned.

SPENCER DRYDEN: When we hired Bill Graham it was going to be that hippie-dippie communal socialistic thing, everybody share and share alike. But Bill pulled out a contract for a specified amount to be paid, and there was a big argument. I remember Jorma walking away, just throwing the contract up and saying, "Fuck this, I'm not going to do it."

The band ultimately prevailed: Graham was given an equal vote in all group-related business decisions, but no papers were signed. He made it clear, however, that they would have to work—harder than they ever had. Although *Surrealistic Pillow* was not yet ready for release, Graham wanted to create a buzz outside of San Francisco prior to the album's appearance, and he knew that the band could never hope to gain a national foothold until it conquered New York. Although the Airplane had played as far east as Chicago, they had yet to venture into Graham's old stomping grounds. With RCA footing the bill, a gala promotional party and showcase performance was scheduled for January 8, 1967 at Webster Hall on the fringe of Greenwich Village.

The Airplane dazzled the New York critical elite. The band played two sets, bringing along a light show, and gave interviews to any member of the media who wished to speak with them. Speaking with *Hit Parader*'s Don Paulsen, Grace's sarcastic sense of humor came bubbling up. Asked how she wrote "White Rabbit," she replied quizzically, "How?" and, with the snap timing of a standup comic, quickly deadpanned, "With pencil and paper."

At the end of the evening, the Airplane was joined onstage for a jam by members of the Butterfield Blues Band, Jorma and the mighty Michael Bloomfield duking it out on their guitars. The journalists went back to their desks sufficiently impressed, and the Airplane returned home. They stayed in San Francisco just long enough to play Basin Street West, sharing the bill with jazz giant Dizzy Gillespie who, recalls Spencer, kept trying to pick up Grace.

• • •

IN FEBRUARY, RCA Victor Records released *Surrealistic Pillow*. You couldn't miss it in the record stores. On the front cover is Herb Greene's black-and-white portrait of the band, posed in front of a wall in the photographer's studio that is covered in hieroglyphicslike graffiti. In the photo, most of the musicians are holding instruments they do not know how to play. Across the top of the cover, in ornate, filigreed capital lettering, is the title. At the bottom right, in much smaller type, superimposed over the banjo Spencer is holding, is the band's name. The entire cover, designed by Marty, is dipped in bubblegum pink.

MARTY BALIN: I did the cover in blue, and when it came out, it was pink. RCA changed things; nobody ever asked.

For the back of the record jacket, Marty picked out a handful of photos of the band members, also shot by Greene, ripped them strategically and shuffled them into a collage. The credits are strewn haphazardly, the most prominent belonging not to the musicians but to producer Jarrard.

The first single taken from the album was "My Best Friend," the Skip Spence composition, backed with "How Do You Feel." Released in January, it never cracked the Top 100, only "bubbling under" to number 103. Clearly, the two slower-paced songs were not what the national record buyers were expecting from the group that was described as the epitome of San Francisco's "acid rock." The album itself also got off to a slow start, nudging into *Billboard*'s Top LPs chart at number 137 in the issue dated March 25. (It was a good week for debuts—the first albums by L.A.'s Doors and Buffalo Springfield also arrived.) But the national hype on the Airplane was building considerably, stimulated by the January press blitz and coverage of the Be-In, as well as a return trip to New York later that winter, when they played a nearly two-week run of shows at the hip Café Au Go Go.

Surrealistic Pillow began its rapid ascent up the album chart in early April, as the second single from the album, "Somebody to Love," with "She Has Funny Cars" on the B-side, began its own run on the Hot 100 singles chart. The single entered at number 88 in the April 1 issue and vaulted steadily upward until June, when it peaked at number 5.

Jefferson Airplane, whose music was supposed to be an antidote to the commercial pop on the radio, suddenly found themselves with a hit single being played on nearly every rock and roll station in the country.

Darby Slick was in India when word reached him that "Somebody to Love" had become a huge hit in America. He thought it might be a valuable experience to witness the success of his masterpiece firsthand so, after four and a half months, he returned home. (Ironically, the Great Society themselves later enjoyed a bit of posthumous acclaim when Columbia Records bought some live tapes of the band recorded at the Matrix and released them on two albums, *Conspicuous Only in Its Absence* and *How It Was*. Howard Wolf, who recalled that it was Grace's idea to release the tapes, so that the world would know the origin of the two songs that established Jefferson Airplane, arranged that deal.)

Surrealistic Pillow, boosted by the heavy airplay devoted to the single, continued to sell steadily, ultimately reaching number 3 in August. Had it not been for the Beatles, who released their era-defining *Sgt. Pepper's Lonely Hearts Club Band* in June, and for the Monkees, whose third album, *Headquarters*, lodged stubbornly at number 2, the Airplane would have had the most popular album in the country during the fabled Summer of Love.

Bill Graham, naturally, wanted to capitalize on all of the attention the band was receiving by setting up as many dates as possible. The Airplane loved nothing more than playing live, but Graham's management philosophy of keeping the band on the road almost continuously, and playing in his own rooms when they were in San Francisco, was wearying to some of the Airplane, who preferred a more leisurely schedule. The hectic pace caused friction within the band, with Grace and Spencer, in particular, objecting to the heavy schedule.

With the hit single and album, media hype now came with little effort. In its May 30 issue, *Look*, one of the most popular national periodicals at the time, devoted four pages to an article titled "Jefferson Airplane Loves You." The author, who largely avoided the men in the group, repeatedly called Grace "Gracie," coining a nickname she soon came to detest.

That spring, the Airplane also made their first major TV appearances since Grace had joined the band. First, in early May, they taped *The Smothers Brothers Comedy Hour*, a progressively minded program in tune with the Airplane's core audience. The band, a light show pulsating behind it, performed "Somebody to Love" and "White Rabbit," and the show aired the following month. Afterward, cohost Tom Smothers and the Airplane hung out together and, invariably, out came the guitars and the sacramental herb.

TOM SMOTHERS: I always said thank God I had a brother who was superstraight, and a show that required that I work under a certain quality of attention. If I'd been running with the bands, I'd probably be dead.

The Airplane also guested on the granddaddy of all rock and roll TV programs, Dick Clark's *American Bandstand*. The show aired on June 3, with both "Somebody to Love" and "White Rabbit" lip-synched, as was the *Bandstand* custom. Being sports, the band played along, Paul, Jorma and Jack tearing into their guitars with abandon, Spencer bobbing his head left to right as was his wont, Marty looking dour stuck behind a piano and Grace giving her most piercing, blasé stare—feigning the commitment they would exhibit had they actually been playing.

DICK CLARK: They were terrific. I was excited and the kids were excited because they were so hot. "White Rabbit" wasn't on the chart when they appeared. It went on two or three weeks later, but "Somebody to Love" had been on and was a two-month-old record, so they were very familiar with it. I remember that Grace had on a Little Red Riding Hood outfit. She was extraordinarily beautiful, very mannequinlike.

In a brief chat segment, Paul gave a quick response when Clark inquired whether the parents of America had anything to worry about now that groups like the Airplane were coming into the fore. Clark must have been surprised when Kantner assured the smiling host, "I think so. Their children are doing things that they don't understand."

WHEN "WHITE RABBIT" WAS RELEASED on June 6, the Airplane were already in the studio in Hollywood working on their next album. But before that, some time during the spring, they recorded something else altogether. Levi Strauss, the blue jeans manufacturer, had approached the band about creating a series of radio ads. The company promised to give the band free rein with the spots—they could go into the studio and do whatever they felt like, as long as they mentioned the product.

At least four spots were recorded. One featured Grace, wailing passionately over an Eastern-sounding group improvisation, insisting that white Levi's came in blue and black, tossing in non sequiturs about cactus, whiskey and whatnot. The other, conceived by Spencer and Gary Blackman, was Frank Zappa–influenced: electronics, mock-'50s Dadaesque rant, the occasional something having to do with the jeans.

To the Airplane, agreeing to the spots was no big deal—they used Levi's and perhaps they even saw this infiltration of the advertising industry as a somewhat revolutionary act. But a handful of radicals viewed the move as a sellout: To Abbie Hoffman, a founder of the fledgling Yippie Party, the commercials were morally abhorrent. In a letter to New York's *Village Voice* in May 1967, Hoffman wrote: "It summarized for me all the doubts I have about the hippie philosophy. I realize they are just doing their 'thing,' but while the Jefferson Airplane grooves with its thing, over 100 workers in the Levi Strauss plant on the Tennessee-Georgia border are doing their thing, which consists of being on strike to protest deplorable working conditions."

When the band learned about the labor dispute, it opted not to record any more jingles for the company, and Levi's let the Airplane out of their contract rather than risk having them bad-mouth the brand. They would never record another commercial.

THE AIRPLANE SPENT NEARLY the entire spring and early summer of 1967 playing dates up and down California. In May they played a trio of San Francisco gigs at Winterland, the former ice-skating rink at Post and Steiner that Graham used as an alternative to the Fillmore. In addition to bringing Graham in as manager, by this time the group had also acquired a booking agent, Todd Schiffman, whose job was to secure gigs for them outside of San Francisco. Although young and inexperienced with rock bands, Schiffman landed a multitude of dates for the Airplane immediately and, in short order, got their per-show fee raised astronomically, from around $3,500 a night to as much as $15,000 for some dates. The accelerated touring schedule caused the musicians to spend more consecutive hours together than they had ever before, providing the first real opportunity to get to know one another as a captive audience, to observe the group dynamic play out.

The first and most eye-popping way in which it was manifested was the sudden inability of Grace and Spencer's hands and lips to spend much time apart. The two had begun gravitating toward each other soon after Grace joined the band, finding they had many interests in common: both loved movies, art, photography and similar music, and they shared a wicked sense of humor and a sardonic worldview—they considered themselves oddballs, even among this bunch. They were the two oldest members of the band and the most recent recruits. The romantic attraction was consummated at the City Squire Motor Inn in New York during that first promotional tour.

Both Spencer and Grace were still married to other partners, but that detail never factored in; besides, both had already strayed. Grace, in fact, had even bedded another member of the Airplane before she became involved with Spencer—while in L.A. for the *Surrealistic Pillow* sessions, she'd delivered a special thank-you gift to Jack for inviting her into the band: a bottle of champagne and herself.

Jack, for his part, had been living for some time with Ginger Jackson, Bill Laudner's ex-wife and Paul's old Santa Cruz flame. Ginger and Jack had been linked since he'd stepped off the plane from D.C., but commitment was not in that pair's future either, something that became obvious the night that Ginger came home from the Fillmore to find Jack with another woman—not that she was being monogamous herself.

GINGER (JACKSON) SCHUSTER: I guess it's really hard for people from another generation to understand how it was okay for us to be as loose as we were. We were all fucking our brains out.

Ginger and Jack kept their relationship going until mid-1967, when he informed her that he was now in love with Melissa Cargill, who had recently given birth to a baby girl sired by acid chemist Owsley. Eventually electing to get off the free-love merry-go-round, Ginger married Steve Schuster of the Santa Cruz crowd, while maintaining a lifelong friendship with Kantner, who even wrote a never-released Jefferson Airplane song inspired by her, "Revolutionary Upstairs Maid."

Paul, since losing Ginger to Jack, had not aligned with one particular woman, preferring to sample from the smorgasbord of available female companionship San Francisco had to offer. Through Jack, Paul was introduced to Barbara Langer, a recent arrival from Chicago who was involved with Elvin Bishop of the Butterfield Band. Although Paul and

Barbara did not have a serious long-term romantic involvement, they remained roommates and close friends for some time. Langer witnessed Paul in all of his various emotional states.

> **BARBARA LANGER:** He's not easy to get to know. He's pigheaded. Paul is a solitary kind of guy, an introvert. I remember tripping on acid and going to Paul for solace, and he looked at me and said, "Don't tell me your bum trips." He could be very caustic and cutting, but on the other hand he could be very sweet too.

Sexual hopscotch had become de rigueur by the late '60s among an ever-swelling segment of the populace, particularly the young and enlightened—it was common to flit from partner to partner without being concerned with marriage or the promise of undying love. Along with shed inhibitions and the widespread availability and acceptance of birth control, a belief that the traditional mating ritual had become obsolete allowed for rampant sexual experimentation. Sexually transmitted disease was always an overhanging threat, but most everything was understood to be curable. Hence, the birth of the groupie. Though the San Francisco variety was not as flamboyant as the groupies in L.A. and New York, the girls often providing loyal friendship as much as anything else, there was no shortage of female companionship for rock musicians and the Airplane guys enjoyed their fair share.

A pair of free spirits who bounded into the Airplane's inner circle were recidivist teenage troublemakers from Marin County named Julia Dreyer (later Brigden) and Martha Wax, the girl who'd arranged the initial meeting between Skip Spence and the Airplane in 1965. The girls had taken to running away on a number of occasions, their parents understandably becoming more exasperated with each new incident. When the 17-year-old Julia—who came to be known as Girl because she was the only one in a family that included five brothers—was picked up in Mexico, and the juvenile court threatened to put her away until she reached 21, she instead found a way to become an instant adult, marrying Quicksilver's David Freiberg, veteran of two recent dope busts.

Martha, for her part, had also been living the nomadic life for some time, once going to stay with David Crosby in L.A., an event that stirred up her father—the mayor of Sausalito—big time. Eventually, she headed back to the Bay Area, staying for some time with Kantner. Paul, inspired by her spirit, wrote a song for her. He called it, simply, "Martha," and it became one of the highlights of the third Jefferson Airplane album.

WORK ON THAT NEXT RECORD began May 22, 1967, with the recording of another new song by Kantner bearing the intriguing title of "The Ballad of You & Me & Pooneil," the mysterious third party in the title being a fusion of two of Paul's greatest inspirations, A. A. Milne's lovable bear of children's literature, Winnie the Pooh, and folk singer Fred Neil.

From its first seconds, "Pooneil" is like nothing the Airplane had previously recorded. It blasts off with an eardrum-shattering detonation of feedback from Jorma, then shifts into a quick-paced stomp punctuated by staccato bursts of guitar. There's a new freedom to the sound that was missing from the carefully manicured and pristine-sounding *Pillow*. The playing is loose, carefree and improvisational—just like the Airplane's live shows. Paul's lead vocals are also less structured, apropos of the song's opening lyrics:

> *If you were a bird and you lived very high*
> *You'd lean on the wind when the breeze came by*
> *Say to the wind as it took you away, "That's where I wanted to go*
> *   today."*

As "Pooneil" shifts into its chorus, Marty and Grace respond to Paul by flying off in divergent directions. Grace converts her voice into a soloing instrument, complementing and sometimes imitating Jorma's guitar (a technique she would employ often). At one point, in a vaguely Middle Eastern–inspired scat, she vamps: "Ah, ahhh, ah, whoa, whoa-oh, ah, ar-ma-dillo-oh."

Armadillo? In the wonderful, wacky world of Grace Slick, nothing can ever be taken for granted.

To support Paul's free-form verse, which incorporates other Milne-originated bits—"I have a house where I can go when there's too many people," "Halfway down the stairs is a stair"—each of the musicians is allowed free rein within the song's structure. Jack lets loose with a driving bass solo midsong that seems to come out of nowhere, conquer the world and go back where it came from.

• • •

THAT THE AIRPLANE COULD RETURN to the RCA studios just months after finishing *Surrealistic Pillow*, and get away with experimenting without restraint, was solid evidence that RCA had no clue how to nurture a modern rock band—rather than attempting to coax another tidy, commercial set out of the Airplane, the label allowed the group to run with its own unfettered instincts and made no effort to dictate direction. At the same time, that very lack of interference was a feather in the label's cap as it gave the Airplane the leeway they needed to grow artistically.

> **PAUL KANTNER:** [Up until then] we kind of inflicted ourselves into the process but we didn't overtake it. By the third album we were doing acid in the studio, and bringing in motorcycles and nitrous oxide tanks. We got away with stuff just by doing it.

After Bathing at Baxter's was wholly indicative of the Airplane's rapid evolution. Much of the credit for the album's farsightedness can be shared with the Airplane's new producer. Finally, in Al Schmitt, they found a sympathetic ear, someone who not only understood the band's need to be free to create and keep pushing, at their own pace, but who got along with the Airplane on a personal level. Schmitt had been the first RCA staffer to see the Airplane perform, and it was he who recommended the label sign the band. But until now his other commitments at the label had made him unavailable to produce them.

Schmitt had become an RCA staff engineer in 1959 and offered to the Airplane a résumé that was impressive and diverse, his credits including Elvis Presley, Sam Cooke, jazz greats Chet Baker and Gerry Mulligan, and the megaselling *Peter Gunn* soundtrack album, as well as rock artists such as Duane Eddy. From the start of the *Baxter's* sessions, Schmitt and the Airplane agreed on how to make records. Basically, that boiled down to leaving the musicians alone, Schmitt's role being to help them capture their ideas on tape.

Anticipating a long recording process, the Airplane rented a house in Beverly Hills (once occupied briefly by the Beatles) and commenced work on *Baxter's* in late May, with Schmitt's younger brother Richie replacing Dave Hassinger as engineer. Using the newly developed 8-track recording technology for the first time, much of the album was molded directly from studio experimentation—the band went in, fooled around and, eventually, something emerged.

Marty and Paul's "Young Girl Sunday Blues"—written about the same young lass who'd inspired the earlier "Come Up the Years"—was the second song they attempted, but the band couldn't get it right and decided to sort it out later. In concert the song had proven a consistent winner: the rhythm section swung beautifully, and Jorma, in particular, reeled off one exquisitely tasteful lick after the other. So the group and Schmitt elected to employ a different technique to achieve the desired effect with "Young Girl Sunday Blues": They took a live version of the song recorded at the Fillmore, stripped off the lead vocal in the studio, and had Marty record a new one. The result was perfect, a natural-sounding, easy-rolling, bittersweet love song.

That song would also prove to be Marty's only writing contribution to the album. After dominating *Takes Off* and supplying *Surrealistic Pillow* with some of its most memorable songs, he essentially sat this one out while Paul and Grace took over the bulk of the writing. Marty's writer's block was compounded as he found himself increasingly on the receiving end of jabs from Jorma and Jack about his love-oriented lyrics, which they found trite.

Marty's partial withdrawal from the creative process should have served as early notice to the others that the founder of their band was beginning to feel stifled, on the outside looking in. But, as Marty recalls, no one other than he seemed to notice that anything was amiss within the Airplane's insular world. Even as he became more sullen and silent, no one asked what was bothering him.

MARTY BALIN: I got disgusted with all the ego trips, and the band was so stoned out I couldn't even talk to them. Everybody was in their little shell.

If the beginning of the band's long demise can truly be traced this far back, to 1967, the very year that the Airplane first experienced success on a wide scale, a period when they should have been having the time of their lives, then two developments can probably be blamed. One was the introduction of cocaine and other hard drugs to the scene, and the other was the tendency of the band members to form factions: in one corner were Grace and Spencer (with Paul sometimes joining them), and in another Jorma and Jack. All alone in the middle, fending for himself and tired of being the referee, was Marty Balin.

It was the Summer of Love, and the most famous of the San Francisco bands, the designated emissaries of peace and love, could not seem to get along.

15
THE LOVE CROWD

THE TOUR BUSES began rolling down Haight Street around April of '67. The Hippie Hop, they called it. With their cameras sticking out of the windows, visitors could now gawk at the aliens—genuine San Francisco hippies!—from a safe distance. "Look at the hair on that one, Maude! Is it a boy or a girl? They all look like they're on something!"

Thousands of young people, many of them runaways, were, for better or often worse, streaming into the district, with no end to the incursion in sight. A carnival atmosphere overtook the Haight, and the only entertainment one needed could be found right on the street, day and night.

But to many Haight-Ashbury pioneers who had watched the phenomenon unfold, this sudden influx of newcomers did not spell a final victory over antiquated lifestyles, or a new American way, but rather the beginning of the end. The greater the number of thumbs and Volkswagen Bugs pointing toward San Francisco from all points east, north and south, the more difficult it became for the Haight to maintain its community spirit.

As more and more immigrants arrived, the hungry vultures swooped closer: the boutiques and head shops were soon joined on Haight Street by dives selling "Love Burgers," and by hollow-eyed wastrels dealing hard drugs.

The problems within the Haight expanded exponentially. Before long, there was nowhere to put all of the new arrivals, and no way to feed or care for them. Recently organized, mostly community-supported operations like the Haight-Ashbury Free Clinic and the Haight-Ashbury Legal Organization dealt with the situation as best they could, dispensing free health care and legal assistance. But there was no stemming the tide of opportunists, entrepreneurs, strung-out burnouts and outright thugs moving in alongside what had been a tight-knit population of artists, activists, anarchists, intellectuals and seekers.

> **MARTY BALIN:** It was really beautiful there for a year or two and then *Time* magazine came out and they were interviewing me. I told the guy, "This is great that you're publicizing this scene out here."
> He said, "Fastest way to kill it." He was right.

As might be expected, the city authorities were also unhappy about the goings-on in the Haight. No government or police department looking to stay employed would welcome jobless, homeless, drug-using, long-haired, draft-resisting kids who had no intention of fattening the city's coffers or voting for its politicians. San Francisco's leaders were in a quandary: the city's implied social policy was one of tolerance and acceptance, but that didn't mean the power brokers wanted the city overrun.

To San Francisco officials, the hippies were pests and an embarrassment—their city was being viewed by outsiders as a symbol of all that was wrong with America. The right-living, God-fearing citizens of the rest of the country equated San Francisco with the decay of the value system they held dear. And they were quite right, that system *was* being attacked. But there was little that the officials could do about their headache, except to harass it, arrest it, keep it from having too much fun and hope it would go away soon.

The Airplane was as guilty as anyone of encouraging the deluge. As Kantner told Ralph Gleason in 1967, "We invite everybody to come to San Francisco. . . . There's not much going on around the United States. People just stay home or go out to a movie or go down to the drive-in and have a shake."

And the curious flocked from everywhere. In April, Beatle Paul McCartney visited San Francisco for the day, stopping by to meet the Airplane. Two years earlier Marty and Paul Kantner were first learning how to rock and roll by listening to Beatles records—now here was Paul McCartney, seeking them out. He had been knocked out by their music, particularly Jack's bass playing. After some small talk during a break in an Airplane rehearsal, Paul, Marty, Thompson, Jack and Jorma showed McCartney around San Francisco.

MARTY BALIN: We went up and down Haight, then we went back to our apartment. I said, "Well, what's new with the Beatles?"

He said, "Well, I have a tape here with something new." It was "A Day in the Life." Imagine, being a little stoned, with McCartney, hearing that for the first time. I about died.

BILL THOMPSON: I remember we were smoking grass. I said, "What's happening in England? Anybody new coming along?"

And he said, "Man, there's an unbelievable guy named Jimi Hendrix."

THE AIRPLANE WOULD HAVE A CHANCE to find out just how unbelievable Jimi Hendrix was when he performed at the Monterey International Pop Festival. Hendrix's show-stopping performance, along with those of the Who, Otis Redding, Ravi Shankar and the Airplane's cohort Janis Joplin, helped catapult the festival to rock milestone status, and made Monterey one of the high points of the Summer of Love.

The pop festival was an idea whose time had come, a weekend gathering of some of the greatest talent from both San Francisco and L.A., as well as from the East Coast, England and points beyond. To be held at the Monterey County Fairgrounds, just over a hundred miles south of San Francisco, the festival was set for June 16 to 18. Nearly all of the performers would play for free, with the proceeds slated to go to youth-friendly causes.

The organizers, including John Phillips of the Mamas and the Papas, enlisted Ralph Gleason to convince the wary San Francisco bands to take part, and he did. With Jefferson Airplane, the Grateful Dead, Quicksilver Messenger Service, the Steve Miller Band, Berkeley's Country Joe and the Fish, Moby Grape, Big Brother and the Holding Company and the Electric Flag (the new soul-rock band led by ex-Butterfield guitarist Michael Bloomfield) all committed, San Francisco was well represented.

By May, the festival's producers had also lined up a documentary filmmaker, D. A. Pennebaker, best known in the rock community for his Dylan film *Don't Look Back*, to capture the proceedings.

With anticipation building, Phillips wrote a new song, "San Francisco (Wear Some Flowers in Your Hair)," and had an old folkie friend of his, Scott McKenzie, record it. By the weekend of the festival, the rush-released single had reached the Top 20 across the United States. McKenzie appeared at Monterey, but among the festival's performers the Airplane was riding the highest commercially that weekend. They were, arguably, the number one group in America when they took the stage on Saturday night, June 17, with "Somebody to Love" at its peak on the charts.

Introduced onstage by Jerry Garcia as "a perfect example of what the world is coming to," the Airplane, as did nearly all of the other artists, played an abbreviated set at Monterey, showcasing a cross-section of their best-known material. With Glenn McKay's Headlights, one of the newer San Francisco light shows, pulsating on the screen behind them, the Airplane gave a storming performance that was among the festival's many highlights.

Pennebaker included "High Flying Bird" and "Today" in *Monterey Pop*, the film that came to theaters the following year. For the first song, the cameras focus primarily on the three vocalists as they trade riffs—although there's a great opening shot of Jorma coaxing razor-sharp chords out of his guitar—offering a close-up of the Slick–Balin dynamic in action. Marty sticks close to the lyric, Grace dances around it, and when the two meet in the middle, they become one.

"Today" is a perplexing few minutes of cinema, however. Although Marty is the sole lead vocalist on the tune, Grace and Paul joining only for harmonies, the camera never leaves Grace Slick. Seated at her keyboard, she is lost in the music. Her lips move, but Marty's voice emerges.

MARTY BALIN: You don't even see me. When the movie came out, I was really hurt. I was young and I was like, "Awwww, I sing the whole song and I don't even get to be seen."

SPENCER DRYDEN: That was all of the stupid media focus on Grace. She didn't really want it. She wanted to be one of the guys, and not the focus of the band. But how could you not think that she would be the focus?

GRACE SLICK: I just thought, any time you have four goats and one pig, you're gonna look at the pig. I didn't think it was anything other than I was a girl.

D. A. PENNEBAKER: It was a dumb problem. We didn't know until we sent the film up [to be processed] that there was no microphone on her. And the only lighting was not on him, but on her. We thought we could get by on psychedelic.

For the entire band, Monterey was one to savor. Whatever was happening at home to cause the Haight to descend, whatever was happening out in the frightening real world of war and strife, for three days and nights in Monterey, it was forgotten. Most who were there remember Monterey being honest and spontaneous, smiles and colors, high and happy. It was about music, but it was also about more than that.

On the last night of the festival, Jimi Hendrix, his guitar and his lighter fluid, all flash and genius, something from another galaxy, made the announcement that rock and roll had just been propelled to the next level.

DAVID CROSBY: I remember Paul Kantner and I and David Freiberg sitting on the left-hand side of the stage, watching Jimi Hendrix, and going, "You can't do that. That's impossible. What is he? Wait-a-minute! Holy shit!"

Late Sunday, after a long day and night filled with superior music, some of the musicians still had adrenaline (and then some) inside of them. Jack wandered over to a hut near the arena, spied Hendrix—zonked on a few hits of freshly minted Owsley acid—plunking at a bass and joined him in a duet that must have been something to behold. When the sun came up, everyone returned home.

With only a couple of days off to catch their collective breath, the Airplane headed over to the Fillmore for the opening of Bill Graham's summer series. Six nights were scheduled, with the Airplane headlining, the Hungarian jazz guitarist Gabor Szabo in the middle spot and, to open . . . the Jimi Hendrix Experience. Hendrix had been an unknown when Graham had booked the Fillmore show. By the time he got there, the guitarist was the talk of the rock world.

What exactly happened that week at the Fillmore is a matter of conjecture, but from most accounts, the Airplane played the first night, June 20 (and perhaps the second), then canceled out of the rest. The official word was that Grace's voice gave out, forcing the Airplane to pass on the other shows, with Janis Joplin—newly benefiting from the Monterey raves—and Big Brother and the Holding Company replacing them. That's how Mitch Mitchell, drummer of the Jimi Hendrix Experience, Sam Andrew of Big Brother and Bill Thompson all remember it.

Another popular version of the story goes like this: The Airplane, on that first night, saw what Hendrix was capable of doing to an audience and, although they did finish out the week, they switched the billing so that Hendrix could close the show. Yet another assessment—a minority opinion—has it that the Airplane stayed the whole week, closing the show as planned.

But one thing everyone agreed upon was that Hendrix took the old rulebook and threw it out the window. He married technology and technique in a visionary way, yet for all of the pyrotechnics and drama of his act, his music oozed soulfulness, sensuality and spirituality—there was nothing phony about it. As musicians who were themselves always attempting to push beyond known boundaries, Jack and Jorma especially looked at what Hendrix was doing as confirmation of their own instincts: there were no limits.

AFTER BATHING AT BAXTER'S was coming along slowly. It wasn't that the Airplane didn't want to finish the record, they simply couldn't squeeze it in. They'd been living their lives at such an accelerated pace, and spending so much time on the road, they hadn't been able to write new material, let alone record it. At one band meeting, tempers flared as the musicians told their manager that they wanted only to play big cities, and then only those where a hip community was in place.

"Let me ask you something," Bill Graham countered. "Outside of Chicago, New York, L.A. and San Francisco . . . what the *fuck* do you think the country is made up of?! All New York? All prime, plush, beautiful locations?"

The conversation that day deteriorated even further, with the band members turning on one another. Spencer and Jorma argued vociferously, the drummer complaining about the length of the guitarist's solos.

SPENCER DRYDEN: The band's relationship was like any typical marriage but there were six people, and even more when you include Graham and Thompson and Laudner. Everybody wanted something different. But when we weren't arguing about the music or being too serious about it, we had a black sense of humor. The best thing we did was laugh.

There were other arguments that summer as well. One involved Graham's percentage of the take from live performances—should it come from the net or the gross? And there were differing opinions regarding the next single. Graham, like Al Schmitt, thought Grace's "Two Heads" had a shot, as the public had responded so favorably to her lead vocals on the last two singles. But Grace herself nixed that one—she didn't want to advance the notion that the Airplane was nothing more than Grace Slick's backup band. They argued over the artwork for the new album as well, something that no one had bothered to do anything about just yet.

A year earlier, the Airplane had been lucky to be splitting $1,000 six ways after a gig (not counting Matthew's take)—*when* they even got paid. Now they were commanding several thousand dollars a night, often more, and talking in terms of six-figure individual annual incomes from their recordings and performances. The media loved them. Their records were played everywhere, their images appeared on posters hanging on bedroom walls across the country. They were well respected by fellow musicians and were considered a top priority by their record company. They were rock stars, symbols of a burgeoning movement.

Yet, as the Summer of Love shone on and the flower children gamboled on Hippie Hill, as the San Francisco scene they helped to spawn underwent the scrutiny of the world, the Airplane and their handlers, rather than enjoying the fruits of their labors, were cooped up in offices, poring over contractual minutiae, debating the relative merits of gigs in Monticello and Colorado Springs. Those differences that had given them their uniqueness were now working to tear them apart.

PAUL KANTNER: Had we been a single organism, Jefferson Airplane would have been diagnosed schizophrenic. We were an orchestra without rules. No leaders, no rules.

For the most part, the Airplane still put up a united front, still shared ideas and ideals and still loved making music together. But now they were a business—one in which everyone was a CEO—as well as an artistic collective, and the parties were getting on each other's nerves. Marty, in particular, was beginning to lose the drive that had been so strong in him when he formed the group. He felt the walls closing in.

MARTY BALIN: Fame changes your life. It's a bit like prison. It ruined the band. Everybody became rich and selfish and self-centered and couldn't care about the band. That was pretty much the end of it all. After that it was just working and living the high life and watching the band destroy itself, living on its laurels.

Whatever was going on between them, after Monterey they needed to get serious about *Baxter's*. Up until that time, they'd worked only on "Pooneil," the unsatisfactory takes of "Young Girl Sunday Blues" and a rudimentary version of "Martha." At the end of June, the band went back into the studio to finish up "Pooneil" and to cut Grace's "Two Heads," one of the two songs she contributed to *Baxter's*. Grace's writing, since the Great Society days, had always been impressionistic, provocative and rich in imagery. Her subject matter leaned increasingly toward the esoteric. But with these latest songs, she was heading deeper into free-form territory.

"Two Heads," like much of Grace's songwriting (and, for that matter, many compositions by Paul, Jorma and Marty), seemed capable of conveying great insights when placed under a microscope, each line worthy of serious pondering. But viewed under a different lens, by a music lover not predisposed toward the opaque, those same words might seem nothing more than drug-induced gibberish. Perhaps Grace's lyrics were penned quickly in a stream-of-consciousness manner, or perhaps each word was carefully considered—only she knew. But that was their beauty as well: Her writings were engineered to make a cerebral impact, subject to reinterpretation by all who heard them—including Grace herself, who would, over the years, often revise her theories as to what her own songs were about.

"Two Heads" would have been an improbable choice for most AM radio stations' playlists. Jorma's sinuous, Middle Eastern–inspired guitar line, drawing from his exposure to world music in his pre-California days, was pure psychedelia and, added to Grace's elliptic verse, it made for a beautiful, rapturous piece of music, but hardly the stuff of hit singles. Even compared to the Beatles' recent work, like the ultratrippy "Strawberry Fields Forever," this was weird—and Jefferson Airplane, popular though they were, could not get away with things the Beatles could get away with.

When the first single from the new album was released, "Two Heads" was indeed on it, but as the flip side. "Pooneil," shortened for time-conscious AM radio, was pushed as the A-side to disc jockeys. Neither song proved safe enough for Top 40 radio, though, and the single only reached number 42 nationally, a huge disappointment to RCA after the two previous smashes.

There was, however, another outlet for this new, more adventurous kind of music: FM radio. Until recently, FM was populated almost exclusively by classical stations, college stations and public or listener-supported stations that offered an eclectic—but usually dull—range of programming. Then, in July 1964, the Federal Communications Commission prescribed that stations broadcasting the same programming on both their AM and FM outlets would no longer be permitted to do so. The dictum forced station owners to create new programming for their FM outlets, which led, among other sweeping changes, to the discovery of FM by the rock and roll crowd. Here was a radio band that offered clean, static-free sound, often in stereo, perfect for the new, more sophisticated rock.

Without the long-established restrictions of AM, the new FM DJs were free to play almost anything they wanted to play—if a disc jockey felt like spinning the long, album version of the Doors' "Light My Fire" instead of the edited single version, that was no longer taboo. If a jock wanted to program an hour of music that featured Ravi Shankar, B. B. King, John Coltrane, Dylan, a poetry recitation, an entire side of a Hendrix album and the Airplane's "Pooneil," that was now okay. If music was too weird or controversial for AM Top 40, it was probably just right for FM.

Now the advertising could be slotted in around the music, instead of the other way around. And the DJs no longer needed to shout or try to squeeze in a million words per minute, the way most AM rock jocks did. FM was more conducive to a relaxed, soft, soothing voice. Perfect for lighting up some incense and a joint, turning down the lights and listening.

FM rock radio came to San Francisco in April of '67. Tom Donahue had left his AM job at KYA and, along with his wife Raechel and a couple of other DJs, inaugurated the new KMPX on the FM band. It was an instant success with the city's rock fans. Here was a station tailored for the catholic tastes of the city's younger listeners. Rock, jazz, raga, blues and folk were all fair game. KMPX immediately took its place as an integral element of the San Francisco scene.

THE AIRPLANE WAS BOOKED TO PLAY the O'Keefe Centre in Toronto at the end of July and beginning of August. Graham had arranged for them, along with the Grateful Dead, to bring a "Sounds of San Francisco" show to Canada, still largely unexploited by purveyors of the new music. If this was going to be an authentic San Francisco experience, though, it would require a light show. Graham, at the request of the Airplane, hired Headlights, the team that had wowed the crowd at Monterey.

Headlights at that time was run by two people, Glenn McKay and Jerry Abrams, and they in turn used three other technicians and artists to make the components of their show work in harmony. For some time the band had considered using one light show exclusively and after seeing Headlights in action, they decided that that was the one. After about five months, Abrams dropped out and started his own Headlights, but for the next few years, the name Glenn McKay's Headlights was synonymous with the Airplane's live shows.

McKay was a minister's son from Missouri who'd set out for San Francisco in 1963 to paint. But a revelation at one of the Acid Tests inspired him to work with the medium of light. The ever-moving images of Fillmore-style light shows were created using hand-painted slides, films, large color wheels and other tricks of the trade. The undulating amoebic blobs that gave the shows their most familiar characteristic were created on oil dishes, made from the face glasses of old clocks. McKay and his crew used high-quality watercolors to color the liquids, pouring the mixture onto the glasses and moving them in time to the music. He used a couple of overhead projectors to send the swirling, formless colors to the screen behind the band, using rear projection.

The total effect of the multimedia creation was dazzling, doing for the eyes what the music of the Airplane, the Dead and the others did for the ears. It was a welcomed sensory overload. The light shows were an art form indelibly associated with their time. What McKay loved most about his art was its very lack of permanence. It was for the moment, made to be experienced only while it was being created.

GLENN MCKAY: It's ephemeral. You can't own it. You can't take it home. And I don't have to store it. I don't have to be responsible for it.

TORONTO WENT WELL. The Airplane got things rolling with a free show attended by some 40,000 sweating Canadians. Both the Airplane and the Dead were well received the following week at the O'Keefe shows. Said the *Toronto Star,* "The Airplane captured the crowd without effort. The quality of their music, its intelligence and imagination superimposed on the necessary beat, drew them out to experience total involvement with sound and color."

Back in San Francisco, the real world intruded again when the Airplane was hit with yet another annoyance. A new lawsuit had been filed against them, this time from the former partners in the Matrix, Ted Saunders, Elliot Sazer and Paul Sedlewicz. *U.S. Pizza v. Jefferson Airplane* was put in motion in civil court on August 10, the plaintiffs arguing that the Airplane failed to fulfill their end of the contract drawn up in 1965. With the Airplane arguably the biggest group in the country, a lot of money was at stake. The Pizza people asked for $600,000 to make things nice again. It took three years, but eventually the case was settled out of court.

In late August the band returned to the studio to work on "Martha," one of a half dozen songs written in part or wholly for the album by the suddenly prolific Kantner. Paul's frothy acoustic guitar is matched by Jorma's muted electric and puffs of Grace's subtle recorder, the song skipping along lightly to a springtime rhythm, as ebullient as a bossa nova. Jorma injects a brief, unexpected solo that is simultaneously wicked and proud, Jack and Spencer maintaining a feathery hop underneath.

"The Last Wall of the Castle" was Jorma's first composition for the Airplane to feature lyrics as well as music. As so much of Jorma's writing would throughout his career, "Last Wall," though on the surface a basic cheating/breakup song, possesses an embedded moralistic twist, a greater life lesson.

The song is a supercharged blues doubling as a showcase for Jorma's blistering fuzz-guitar soloing. Guitar and amplification technology had much to do with where electric rock music was heading at the time, developing as swiftly as the music itself in the late '60s, and the Airplane tried out all of the new machinery. The guitarists, especially, were constantly upgrading their equipment, buying the newest models and the loudest, most durable amps—whatever it took to discover their capabilities and ceaselessly reinvent themselves.

JORMA KAUKONEN: It was a growth period. I was starting to use multiple amplifiers. There are different kinds of fuzztones and the wah-wah pedal, which was a really integral part of my sound for a number of years. It certainly does evoke that period. You hear a wah-wah and you're thinking Cream and "Strange Brew."

Cream: Eric Clapton, Jack Bruce and Ginger Baker. Virtuoso musicians. English hard-rock/blues power trio. The first supergroup. The effect that Cream had on Jorma Kaukonen and Jack Casady after the San Franciscans heard them at the Fillmore was profound. From that night forward, Jefferson Airplane would never be the same.

16 DOING THINGS THAT HAVEN'T GOT A NAME YET

STUCK IN BAKERSFIELD, CALIFORNIA. Another gig in a godforsaken, dusty cattle trough. Another loser job set up by Bill Graham. But what really burned them was that, back at the Fillmore, Cream was blowing the roof off the place. Miss Cream to play for a bunch of cowboys? He had a lot of nerve!

And leave it to Paul to make things even worse. Now his mouth had gotten them all into trouble with the law. The charge: inciting a riot.

It all started around 10:30 on the night of September 2. The Airplane was only a couple of songs into their set at the Bakersfield Civic Auditorium when Kantner took it upon himself to inform the audience that it was not necessary for them to sit on their hands and stare as if they were watching a movie. "We came up here thinking this was a dance concert, so why don't you dance?" he asked. "Push your chairs back and dance!"

But it wasn't a dance concert, not in the eyes of the aggravated Bakersfield police officers on duty that night. Dancing was not for people under the age of 16 in Bakersfield, and as there might very well have been persons fitting that description in the room that evening, enforcement of that provision was imperative. Couldn't take any chances.

Kantner kept it up, the cops growing more pissed off by the minute. Bill Thompson attempted to cool things down: "I've told them over and over not to do this but I can't stop them," he told the officer in charge.

With the show coming to an end, Kantner again exhorted the crowd: "What's the matter with you guys out there? Remember, there are only five of them and 5,000 of us."

That did it. They *could* get away with dancing! What were the cops going to do, throw the whole damn audience in jail? The fans surged forward, pinning the officers to the front of the stage. Bakersfield danced.

The officers pushed the crowd away. The kids pushed their way back. As the police mounted the stage and the auditorium manager grabbed a microphone to announce that the show was over, the band played louder and louder, ignoring the melee that was ensuing.

Finally, the Airplane finished their last number. But now the writhing, ecstatic mass wanted an encore. The show's promoter tried to convince the police, who had called in for backup, that if they did *not* allow the group back, they would have a riot on their hands. With the scene about to turn violent, the band was finally persuaded to leave and the disgruntled fans were escorted outside. But the Airplane had learned a new trick, and a new truth: There is power in numbers.

> **MARTY BALIN:** We began to pull that all the time. Sometimes the cops would turn off the electricity. Grace and I would pick up megaphones and just keep on. Then they'd come out and grab the megaphones.

Ultimately, no one was charged in the Bakersfield incident, and as far as the Airplane was concerned the whole ruckus was old news even before they touched down at the Fillmore later that same night, a few of them already loaded on double doses of Owsley acid. But first Paul almost got them busted again.

The band had rented a private plane to take them back to San Francisco, but the pilot, none too happy with his passengers, was giving Paul a hard time about his chain-smoking on board. So Paul shrugged and got rid of his cigarette—by opening the plane's door and flinging it out.

By the time they arrived at the Fillmore, Jefferson Airplane, like many other rock fans in San Francisco that weekend, was more than ready to experience the power trio that was supposed to give even the Jimi Hendrix Experience some serious competition in the musicianship department.

Cream, formed in England in the summer of 1966, raised the art of improvisation to a whole other level. Bruce and Clapton were skilled, expressive vocalists, but singing was clearly not their forte. The power of Cream lay almost exclusively in the telepathic communication between masters of their instruments.

Jorma and Jack felt vindicated. For some time, they'd been attempting to push the Airplane into a similar direction, extending the improvisational nature of the songs, introducing new ideas to keep the music fresh. Cream confirmed to them that they were on the right track.

JORMA KAUKONEN: When I saw Cream, I thought they were the most incredible performing band I had ever seen in my life. That might still be true. And, of course, as a guitar player I wanted to be able to do stuff like that.

MARTY BALIN: One night we were playing and Jorma just took off. He started playing amazing, and it was just real and free. Pretty soon we got to a place where the music was playing us, we weren't playing it. That's where you want to get to.

This wasn't just about going crazy and making more noise—there was still a necessity to rein in the experimentation, to confine the musicians' exploratory zeal within the bounds of the increasingly complex song structures being conjured up by the group's writers. But Jorma and Jack now became even more antagonistic toward Marty and his pop-oriented songwriting. They needled him openly, causing the already browbeaten Balin to retreat even further into the shadows of the band he'd created.

THE AIRPLANE RETURNED TO RCA for more recording in early September. "Pooneil" had already been released as the new single, but the album was still far from completed. They worked at an easy pace, exploiting the luxury of the unlimited studio time that RCA was willing to bestow on its hottest band (even if the company wasn't thrilled about the money the band was spending making the record). The Airplane let the tapes roll, doing whatever they felt like doing. Sometimes it worked, sometimes it didn't, but that was a chance they were willing to take: their only concern was making an album they were happy with, not one that would echo *Pillow*'s sound or sales. *Pillow* had taken weeks to record, *Baxter's* would take months.

RCA had never seen their like before, but the label executives knew that these crazy dope fiends were making them richer by the day, and that was reason enough to turn a blind eye toward the group's eccentricity and irresponsibility. Visitors came and went from the studio constantly, and sometimes one or two of the musicians might not show up at all. The Dead hung out when they were in town to perform or record, and Buffalo Springfield, who also recorded nearby, dropped in. Another group that stopped by to party was the Monkees. The Airplane got along well with the band, and more than a few evenings found the two groups, both well aware that they were living inside of an absurd dream, picking at guitars, passing around the smoke and, when they got tired of behaving, tossing water balloons and drawing on the studio walls.

One RCA employee who witnessed some of these hijinks was Pat Ieraci, an amiable Italian-American from Brooklyn. Ieraci (pronounced eye-RAY-see) had started at RCA in 1963 as an assistant to engineer Dave Hassinger, witnessing sessions not only by RCA artists, but by others using the studio. When RCA sent Al Schmitt to San Francisco and pondered taking on the Airplane later that year, Ieraci was instrumental in convincing the label to take the risk.

In time, Ieraci became an increasingly important presence in the Airplane's inner circle. Although he did not receive a published credit until the fourth album, he made himself available to the band whenever they came to L.A. to record. He became both confidant and personal caretaker, doing whatever it took to make their stay more productive and comfortable, from fetching their lunch to meticulously documenting their every expenditure and filling in the studio session logs. At some point, the band decided he needed a nickname.

PAT "MAURICE" IERACI: Either Kantner or Balin says, "You know, you don't look Italian to me. You look like a Frenchman." So they went out, they bought a beret, an ascot, a cigarette holder, the whole thing. And they said, "We're gonna name you Maurice." And it's stuck to this very day.

The two tracks the Airplane cut that week, "Watch Her Ride" and "Wild Tyme (H)," were both Paul's. "Watch Her Ride" was not unlike Marty's "Today" in its sentiment, an unabashed love song, practically worshipful in tone. Unlike the *Pillow* ballad, though, "Watch Her Ride" is a blazing rock and roll song, leaving plenty of room for both the musicians and vocalists to reach for the sky. "Wild Tyme (H)," with its chiming rhythm guitar and tight harmonies, could have been Kantner's farewell tribute to the Byrds' David Crosby era—the H in parentheses deliberately tied it to the Byrds' own song "Wild Mountain Thyme." Or, with its declaration of seeing "changes all around me," it could have been Paul's joyful celebration of the Summer of Love as it passed into history. It's a mystery why RCA didn't choose it as a single, as it was one of the more accessible tracks on the album-in-progress.

The group's next trip to the studio was to record one of the most complex, masterful and moving songs in the entire Jefferson Airplane canon, Grace's "rejoyce." Having already translated Lewis Carroll and Lenny Bruce into Slick-ese, here Grace went after no less than James Joyce's landmark novel *Ulysses*. Although only four minutes in length, Grace's piece is, like the work on which it's based, epic in scope. She takes liberties with Joyce's narrative, borrows a few of the book's characters (as well as a few lines of text) and redirects the course of their lives. Grace's "rejoyce" turns up the volume on the book's antiwar subtext.

> **GRACE SLICK:** I wrote about what was interesting to me, assuming people had read this stuff or that people would be amused by mothers saying how wonderful their kid was because he killed a lot of people. But there's a larger record-buying audience out there that doesn't know shit. "rejoyce" is verse from beginning to end, and it moves around. That's difficult for people. It's almost impossible to dance to and it's difficult to sing along with.

If the lyrics were demanding, the music for "rejoyce" was Grace's most ambitious to date, a stroll in various time signatures through her favorite elements: the hypnotic flamenco and Arabian tones, the discordant, brooding, ominous chord sequences, the vocal calisthenics, a horn arrangement crafted by Spencer, whose drumming is adventurous as well. Despite its precisely composed twists and turns, the song's second half veers as close to straight jazz as the Airplane ever ventured. The specter of both John Coltrane and Gil Evans hovers and a McCoy Tyner influence colors Grace's piano, an instrument on which she proves more polished than she'd ever admit.

Accompanying Grace, Jack plays a complementary bass line, but otherwise "rejoyce" is virtually guitarless. Nonetheless, its sparseness is affecting in the way the Beatles' "Yesterday" was—just as McCartney's solo triumph was still very much classic Beatles, "rejoyce," even without half the band, is quintessential Airplane.

The rest of the fall was spent shuttling between gigs and the studio. Among the tracks completed for *Baxter's* was Paul's paean to the Be-In,

"Saturday Afternoon," which he had since coupled into a medley with another new composition, "Won't You Try."

On Halloween, the madmen took over the asylum. With the band's main vocalists nowhere to be found, Jorma, Jack and Spencer got down to some serious open-ended jamming, their nine-minute excursion gliding from pure sound collage, as avant-garde as anything the jazz world had to offer, to consummate Fillmore-style acidic/electric orgy. The unedited results were given the title of "Spare Chaynge" and added to the album's track list.

For the final blowout, it was Spencer's turn to take the reins. In tribute to his muse Frank Zappa, Dryden took command of every instrument in sight—xylophone, cowbell, marimba, piano, harpsichord— added three layers of overdubbed drums and let the tapes roll. Afterward, he called in Thompson and Gary Blackman, and the trio— calling themselves the Walking Owls—blurted out whatever came to their minds, going nuts and getting paid for it. At the very end, Blackman, conjuring the ghost of poet John Donne, bellows, "No man is an island, no man is an island!"

To which Thompson responds, equally sensibly, "He's a peninsula," inducing hysterical laughter from all. Just over a minute and a half long, "A Small Package of Value Will Come to You, Shortly"—its title taken from a fortune cookie—is the sound of LSD at work.

That do-anything-you-want-to-do philosophy only went so far outside of the studio, though, even for this freethinking bunch. After returning from a gig in Santa Barbara, the band had been surprised to find its rented house taken over by uninvited squatters, having a grand time splashing in the swimming pool.

JORMA KAUKONEN: They didn't want to leave. Bill Laudner and I had a couple of pellet pistols, so we popped them into the water and that got the people out.

SPENCER DRYDEN: We all—Paul, Jorma, Grace and myself—had guns. We weren't hippies. Hippies were the people that lived on the streets down in Haight-Ashbury. We were basically musicians and art school kids. We were into guns and machinery.

After more than five months and a cost of nearly $80,000—unheard of in those days, and more than 10 times the cost of *Pillow*—*After Bathing at Baxter's* was completed. When the album was released on November 27, just weeks after the final tracks were completed, its 11 pieces had been arranged into a conceptual whole consisting of five interlocking minisuites. The album's title came from a poem/song written by Blackman and printed on the album's inner sleeve—the word "Baxter," Kantner has explained, was Airplane code for acid, and rather than titling the album something as obvious as *After Taking LSD*, they named it *After Bathing at Baxter's*.

For the cover art, the Airplane hired Ron Cobb, a popular political cartoonist who drew for the *L.A. Free Press*. Cobb's elegant design was all-American all the way, from the red, white and blue coloring to the depiction of consumerism and urban decay along the bottom of the bifold album jacket. And it was as San Franciscan—with its R. Crumbesque biplane cleverly built from a Victorian house—as Jefferson Airplane.

RCA had no dispute with Cobb's work, nor did the company mind at all the inside spread, a grouping of dark, disembodied photographs, some of band members, some not, taken by Alan Pappe. But the paper inner sleeve that housed the actual vinyl record was another matter. Even after finding nothing to red-pencil in the album's lyrics, corporate paranoids still managed to come up with something they deemed offensive on a Jefferson Airplane album. Among the various drawings on the sleeve, contributed by the band and their friends, is a circular object with what appears to be a big exclamation point turning into an eye with fluffy lashes—or something. To RCA, though, any crevice with hair coming out of it could only be one thing: a vagina.

> **GRACE SLICK:** We'd had some cupcakes in the studio and somebody outlined the cupcake holder, for no reason at all. Somebody at RCA decided that it was a cunt. It's not even shaped like one. Nobody's cunt is that big, unless you're a horse or something. We said, "It's an upside down cupcake."
>
> "Well, then, why do you have it on there?"
>
> "*Because* it doesn't mean anything. You decided it was a cunt, so don't have us take it off there because your imagination is screwed up."

After Bathing at Baxter's was released while *Surrealistic Pillow* was still selling well and continuing to garner press notices. All of those clippings helped to further the band's standing, but the launch of *Rolling Stone* magazine in the fall of 1967 signaled a new era in the evolving area of rock music journalism. It was started by Jann (pronounced Yon) Wenner, a 21-year-old college dropout who sensed the need for a magazine that spoke directly to the young rock generation yet was published on a regular schedule and adhered to high professional standards. With Wenner editing and Ralph Gleason as its guiding light and patron saint, *Rolling Stone*, which covered the Airplane regularly, soon established itself as the unofficial bible of hipdom.

TENSIONS WITH BILL GRAHAM ESCALATED when *Baxter's*, which made the *Billboard* chart during Christmas week, failed to come close to matching *Pillow*'s success. For most American record buyers, even those who took "White Rabbit" and its druggy imagery to heart, *Baxter's* was too much too soon. Graham switched to I-told-you-so mode, but the band shrugged him off.

> **SPENCER DRYDEN:** He said, "You guys are pushing all the wrong buttons. You're alienating yourself from RCA. This is not what they expected to follow up *Surrealistic Pillow*. It's too far ahead of its time. Maybe two or three albums down the road you could get away with this. But to do this now, you're just flying in the face of fate." We didn't care. Of course, it was true.

Baxter's' hue was notably darker than its predecessor, a deeper, more mysterious—and fragile—beauty replacing *Pillow*'s pinkish glow. *Baxter's* was almost cinematic, a sweeping, oversized declarative on the state of the American being in 1967.

Some critics raved. *Rolling Stone*'s Wenner reviewed the album himself, suggesting that the Airplane "could be the best rock and roll band in America today" and that in *Baxter's* the band had "come up with probably the best, considering the criteria and the exceptions, rock and roll album so far produced by an American group."

> **JACK CASADY:** To us, [*Baxter's*] was a performance and artistic success because, like spoiled little brats, we got to do whatever we wanted to do. But I say "spoiled little brats" with a certain amount of fondness.

At the close of 1967, Jefferson Airplane was a star attraction. The music industry may not have understood what they were all about, but it understood success: The group received a Grammy nomination for the Best New Artist of 1967, losing out to country singer Bobbie Gentry. Those "changes all around me," of which Paul Kantner had sung, seemed to be taking place everywhere. There would be many more to come.

17
LIFE IS CHANGE, HOW IT DIFFERS FROM THE ROCKS

HIPPIE WAS DEAD. With 1967's Summer of Love now turned into the fall of something else, Ron Thelin, the proprietor of the Haight's Psychedelic Shop, announced that he was closing the store. In order to mark the solemn occasion, the Diggers arranged a "Death of Hippie" march along Haight Street, pallbearers and all. Then even the Diggers vacated the Haight.

They weren't the only ones. Four days before that parade, a team of dope cops had swooped down on the Grateful Dead's house at 710 Ashbury and arrested its occupants on drug possession charges. Most of the band soon left the city for the solitude of Marin County.

Jefferson Airplane loved San Francisco, and they vowed to stay put. But there would have to be some changes made. The first was the matter of Bill Graham. Grace and Spencer, tired of being overworked and weary of the arguing, had come to a decision: If Graham stayed on as manager, they were leaving the band.

Grace was the band's star, and if anyone could thrive outside of its structure, she could. She'd been told as much by more than a few big shots in the music industry, and twice, recalled Howard Wolf, Grace came to the former Great Society manager and expressed a desire to leave the Airplane. Wolf convinced her it was unfair to leave the band on the eve of a tour, but when she approached him yet again he brokered a solo deal for her with David Anderle, an executive with Elektra Records. As part of the arrangement, Jerry Slick would receive a sum of cash to make a film of whatever song served as the title track of Grace's album— this more than a dozen years before the birth of MTV.

Ultimately, though, the label's president, Jac Holzman, unhappy with the dollar figures being bandied about, negated the deal. Wolf recalls him saying, "Judy Collins doesn't get that much, why should Grace Slick?" Grace stayed with the Airplane, but Graham was gone. The only question was, which unfortunate soul was going to break the news to him? At a band meeting in late January of 1968, Thompson and Balin performed the deed.

The only candidate for the management position now was Bill Thompson, and he readily accepted. Thompson had been with the Airplane since the inception, had been involved in the group's affairs and had witnessed enough of the inner workings of the music industry at this point to have an inkling of how things worked.

BILL THOMPSON: I don't know if they really thought I could do it. And to be honest, I didn't know either.

With Graham out of the picture, the Airplane took the Grateful Dead up on an offer to partner in a dance hall that would compete head-to-head with both the Fillmore and the Avalon—Quicksilver also jumped in and each band held a 10 percent interest in the new business venture, which they called Triad. They leased a room called the Carousel Ballroom, formerly the El Patio, above a car dealership on the much-traveled corner of Van Ness and Market. With twice the capacity of the Fillmore, the lushly decorated Carousel had, in another era, presented popular big bands. The venue opened under its new management on January 17, 1968 with a show by the Dead and Quicksilver. During its short life as an independently operated dance hall, the Carousel hosted all of the major San Francisco bands, as well as leading artists from the worlds of jazz (Thelonious Monk), gospel (Clara Ward), country music (Johnny Cash) and classic rock and roll (Chuck Berry).

But ultimately, and not surprisingly, the Airplane and the Dead came to the realization that running a concert hall wasn't their forte. By the summer of '68, the mismanaged Carousel, despite drawing crowds, was becoming a losing proposition. Graham, feeling threatened by the changing vibes in the mostly black Fillmore district after the recent assassination of Dr. Martin Luther King, stepped in to take it over. Vacating the now legendary hall that he'd called home since 1965, Graham shifted his operation to the Carousel and renamed it Fillmore West. He inaugurated his new home with a series of blockbuster bills in July featuring old standbys Big Brother, Moby Grape and Butterfield, and shining newcomers Santana, Sly and the Family Stone and England's Jeff Beck Group.

Graham also took the opportunity to spread his wings eastward in early 1968. He'd always harbored an urge to return to New York and make his mark there too. Taking over a rundown theater at 105 Second Avenue, at the corner of East Sixth Street in the East Village, Graham went to work creating a rock venue the likes of which New York had never seen.

Originally called the Loews Commodore East, the theater was erected early in the twentieth century. When Graham first spied the property in 1967, it was the Village Theater, used for occasional jazz and rock concerts. Graham made repairs to the building, spruced up the lobby and the marquee and brought in a state-of-the-art sound system. Finally, on March 8, the venue that Graham christened Fillmore East opened, with a show starring Big Brother, singer-songwriter Tim Buckley and blues guitarist Albert King.

Unlike the Fillmore Auditorium or its San Francisco competitors, Graham's New York outpost was not intended for dancing. With seating for 2,400 customers, Fillmore East was set up for viewing a performance, not for participating in an interactive event. With its opening, Graham was both acknowledging and, in some ways, ensuring that the era of the San Francisco–style rock and roll dance was coming to an end, to be replaced by the rock concert. Although Graham used light shows at Fillmore East, most of the other vestiges of the dances were eradicated—the focus was now squarely on the musicians.

Despite their dismissal of him as manager, Graham maintained a cordial relationship with the Airplane. The friendship that he and the band had forged overrode Graham's bitterness at being fired—besides, as a promoter he couldn't afford to ignore one of the hottest bands in the country. The Airplane played their first Fillmore East sets over the weekend of May 3 to 4. Ultimately, they would perform there on seven different occasions into 1970. It quickly became one of their favorite places to play, and the New York audiences became some of their most fanatic supporters.

PAUL KANTNER: We were like missionary Jesuits, coming into a foreign land. New York and the East Coast were inordinately fond of the whole West Coast experience, probably with good cause.

SPENCER DRYDEN: We used to play these monster long shows and walk out after the sun was up, all high as a kite. I never thought we'd do it in New York. But for some reason, New Yorkers took us to heart.

While they were in town for the Fillmore East gigs, Michael Klenfner, one of Graham's first employees at the new venue, arranged for the Airplane to give their first free concert in Central Park. Also performing on that spring afternoon were Butterfield and the Dead. The bands set up on a flatbed truck, using generators for power, with Klenfner and his Brooklyn buddies serving as security. Mickey Hart, one of the Dead's two drummers, recalls the many Airplane–Dead bills being particularly beneficial for both bands.

MICKEY HART: We stirred each other's juices. *We* would play better when we would play with the Airplane and I can remember specific moments when *they* were the best band in the world.

BY 1968, MANY FANS AND CRITICS WERE IN AGREEMENT. Each individual component was operating at full throttle, and each personality within the unit had become wholly assertive. That tension fired their artistic creativity but, more and more often, it also caused interpersonal problems.

Grace and Spencer, in particular, were becoming a nuisance to some of the others. When Grace first joined the Airplane, she had been content to sing her parts and confine her trademark acerbic remarks to her private interactions. When she did speak during shows, she had generally been amiable and witty, often conversing one-on-one with audience members between songs, bringing a warm, living-room intimacy to the proceedings.

But now the old sarcasm and spleen that had alienated her from friends in the past often came to the fore onstage. Before, Grace had been known to tear into a total stranger at a party, needle them about their clothes, their boyfriend's lisp—whatever she felt like saying, she just said—and most people meekly put up with it or walked away. But now she was elevating her brutality into a fine art and a trademark, berating audiences, donning bizarre costumes for the shock value, constructing a new role for herself as an unpredictable sideshow. And because she was Grace Slick, rock star, her erratic behavior made news.

Not coincidentally, during this period Grace became increasingly reliant on alcohol. Although she'd been a drinker since high school, Grace had usually managed to keep her boozing under control. Some who were close to her say that they never knew anyone who could conceal acute intoxication as well as she could, and Grace's excesses had rarely been questioned by those in her peer group—the tenor of the times was such that one tended to overlook a fellow stoner's indiscretions, regardless of how annoying they might get.

Before bonding with Spencer, Grace had often been alone in her drinking. Alcohol was considered gauche in the doper community—an uncool high, your parents' drug—and Grace often found herself the only one nipping while everyone else was toking. Spencer, however, shared Grace's affection for the bottle, and in him she found a compassionate accomplice. In the verbiage of a later time, they both became enablers.

As for the others in the band, they were hardly innocent teetotalers: as the use of psychedelics began to wane, some now took to harder substances. Methamphetamine, or speed, was a special favorite, and cocaine was rising up the charts. The drugs, the simmering hostilities, boredom, the musicians' lust for spontaneity and excitement—all of these factors fueled the internal battles, which now were manifested during the band's performances. Jorma and Jack, feeding off of their ever-accelerating yearnings to take the music to the edge—and reeling from the considerable quantities of speed they were taking—continually pushed back the boundaries of the jams, often ignoring the desires of the others in the band. On more than one occasion, Spencer's hands literally bled from the workout the lead guitarist and bassist put him through.

JACK CASADY: It got a little mean after a while. At that time Spencer was very slender; and his health was frail. He would have a hard time holding up on the road.

JEFFERSON AIRPLANE BROUGHT ALL OF THIS ANGST with them when they returned to Los Angeles to record. For several months they had been run ragged by the constant touring, the press interviews and TV appearances. With Graham no longer telling them where they had to be, the band members who'd hoped for some time off thought they'd finally get it. But now it was time to start work on album number four.

There had actually been an attempt in late 1967 to begin another record, and two new songs penned by a recharged Marty—an unnamed ballad (later christened "Things Are Better in the East" when it appeared on the *Jefferson Airplane Loves You* boxed set) and a bluesy rocker called "Don't Let Me Down" (no relation to the Beatles' song)—had been committed to tape at RCA Studios. But the label, or the band, apparently didn't agree with the direction in which those songs were taking the Airplane (Grace's absence from both could be one reason). That project was scrapped and work on an all-new album began in earnest in early '68.

RCA wanted a single immediately, so the first item of business was to come up with one. This time Grace bowed to the pressure and agreed to donate one of her new compositions, "Greasy Heart," for that purpose. For two weeks during the end of February and the beginning of March, the Airplane laid down tracks for the combustive A-side and the Marty-penned B-side, the melancholic ballad "Share a Little Joke."

It was already apparent from the single that the experimental zeal that had impregnated *Baxter's* was going to be toned down for the new effort, or at least channeled into more traditional song structures. Both tracks clocked in at just over three minutes, but they were still far from typical radio fare. "Greasy Heart" took Grace's sharp-tongued rancor, trained it on the subject of the superficiality of relationships and beauty and set it to a convulsive stomp; to give it an even greater dynamic, Slick took advantage of the 8-track recording facilities to double-track her vocal. "Share a Little Joke," meanwhile, rings with sadness, yet the singer empathizes fully with his subject's solitary existence, a life lived in peace but outside of "normal" social bounds. Marty, who plays guitar on the song and sings it solo, has said that Gary Blackman provided the motivation for the person described in "Share a Little Joke."

"Greasy Heart" entered the *Billboard* chart on April 20, but only stayed for three weeks and never rose above number 98. Clearly, the widening dichotomy between the sensibilities of Top 40 and underground FM had taken its toll on the ability of Jefferson Airplane to rack up another hit. In the months since they'd put San Francisco on the map with "Somebody to Love" and "White Rabbit," much had changed. The Airplane now fell clearly into a category of bands that would soon have a genre and a radio format to call their own, AOR (album-oriented rock). AOR stations largely avoided the effervescent, young teen-oriented singles that dominated AM and instead offered a steady barrage of the more progressive (mostly white) rock of the day, in all of its many permutations (jazz-rock, raga-rock, blues-rock, etc.). The Airplane was an easy choice for the new breed of AOR DJs and programmers.

The group continued to alternate recording dates and concerts as 1968 unfolded. In March they cut one of Jorma's two songwriting contributions to the new album, "Ice Cream Phoenix," cowritten with Charles Cockey, an old folkie friend who was living with him and Margareta at the time. The song is emblematic of a searching, often-times confessional focus that would come to mark Kaukonen's writing through the years. There is love, the greatest emotion one can experience, and then there is the unknown, oblivion, fear, pain and death— a Kaukonen fixation in much of his writing. Like the great bluesmen whose work he'd absorbed so thoroughly, Jorma asked, time and time again, how one lived within that balance.

Two weeks later, Grace unveiled another new masterpiece, "Lather." Where Jorma's song had asked whether its subject was too far removed from childhood to even remember it, Grace's Lather was wondering why everyone thought he should grow up.

> Lather was 30 years old today
> They took away all of his toys
> His mother sent newspaper clippings to him
> About his old friends who stopped being boys.

"Lather" was written for Spencer, who would reach 30 a few weeks after the track was recorded.

GRACE SLICK: Spencer was older than anybody else in the band. We had a saying that once you turn 30, you're dead, you're not interesting anymore. You're still a baby and you still like to goof around, but you're expected to be responsible. But there's also the determination to maintain that somewhat useful, childlike openness to new ideas and experiences.

Apropos of the song, Grace employs a nearly childlike singing voice, devoid of the hard, robust edge she brought to most of her other lead vocals. To annotate the largely acoustic recording, Spencer, abetted by Gary Blackman, unleashed a virtual arsenal of sound effects, cramming the extra tracks with everything from a typewriter to exploding bombs and screaming rock fans. The album, on the whole, was something of a weird sounds laboratory: among the odder credits were a Blackman "nose solo," Jorma's "Electric Chicken" and Jack's Yggdrasil Bass (Yggdrasil being the Norse sacred tree of life).

With the first four tracks for the new record wrapped up (the version of "Share a Little Joke" on the album is actually a completely different take than the single), the Airplane returned to the touring circuit. It was a musically fertile time, particularly for Jack and Jorma, who took every opportunity not only to continually retool the Airplane's own music, but to sit in with other musicians.

The night before the Airplane played their first Fillmore East show, Jack dropped by to see Jimi Hendrix at the Record Plant studio, where the guitarist was recording his *Electric Ladyland* album and gearing up for a Fillmore East show of his own. Also joined by organist Steve Winwood, the remarkable young British musician whose band Traffic had just played the venue the weekend prior to the Airplane, Jack plugged in his bass and supplied the bottom on Hendrix's classic recording of "Voodoo Chile."

The Airplane also appeared on *The Tonight Show* while in New York, which brought them to a larger television audience than they'd yet encountered. Introduced by Johnny Carson, the band played two older songs from *Surrealistic Pillow*, a lethargic "Today" and the more inspired "Somebody to Love."

BILL THOMPSON: Carson did not like the band. He had put a little carousel [on the set], and Grace sat backwards on the horse singing "Somebody to Love." At the end of the song, she took the microphone and shoved it up the horse's ass, looking right at Johnny Carson. I thought he was going to fall right off his fucking chair.

18
CAN'T HELP BUT SEE THE RHINOCEROS AROUND US

THE COLONIAL REVIVAL STYLE HOME at 2400 Fulton Street was like no other in that part of San Francisco, perhaps none in the entire city. Directly across the street from the northern border of Golden Gate Park, not far from Stanyan Street at the eastern end of the park and within walking distance of the Haight, it was designed and built in 1901 by R. A. Vance, whose family owned the Vance Lumber Company of Eureka, California.

A three-story building, it boldly declared its preeminence through Ionic and Doric columns. Inside the 17-room mansion were mahogany wood paneling from India, crystal chandeliers, exquisite carpeting, a stained glass window, tapestry wallpaper, ornate scrollwork and eight fireplaces. On the octagonal top floor were five oddly shaped bedrooms. A fresco on the ceiling of the second story master bedroom depicted reclining, seminude women. Behind the house were three separate gardens.

In April 1906, when the Great Earthquake leveled much of San Francisco, it spared the new building, and rumors have persisted for years that Enrico Caruso, the legendary operatic tenor, sought shelter that night inside the walls of 2400 Fulton. Caruso's own diary actually placed him nowhere near that part of town, instead stating that he fled eastward from the Palace Hotel near Market Street and paid a ferryman a small fortune to take him to Oakland, but the story has resonance nonetheless.

In the 1930s, Vance sold the house to his niece, Mrs. T. E. Connolly, and it remained in the Connolly family until 1968, when it was sold for $73,000 to a local rock group called Jefferson Airplane. They quickly customized the interior, installing a 4-track recording studio in the huge basement, bringing in Ping-Pong and pool tables, strewing electronic gadgets everywhere, throwing posters on the walls and taking in stray cats.

Immediately the home, henceforth known in rock lore simply as 2400 Fulton, the Airplane House or the Mansion, became a magnet for all manner of visiting fans, musicians, groupies, dope dealers, shysters, oddballs and those simply curious about what the house and its occupants might offer them. The parties became legendary.

> **BARBARA LANGER:** I remember one banquet when there was a big fat joint on every plate, and a roasted suckling pig with an apple in its mouth. It was incredibly lavish and extravagant, ridiculous at certain points.

For some time the Airplane had been discussing the purchase of real estate to serve as their headquarters; 2400 Fulton became all of that and more. The Airplane later titled an album that compiled their biggest hits *2400 Fulton Street*, and an Internet mailing list for fans of the group also honors the address.

Shortly before purchasing the building, Bill Thompson hired Jacky Watts as his and the group's clerical assistant. Her job duties were to include creating itineraries, banking, handling the phones, the bookings—whatever was needed to keep the band's affairs running as tidily as possible—and to give Thompson a break from the day-to-day tedium of paperwork and other managerial drudgery.

> **JACKY (WATTS KAUKONEN) SARTI:** Thompson sent his girlfriend Judy over to see if I was hip enough. I had a great little house, I had blacklight posters all over the place, I had a kitty cat, I was wearing paisley. I passed the hipness test.

One of Jacky's first good deeds was finding the Fulton house.

> **BILL THOMPSON:** The lecherous old guy who lived there liked Jacky. It was the greatest investment we ever made.

With Thompson as manager, employee roles were defined more clearly. Jacky took care of the office, Maurice kept things in line in the studio and Bill Laudner began taking on greater responsibility as road manager. He made travel arrangements, booked flights, hired trucks, scouted show sites, made food arrangements and hotel reservations, rented cars, arranged bail. He left the financial dealings relating to the tours to Thompson as much as possible, but when Thompson was unable to make a gig, Laudner collected the money and paid expenditures.

Finally, somehow, after nearly three chaotic years, the Airplane had their business affairs more or less in order.

CROWN OF CREATION, as the Airplane's fourth album came to be called, was wrapped up in the spring of 1968. Among Grace's contributions was her interpretation of a mostly acoustic ballad written by David Crosby. Sung beautifully and confidently, in a mature, bell-like voice, "Triad" dealt with a ménage à trois in a most casual, if-it-feels-good-do-it manner. Even in the sexually liberated '60s, the notion of a three-way relationship was still considered taboo, and the Byrds, although they had recorded it, refused to allow Crosby's own version of the song to be released, facilitating his departure from the group.

> **GRACE SLICK:** I would have gone, "What?! This is 1968, what do you mean you don't want me to play that?" What is he saying that is bad? If the two women want to live there, and he wants to live there, who cares? His band wouldn't let him and, yeah, I'll sing it! I wouldn't do that [a threesome] personally, but I don't have a moral issue with it.

The album's title track, "Crown of Creation," has become one of Paul Kantner's most time-tested anthems. The song pulsates with a martial rhythm that Paul called up from his military school days, "that vainglorious, epic movie thing, Moses and Catholic military mass, all that stuff," as he describes it. The agitated energy reflects its time and provides the ideal setting for a scenario—and some lyrics—borrowed directly from one of the most celebrated science fiction novels of the Cold War era, John Wyndham's 1955 *The Chrysalids*.

In a 1996 interview with the late Italian Airplane historian Johnny Blasi, Kantner was asked about his penchant for dropping the words of others into his own work. "I have thousands of influences in literature and find it a turn-on to leave a little thing like that for people to find, and then go to the writer who it came from and read him," Kantner said. "I've never thought of it as plagiarism."

Next, the band recorded two pieces that were ultimately bumped from *Crown:* "Would You Like a Snack," two and a half minutes of quasi-free jazz improvisation cowritten by Grace and Frank Zappa (who later borrowed the title for an unrelated tune on one of his own albums), and Spencer's 12-minute "The Saga of Sydney Spacepig."

"Star Track," Jorma's second donation to *Crown*, provided another impressive opportunity for the Kaukonen–Casady–Kantner–Dryden axis to indulge in some delicious interplay. The song borrows its chord changes from Reverend Gary Davis's "Death Don't Have No Mercy," while lyrically it finds Jorma again pondering those weighty topics of love, life, the passing of time and where it all leads.

"If You Feel" was copenned by Marty and Blackman. The tune is alternately whimsical and mischievous, propelled by a driving bass line and taut, skipping guitar riffs from Jorma that lead up to a stunningly wicked solo. "The House at Pooneil Corners," on the other hand, represents *Crown's* dark, foreboding side. Just two years earlier the Airplane was spreading the love vibe, vowing to stay away from the depressingly topical and political. Even at the start of 1968, at a press conference in New York, they had brushed off a question about their political leanings: "Don't ask us anything about politics. We don't know anything about it," one of them had said. "And what we did know, we just forgot."

Now here they were, closing out their 1968 statement with a vivid snapshot of a stark, portentous nightmare, a tour de force of cataclysm. "The House at Pooneil Corners" is ostensibly, but not blatantly, an expounding on the themes put forth in "The Ballad of You & Me & Pooneil." In the original, they sang, "You and me go walking south and we see all the world around us." Now, in the dirgelike sequel, despite a glimmer of optimism in the chorus, the world has become less inviting: "You and me we keep walkin' around and we see all the bullshit around us."

THE SENSE OF DREAD exhibited in the song had rained down upon Jefferson Airplane, the same as it had everyone else under its cloud. Already the year had seen the bloody Tet offensive in Vietnam, the assassination of Dr. King, race riots and campus unrest. Then, just a day after recording "Pooneil Corners," as they were readying for the trip back to San Francisco, the Airplane, along with the rest of the world, learned that Senator Robert F. Kennedy had been shot in Los Angeles, not far from the studio where they were ensconced. The band turned off the tape machines and spoke to one another the best way they knew how: by getting lost in a howling, primal blues jam, playing until they could no longer play.

Although they had stuck to their guns and endorsed no political candidates, the Airplane admired "Bobby," who had emerged as the leading contender for the Democratic presidential nomination. And Kennedy was an Airplane fan. Earlier that year, RFK had invited them to be the only rock band to perform in Washington at a pay-per-view television event, the Junior Village Telethon. Ethel Kennedy, the soon-to-be-candidate's wife, had arranged the program as a benefit for the Kennedy Foundation for Retarded Children.

The band willingly agreed to participate. To the Airplane and many of their generation, Bobby Kennedy was the last hope of the liberals—at a time when radical thought was spreading rapidly among the youth, as conventional party politics proved less and less responsive to their concerns, Kennedy offered an acceptable compromise. He was unapologetically antiwar, pro-civil rights, and supported social programs to help the poor and underrepresented. If America's leftists were going to remain a part of the system, many felt Kennedy was the best they were going to get.

The Airplane was flown from San Francisco to D.C. on a government Lear Jet. When they arrived at the site of the telecast, Thompson worked up the nerve to ask Pierre Salinger, the legendary press secretary to the Kennedys, and an accomplished concert pianist, to "sit in" with the Airplane. There was no need for him to actually learn the music they'd be playing since they would be lip-synching anyway—Thompson just thought it would look cool on TV.

What Salinger didn't realize was that he'd be taking part in a song in which Grace Slick openly challenged the most famous line from John F. Kennedy's historic 1961 inaugural speech, indeed from his tenure as president: "Ask not what your country can do for you, ask what you can do for your country."

BILL THOMPSON: We did "rejoyce," and in the middle of the song, "War's good business, so give your son, but I'd rather have my country die for me." Oh, man, there was a big fallout from that, with all the politicians. And Salinger was caught in the middle of it, because he didn't know what he was playing. I had just talked him into it.

At a party at the home of LBJ's Ambassador-at-Large W. Averell Harriman following the benefit, the band mingled with the VIPs. Thompson, still new to his job, was shell-shocked to find himself not only commiserating with the Kennedys but all manner of celebrities, from comedian Woody Allen to football legend Rosey Grier.

The next day, the band was limoed to Hickory Hill, the Kennedys' Virginia compound. The Airplane breakfasted with the family and met Brumus, their Newfoundland dog, whose portrait would grace the inner sleeve of the *Crown of Creation* album cover later that year.

Back in San Francisco following Kennedy's death, the Airplane and the Dead set up in Golden Gate Park, attempting to play an impromptu "wake" for the fallen senator. But the Speedway Meadow had been reserved for a Cub Scout pack and the rock bands didn't have a permit to play. Although a sympathetic police sergeant told the bands he felt terrible about having to send them packing—he too admired RFK—there would be no music that day.

Filling out *Crown of Creation* was "In Time," a Balin–Kantner collaboration with a sweet solo from Jorma, and Spencer's "Chushingura," another instrumental sound collage, which took its title from an epic 1962 film directed by Hiroshi Inagaki. Spencer, along with some percussionist pals, also cut a minute and a half of heavily reverbed drums and more Zappa-fied vocal silliness, "Ribump Ba Bap Dum Dum." Originally intended to close out the album, it was instead snipped from the master tape and tossed onto a shelf, where it remained (along with "Would You Like a Snack") until being remixed for the *Loves You* boxed set 24 years later.

Produced by Al Schmitt and engineered by Richie Schmitt, *Crown of Creation* was more accessible than *Baxter's*, perhaps, but still marked forward movement for the group.

GRACE SLICK: We still had the freedom to do what we felt like doing. It hadn't gotten to, "You better repeat yourself." We're still more or less open to each other's stuff, and still at a point where information is moving relatively freely within the band.

The album was released in late August with a cover designed by John Van Hamersveld, a Los Angeles–based graphic artist and a member of Pinnacle Production Company, which had promoted an Airplane show in L.A. at the Shrine Auditorium. In planning the artwork, Van Hamersveld, who had previously created the popular poster for the surfing film *The Endless Summer*, asked each member of the band to come up with a single word to describe what he or she would like the cover to represent.

> **JOHN VAN HAMERSVELD:** Grace said "stump." And then, just like a child, Marty says "rainbow." Spencer didn't say anything, he just nodded, and Casady and Jorma were in a corner working on their feedback. Paul said "bomb."

Kantner's image stuck with Van Hamersveld—it seemed to capture the tenuous spirit of the music, and the volatile nature of the times. Thompson located a U.S. Air Force file photo of the atomic bomb exploding over Hiroshima. Perfect.

Van Hamersveld needed a photo of the Airplane to complete the design he had in mind, and Thompson suggested he look at a series of shots taken recently at a session in New York by—and the irony didn't escape them—the Japanese photographer Hiro, a lensman for *Harper's Bazaar* magazine and assistant to the famed portrait photographer Richard Avedon. Van Hamersveld had the photos of the band and the bomb combined and colored and the final cover depicted the Airplane—double-exposed and looking more than a bit freaked out—ascending to the heavens amid the bright orange mushroom cloud of annihilation.

The Summer of Love was definitely over.

For the inner sleeve, the Airplane used the photo of Brumus the dog, and one of Maurice, replete with beret and cigarette, standing in front of RCA's 8-track recorder. For the first time, the band also included in the packaging the lyrics to all of the songs. Which, of course, meant that RCA had to find something to censor. "The House at Pooneil Corners" gave the company a few opportunities to keep America's youth from being corrupted: the word "bullshit" was cleverly disguised as "bulsht," while the pleasures of indulging in sex and drugs became "And you do what you can to get bald and hi."

• • •

IF THE *TONIGHT SHOW* and an invitation to schmooze with the Kennedys served notice that the Airplane had traversed the underground and moved up another rung on the recognition ladder, several events in the spring of '68 confirmed the absurdity of it all.

First was the airing of a brief promotional radio spot for the United States Army, of all things, spotlighting the Airplane. Hosted by New York disc jockey Harry Harrison, the "In Sounds" program attempted to lure young Americans into the Armed Forces by associating military service with something hip, like a happening antiwar rock group.

After playing some Airplane, the DJ gets "Gracie" on the phone for a chat. "How would you describe your singing voice?" he asks her.

"Loud."

And how does that loud voice compare to that of Mama Cass of the Mamas and the Papas? Cass is better, opines Grace. Then it's good night, Gracie.

But it was the publication of the June 28, 1968 issue of *Life* magazine that provided unassailable confirmation that the Airplane had broken through the psychedelic haze. *Life*, one of America's most popular and highly respected periodicals, brought the latest news and issues into millions of American homes. *Life* was as mainstream as it got—everyone's parents read it. And now, occupying the entire cover, under a banner headline reading "Music That's Hooked the Whole Vibrating World—THE NEW ROCK," was Jefferson Airplane.

The photo was a classic. It was taken by Art Kane who, 10 years earlier, under assignment from *Esquire*, had shot 57 of the leading figures of jazz on a Harlem street, assembled together for the first time. For the Airplane shoot, Kane created—at great expense to *Life*—a pyramid of Plexiglas cubes and piled them atop one another at a gypsum plant in Queens, New York, in the shadow of an abandoned factory. Full of huge piles of volcanic ash, the site gave Kane the barren, desertlike atmosphere he sought, even if it was just across the river from Manhattan. The photographer had each band member occupy a cube, and snapped a series of photos of a very bored-looking Airplane, the lotus-positioned Grace at the top.

Later, Kane presciently wrote, "By placing each member of the group into their own container in this rising pattern we create the illusion of 'flying,' if you will. The group appears together but apart, suggesting the loneliness that sets in with the rise of individualism."

One shot made the cover, another made the two-page inside spread. Why the Airplane was chosen for the cover over the Who, Cream, Jim Morrison, the Mothers or Country Joe and the Fish—the other artists featured—is a matter of conjecture. The text, rather ridiculous, consisted of one long paragraph that began, "The Jefferson Airplane flies the runways of the mind and the airways of the imagination," and went downhill from there.

> **GRACE SLICK:** I thought [being on the cover] was amusing more than anything else.

"NEW WORLDS TO GAIN," Paul had written in "Crown of Creation," and now, Europe was next. Although the Airplane had yet to score a hit single or album anywhere outside of the U.S., a buzz had been generated regarding the West Coast scene. A series of dates was booked beginning in late August, some coheadlining with the Doors. Their keyboardist recalled the excitement his group felt.

> **RAY MANZAREK:** When we heard we were playing with the Airplane, it was like, holy fuck, West Coast psychedelic goes to London! We were on a mission to bring to the heart of the British Invasion what we were.

Gigs were set up in Stockholm, Copenhagen, London, Hamburg, Dusseldorf and Amsterdam. The majority of the shows found the Airplane in superb form, playing material from all four albums. They headlined the first rock festival at the Isle of Wight in England and played a pair of London shows at the Roundhouse. There was also the obligatory freebie, at London's Parliament Hill.

But the show that everyone remembers from this tour—not so much for the Airplane's performance per se as for the guy who crashed the stage during their first set—took place at the Concertgebouw in Amsterdam. Things got interesting when the Airplane, opening the show that night, launched into "Plastic Fantastic Lover." Jim Morrison suddenly materialized onstage.

> **RAY MANZAREK:** They started playing faster and faster and faster. Morrison is singing with them, doing a dervish dance, obviously

completely gone. He gets caught up in the cords and falls down on the stage, gets back up, extricates himself, keeps on whirling. The song comes to an end. Morrison waves to the audience, bows and comes backstage. He leans up against the wall in the dressing room and very slowly, with a beer in his hand, slides down the wall and passes out. And that was it. He was gone.

SPENCER DRYDEN: The audience probably thought it was part of the show. It seems that he drank something like a six- or 12-pack of Heineken to chase down an ounce of blond hashish.

RAY MANZAREK: The paramedics loaded Jim Morrison onto a stretcher, covered him in a rubber sheet, put an oxygen mask on his face and proceeded to carry him out into an ambulance. We played our set without him and I sang.

The band returned to New York at the end of September to play the most popular television variety show of the time—of all time—*The Ed Sullivan Show.* All of those other TV appearances were good exposure, but getting on Sullivan meant they had truly made it in "the biz." Now even their own parents—in case the folks still concealed any lingering doubts about their child's career choice after the *Life* cover—had to acknowledge that Jefferson Airplane was a success. Every Sunday night, millions of Americans sat religiously in front of their sets and watched the hunched-shouldered Sullivan's "really big shoe" with its parade of jugglers, opera singers, comedians, Broadway stars, plate spinners, rock groups and, of course, Topo Gigio, the Italian mouse. Elvis Presley had made his major TV breakthrough on *Ed Sullivan*, as had the Beatles.

It was in fact a Presley connection that landed the Airplane the booking—Colonel Tom Parker, Elvis's manager, undoubtedly at the urging of someone at RCA, had personally suggested the band to the high-powered host. Now here was Ed Sullivan himself, introducing "the number one rock group in the country . . . for the youngsters, let's hear it, the Jefferson Airplane." The Airplane, with Glenn McKay's lights behind them, performed "Crown of Creation," the majority of the audience no doubt having nary a clue what the band was singing about or why they had to have those blinding, pulsating, colored blobs behind them.

The day after the Sullivan appearance, the Airplane put on another free concert in Central Park. Then, later that week, they appeared at the

Whitney Museum, where an organization called Friends of the Whitney was holding a fund-raising event. From the beginning, the night was a disaster. Jack was nearly denied admission when the security guard at the door didn't believe that he was one of the scheduled performers, then McKay found out that his rear projection system could not be used in the space allotted for him; he had to rearrange his show to project from the front.

But Grace was the real problem. Mingling with the moneyed, well-dressed, smug upper-classers reminded her too much of Palo Alto and the life she'd chosen not to live. Her head full of alcohol, deliberately setting herself up for the kill, Grace uncoiled, hurling insults at the museum's guests, and singing off-key to boot. She went into a midsong monologue, calling the assembled rich "filthy jewels," which some misheard as "filthy Jews." As Marty cringed and the others played on, she castigated the women, among them the curator's wife, asking if they ever saw their husbands in the bedroom or only at functions such as this. She wasn't making many new fans.

Although the band played well despite the singer's indiscretions, the audience didn't know what to make of Grace's display and—except for one couple that got up to dance the foxtrot—either sat on the floor in utter bewilderment or headed for the door.

But perhaps Grace's acting out was a nervous reaction to the confusion that had been hanging over her since the European trip and a swiftly curtailed Virgin Islands vacation that had followed. Grace had vacated the Caribbean, where both Spencer and Paul had joined her, after deciding that Spencer was causing her time off to be anything but relaxing. Their relationship was clearly reaching its denouement, although they'd continued presenting themselves to others as a committed couple. But now, as sexually liberated citizens of the '60s, it seemed hypocritical and silly to Grace to put up a front.

Besides, she already had her eyes on someone else.

19

WHEN SPENCER MET SALLY

GRACE SLICK LOOKED at the makeup spread out on the table in the TV studio's waiting room. Every color in the rainbow. Digging in, she covered her entire face and neck with the darkest brown she could find.

The Smothers Brothers had sought the return of the Airplane to their show ever since that first successful appearance in '67. In October of the following year, the band obliged.

When none of the program's makeup assistants protested her instant transformation, Grace sauntered out nonchalantly in front of the cameras and, during a year when racially motivated violence was polarizing the nation, sang in blackface in front of millions. As a final gesture, she raised her fist in the black power salute.

When the show aired a few weeks later, many viewers, both white and black, were outraged.

TOM SMOTHERS: I asked her what it meant, but she said, "I don't know." It was never explained to us. If she did it today there'd be all kinds of people screaming and yelling, but everybody who came on the show was our guest and they could do whatever they wanted to do.

BILL THOMPSON: At the summer Olympics in 1968, two black runners [Tommie Smith and John Carlos] had raised their fists in the black power salute to protest injustices against blacks. Grace's gesture was to show solidarity with them.

GRACE SLICK: It wasn't political. Women wear makeup, and it's very standardized: you wear this color if you're this kind of person. And I thought, Well, why not wear black? Black just seemed interesting because I had white on and it was so antithetical to my features. But it didn't work very well because I looked almost East Indian. It was just last-minute stuff, and the Smothers Brothers were very lenient. I think if I'd done a regular Al Jolson with the lips that might've made people even more furious.

On the program, the Airplane performed both sides of their latest single. "Crown of Creation" was played live in the studio, followed by "Lather," which was lip-synched. But if the TV appearance was intended to boost sales, it didn't: the "Crown" single charted shortly before the program's airing but never rose above number 64.

The album itself, which landed on the charts during the week of September 7, fared much better sales-wise, aided by positive press and substantial FM radio airplay. *Rolling Stone's* half-page review, written by Jim Miller, suggested that, "Style is both the curse and the achievement" of the Airplane and, "the problem with style is the danger of degeneration into stylization which can become a crutch and a refuge from artistic development."

Only a few nights before taping the Smothers Brothers' show, in late October, the Airplane had wrapped up a three-night stay at Fillmore West. There, with Al and Richie Schmitt at the controls, they recorded all of the shows with the intention of compiling the best of the performances into the group's first live album.

It was time for a sampling of the rapturous delirium of the Airplane concert experience to find its way to a record. They had evolved in three years into one of the most stunning performing bands of their time, a supersonic, hyperinventive rock and roll machine. Whatever might have been gnawing at their interpersonal relationships, when they took the stage, those differences were put aside, or put to good use; the Airplane was untouchable.

From the October shows, six tracks made it to the final live album. Half were songs that had originally appeared on *Surrealistic Pillow:* "3/5 of a Mile in 10 Seconds," "Somebody to Love" and "Plastic Fantastic Lover." From *Takes Off* came "It's No Secret." On the studio albums, those songs had been tightly constructed and tough, but live in '68 they were textbook examples of improvisational, electrified rock and roll at its finest, at times so far removed from the prototypes as to be virtually unrecognizable. A solid foundation is always present underneath but the embellishments match those of the Airplane Mansion in majesty.

Also taken from the October shows was "Rock Me Baby," an eight-minute, hard-core blues juggernaut placing Jorma, Jack and Spencer (and, to a lesser degree, Paul) at center stage. Both B. B. King and Muddy Waters had previously claimed songwriting credit for the tune, so perhaps it was mere confusion that led the Airplane to attribute it to "Traditional" when the album was released. The last of the October tracks is "The Other Side of This Life," the Fred Neil favorite that had been a mainstay of Airplane shows since day one. Although the song had been recorded by the Lovin' Spoonful, the Animals, the Youngbloods and others, the Airplane had never committed their interpretation to record before. They attacked the song savagely, leaving no doubt that they'd not only visited that other side, but that they resided there.

Jack remained industrious outside of the group during this period. The current owner of the Matrix had repositioned the club as a place where musicians could stop by on nights off and jam to their hearts' content. Most of the sessions were organized loosely around Grateful Dead members Mickey Hart, Bill Kreutzmann, Jerry Garcia and Phil Lesh, going under the name Mickey and the Hartbeats. On several occasions, Jack sat in, playing along happily on the mostly-Dead repertoire.

Casady had become recognized by 1968 as one of the most respected bassists in rock. His unique approach to the instrument, what Dan Schwartz of *Bass Player* magazine later described as "an equal voice, supportive and contrapuntal, painting with huge swatches of deep chords, limning the landscape with melodies and countermelodies, hammering down the bottom with pedal points of gigantic scale," had redefined its role.

Some have described Jack's style of playing as "lead bass," but while he was one of the dominant forces within the Airplane, Jack was, in his own way, a classic team player. Not content to stay in the background and plunk out simple rhythms, to provide the music with an anchor, he saw it as his job to add another harmonic voice to the mix. Jack interacted with Jorma, Spencer and Paul in a manner not unlike that in which the singers up front were doing with one another.

Lesh was one admirer, quoted in the 1970 book *Rock: A World Bold As Love* as saying, "Jack Casady is the world's greatest electric bass player. . . . He's the most evolved product of rock and roll bass playing. . . . Even in jazz, they don't play the bass like that."

It's not surprising, then, that other musicians sought Jack out, and when he dropped in on Hendrix during the guitar star's three-nighter at Winterland that fall, Casady again ended up sitting in with the Experience. One track from those shows featuring Jack on bass, Howlin' Wolf's "Killing Floor," later made it to a Hendrix CD called *Live at Winterland*.

IN NOVEMBER, the Airplane was back on the East Coast. They met with the renowned French filmmaker Jean-Luc Godard, whose masterpieces, including *Breathless*, *La Chinoise* and *Weekend*, were considered groundbreaking. Godard had begun leaving conventional filmmaking techniques behind by the late '60s, and had become increasingly politicized, infatuated with the revolutionary struggle. Understanding the vital role of rock music at that time, he had already made an as-yet-unreleased film featuring the Rolling Stones, *One Plus One* (also known as *Sympathy for the Devil*), and now he set his sights on Jefferson Airplane.

Godard, in collaboration with documentarian D. A. Pennebaker (*Monterey Pop*) and his team, was involved with a work-in-progress he called *One A.M.* (for *One American Movie*). For the film, Godard trained his camera on such leading movement figures as Eldridge Cleaver and Tom Hayden and simply let them speak. And speak they did. Their rambling revolutionary rhetoric occupied nearly the entire film: traditional storyline and direction were abandoned, and what emerged was a stark portrait of the underbelly of a nation on the verge of a massive overhaul.

Considering the Airplane an important revolutionary voice, Godard wanted the band in his film. This wasn't the first time the group had been approached by a famous director seeking their drawing power. Otto Preminger (*Exodus*, *The Man with the Golden Arm*), working on a hippie exploitation film called *Skidoo*, had sought Grace for his project, but she found his attempts to be hip rather pathetic. The final film, which featured Jackie Gleason on acid and Groucho Marx as a mob boss named God—with music by Harry Nilsson, who sang the credits—was rather surreal.

Godard's idea was more in line with the Airplane's: all they had to do was play music. On a chilly autumn afternoon, Laudner and the crew set up the Airplane's equipment atop the condemned Schuyler Hotel on

45th Street in New York. Pennebaker positioned his camera crew there and directly across the street, in his office, and film rolled. Jefferson Airplane, padded in their winter coats and gloves (and Jack in an imposing hat), churned out a particularly nasty rendition of "House at Pooneil Corners." Marty—temporarily putting aside his grievances and looking as if he'd never been happier to be a part of this band—barked the words, mocking and mugging for the cameras, lulling even the usually poker-faced Grace into laughter.

On the rooftop, crew, friends and the curious gathered to listen, and dance. On the street below, New Yorkers—usually fazed by nothing—stopped in their tracks to gaze skyward. At the song's conclusion, the band ran over to the edge of the roof, climbing the chain-link fence to peer down at those peering up at them. Grace, enjoying it all, danced a jig.

To no one's surprise, New York's Finest soon arrived, with orders to end this disruption of the more common New York sounds of car horns, construction equipment and their own sirens. "If they continue the music, lock 'em up," warned one cop. The camera then turned toward the patrol cars on the street, where actor Rip Torn, a friend of the band, was being hauled away for disturbing the officers, while Marty glided by, a contented smile plastered across his face.

Godard later abandoned the project, and *One A.M.* was finished by Pennebaker, retitled *One P.M.* (for *One Perfect Movie*). The film opened more than a year after the Airplane's sequence was filmed, playing to limited audiences in art houses and receiving indifferent reviews. It has remained out of circulation since.

Two months after the Airplane's impromptu rooftop performance, the Beatles ascended to the roof of their Apple building in London and played for the folks below. The cameras were still rolling as the police arrived to put a stop to the Beatles' final public performance.

FOR THREE NIGHTS during the 1968 Thanksgiving weekend, the Airplane played Fillmore East, where they again set up recording equipment in order to grab material for the proposed live album. They ultimately chose two epics and a couple of trifles to top off the project.

"Fat Angel," the Donovan-penned song that included the by-then oft-quoted "fly Jefferson Airplane" reference, had been a staple of the

Airplane's shows since they'd heard it two years earlier. Now transformed into a ragalike excursion through mysterious psychic lands, it was a highlight of Airplane shows and an unusual number in that Marty strapped on Jack's Guild Starfire II bass and Jack switched over to a Fender Telecaster to play rhythm guitar. Paul, who sang the song, spent most of it coaxing drone sounds out of his Rickenbacker 12-string while Jorma played an exotic lead. The live album was a perfect home for "Fat Angel," and a seven-and-a-half-minute take was culled from the Fillmore East tapes.

> **DONOVAN:** The song was inspired by Cass Elliot of the Mamas and the Papas. I hung out seriously with this band and made a drawing of Cass as a fat angel sleeping under a tree in a meadow. The rest of the lyrics describe various happenings in Hollywood. The guy on the bike was Barry McGuire, who recorded "Eve of Destruction." "Fly Jefferson Airplane" was of course a reference to the astral flying we all were doing. I love the Airplane's version of the song.

"Bear Melt," the 11-plus-minute bluesy magnum opus that would close out the finished live album, was a new title given to an old Airplane idea: the free-form improvisation. During most of their shows, the band, usually near the end, took off on an open-ended jam they dubbed "Thing." Inflating exponentially from only the most tenuous of predetermined chord progressions, the group, minus Marty, who usually sat these jams out, fed off of one another's cues, going wherever inspiration led them.

For the first half of the piece on this night, a versatile and surefooted Grace provided much of the glory, putting her jazz exposure to good use. She flexed her voice, riding the waves of sound where they took her, setting the scene for the others. "You can move your rear ends now," Grace chided her audience at the end, but they were too shell-shocked to even consider it.

"Turn Out the Lights," a whimsical, off-the-cuff, minute-long instrumental hoedown, and "Clergy" (original title, vetoed by RCA: "King Cong," as in Viet), which was nothing more than the last minute and a half of the original 1933 *King Kong* film ("Oh, no, it wasn't the airplanes, it was beauty killed the beast"), shown to the Fillmore East audience as the band took the stage, were added to the album.

Gary Blackman was handed the task of designing the packaging for the completed record. On the inside of the jacket, he inserted a poster, a piece of artwork by Bill Thompson that resembled a trio of demented potatoes as drawn by a three-year-old. For the black-and-white album cover itself, Jim Smircich, who'd often photographed the band in its infancy, was invited back to shoot the Airplane during the various stages of a party at 2400 Fulton. On the back cover of the album, the full band, considerably damaged, gets a bit cozier than they're accustomed to getting. On the front, Jack, grabbing a little shut-eye before the feast, makes the mile-long banquet table his personal headrest, clutching for dear life a bottle of the evening's liquid refreshments.

Upon seeing that photograph of Jack, Grace, paraphrasing from a Philip Whalen poem, reportedly proclaimed, "Well, bless its pointed little head," and a title was born.

> **JORMA KAUKONEN:** *Bless Its Pointed Little Head* is an archetypal live album, and it really is a live album. There's no overdubbing. There are no redone vocals. That is the Airplane at its peak.

While the Airplane was recording the concerts that would become *Bless Its Pointed Little Head*, the *Billboard* album chart was providing concrete evidence of the turning of the musical tide. In October of 1968, the Airplane was at number 9 with *Crown of Creation*, sharing the Top 10 with such hip bands as Iron Butterfly, the Chambers Brothers, Steppenwolf, the Doors and the Rascals. Just a few notches below the Top 10 stood both Hendrix and Cream.

But it was the occupant of the top position on the chart that was really raising eyebrows: the second release by Janis Joplin and Big Brother and the Holding Company, *Cheap Thrills*. Now San Francisco boasted two superstar rock women, and the media couldn't help but compare them: A poster of Grace and Janis together, from a 1967 photograph by Jim Marshall, was a best-seller, and magazine articles persistently mentioned the two singers in the same breath, attempting to pigeonhole the personalities of these two disparate people.

Grace, with her cool, hard demeanor, biting tongue and intense blue eyes, was "ice." Joplin, the Southern Comfort slugger (the media didn't yet know that Grace could match her swig for swig) with the Texas drawl, wild onstage moves and tough-broad stance, was "fire." While there was some truth to the characterizations, the stereotyping was an oversimplification.

GRACE SLICK: We were so different. It's like comparing an apple with a Hershey bar.

SAM ANDREW: Fire and ice doesn't begin to describe them. Janis was an artist and Grace was a terrorist.

MICKEY HART: There was a symbiotic relationship between Janis and Grace. They were twin pillars.

By the time *Cheap Thrills* had reached number 1, Janis Joplin had already announced her departure from Big Brother, convinced by friends and handlers that she could do better without them. Disarray was also, once again, rampant in the Airplane camp. On the last night of the band's Thanksgiving run at Fillmore East, Spencer had made a demonstration—for Grace's benefit—of snatching a groupie out of the audience. Grace not only displayed no heartbreak over the blatant snub but shared a taxi back to the hotel with them.

Spencer stayed behind in New York for a few days after the one-nighter while the others flew home. When he finally arrived back in San Francisco, Dryden was more than a little surprised to see a charred shell where his apartment used to be. In his absence Spencer had entrusted the place he shared with Grace—the building also housed Jorma and Margareta Kaukonen and their friend Charles Cockey on the floor above them—to a pair of hippies who got careless with matches while smoking dope. Spencer, the Kaukonens and Cockey all moved to 2400 Fulton after the fire, but Grace had taken one look at the remains of the building, shrugged and headed directly to L.A., where she joined Paul in the task of mixing the live album.

If it had ever crossed either of their minds before that coupling up might be a good idea, they'd kept those thoughts to themselves. But not anymore. Their union had, perhaps, been inevitable: One night in Europe, when Paul was feeling troubled during an acid trip, Grace had talked him down and, unexpectedly, found herself feeling passionate toward him. Then, when Paul had followed her and Spencer to the Virgin Islands after the tour, Grace couldn't help but notice that her feelings had returned. She even began experiencing jealousy—now that was something new!—whenever she saw Paul in the company of one of his many female acquaintances.

Alone now with Kantner in the recording studio in L.A., a couple of weeks before Christmas, Grace, accidentally brushing Paul's hand, felt that spark again. But this time she sensed it coming back from him.

Meanwhile, back in San Francisco, Spencer was retrieving what was left of his belongings from the apartment when Jorma and Margareta called him over to meet a woman named Sally Mann. She came, he learned, from a politically powerful Houston family. Having graduated from the University of Texas in 1966, still in her teens, she'd set out for Los Angeles with the Sir Douglas Quintet, the fine band led by multi-instrumentalist Doug Sahm. Being underage, there was some concern that Sally would get the band arrested, so she married her boyfriend, the Quintet's road manager, and the newlyweds shared an apartment with Sahm.

SALLY (MANN) ROMANO: We all thought we were grown up but when we got away from our mommies we all wondered who was supposed to be making breakfast and stuff. So my mother came out and was sort of the den mother for Doug. This was even before people were brave enough to grow their hair long—Doug was actually wearing a wig onstage.

One night Sally went down to the Whisky, where she met Kantner. The two became fast friends and Sally, already split from her husband, soon found herself spending considerable time in San Francisco. The new mother of a baby boy, courtesy of a cast member of *Hair*, Sally was now involved with Big Brother guitarist James Gurley. Kantner introduced her to the Kaukonens, who often put her up when she needed a place to stay, and eventually, after both Sally and her mother were arrested in a pot bust in L.A. (the charges were dropped), Sally moved up north. She and Spencer, soon after meeting, consummated their budding friendship one evening in Marty's bedroom at the Mansion.

Although Grace was also still nominally involved with Spencer, she readily accepted that he and Sally were spending an awful lot of time together. And the more Grace got to know Sally, the more she liked her. Although there was nearly a 10-year age difference between them, Grace appreciated Sally's intelligence and wit, and they obviously shared the same taste in men.

SALLY (MANN) ROMANO: Grace had already made the decision to break up with Spencer and they were not physically together at all.

There were lots of bizarre evenings. The three of us would be up real late, drinking, and at some point some little emotional cog would switch on in Spencer's head. Grace is a master at avoiding emotional attachments she doesn't want to have, and she would either split—she had just moved—and we'd be dealing with the fallout, or she and I would go.

AFTER THE APARTMENT HAD BURNED DOWN, Grace, rather than moving full-time into the Fulton Street mansion, chose to get her own apartment in Sausalito. Complicating the relationship maze even further, Grace asked Jerry Slick, to whom she was still legally married, to move back in with her, which he did for a brief while.

Like all of the Airplane, though, Grace still spent a great deal of time at Fulton Street—she maintained a bedroom there for those nights when she just couldn't make it home. Sally, meanwhile, was also living at the Mansion, having been hired to serve as housekeeper. One night while Grace was visiting, she found Sally downstairs—Spencer, it seemed, was upstairs entertaining some groupies. Sally and Grace passed a bottle back and forth, talking about what a cad their mutual lover was. Eventually, Grace became so incapacitated that Spencer called Jerry Slick to come into the city and retrieve his wife, but not before Grace made it clear that the man she really wanted to be with, more than either of them, was Paul Kantner.

Paul, for his part, was being his resolutely noncommittal self. While living at Fulton Street with his own housekeeper, Barbara Langer, Paul was presently involved with a friend of Sally's named Karen Seltenrich, a waitress and booker at the Matrix who would later appear on the cover of a *Rolling Stone* magazine issue devoted to groupies. (Years later still, when Karen presented Paul with a boy named Gareth and informed Kantner that he was the father, Paul readily and willingly accepted the child as his own and adopted him legally. Gareth, who grew up in Paris and later in life became a respected Los Angeles restaurateur, and Paul have remained close since.)

As for Jack, in late 1968 he was the only Airplane member beside Grace not living at Fulton Street—he shared a home in San Francisco with Melissa Cargill and their pet owl. By early '69, though, the Airplane house began losing tenants as the old gang dispersed yet again:

Marty vacated Fulton and bought a house across the Golden Gate in Mill Valley and the Kaukonens picked one up in the city. Only Paul and Spencer from the band now remained at the Mansion.

It was a strange and taxing time for Jefferson Airplane. In January, Grace, who had occasionally experienced vocal strain, checked into a hospital to have nodules removed from her throat. When she came home to Sausalito, she found that her place had been burglarized. Marty's new home was also the target of thieves. Paul's new Porsche was stolen and Jack's car was broken into. It wasn't a good time to be a nouveau riche rock star, especially one in a band noted for flaunting its newly acquired wealth in the form of expensive possessions—like Grace's brand new 1969 Aston Martin, paid for in cash.

Meanwhile, despite the fact that the musicians were moving out, Fulton Street was becoming a destination not only for colleagues of the band, but for an increasing number of intruders, some benevolent, others with more malicious intent.

SPENCER DRYDEN: One night, we were on the top floor and we heard some noise. There's a weird guy walking down the hall; he had crawled up the drainpipe and come in through a window!

JACKY (WATTS KAUKONEN) SARTI: I used to keep Thorazine in my bottom drawer, to bring people down from acid trips. People would be sitting in Golden Gate Park thinking that Grace was calling to them.

There was also a growing sense of restlessness among the musicians, particularly within Jack and Jorma. Jack took advantage of the Airplane's downtime by playing gigs with Country Joe and the Fish, whose bassist, Bruce Barthol, had left the band. Some of the shows—which also included appearances by Jerry Garcia, Mickey Hart, Steve Miller and Big Brother's David Getz—were recorded and selections were released many years later as a CD titled *Live! Fillmore West 1969*.

In February, *Bless Its Pointed Little Head* was released, soon thereafter beginning a respectable climb up the *Billboard* charts to number 17. Reviews of the album were almost universally glowing, several writers stating outright that it was the most sensational live rock album ever released. Gushed the *Village Voice*, "It's the Airplane sounding like the

Airplane, for the first time on record. . . . The others were blueprints, this is the real thing. In many ways the Jefferson Airplane's fifth album is actually their first."

For the band, *Pointed Head* was a way of explaining, to those who'd judged them by their studio albums and found them lacking, what they were really capable of doing. In the studio, they'd been unable to replicate the live experience and quickly learned not even to try, to instead treat the studio as the radically different medium it was. Yet when they'd attempted to record live shows before, they'd also found those results to be a shadow of the real thing.

Finally, by late 1968, aided by advances in technology and qualified recordists, the Airplane had gotten it right. Even if there was still no way for the uninitiated listener to play *Pointed Head* and understand what it felt like to be inside one of the Fillmores as these musicians worked their charm, at least now people could get an inkling of how monstrous Jefferson Airplane sounded on a good night.

20 OUTLAWS IN THE EYES OF AMERICA

BILL THOMPSON SAW GRACE AND PAUL coming down the stairs of the Mansion together one morning, big smiles on their faces: "Oh, shit, here we go again," Thompson muttered to himself.

The band had been in Honolulu a few weeks earlier for a gig at the International Centre and had rented a castle on the ocean. Grace spent her time in Hawaii with Spencer at first, giving it one last try, but he was being cantankerous, staying in the hotel room and getting loaded. Forget this, Grace thought. She headed down to the pool, where Paul offered her some acid. After a while the two of them went for a drive with Jorma and Margareta and, as they all admired the breathtaking countryside, for the first time Grace and Paul became aware that they might be heading into something deeper together.

Nothing happened between them in Hawaii—Paul had brought a girlfriend along and Grace was still, in theory, attached to Spencer—but when they returned home, Grace and Paul spent the night together and made no attempt to shield their newfound passion from the others. The latest intraband romance was now out in the open.

Said Paul in one interview, "I fell in love with Grace the moment I first saw her, but I had to wait my turn."

SALLY (MANN) ROMANO: Spencer was really the one suffering from the fallout, because it is true that there is a great power base there. Spencer was a latecomer to the band and there were differences that were going to be accentuated if he didn't have that connection anymore.

Like a game of checkers, Grace and Paul were now the kings on one side of the board, Jorma and Jack on the other, with Marty and Spencer lone pieces trying to get anywhere they could without getting jumped.

Although hobbled internally by this Peyton Place situation, the Airplane as a musical unit continued to function. Due to Grace's throat problems, they played no live gigs between Thanksgiving of 1968 and the March '69 Hawaiian excursion. During this hiatus, into the midst of the Jefferson Airplane psychodrama came Joey Covington, a Los Angeles–based drummer Marty had met in early '68 while the group was in L.A. recording.

Covington's roommate at the time was friendly with Todd Schiffman, the booking agent, who'd heard Joey play and asked if he might bring some friends over to listen to him. Marty and Thompson, knowing even then that it was just a matter of time until Spencer would be booted from the band, had leaked word to Schiffman that they were looking for a drummer who could handle the endurance test that Airplane gigs had become. They'd already tried out a young kid named Michael Shrieve, but he instead threw his lot in with Carlos Santana, the remarkable guitar player who was the new talk of San Francisco. Todd thought that Joey would be perfect for the Airplane job.

Covington wasn't his real name. He was born Joseph Michno in 1945, in Johnstown, Pennsylvania, and raised in the nearby small town of East Conemaugh. His father, a truck driver named Louis, was a one-time minor league baseball player who would have been headed for the pros had World War II not drafted him first. Joey's mother, Elizabeth Sisco, known as Betty, was an aspiring country singer until marriage and children scotched that dream.

Joey taught himself drums and, in his late teens, joined a rock and roll band called the Vibra-Sonics. In 1965, the band's car was blindsided by a drunk driver, killing one member, and Joey broke a leg, his pelvis and several other bones. His recuperation took six months, after which Joey took off for New York and Florida, picking up whatever drum jobs he could. Returning home, he hooked up with two other bands, the Charms and the Fenways.

By 1967, though, restless Joe Michno had moved to Los Angeles and become Joey Covington. He began putting together a new band, including an older man, a violinist he had met at the musicians' union hall, John Creach. The band never coalesced but Joey kept in touch with the gentleman he nicknamed Papa John, admiring the high-spirited musician's versatility and undeniable charisma.

After auditioning for Marty and Thompson, Joey went to see the Airplane—with whom he was largely unfamiliar—at the Whisky. Marty invited him to watch the band record at RCA and Joey brought along his new neighbor, the acclaimed British blues pianist and saxist Graham Bond, who had recently relocated to L.A. Fortified by a tank of nitrous oxide—laughing gas—smuggled into the studio, Joey, Jorma, Jack and Bond jammed for more than an hour during one of the band's breaks, capturing the moment on a never-released tape that reveals Joey to be a powerful and creative rock drummer, lacking Spencer's jazz touches but making up for that with sheer strength, dexterity, imagination and sensitivity.

Following that evening, Joey didn't hear from anyone in the Airplane for several months, during which he formed another band, Tsong, which included Mickey Rooney Jr., son of the famous actor. Joey soon left that band and was biding his time again. He was dating Dianne Linkletter—the daughter of TV personality Art Linkletter—who would later become a poster girl for the antidrug movement when she jumped (or, as some claim, was pushed) from a window to her death, supposedly while high on LSD. When Joey heard from Marty Balin again in early 1969, asking him if he'd like to come up to San Francisco to audition for Jefferson Airplane, he didn't have to think long.

> **JOEY COVINGTON:** They kept playing "Triad." I'm playing and playing and I hear someone snicker. Finally I stopped and I went, "Wait a minute. This song doesn't need drums."
> Marty walks up to me and says, "You just passed the audition."

Joey moved to San Francisco, spending most of his time hanging around the Airplane house. He was made to feel a part of the family, but if he thought that any full-time employment opportunity was imminent, he was wrong. Although Spencer had threatened to leave the band many times, and they had talked about canning him equally as often, Spencer Dryden was, for the time being, still very much the drummer for Jefferson Airplane.

> **JOEY COVINGTON:** I walked into a situation where there were a lot of negative vibes already festering. And nobody would talk about it—it was like a secret society.

Joey remained a member of the inner circle throughout that long year of 1969, jamming with Jorma and Jack on old blues tunes in a heavy rock style inspired by Cream and the latest British supergroup, Led Zeppelin. Their moonlighting soon became serious as the trio took it public, playing gigs on their own when the Airplane wasn't working. Much of the music consisted of nameless instrumental jams, but Jorma also drew from the Airplane's repertoire and his old solo set lists, electrifying those songs by Reverend Gary Davis, Lightnin' Hopkins and the other blues heroes that had sustained him during the pre-Airplane years.

The Airplane got back to work in March, flying en masse, crew, lovers and all, back to Hawaii for a pair of concerts, a paying gig in Honolulu and a freebie in Waikiki. The Honolulu show ended up costing *them*, however, when a stoned-out Marty, having more than a little trouble at the wheel, had a run-in with a bank wall. Only when the Airplane managed to convince the local police that he was the singer with a band and not a bank robber—and that they would pay for the damage out of that night's box office receipts—was Marty sprung.

A COUPLE OF WEEKS AFTER RETURNING FROM HAWAII, the Airplane began work on their fifth studio album. This time their commute would be much shorter. Wally Heider, a top-tier recording engineer who had run one of the most popular studios in Hollywood, decided in 1969 that it was high time that San Francisco also had a facility worthy of the city's music scene. Wally Heider Recording Studio, in the seedy Tenderloin district, was state-of-the-art in every way. Heider installed the first 16-track Ampex recording machines, a remarkable advance in technology that allowed for layer upon layer of overdubbing to take place. And he installed the first Quadraphonic 8 board, an experimental system that doubled the effect of stereo by playing music back on four distinct channels.

For the San Francisco bands, the spanking new equipment and the hometown location of the studio was a most welcomed development. But Heider's went one step further, catering to the musicians' quirky whims: There was space to hang out, eat, relax and play games, even a rehearsal room upstairs.

RCA wasn't overjoyed about the Airplane wanting to record someplace other than the company's own Los Angeles studio, but the group was too hot a commodity to boss around, and the label gave in. Al and Richie Schmitt and Pat Ieraci were dispatched north and recording commenced on a new song by Grace, "Hey Fredrick," whose title may or may not have been in keeping with the latest Airplane in-joke, whereby the word "fuck" was replaced by the name Fred to keep the censors happy.

The expansive, eight-and-a-half-minute opus is another Grace Slick compositional tour de force. "Either go away or go all the way in, look at what you hold," she sings to ominous-sounding chords in the first line, perhaps—if the lyric is to be taken on its surface—supporting the title's sexual innuendo or, if one is inclined to dig further, alluding to something larger, a doorway into another conscious plane.

The vocals are disposed of during the song's first half, giving way to a blistering jam. Jorma's solo is one of his most adventurous yet, incorporating a number of innovative sonic textures and harmonics. But the key melody is, for much of the song, provided by piano, played by the British session pianist Nicky Hopkins, a legend who'd recorded with most of the hottest English bands and, after he moved to the Bay Area, the Steve Miller Band and Quicksilver.

The same weekend that "Hey Fredrick" was recorded, the band also cut Spencer's newest contribution, "A Song for All Seasons." This time there were no weird sound-effects collages, and no Frank Zappa references. Instead, Spencer wrote both words and music to a straightforward, semi-autobiographical country tune about a rock band whose success goes to its head and soon finds itself on the verge of falling apart, pushed to the brink by the cannibalistic music industry. "A Song for All Seasons" includes a vocal part by road manager Bill Laudner, and spotlights Hopkins on tasty honky-tonk piano.

Hopkins also appeared on the new Paul Kantner song being committed to tape at the time. Chosen to open the album, "We Can Be Together" was the most outwardly political song he'd written. Set to a churning martial beat, it immediately became a staple of the Airplane's repertoire. In the song, which incorporated snippets of political graffiti spotted on walls by the author, a defiant Kantner presents an in-your-face declaration:

We are all outlaws in the eyes of America
In order to survive we steal, cheat, lie, forge, fuck, hide and deal
We are obscene, lawless, hideous, dangerous, dirty, violent and young.

Keeping a positive frame of mind, the Airplane then appeals for solidarity:

But we should be together
Come on, all you people standing around
Our life's too fine to let it die and we can be together.

There's an admonition:

All your private property is
Target for your enemy
And your enemy is we.

We are forces of chaos and anarchy
Everything they say we are, we are
And we are very
Proud of ourselves.

Now the die is cast, and the band has its collective fist raised in the air. It's time for the slogan:

Up against the wall
Up against the wall, motherfucker
Tear down the walls
Tear down the walls.

"Won't you try" is the last line, borrowing a phrase from an earlier song, taking on a new significance here.

"We Can Be Together" would be dissected and critiqued many times upon its release and in subsequent years. What did they mean by "tear down the walls" (a phrase that Paul actually borrowed from a 1964 Fred Neil album title)? Was this a literal call for rampant and random violence in the streets, or a symbolic plea to eliminate all barriers?

As the opening salvo on the new album by a top American rock band during a precarious time in our history, "We Can Be Together" hit the streets as a controversy. Not surprisingly, the blatant use of the phrase "up against the wall, motherfucker" also brought some attention to the song—it was, after all, only three years since RCA had made the group remove the word "trips" from a track because it was deemed too inflammatory.

How did the Airplane get away with including the phrase (which Kantner first heard uttered by members of the Black Panther Party) so prominently? In essence, RCA dug its own grave this time. As it turned out, another of the label's top-selling albums, the original cast album from the Broadway pseudo-hippie musical *Hair,* had already gotten away with a number of obscenities—among them the word "motherfucker." If they could do it, argued the Airplane, why can't we? For once, RCA had no good answer.

"We Can Be Together" was as strong a statement as Jefferson Airplane had made. And to push the point home, they book-ended the album with another hard-rocking broadside, placing the album's title track, "Volunteers," an equally powerful anthem, at the end of the record. With music cowritten by Marty and Paul and the words penned by the usually apolitical Marty, "Volunteers" became another instant rallying cry.

Like "We Can Be Together," "Volunteers" celebrated the uprising of a generation against the wrongs that it witnessed. It assumed that change was already in progress, and invited the listener not specifically to commit civil disobedience or engage in combat, but to "pick up the cry" and marvel at the sheer number of them working to make a difference:

> *Look what's happening out in the streets*
> *Got a revolution, got to revolution,*
> *Hey, I'm dancing down the streets*
> *Got a revolution, got to revolution*
> *Ain't it amazing all the people I meet*
> *Got a revolution, got to revolution.*

"Volunteers" shares a basic chord structure and rhythm with "We Can Be Together." The songs are meant to be of a piece. (The chord changes to both songs are variations on an old banjo lick that David Crosby showed Paul; they also form the basis of "St. Stephen," a song the Grateful Dead wrote and recorded around the same time.)

Once the two songs were released, the Airplane fielded complaints by some critics that they were sitting on the sidelines while pushing others to become involved. Some of the most fervent detractors of "We Can Be Together" were not only the antihippie, prowar conservatives but radical members of the New Left, who called the Airplane bourgeois phonies. How hypocritical, they said, of Jefferson Airplane to claim that private property was fair game for destruction when they were rich, pampered, limousine-riding rock stars. Why were they not on the front lines making the revolution happen? What were they doing personally to help the poor and dispossessed, to end the war and bring home the troops, to change the capitalist society they supposedly found so loathsome? Why were Paul and Grace not more like John Lennon and his new wife Yoko Ono, who not only sang "Give Peace a Chance" at every opportunity—particularly when the cameras were pointing their way—but used their enormous fame as leverage in helping to spread their political agenda?

Kantner's response was that his role was to act as an observer and commentator, like war correspondents who record and spread the information without ever picking up a gun. "We Can Be Together" and "Volunteers," he explained, were position papers. By 1969, American troop strength in Vietnam had topped a half million. Opposition to the war was still growing, but so was opposition to the antiwar protesters. The trial of the Chicago Eight—a collection of radicals, including Yippie leaders Abbie Hoffman and Jerry Rubin, accused of sparking riots during the 1968 Democratic convention—had become a mockery, a farcical if entertaining piece of theater. On the college campuses of America, student strikes prevented business as usual from taking place inside the halls of academia. By exhorting their fans to become aware and involved, the songwriters were saying, they were serving the movement in their own vital way.

"Volunteers," which the Airplane began recording in mid-April, just days after finishing "We Can Be Together," had its origin when Marty, sleeping at the Mansion, was awakened one morning by a noisy truck outside of his window. Rubbing his eyes and peeking outside to see what the racket was, he noticed the lettering on the side of the vehicle: Volunteers of America. He wrote down those words and began crafting a song around them—his only contribution to the album-in-progress. Paul finished the job and a classic was born.

Originally, they had planned to call the song, as well as the album itself, "Volunteers of Amerika," the misspelling a then-prevalent leftist means of expressing dissatisfaction with the nation's state. But when the real Volunteers of America—a nonprofit organization similar to the Salvation Army—got wind of the band's plans, they nixed that idea with threats of a lawsuit.

Not all of the Airplane members agreed wholeheartedly with the stepped-up politicization of the lyrics, but neither did they have a strong objection to it.

JACK CASADY: Naturally, nobody wanted people to die in a war, but I don't think there was tremendous deep thought about the situation. Paul waving his guitar over his head like Che Guevara, and pumping his guitar in the air in military fashion, was all okay theater at the time.

JORMA KAUKONEN: I always thought that Paul was very politically naive. And I always thought that I was very politically savvy because my dad was a government guy. After the fact, I suspect neither one of us really knew very much about what was going on. But it was better to have an opinion than to have none.

Jorma's newest song, "Turn My Life Down," inspired by Smokey Robinson and the Miracles' "The Tracks of My Tears," was a rare example of true collaboration among the feuding band members, Jorma yielding the lead vocal to Marty, who was joined by Paul and Grace in harmony.

Joey Covington made his first appearance on an Airplane record on that track, supplying the conga drums, and a local female vocal quartet called the Ace of Cups added background vocals. A swirling Hammond organ was contributed by Stephen Stills, who'd been spending his time recently with David Crosby and former Hollies singer Graham Nash in a new ensemble that would soon take on a fourth member, Neil Young.

Crosby and Stills's larger contribution to *Volunteers*, though, was their coauthorship, along with Kantner, of "Wooden Ships." One of the most fondly recalled songs of the era, it was recorded by both the Airplane and Crosby, Stills and Nash on their debut album.

"Wooden Ships" had its genesis during a weekend in paradise off the coast of Florida in 1968. There Crosby had anchored his boat, the *Mayan*, while Stills, Grace and Paul, and two or three of Crosby's girlfriends, cavorted aboard, diving, getting high in the sun, playing music and dreaming. Crosby had some music but no words, and Paul had one line—"Wooden ships on the water, very free and easy." Stills contributed the "horror grips us as we watch you die" verse, and before the musicians docked, they'd crafted another '60s anthem.

DAVID CROSBY: It was a very organic process; we really wrote it together. I'm amazed we never wrote anything else together.

"Wooden Ships" is certainly one of the lovelier songs ever written about the quest for survival in a postapocalyptic world, and the enduring human spirit that motivates the living to rebuild from the ashes of destruction, in this case a new civilization free from the madness that felled the old one.

Paul grafted part of the lyrics, including "Take a sister by the hand, lead her far from this foreign land," from the very first song he wrote, "Fly Away," dating back to his college days. And the first couple of lines in the song—"If you smile at me, you know I will understand, 'cause that is something everybody everywhere does in the same language"—were modified from a message that Crosby found on the side of a Baptist church in Florida.

The Airplane's version of the song includes a couple of verses—by Paul (who is deliberately not listed as a cowriter on the CSN version because he did not want Matthew Katz, still in litigation over the Airplane's publishing rights, to hold up any royalties due Stills and Crosby)—that CSN's did not. And there is a prelude, included in the lyric sheet but unsung. It leaves no doubt that the song isn't about a weekend pleasure cruise:

Black sails knifing through the pitchblende night
Away from the radioactive landmass madness

From the silver-suited people searching out
Uncontaminated food and shelter on the shores
No glowing metal on our ship of wood only
Free happy crazy people naked in the universe
WE SPEAK EARTH TALK
GO RIDE THE MUSIC.

The Airplane, but not Crosby, Stills and Nash, took hold of that last line, "go ride the music," and riffed on it as a coda to the main body of the song. It puts a glimmer of hope to an otherwise numbing scenario—stay with the music and it will take you to a freer place.

The same busy week that found the Airplane laying down basic tracks for "Volunteers" and "Wooden Ships" also gave rise to "The Farm" and "Good Shepherd," easygoing songs that deliberately eschewed harder rock edges. The former, with lyrics by Gary Blackman set to a country melody by Kantner (with Jerry Garcia playing pedal steel guitar on the record), was a commentary on the back-to-the-land movement finding favor with many hippies at the time.

Apropos of the withdrawal from urban chaos, a new, nonacidic, country-based brand of rock—Dylan's *John Wesley Harding* and *Nashville Skyline* albums, the Band's highly touted debut *Music from Big Pink*, the Byrds' *Sweetheart of the Rodeo*, and others—had risen. The agrarian movement and the formation of dozens of communes in remote, rural parts of the country put forth a signal, perhaps, that some were opting to forgo changing the world, choosing instead to alter their own living situation—and their inner consciousness—by creating self-sufficient utopian societies away from the confused and crumbling one around them.

"Good Shepherd" is Jorma's major showcase tune on *Volunteers*. A hymn credited to "Traditional," Jorma learned the song in the early '60s from a folk singer named Roger Perkins. It rides the cusp between gospel and blues both musically and lyrically.

WITH THE BULK OF THE ALBUM RECORDED, the Airplane returned to live performance, playing shows both locally and out of town. One of the more memorable was a free show attended by 50,000 at Chicago's Grant Park, the site of the great confrontation between protesters and police during the '68 Democratic convention.

Two nights later, on May 16, in New Orleans, the Airplane experienced firsthand how law enforcement officials in the South felt about hippie liberals coming into their neck of the woods. Some time after midnight, several persons were partying in Jack's room at the Royal Orleans Hotel. Without warning a team of police burst in and arrested Jack, his brother Chick, Bill Thompson, Bill Laudner and two female friends of the band for possession of two joints of marijuana.

Drug arrests were serious business in Louisiana at the time. Convicted offenders had been known to receive years of imprisonment for the possession of a single joint or even marijuana seeds. Jack and the others faced real jail time. Bail and a trial date were set and it was made clear that this bust was not something to be disregarded.

With anxiety and gloom in the air, the Airplane headed to the next night's show, at Pirate's World in Miami. More trouble awaited them. When the power was cut off after the band played past the designated curfew, Paul cursed out the police and pressed the crowd—shades of Bakersfield 1967—into action. "Wait till we burn down *your* society!" he shouted, as the audience of 10,000 cheered him on. Before Thompson could reach the stage to try to defuse the situation, Paul was surrounded by cops and carted away, hit with a disturbing the peace charge.

Sitting in an interrogation room, Paul spied a bottle of liquor that he assumed the police would soon be swigging from. He took a vial of liquid acid from his pocket and emptied it into the cops' stash. Unfortunately (or fortunately), Paul was out on the street before he could witness the spectacle he hoped would ensue.

By this time, governmental authorities were well aware of the effect that rock stars were having on America's youth. Many musicians, Jefferson Airplane included, became the subject of surveillance and outright harassment. Some began to wonder, not unjustifiably—as became clear decades later when FBI files on the Airplane, the Dead, John Lennon and others were made available to the public—whether the bands were being directly targeted. Despite several busts, though, no Airplane member ever served time.

PAUL KANTNER: Jorma used to think we were a CIA experiment: "Don't arrest them. We've got an eye on them."

Rock and roll had always been an easy—and particularly enjoyable—target for the powers that be, but lately the stakes had been raised even higher in the war between young ideals and the old. As the '60s began drawing to a close, it became apparent that Vietnam wasn't the only battlefield where young people were dying and being taken prisoner. At home, all over America, another war was raging.

21
BLUES FROM AN AIRPLANE

NO ONE IS QUITE SURE when exactly their auxiliary band acquired a name, but by the fall of 1969, Jorma and Jack were Hot Tuna, blues-rock gods. Although the pair had long kept occupied during Airplane downtime by playing together acoustically, the switch to electric instruments and the addition of a drummer—as well as the establishment of a real repertoire—gave their supplemental activities a new legitimacy. Now they were ready to take it public in a more high-profile way.

At first, Joey Covington was cobilled with the Airplane mainstays. Sometimes the trio folded its set into the context of an Airplane show and, increasingly, the musicians gigged on their own at clubs around the Bay Area. The loose conglomeration at first also included Marty on vocals and, joining Jorma on guitar, Peter Kaukonen. But by 1970, Peter was out, replaced by Paul Ziegler, a folkie friend of Jorma's dating back to the Peninsula days, when Ziegler ran a club in San Jose called the Shelter.

In the minds of most fans, however, regardless of who the support players were, from its inception, Hot Tuna equaled Jorma and Jack.

That the two of them would augment their Airplane work, particularly during this fallow period for the larger band, was inevitable. They were working musicians first and foremost, they needed to play and they weren't getting their fill with the Airplane.

JORMA KAUKONEN: In the dark ages of rock and roll, when we were still sharing hotel rooms—and many hotel rooms didn't have TVs in those days—you'd go back to your room and, contrary to popular belief, the groupies weren't knocking the door down. Jack and I would drag the guitars out and play blues songs.

"With the Airplane's concert format becoming more standardized, leaving less room for true spontaneity, Jack and Jorma began channeling more of their energy into the sideshow, working up material that they didn't play with the parent group and tinkering with the configuration. Hot Tuna in its early stages was an experiment in search of a band.

As for the name, like Jefferson Airplane itself, Hot Tuna can be attributed to a play on the language of traditional blues. In "Keep on Truckin'," a song Hot Tuna would record on their third album, and whose lyrics are derived from a couple of '20s and '30s blues recordings, the singer asks, "What's that smell like fish? Oh, baby, I really would like to know."

JORMA KAUKONEN: Somebody suggested the answer just might be Hot Tuna.

Since the band's inception, a rumor has circulated that Jorma originally called the band Hot Shit, and that RCA, preparing to release their debut album, said no way. Joey is among those who remember that being the case, but Jorma rejects the persistent tale as utterly untrue.

Call it what they will, Jorma and Jack were happy to have a drummer in Covington who was on 24-hour call to play their "other" music. It may have been Marty who'd invited Joey to San Francisco, but so far Jorma and Jack were making the most use of Covington's talents—they valued his muscular drumming and his enthusiasm and jumped at the chance to play regularly with someone other than Spencer.

For Joey, though, the Tuna gig was a mixed blessing. He was happy to be working with well-known, gifted musicians, and the music they were making together was admittedly superb. But he was a rock drummer and he'd come to San Francisco to play with Jefferson Airplane, not their blues offshoot. Now he was finding himself in the midst of a battle royale, an unwilling pawn in the Airplane's ego games. His time would soon come, he was assured, but Joey's patience was wearing thin.

Volunteers was wrapped up in June. The last major track to be cut, Grace's "Eskimo Blue Day," was, like her "Hey Fredrick," cinematic in scope, a broad stroke that places the puny biological accident called mankind into its proper perspective. Its tag line, that the "human name doesn't mean shit to a tree," resonates long after the musically ambitious song has concluded.

GRACE SLICK: We think we're such hot stuff, but a redwood tree has been around for about a thousand years, and who do we think we are, really? Our greed *does* mean shit to a tree. The trees are dying. All of our separating ourselves from the planet is stupid because, in the larger picture, whether or not you become president of Bank of America has nothing to do with evolution.

Grace is also credited with arranging for the album the minute-long "Meadowlands," a church organ solo that she plays. Credited to "Traditional," the piece actually had its origin as a hymn of the Soviet Red Army Chorus.

Volunteers, the band members all agree, was one of the great Jefferson Airplane albums, possibly the last great Jefferson Airplane album. It was also producer Al Schmitt's favorite, and his final one for the group. He'd done all he could with them. Schmitt stuck around long enough to work with Hot Tuna on their first album, and with the Airplane on one more single, but after that it was time for him to move on.

As the summer of '69 got under way, the Airplane took turns helping to master the album, and there were sporadic gigs up and down the West Coast—including a free show in L.A.'s Griffith Park in July—and scattered points east of the Rockies. A run of high-profile appearances in the Northeast occupied the group during the first part of August. First came the Atlantic City Pop Festival, the first major rock gathering of its kind in the New York/New Jersey/Philadelphia area. The event has been forgotten by time despite attendance by more than 100,000 people and a diverse lineup that included B. B. King, Creedence Clearwater Revival, Janis Joplin, Santana, the Byrds, Frank Zappa, Little Richard and a new singer-songwriter from Canada, Joni Mitchell, who left the stage in tears after 10 minutes, chastising the crowd for not paying attention to her.

The following weekend, it was back to the Fillmore East for a quartet of shows headlining over the British soul man Joe Cocker, and another freebie in Central Park. The caravan headed next to Tanglewood in Lenox, Massachusetts, where the Airplane headlined a knockout triple bill, presented by Bill Graham, with B. B. King and the Who. Then, from Tanglewood, it was off to upstate New York. The Woodstock Music and Art Fair was the next stop on the tour.

• • •

DESPITE ITS SIGNIFICANCE as a cultural marker, Woodstock had some tough acts to follow in the news-heavy summer of 1969, not the least of which was the landing of Apollo 11 on the moon. Like Woodstock itself, the accomplishment of astronauts Neil Armstrong, Edwin E. "Buzz" Aldrin Jr. and Michael Collins reassured us that hope and cooperation could build a better future.

But some of the other news of the day was less encouraging. After a series of grisly murders in the Los Angeles area led to a former resident of Haight-Ashbury, a long-haired, drug-taking, guitar-playing career criminal named Charles Manson, the antihippie forces had plenty of fresh ammo for their cause. With an increasing number of angered mainstream Americans already believing that the vast majority of the youth population did nothing but smoke pot all day and plot to over-throw the government, it was getting dangerous to look like a "freak."

That dread was manifested vividly that summer in the film *Easy Rider*, which depicted two long-haired bikers, played by Dennis Hopper and Peter Fonda, on the road discovering America and themselves. The ha-tred and hostilities they faced on their freedom ride were familiar to many of the young people who filled the theaters.

Woodstock, like *Easy Rider*, was also about freedom. The festival set the record straight for the skeptical elders, demonstrating that this was indeed a peaceful generation—its slogan made it clear: "Three days of peace and music." Like Monterey two years before it, Woodstock was an idea whose time had arrived.

But just getting the show together proved more challenging than its organizers had imagined. Securing a site proved problematic, and even as the hour approached, the young promoters—John Roberts, Joel Rosenman and Michael Lang—were not quite sure which of the acts they'd booked would actually show up. In the end it didn't really matter: the music was the nominal lure, not the main attraction. The entertain-ment on the stage served mostly as a soundtrack to the festival's greater purpose, the celebration of what would come to be called the Wood-stock Nation.

As history has noted adequately, the crowd that showed up that weekend of August 15 to 17, 1969—estimated at half a million—far ex-ceeded expectations. Roads became parking lots for miles around, and the site itself—Max Yasgur's farm near the town of Bethel, New York—

resembled a large tent city. Tickets became scrap paper as fences were torn down—Woodstock became synonymous with the concept of the free festival. The mud, the rain, the chanting throng, the sharing of dope, water, food and sex—all of it became part of the legend.

After checking into their hotel, a Holiday Inn in the town of Liberty where many of the bands were staying, the Airplane made their way to the site on Saturday, prepared to go on at their appointed 9:00 P.M. slot. As it transpired, they didn't take the stage until 7:00 A.M. Sunday morning, following the Who's well-received set.

"All right, friends," Grace addressed the sea of sleepy humans, "you have seen the heavy groups. Now you will see morning maniac music. Believe me, yeah, it's a new dawn." She looked particularly ravishing in a simple white, fringed top, laced up in the front, and white pants, her hair no longer stick-straight but billowing out into a tasteful perm.

With Nicky Hopkins sitting in on piano, the Airplane, who were paid $15,000 for their morning's work, were certainly far from horrendous, but they felt they were anything but inspired. When the filmmakers assembling the Woodstock documentary later approached the group about being included, they were given the thumbs-down. Although the Airplane's performance of "Volunteers" appears on the successful three-record soundtrack album released in 1970, and a couple of tracks show up on the *Woodstock Two* follow-up album, there was no way they were allowing their ragged selves to appear on screen. Most of the band members have mixed emotions about their Woodstock experience.

> **GRACE SLICK:** Woodstock everybody remembers with a little more fondness than I do. I have a bladder about the size of a dime and you couldn't get off the stage to go to the bathroom. It was not that well organized. But it was unique in that there were a half-million people not stabbing each other to death. And it was a statement of, look at us, we're 25 and we're all together and things ought to change.

Without even a day's rest, the band headed directly from the festival site to New York City, where they were booked to appear on ABC-TV's *The Dick Cavett Show*, along with Hendrix, Crosby, Stills and Joni Mitchell, who hadn't been able to make it to Woodstock (although she would write the most famous song about the festival) and stayed in New York watching it on the news. Hendrix was a no-show, sleeping it off after closing out the festival on Monday morning, but the others arrived eager to share their experiences. Stills made a point of showing off the genuine Woodstock mud on his boots.

Sitting in a circle on the floor, the musicians talked casually about Woodstock; already there was a sense that something epochal had just taken place. They played a few songs and jammed as the closing credits rolled. When the Airplane performed "We Can Be Together," there was no bleep when they came to the "motherfucker" line—as far as anyone remembers, that was the first time *that* word had been uttered on national television.

JORMA KAUKONEN DECIDED it was time to make a Hot Tuna record. In September 1969, Thompson, now managing Tuna as well as the Airplane, booked several nights at a tiny club in Berkeley, the New Orleans House, which customarily featured acoustic folk and blues acts. It was an appropriate venue for the recording because Jorma had every intention of making an all-acoustic album. Joey Covington didn't even know the shows had taken place until he stumbled across Jorma and Jack mixing down the live tracks at Wally Heider's studio.

Owsley was recruited to mix the sound inside the club, Al Schmitt was brought in to produce and engineer Allen Zentz twiddled the knobs. Over six nights, Jorma and Jack regaled the small Berkeley audience with the songs they'd played together in hotel rooms for eons. From the Reverend Gary Davis songbook they borrowed "Death Don't Have No Mercy" and "Oh Lord, Search My Heart," and from Jelly Roll Morton "Don't You Leave Me Here" and "Winin' Boy Blues." "How Long Blues" Jorma got from pianist Leroy Carr, and "Hesitation Blues," which had been recorded by Leadbelly and many others, Jorma learned in college from Ian Buchanan, who got it from Davis. "Know You Rider" Jorma used to play when he backed Janis Joplin, and "Uncle Sam Blues" came from an album by Snooks Eaglin, by way of Buchanan.

Jorma performed a few original compositions as well. "Mann's Fate" was an instrumental he had written in 1964, its title a tribute to his guitarist friend Steve Mann. "New Song (for the Morning)" was one of the first pieces Jorma had written with lyrics—he never could think of a title, hence it remained "New Song."

It was specifically to sit in on that song that Jorma invited a friend of Mann's, local harmonica player Will Scarlett, to the New Orleans House. Scarlett, who had played in a group called the Cleanliness and Godliness Skiffle Band, added harp to "New Song" as asked, and ended up staying onstage with Jack and Jorma throughout the week.

With the first Hot Tuna album in the bag, the full Airplane family flew for the second time that year to Hawaii. It was during this trip that Jacky Watts, Thompson's assistant, fell into a relationship with Peter Kaukonen, still in Tuna at the time. They married in 1971—with Bill Thompson, a minister in the Universal Life Church, officiating—and stayed together until 1980. Honolulu also marked the occasion of the next Airplane bust, when Paul was caught with marijuana that he claimed was planted on him by narcotics agents. Kantner was convicted of the misdemeanor offense the following June, but got off with a $150 fine.

VOLUNTEERS WAS RELEASED in late October, delayed because the label and the band fought over the album title, the "motherfucker" and "shit to a tree" lyrics and the Airplane's desire to depict the American flag on the album cover. RCA felt that some retail chains might boycott the album for any of the above reasons, to which the Airplane responded that record stores like that sucked anyway, so who cares? Eventually, the differences were ironed out, the band winning most rounds—the flag and the lyrics stayed, but *Volunteers of Amerika* (or even *America*) had to be shortened to the now familiar title.

The cover art was some of their most ambitious yet, and a drastic about-face from the serious images that had graced *Crown of Creation*. In keeping with Kantner's idea that the title track and "We Can Be Together" were reportage, the entire cover, outside and in, was designed to resemble a mock newspaper.

For the front cover, in a photo shot by Jim Marshall, the band members posed in all manner of wigs, funny hats, eyeglasses, big lips and a giant lampshade. Behind them waved the American flag that RCA had wanted to remove. On the back cover, with photos by Jim Smircich, was the newspaper, the big happening of the day a gala event called the Paz Chin-In—*paz* being Spanish for peace—held in a fictional locale in South Dakota.

In the upper left corner of the back cover, Pat Ieraci, in robe, beret and newly sprouted facial hair, leaned proudly against one of the Wally Heider recording units, giving the official hippie two-fingers-for-peace symbol. "Maurice Sez," the caption read.

Inside the album cover was an insert which, in addition to displaying the lyrics—and a suggestion to "Feed and Water Your Flag"—offered "news" regarding the pot bust of a group called Jefferson Airplane and other silliness, including a sports section featuring batting leaders of the Amerikan League (among them, R. Nixon, J. Casady, J. Lennon and predisgrace O. J. Simpson).

Finally, the interior of the foldout cover revealed an oversized peanut butter and jelly sandwich, photographed by Herbie Greene. The actual sandwich was later eaten by Gut, an ex-Hell's Angel and manager of the hard rock band Blue Cheer who, along with one Milton Burke and an uncredited Gary Blackman, designed the cover.

> **MARTY BALIN:** I personally hated that cover. I had no idea why they would put a peanut butter and jelly sandwich on there. I guess they thought it was funny.

The album was released to generally supportive reviews. Ed Leimbacher, writing for *Ramparts*, was cautious in his approval, but in the end, couldn't help but fawn. "In terms of sheer music," he said, "*Volunteers* is the greatest Airplane album yet; they may have taken off four years ago, but they didn't reach the stratosphere till now."

The album's title track was released as a single, but it rose only to number 65. The *Volunteers* album itself entered the *Billboard* chart on November 22, and stayed there for an impressive 44 weeks, ultimately peaking at number 13.

(In 1973, RCA issued *Volunteers* as a quadraphonic album that contained alternate takes and noticeably different mixes of some tracks. The quad *Volunteers* is one of the most collectible Airplane recordings.)

As the *Volunteers* album began its climb in the fall of 1969, the band was on tour. Grace experienced a scare one night in Pennsylvania when she returned to her hotel room after a gig to find a man in her bed, and not one she'd invited. Even as Laudner dragged him out into the hallway and the police eventually hauled him away, the intruder kept insisting that he was the father of Grace's nonexistent child.

At Fillmore East, for the first night of a Thanksgiving weekend run,

Grace took the stage with her hair slicked down, a frighteningly familiar rectangular mustache glued in place and wearing a uniform that still symbolized horror more than two decades after its peak as a fashion statement. How the hall's proprietor, Bill Graham, a Holocaust survivor, felt about the Airplane's singer decked out as Adolf Hitler and goose-stepping all over the New York stage one can only ponder, but he couldn't have been too delighted.

Florida was next on the itinerary, the West Palm Beach Pop Festival—headlined by the Rolling Stones—and then a couple of college gigs. From there, it was right back in the air for a return trip to California, and a free show in a hell called Altamont.

22

NEVER SAY "FUCK YOU" TO A HELL'S ANGEL

ALTAMONT WAS SUPPOSED to be the West Coast Woodstock, a one-day lovefest with the Rolling Stones headlining. Instead, on December 6, 1969, more than 300,000 souls found their way to one of the most desolate, depressing locations in the state of California to witness one of rock's darkest moments.

It began as a more modest idea. On July 3, Brian Jones, who just a few weeks earlier had left the Stones, was found dead at the bottom of his swimming pool in England, a victim of "drowning while under the influence." Two days later, the Stones introduced his replacement, the young guitarist Mick Taylor, at a free concert in London's Hyde Park, which drew a quarter of a million fans.

With that—and the success of Woodstock—in mind, the Stones, when they launched their first American tour in three years in early November, toyed with the idea of playing a free concert in San Francisco. At first they thought small—an unannounced show at Fillmore West— but before long they decided they wanted something grander, an outdoor concert, and a team was assembled to pull it together. In short order, support groups were signed: Santana, Crosby, Stills, Nash and Young, the Grateful Dead, the Airplane and the hot new country-rock band the Flying Burrito Brothers.

Of course, an event of such magnitude had to be commemorated. Mick Jagger had already arranged for brothers David and Albert Maysles to film the Stones' tour, with the intention of creating a documentary like the one then being cobbled together from Woodstock footage. They would capture the free concert, in all of its glory, for posterity. It was to be the last date of the Stones's tour—what a dramatic way to end their film.

When a couple of proposed sites, among them Golden Gate Park, didn't pan out, Dick Carter, who ran the Altamont Speedway, about an hour's drive east of San Francisco between Livermore and Tracy, came through with his facility. The promoters quickly discovered that the place was a dump, but it was all they had. With less than a day to prepare and pilgrims already making their way, they did all they could to erect a stage and arrange for food, water, toilets, medical help and, a necessity at such a large gathering, security.

The Hell's Angels, it was suggested, could handle the latter easily. They'd worked for the Dead before and managed to keep order without invoking the paranoia that a police presence would in such a crowd. The Stones had also used bikers for security in England, and readily agreed to enlist the Angels for Altamont, their payment to be made in beer.

By Friday evening, most of the work had been miraculously completed. Radio stations repeatedly broadcast the concert information and the crowd streamed in, thousands winding their way toward the Speedway along the lone road that led to it. By the time the music began on Saturday, over a quarter of a million fans, many of them well on their way toward being hungry, thirsty, tired, agitated and stoned to oblivion, found themselves jammed together, sweaty, dirty and cranky, an ominous feeling hanging over the entire proceedings.

Even before the Airplane left San Francisco for the site, something about the event smelled wrong to Spencer, and he refused to go. He and Jorma argued vociferously, the guitarist telling the drummer they would play the gig with or without him. Only when Bill Thompson physically threatened Spencer did he capitulate, and Jefferson Airplane headed off to their date with mayhem.

The violence at Altamont had begun before the Airplane even arrived, when a number of Hell's Angels, who had been amassing near the stage, wantonly attacked several concert-goers who'd objected to their overbearing presence or didn't appreciate motorcycles being driven through the crowd. Even while Santana played the show's opening set, fights broke out, prompting Carlos Santana to beg for the peace and love he'd seen at Woodstock only four months earlier.

The Airplane was scheduled to go on next. Like everyone else involved with the show, they hadn't found out until the last minute that the venue had been changed to Altamont. They'd only just returned to San Francisco from Florida at 3:30 that morning, and were expected to meet Thompson to helicopter to the site at 7:00. As soon as they arrived at the speedway, the musicians were struck by its ugliness—this place had seen one too many demolition derbies; broken glass and rusted metal were everywhere.

SPENCER DRYDEN: It was just a horrible, pink-sky Hieronymus Bosch dustbin, not a tree in sight, just a hellhole. It was the beginning of the end. No, not the beginning, it *was* the end.

There was a palpable tension in the air, and the colder-than-usual weather exacerbated the foul mood. The Angels, bearing chains, pool cues, knives and other weapons, were getting testy, having already consumed the lion's share of their sizable beer stash. Acid was plentiful too, but much of it was reported to be tainted.

The Airplane took the stage playing "We Can Be Together," perhaps thinking that the song's plea for unity would somehow calm the audience. But the violent behavior only increased, and the atmosphere both on and surrounding the stage—itself overpopulated with bikers and fans trying to escape the melee—proved inhospitable to the band. Rolling Stones tour manager Sam Cutler's appeal for the stage to be cleared so the Airplane could play its set—"There are 200 people breathing down their necks"—went unheeded.

As the Airplane launched into their second number, "The Other Side of This Life," the Maysles brothers' cameras sampled the crowd: some danced happily, unfazed; others appeared nervous and fearful. Hell's Angels, ripped on liquid and chemical substances, menaced and pushed. Most of the fans just sat there, guarding their inch of space, stunned. Then, a bustle below the stage caught Grace's eye.

"Easy," she pleaded in a calm tone as a scuffle broke out. "Easy, easy, easy, easy . . ."

The band stopped playing momentarily, shaken by the brutality. Spencer, Jorma and Jack returned to riffing absentmindedly, one eye on the chaos offstage and another on their fellow musicians. Paul stood at the lip of the stage, his guitar dangling as he surveyed the weirdness.

Then a scream came from below. Marty, standing a second ago at center stage peering at the melee intently, leaped from his perch, disappearing into the thick of the crowd. More movement followed, but there was still no sign of Marty.

He had been knocked out cold.

MARTY BALIN: I had my eyes closed and I heard a commotion. I opened my eyes, and the Hell's Angels are beating this guy with pool cues. I saw the whole crowd, this mass, just back up and allow it to happen. I said, "To hell with the song, this guy needs some help." So I went down there and started fighting, helping the guy out.

When I woke up I had all these boot marks tattooed all over me. Jorma said to me, "Man, you're one crazy motherfucker."

GRACE SLICK: I didn't have my contact lenses on so I could see to a point, but not clearly. I looked at Spencer and he looked horrified. I said, "What's going on?"

He said, "The Hell's Angels are beating up Marty."

Apparently the Hell's Angels were beating up somebody else and Marty said, "Don't do that, fuck you."

The Hell's Angel said, "Never say 'fuck you' to a Hell's Angel!"

Marty was lying on his back. And from the floor, Marty says "fuck you" again.

Grace and Paul tried reasoning with the Angels from the relative safety of the stage, but the bikers would have none of it. "No! Stop it! That's really stupid," Grace shouted. "You've got to keep your bodies off each other unless you intend love." But this was not the love crowd of Monterey or Woodstock. Something else, something more demonic, was taking place here.

Demoralized and just wanting to be someplace else, the Airplane finished their set, followed by the Burritos, CSNY and, ultimately, the Stones. The Dead, upon sizing up the situation, had decided not to perform at all and headed home.

In the worst of the violence, a young black man, Meredith Hunter, who some witnesses said had flashed a gun, was stabbed and beaten to death by Hell's Angels during the Stones' set. His murder was caught on film, and a Hell's Angel was subsequently tried but acquitted. The very mention of Altamont still causes shudders among those who had the misfortune of being a part of it.

THE '60S DIDN'T CONCLUDE with any special fanfare. There was little deep philosophical reflection, no real sense that one of the most exciting, and tumultuous, decades in American history was coming to an end. It wasn't as if acid and revolution faded away on December 31 and shag haircuts and disco came in on New Year's Day. In most respects, it was business as usual as the decades rolled over, and Altamont did not become a symbol of the turning of the tide until well into the '70s—the event was viewed first merely as an unfortunate blip on the countercultural radar screen, an anomaly. For many, just as the '60s had not really kicked in until JFK was assassinated and the Beatles, Vietnam and other key events came along mid-decade, the conceptual '60s did not truly die until well into the physical '70s, Richard Nixon's resignation in 1974 being the most often-cited final nail in the coffin.

The Airplane finished out the chronological '60s in a familiar setting, playing a concert at Winterland, with Quicksilver, the Sons of Champlin and Hot Tuna sharing the bill. In January, the Airplane celebrated the wedding of Spencer Dryden and Sally Mann. Paul served as the best man, and Grace as the matron of honor. At the party that followed, Paul produced a thousand-dollar bill and a silver tray, and the two couples snorted a pile of Orange Sunshine acid laced with cocaine.

Early in the new year, the Airplane got back to business, recording a new song Paul had written, "Have You Seen the Saucers." Reaching back to his childhood interest in science fiction, Paul crafted one of the more poignant latter-day Airplane tunes, an elucidation of his belief that there is someone else out there, an indictment of government cover-ups, and a reminder that we're living on a fragile spaceship ourselves.

In February the Airplane, Santana and the Dead gathered at the Family Dog's new space on the Great Highway to videotape an hour-long concert for later broadcast on KQED-TV. Produced by Ralph Gleason, the program, called *A Night at the Family Dog*, concluded with a jam featuring members of all three bands.

That same month they recorded "Mexico," a new composition by Grace, written in response to President Nixon's 1969 implementation of Operation Intercept, a program designed to curtail the flow of high-grade Mexican marijuana into the United States by poisoning it with a substance called paraquat. Stephen Barncard, a young assistant engineer at Wally Heider's, observed an Airplane whose members seemed to have little to do with one another.

STEPHEN BARNCARD: The band was already falling apart. Jack came in and took five days to do a bass part. Then Jorma came in and did his part. Paul was pretty much running the show and Grace was hanging out and grossing everyone out.

With no new album on the horizon, RCA released the two new songs as a single, but with "Mexico" banned from many radio stations due to its drug content, and a near-total lack of airplay except on underground FM stations anyway, it stood no chance of making the charts.

SPENCER DRYDEN WAS SETTLING COMFORTABLY into his third marriage when he was summoned to a meeting. "It's time for you to leave the band," he was told. "We don't think you're happy."

Spencer polled each person in the room. When Paul and Grace—who had only recently helped officiate at his wedding—agreed with Jack and Jorma, Spencer knew it was over.

Although Joey Covington had been a part of the Airplane family for over a year, he wasn't the only choice for Spencer's job—they had also discussed hiring Tim Davis, the drummer with the Steve Miller Band. But when Joey got wind of that, he made his position clear: He'd been waiting a long time and now wanted in. There was some concern among the others whether he had the stamina to play with both Tuna and the Airplane, but Joey insisted he did. Finally, more than a year after first being groomed for the position, Joey Covington was hired as Jefferson Airplane's drummer.

JACK CASADY: If Spencer had the power to drum like a madman, I think that it would have been tougher [to fire him], but he was hesitant to go out on the road, and we were looking for a drummer who could play a little harder.

JORMA KAUKONEN: I think Spencer is the most articulate drummer that the band had, and we might have grown in other musical directions had we stayed with Spencer. But that's in retrospect. At the time I just wanted to be louder, and I got louder.

Rolling Stone introduced Joey to the world with a news item, "The Airplane's New Drummer." In it, Joey said, "I want to change the Airplane's sound. I consider myself to be the Airplane's new rhythm more than a drummer. I'd like to see us become more of a dancing band."

GRACE SLICK: Joey was just so naive, a nice little guy. He's like a farm boy. Used to wear overalls and long blond hair, kind of a John Denver deal.

Joey brought a sharper edge to the Airplane's sound, a more pronounced rock and roll thump, with less of the ornamentation in which Spencer had specialized. With Hot Tuna, Joey went further, introducing material of his own, most notably a hard, funky, politically incorrect soul-rock song called "Whatever the Old Man Does Is Always Right."

Jorma also continued to expand the Tuna repertoire, introducing songs like "Come Back Baby," "True Religion" and his own "Sea Child." Marty, who was still involved with Tuna, got a chance to indulge his soul-man fantasies, bringing to the proceedings a handful of R&B-based tunes he'd been tackling of late: "Emergency," "You Wear Your Dresses Too Short," "Drifting" (by Bay Area writer Jesse Osborne) and Peter Kaukonen's "Up or Down."

Hot Tuna began to develop not only their own musical identity but a distinct audience, fans who were more in tune with their brand of no-nonsense rocking blues and intense jamming style than with what the Airplane was becoming.

JACK CASADY: With Hot Tuna, there wasn't an agenda that you had to hate Nixon or had to march in the streets. Hot Tuna was our way to get a band together that made people jump up and down a little bit.

IT WAS THE POLITICAL AGENDA and the anti-Nixon fervor, however, that accounted for the next newsworthy display by Grace. It had been a long time since she had thought about her days at New York's tony Finch College, another lifetime since she'd bothered with the social graces she was to have learned there.

The president's oldest daughter, Tricia Nixon, several years younger than Grace, was undoubtedly unaware, when she sent out invitations for a White House tea party to fellow Finch alumni, that the Grace Wing on her mailing list had morphed into Grace Slick, radical rock star.

Grace beamed when she received the invitation to the April event. This was too good to be true: Richard Nixon's daughter was requesting her presence at the White House. Only in her wildest dreams.

There was only one man who could accompany her as her escort: Abbie Hoffman.

Although Hoffman had castigated the Airplane for recording the Levi's commercials a few years earlier, he and Grace had since met and found kinship. Abbie and his wife Anita had recently conducted a joint interview with Grace and Paul for the New York underground newspaper the *East Village Other*, in which they discussed, not surprisingly, the relationship between music and politics. Grace and Abbie discovered that they shared a wicked sense of humor and disillusionment with the state of the nation.

> **GRACE SLICK:** I got the invitation in the mail and went, "Oh, yes!" I assumed that they were bringing their husbands, so I thought, I'll dress up Abbie. But there's no way to dress up Abbie. We put a suit on him and put his hair back and he looked like a Mafia guy. I had on the boots and the miniskirt and all these other women were dressed the way preppy women dressed, with the camel's hair coat and the gold pins and a pageboy hairdo. So we stood out right away and the security guards came right over and said, "Sorry, this is invitation only."
>
> I said, "Well, I have an invitation."
>
> He took it over to the security booth and came back and said, "You can't come in, you're a security risk." And he was right. He didn't know why, but he was right.

Grace, unaware that Nixon himself wouldn't even be in attendance, had brought along a gift, a little something to help him see things in a different light. The Secret Service, though, was not about to let her have an opportunity to slip LSD into the drink of the President of the United States. Grace and Abbie left together, riding away from the scene thinking of the possibilities, chauffeur Paul Kantner at the wheel.

23
AND YOUR ENEMY IS WE

ON MAY 4, 1970, America declared war against her children. At Kent State University in Ohio, four students were shot dead by National Guardsmen for the crime of opposing the war in Vietnam—or, for some of them, just being in the wrong place at the wrong time.

The Guard had been called out to quell protests that had erupted in the wake of President Nixon's April 30 announcement that the United States military had invaded Cambodia, and that he was drafting 150,000 additional troops. In effect, Nixon was widening a war that many believed might finally be winding down.

Student response across the country was swift and angry. More than 400 colleges and universities experienced some kind of protest; many were the target of student strikes, others were shut down entirely. The repercussions were felt throughout the world; photos of the horror remain some of the most painfully poignant reminders of the turbulent era, and proof that the '60s were not really over.

Typically, the nation's leaders responded with indifference or outright scorn. Vice President Spiro Agnew said, "The real pity is that many of the students of our universities really feel that the theatrical radicals are the architects of a brave, new compassionate world, spiced with rock music, acid and pot. There is a group of students committed to radical change through violent means."

Ten days after Kent State, police killed two black students, this time at Jackson State University in Mississippi, the heart of the conservative South.

The campus deaths were only the latest assaults on America's dissidents, albeit the most startling. Demonstrations and rioting had taken place throughout 1969 and into 1970. One of the most widely reported confrontations had occurred in Berkeley, where students and local residents attempted to defend a three-acre plot of land that had come to be known as People's Park. There, a crowd of several thousand was met with tear gas and buckshot, leaving one man dead and dozens injured. That night, Governor Ronald Reagan sent the National Guard into Berkeley and imposed a curfew.

Opposition to the war was hardly limited to the campuses though. In October 1969, millions across the country had observed a moratorium against the war. A second moratorium a month later culminated with a gathering at the Washington Monument, attended by 250,000, the largest antiwar protest in the nation's history.

On the domestic front, the "other" war was also escalating: two members of the Illinois branch of the militant Black Panther Party were shot and killed in a morning raid by a squadron of heavily armed police. And although the Chicago Eight (reduced by one when Black Panther Party founder Bobby Seale was given a separate trial) were acquitted of conspiracy charges, five of the defendants were convicted of inciting to riot anyway. In New York, a Greenwich Village townhouse being used as a bomb-making factory by the radical group the Weathermen exploded, killing three. Turmoil was the order of the day. Fear was everywhere. Anger was in the air.

Some students attempted to forgo the violent approach and proposed working within the system to change it, through voting and even running for office, raising money and petitioning for peaceful means to end the war. But for a short while, at least, it appeared as if the revolution that the Airplane and other groups had sung about was on its way to becoming a reality, that radical changes in society were about to take place.

The weekend of Kent State, Jefferson Airplane was in New York—they'd been playing scattered dates on the East Coast since late April. A few days prior to the Ohio tragedy, some Yale students had tried to coerce the band into abandoning a planned free concert in Central Park and going instead to New Haven, where a student strike was in progress.

The Airplane was in a quandary over what to do. Wrote Robert Christgau in the *Village Voice*, "Reportedly, this request caused some consternation in the band, with Grace and Marty tempted and the others reluctant. The objections were more tactical than political—where another group might have questioned the purpose of the demonstration itself, the Airplane apparently raised a smokescreen of petty and paranoid reservations. Now, rock musicians do have reason to worry about being used by politicos; many movement people regard rock as bait, nothing more, and wouldn't know the Airplane from the Guess Who. That wasn't the case this time, however. Anyway, the Airplane not only has revolutionary pretensions, it sells them."

The Airplane spurned the request and ended up playing Central Park, but in an odd twist of logic Grace, according to Christgau, reportedly berated the audience for not being in New Haven themselves.

The week's weird vibes got even weirder following the Ohio incident, when the band moved its base of operations to Fillmore East. The shows on the first night, by all accounts, were fantastic, charged with electricity. If the events at Kent State had had any effect on the Airplane, it was in a positive sense, energizing them.

On the second night, though, at the late show, things weren't right from the start. Grace—dressed in a short black skirt with a see-through top, her breasts covered with strategically placed black squares—was in a talkative mood, a little too talkative for some. Sensing that the New York audience was more hostile than usual, she fed the dark mood. She wondered aloud how New Yorkers could stand living "stacked up on each other, and our band is going back to California, where it's cool." She accused Paul of never smiling, because "Germans are always serious." She stated that "New York chicks don't fart," and called herself a dwarf. Repeatedly, Grace fielded taunts from audience members, bounced them off her armor and shot back with barbs of her own.

But she really got going during "Somebody to Love," launching into a midsong monologue—the musicians riffing along patiently behind her—that has gone down in Airplane mythology as the "shrimp shit rap." Directing her ire at the audience, the band and herself, Grace didn't let up for several minutes:

"You paid $3.50 to come in here and you probably don't have it, man, but we do. We can ride in cars that are all closed up and nobody sees us. . . . You [referring to the band] can smoke all this dope and nobody gives you any shit. But they give *you* [the audience] shit because you don't have a Cadillac. We do. You know the people you're rising up against? They're right up here on this stage. They're also in the White House but they're also right here. Because you had to pay to get in here.

It wasn't free. You're paying our asses so I can send up and have a shrimp salad and all that shit. You can't. So you know who you're putting down? Right here. . . . And I'm a jerk 'cause I love it. I love that shrimp shit. . . . So get it, man. . . . Take it from me. Grab it from me. I got what you want. Get it, grab it, fondle it."

And so on. Perhaps her rant was meant to be inspirational—*If someone as messed-up as I am can get to be rich and famous, so can you, but you have to go out and fight for it,* she seemed to be saying—but it wasn't interpreted that way. Instead, the audience just felt antagonized.

> **GRACE SLICK:** Dark humor's a very tricky area. Slapstick isn't. You fall down—you're hurting yourself. Sarcasm is usually aimed outward. I turn it on myself too.

Back in the hotel after one of the Fillmore East shows, presumably after finishing her shrimp salad, Grace went to see Paul in his room and matter-of-factly informed him that she wanted to have his child. "She just told me that she was going to do it. I was intrigued but I didn't care if she did or didn't," Paul later told Grace's biographer, Barbara Rowes. Paul took care of his part willingly and the newly pregnant couple returned to the business at hand, leaving for the Midwest, where it was time for another notch on the burgeoning Jefferson Airplane police record. This time it was Marty's turn to get busted for dope, during a tour stop in Bloomington, Indiana. But a fine of $100 took care of business and, once again, a member of the Airplane laughed in the face of the law.

WITH NO IMMEDIATE PLANS for the Airplane, Hot Tuna and an entourage including Maurice and Thompson headed down to Jamaica in the spring, with the intention of recording a live album. Jorma and Margareta, Jack and Melissa, Joey, Marty and Paul Ziegler and his wife arrived in shifts in early June, staying together in a rented house in Runaway Bay. Maurice secured work permits to record at a club in Ocho Rios and arranged for RCA to ship down the necessary recording equipment. But by the time they left Jamaica, the very future of Hot Tuna was in doubt.

> **JORMA KAUKONEN:** We were having breakfast one morning and I was busting Marty's balls about something, and whatever it was just sent him over the edge. I remember him throwing his plate on

the floor and screaming, "Same jokes, year after year!" and he walked out. I really must have been an obnoxious prick, but I thought I was hysterically funny.

Marty was growing increasingly bitter and disgusted. The arguments came more frequently and became more voluble. Thompson recalls Marty drinking a lot at the time, growing an unkempt, full beard and engaging in name-calling. Adding to the tension, Maurice remembers that just getting Jorma and Jack to show up at the club proved challenging.

Finally, toward the end of their stay in Jamaica, the band did manage to assemble long enough to tape a set. But just as they'd gotten it together to actually play some music, the Tuna party found itself in serious trouble, forced to beat a hasty retreat from the island.

BILL THOMPSON: Jorma had a friend who was driving this truck, 90 miles an hour over some road, and he gets stopped by the police. They find 27 pounds of marijuana in the truck and they go, "What's this for?"
And he says, "I'm working with Hot Tuna over here."

JORMA KAUKONEN: The Jamaican government summoned us to come to Kingston and we went through this process at the foreign office:
"How do you like Jamaica?"
"We like it."
"Great, because you're gonna spend 20 years here."

BILL THOMPSON: We got out on the next flight.

Maurice, meanwhile, had to cut his own stay short for another reason: A group of Rastafarian musicians with whom Tuna had arranged to record were more than a little perturbed when the band failed to materialize.

PAT "MAURICE" IERACI: The Rastas were after my ass because no one was showing up at the club. I tried to reason with the leader, because he had all these men come down there. I said, "I'll pay you."
He said, "Mon, you better leave, I'm gonna get you."
So I took off on the next goddamn flight. I said, "I ain't gonna die in Jamaica."

Marty, for his part, didn't stick around Jamaica long enough to witness any of that action-movie stuff. He had already left in disgust after learning from Thompson that the funds RCA had allocated for the Hot Tuna record had already been spent, leaving him with nothing.

Just days after exiting Jamaica, the Airplane and Tuna found themselves in Europe to play the Kralingen Festival in Rotterdam, Holland, a performance later partially released on video as part of a concert film called *Stamping Ground*. The Bath Festival, in England, followed a couple of days later, the Airplane and Tuna sharing the bill with Led Zeppelin, Frank Zappa, the Byrds, Santana and others.

Tuna's appearance went without a hitch and was enhanced by the appearance of nude dancers on the stage. Not so the Airplane's. Rain intervened after they finally took the stage at 3:00 A.M. on a Monday morning. Their set was rather anticlimactic, Grace trying out her sarcasm on the implacable Brits and Paul complaining of electrical shocks.

The next few months were quiet. Tuna's self-titled debut album, featuring Mike Frankel's deliberately blurry photo of Jorma and Jack bathed in intense red light on the front cover, and a painting by Margareta Kaukonen on the back, had finally been released in May. By July it had climbed to number 30, proof that there was life outside of the Airplane, for Jorma and Jack at least. The album's release also coincided neatly with Jack, Jorma, Grace and the Airplane as a group placing high in best-of-category polls in *Jazz & Pop* magazine. In the public eye, the Airplane was still on top of the world. Privately, they were drifting apart.

FOR GRACE AND PAUL, house hunting was on the menu in mid-1970. With Grace now expecting, she and Paul decided to buy a home together, someplace a little less hectic than San Francisco. The Mansion had remained a hub of activity, but not all of it was fun. They no longer felt entirely safe there.

> **DAVID CROSBY:** There was one weirdo who decided that Grace was having the devil's baby, and that he had to save her from having that baby. Paul and I came back one night, and all the front windows were kicked in. The lights were on at the top floor, where Grace and Paul lived. We went inside and found this guy and he was, fortunately, drunk, completely on his ass, and we saved his life.

There was also the matter of cocaine. Paul's intake, especially, was growing with each passing week, and he and Grace thought that this might be a good time to move to a place where there would be less of it in front of them all the time.

> **AL KOOPER:** Grace and Paul once came over to my house in New York and did more cocaine than I'd ever seen before in my life. Just constant. They were totally enraptured.

> **PAUL KANTNER:** It got out of hand. What I did was nothing compared to some rock stars, but for the day it was a lot.

Paul and Grace selected a house in Bolinas in Marin County, a four-bedroom, two-story residence on the beach, with a pool. Thompson bought the house for them with cash, and the couple settled into a comparatively domestic routine, lying around, swimming, reading and watching TV. Grace busied herself decorating. Friends dropped by often, including Garcia and Crosby.

Crosby had been having a rough time of it lately. In 1969, his girlfriend, Christine Hinton, was killed when the Volkswagen van she'd borrowed from Crosby was involved in a head-on collision. Barbara Langer, Paul's former housemate, who was living with Crosby at the time, was seriously injured in the crash.

Thus the first months of the new decade served as a much-needed cooling-down period for Crosby and for Grace and Paul, a brief respite from the maelstrom that was the '60s. The musicians found the laid-back Marin life conducive to creating and they wrote prolifically, testing out their new songs on one another: Crosby played Paul tunes he was working on for a planned solo album, and Paul reciprocated, playing Crosby his own new material.

Not all of the musicians' off-road time was spent making music though. Some of the Airplane also occasionally dabbled in, of all things, baseball. Their team, the Giraffes—with Grace reviving her old high school cheerleading routines on the sidelines—could often be found on weekends in Golden Gate Park playing the Grateful Dead's team, the Dead Ringers, or the Bill Graham Presents club, the Marin Marauders. The Giraffes sometimes even won.

In September, most of the band members gathered at Wally Heider's to record Joey's two new songs: "Whatever the Old Man Does Is Always Right" and "Bludgeon of a Bluecoat (The Man)." Some of the group, though, upon arriving at the studio, were more than a mite surprised to find that Covington had arranged for a guest piano player to join them for the session, none other than the legendary Little Richard. Joey felt that the song needed a Little Richard–style piano and, he reasoned, why get an imitation? A series of phone calls and promises later, and Richard Penniman, resplendent in gold lamé, was pounding the ivories with Jefferson Airplane.

Maurice filmed the lively session (without sound) for posterity, but in the end, the Airplane scrapped the track.

> **JACK CASADY:** I love Little Richard. But we couldn't understand why he was there. "Why, Joey, are you bringing Little Richard in to an Airplane session?" I think we felt at the time that it wasn't the right thing to do. And furthermore, what is *Joey Covington* doing bringing in Little Richard?

Joey had deliberately begun divorcing himself from Hot Tuna following the Jamaican debacle, even while remaining the Airplane's drummer, and neither Jorma nor Jack begged him to stay. Joey participated with them in a handful of electric gigs into the fall but, during this transitional period, Hot Tuna played most of their engagements as the acoustic trio of Jorma, Jack and Will Scarlett. One of their most talked-about shows using that lineup occurred in September at Marin County's Pepperland, where Tuna shared the bill with the quirky Captain Beefheart and his Magic Band.

Just a few days before that, the Airplane put in a weekend at Fillmore West—the last time they would play the historic venue. Philip Elwood, the reviewer for the *San Francisco Examiner*, was not impressed. Describing the show as "a shambles of sound" and a "cacophony," Elwood complained that the group had "forgotten how to balance their sounds for a live audience. Either that, or they just didn't care."

THE NEXT AIRPLANE GIGS were scheduled for the weekend of October 4 and 5 at Winterland, to be simulcast on the local public broadcasting television station, KQED-TV, and in quadraphonic sound on both KQED-FM radio and KSAN, the station that had taken over as the city's leading FM rock outlet since the demise of KMPX.

The Winterland shows, also featuring the Dead and Quicksilver, had been booked by Paul Baratta, Bill Graham's former right-hand man, who had gone into business for himself. The first night was telecast as planned, called "Go Ride the Music," the title taken from the lyrics of "Wooden Ships." But what should have been a triumphant evening for the three great San Francisco bands turned into one of extreme sadness when they learned that their friend and colleague Janis Joplin had died of a heroin overdose in Los Angeles earlier that day.

Baratta tried to keep the news from the bands as long as possible, so as not to put a damper on the show, but word got out. The bands played out their sets, but there was no masking their sorrow.

PAUL BARATTA: I remember Grace being more visibly upset than anybody else. I think she felt a kinship with Janis. It was a guys' world. Grace was probably somewhat threatened by all the other ones that had gone down, but this was too close to home.

Janis was not the first intimate of the San Francisco bands to lose the battle. Only three weeks earlier, Jimi Hendrix had been found dead in London, choking on his own vomit after a night of binging on barbiturates. His death hit the Airplane hard too, as they'd admired him and worked with him—Jack had appeared both on record and onstage with Hendrix. The stakes were higher now—friends were dying. Janis, like Jimi, was only 27. Marty took it especially hard, and couldn't bring himself to perform the next night.

MARTY BALIN: I just didn't want to go onstage and play that crazy music, that cocained, messed-up music that they were into. I stayed home.

The group played without Marty. In his stead, the audience was treated to something else altogether. Joining them that evening was Papa John Creach, the violinist Joey had met a few years back in L.A. A tall, balding, 55-year-old black man, rail-thin and bent over with arthritis, Papa John sawed away at his fiddle and played the Airplane's tunes as if he'd been a member of this troupe of ragged hippie rockers since the beginning. He blew away the Airplane that night with his funky, animated style and elicited a standing ovation from the audience. The band invited him right away to join them on their next tour and it wasn't long before he became the newest member of Jefferson Airplane.

Papa John was not a rock and roll musician by trade, and he'd been making music professionally since before these youngsters were born. But fitting in with Jefferson Airplane came as easily to him as anything he'd ever done.

Like Joey, John Henry Creach hailed from a small Pennsylvania town, Beaver Falls, born to Cathis and Elizabeth Creach in 1916. Many of the 10 Creach children were musically inclined, and during his early teens, John gravitated toward the violin, learning the elements of classical music.

When he was 18, John moved to Chicago and studied violin at the Conservatory of Music. A quick learner, he played as a guest artist with the Illinois Symphony Orchestra. During the Depression, he began playing the violin wherever he might pick up a few coins: in bars, on the street, in supper clubs; he even played hillbilly music at rodeos in Montana and Idaho. "People will do a lot of things to get something to eat," he told *Rolling Stone* in 1970. "I've seen some hard times."

In the '30s, Creach played for a while with a group called the Chocolate Music Bars, then worked for a couple of hotel chains in the Midwest for several years. In 1943, he was given one of the first electric violins, which he alternated playing with the more common acoustic instrument. Throughout the '40s and '50s, Creach played clubs and cocktail lounges—pop, gospel, jazz or the nascent rhythm and blues sound—he loved it all. He worked with, among others, guitarist Slim Gaillard and alto saxist Eddie "Cleanhead" Vinson, and appeared in a movie, Fritz Lang's *The Blue Gardenia*, where he can be seen (but not actually heard) backing up the great Nat "King" Cole during a mimed performance of the film's title track.

By 1945, Creach had moved to California, working with his own Johnny Creach Trio, playing the hotel circuit in matching uniforms. By the early '60s, he could be found on the cruise ship the SS *Catalina*. He stayed with that job for about five years, making a decent living as a member of the Shipmates.

Creach left the groups behind in the late '60s to work as a soloist at the Parisian Room in L.A. That's what he was doing when he ran into Joey Covington at the musicians' union. After their aborted attempt to form a band, they kept in touch and while Joey was in Jamaica with Hot Tuna, he called Papa John back in L.A. to see if he might want to do something with the Airplane. Joey and Marty went to see Creach perform and had dinner with Papa John and his wife, Gretchen. Creach charmed Marty, who agreed with Joey that playing with the violinist would be something different for the band, maybe even the very spark they needed to ignite the Airplane again.

JOEY COVINGTON: Papa John filled a void. Kids would give him a standing ovation just for tuning up.

JORMA KAUKONEN: He wasn't the heaviest violin player in the world, but he was a soulful guy and he had so much experience. His take on our music—it must have been like he dropped in from another planet. Of course, at that time we thought he was a decrepit old coot.

Not everyone in the Airplane camp was immediately taken by the new addition, and a few fans called him "Papa John Screech." But most audiences did come to accept the new member. Creach's association with the Airplane boosted his career profile immeasurably and, for a little while at least, drew attention back to the quickly crumbling Airplane. Following his Winterland debut, Papa John Creach and his fiddle headed out on the road with Jefferson Airplane, less than a week after meeting most of them.

On their return home, the musicians once again headed off on their own. At a Hot Tuna gig in San Diego, Jorma and Jack paid special attention to the drummer in Dry Creek Road, one of the opening acts. A powerhouse named Sammy Piazza, he was first brought to the attention of Bill Thompson, who had previously checked them out at a Fillmore West Airplane gig. Thompson recommended Piazza to Jack and Jorma, who agreed upon seeing him play that he could be right for Tuna.

Following the San Diego set, Jack invited Piazza to sit in with Tuna that night at a local club. From the moment he started jamming with them, there was never a doubt that Sammy Piazza was going to be Hot Tuna's new drummer. Two days later, Jorma told him he was in.

Sammy Piazza was a Texan, born and raised in Waco. While in Dallas in 1968, fresh out of the Marine Corps, he had met a guitarist named Jimmie Vaughan, who hired him to play with his group, the Chessmen. (Vaughan's teenage brother, Stevie Ray, was still working on *his* chops at that point.) Two years later, Piazza was contacted by Billy Gibbons, another local guitar hotshot, who wondered if Piazza might be interested in joining a trio he was putting together by the name of ZZ Top. But Piazza passed, saying he wanted to head out to California. He was there all of three months when he was asked to join Hot Tuna.

> **SAMMY PIAZZA:** They didn't want Joey to play, basically, and they found the guy: "He's got a southern drawl, he doesn't know a damn thing about what's going on out here, but he's our boy."

The Airplane and Tuna toured through the end of November. In Rochester, New York, several days before Thanksgiving, the Airplane played two sets, after which Jorma skipped across town to where the Dead were holding court and jammed with them. The Thanksgiving shows at Fillmore East wrapped it all up and the band headed home for the holidays.

As they said their good-byes, perhaps Marty already knew that it was all over for him, perhaps he didn't. But if he did, he forgot to tell the others.

24
PLANET EARTH ROCK AND ROLL ORCHESTRA

ALTHOUGH THEY ENJOYED the peacefulness and loveliness of Bolinas, Grace and Paul had hardly become country bumpkins. While the hour-long drive to San Francisco precluded much leisurely hanging out in the city, especially as Grace grew larger with child, the couple did commute regularly. They often worked the night shift, laying down tracks at Wally Heider's and another San Francisco studio, Pacific High Recording.

Since the early spring they had been piecing together Paul's new project, *Blows Against the Empire*. Not surprisingly, since Paul rarely did anything in the traditional sense, it wasn't turning out to be a traditional solo album.

Heider's had become a hub of the local rock community, and at any given time several members of the top bands might be found there, working either in an official capacity or just hanging out because it was party central. Inevitably, those in the process of recording would informally invite their friends from other bands to add their ideas to the works in progress.

Grace, Jack and Joey each put their mark on Paul's album. Crosby and Graham Nash contributed, and from the Dead, Garcia, Mickey Hart and Bill Kreutzmann. Quicksilver's David Freiberg helped out, as did Peter Kaukonen, bassist Harvey Brooks and Phil Sawyer, an engineer with a knack for sound effects.

PAUL KANTNER: The album actually started out as demo tracks for the next Airplane album, and Grace was helping me. The demo tracks took on a life of their own.

At some point, Paul dubbed the loose, ever-metamorphosing conglomeration of musicians the Planet Earth Rock and Roll Orchestra. Allen

Zentz served as the engineer, with Stephen Barncard and Maurice assisting. Paul is credited as the album's producer, but Nash helped give shape to the suite that occupies the album's second half. They recorded on 16 tracks, using a Mellotron (an early synthesizer) and any other technological advances available to them.

The songwriting on *Blows* was a collaborative effort as well. Returning to his love of science fiction, Paul peppered his own words with snatches of lyrical ideas originated by Grace, Marty, Blackman, Crosby and Covington. And, once again, Kantner also turned to some of his favorite authors for inspiration. This time, though, he decided to ask one of them, *Stranger in a Strange Land* author Robert Heinlein, if he would mind if he borrowed some ideas. Paul was pleased when Heinlein gave his blessing.

Despite drawing on the brain power of many, the concept behind *Blows Against the Empire* was one that only Paul Kantner could conjure. Taking his cues from "Wooden Ships" and "Have You Seen the Saucers," and zeroing in on his generation's fascination with space exploration, Paul examined the notion of hijacking a starship and establishing an alternative community of free souls in space, far away from the spoiled planet Earth. Kantner applied his generation's pioneering spirit to a story of exploration and rejuvenation, survival and freedom, in a new man-made world above and beyond the only one humankind has known. Some 7000 people would sail "past the sun, and our babes'll wander naked through the cities of the universe," Kantner wrote. There would be "free minds, free bodies, free dope, free music."

Grace stepped in at the outset of the project and contributed voice, words and, most appreciated by Paul, her piano work, which, along with Paul's guitar, unifies the album instrumentally. Her major songwriting contribution to the album was "Sunrise," a minute and a half of spare, extraordinary beauty that launched the suite of interconnected songs on the original album's second side. Crosby, meanwhile, gave Paul the seedling for one of the album's most exquisite tunes, "Have You Seen the Stars Tonite." At this point in the saga, the space cadets have already pilfered the ship and are enjoying their idyllic cruise through the free universe. Crosby and Kantner strum lazily, Garcia and Hart add airy atmospherics via pedal steel guitar and percussion and a chorus of voices joins in celestial harmony.

Cofounder Marty Balin
Courtesy of Joe and Jean Buchwald © 2003

Cofounder Paul Kantner
Courtesy of Paul Kantner © 2003

Cofounder Jorma Kaukonen
Courtesy of Jorma and Vanessa Kaukonen © 2003

The Casadys (left to right: Chick, Mom
Mary, Michael, and Jack)
Courtesy of Jack Casady © 2003

LEFT: The future Grace Slick, acting out *Courtesy of Grace Slick © 2003*
RIGHT: Spencer Dryden in a high school play *Courtesy of Spencer Dryden © 2003*

The Triumphs, 1958 (left to right: Warren Smith, Jack Casady, Jorma Kaukonen) *Courtesy of Jorma Kaukonen and Jack Casady © 2003*

ABOVE: The Town Criers, 1964 (left to right: Jan Ellickson, Larry Vargo, Bill Collins, Marty Balin) at the Hungry i *Courtesy of Bill Collins © 2003*

BELOW: The Great Society, 1965 (left to right: Jerry Slick, David Minor, Grace Slick, Darby Slick, Bard Dupont) *Courtesy of Grace Slick © 2003*

Original Jefferson Airplane lineup, summer 1965, at the Matrix in San Francisco (clockwise from left: Bob Harvey, Signe Toly Anderson, Jerry Peloquin, Paul Kantner, Jorma Kaukonen, Marty Balin in front). *Photo by James Smircich © 2002*

Jefferson Airplane 1966, first album lineup (left to right: Signe Toly Anderson, Jack Casady, Marty Balin, Alexander "Skip" Spence on drums, Paul Kantner, Jorma Kaukonen) *Photo by Chuck Boyd/Redferns © 2003*

ABOVE LEFT: Paul Kantner signs copies of the Airplane's first album,
1966 *Photo by Michelle Vignes © 2003*

ABOVE RIGHT: Spencer Dryden, Jefferson Airplane drummer
1966–1970 *Photo by Chuck Boyd/Redferns © 2003*

BELOW: Jefferson Airplane live at Webster Hall, January 1967—
their first-ever New York gig. *Photo by Don Paulsen © 2003*

Five-sixths of Jefferson Airplane (left to right: Paul Kantner, Jorma Kaukonen, Spencer Dryden, Grace Slick, and Jack Casady) pose before a show at Hunter College in New York in October 1967 . . .
Photo by Don Paulsen © 2003

. . . while Marty Balin conserves energy.
Photo by Don Paulsen © 2003

The classic lineup of Jefferson Airplane, 1966–1970. On the couch
(left to right: Paul Kantner, Grace Slick, Jorma Kaukonen, Marty
Balin) and peeking from behind the window (left to right: Spencer
Dryden and Jack Casady). *Courtesy of London Features © 2003*

Grace studying
lyrics at 2400
Fulton Street, the
group's San
Francisco head-
quarters.
Photo by Michelle
Vignes © 2003

Jorma Kaukonen 1970
Photo by LarsMan © 2003

Jack Casady 1970
Photo by LarsMan
© 2003

"Have You Seen the Stars Tonite" is buffered by "Home" and "X>M," two brief electronic sound collages that Kantner describes as "background landscaping." Those melt into "Starship," Kantner's state of the universe address:

Gotta get back and ahead to the things that matter
Amerika hates her crazies and you gotta let go, you know
Gotta let go, you know
Gotta let go, you know
Gotta let go, you know, or else you stay.

The second half of the album, outlining the actual star trek, received the lion's share of fan and press attention; it's really what *Blows Against the Empire* is, at its heart, all about. But the four songs that comprise the record's first side are no less important to the totality of the work, if presented somewhat less dramatically. "Let's Go Together," the third song, mines familiar Kantner territory, with a twist: Unlike the first Airplane album's "Let's Get Together," it's no longer about smiling and loving. Now it's time to run for your life.

The album's first half ended with "A Child Is Coming," Paul, Grace and Crosby ruminating on the imminent arrival of a wee one, and choosing to keep the birth a secret from those who might later become the oppressor.

What you gonna do when Uncle Samuel comes around
Askin' for the young one's name
And lookin' for the print of his hand for the files in their numbers game
I don't want his chance for freedom to ever be that slim
Let's not tell 'em about him.

The sci-fi community took the album to heart: *Blows* became the first record album ever to be nominated for the prestigious Hugo award, given out annually by the World Science Fiction Society for outstanding work in the field. Although the album didn't win, its nomination went a long way toward validating the record's concept, which some critics felt was more than a bit spaced-out.

Like Hot Tuna's album, *Blows* found favor with the Airplane faithful, hitting the charts at the end of 1970 and rising to number 20. Few buyers gave it any significance at the time, but in order to distinguish the project, to make fans aware that it wasn't an Airplane album—and yet to indicate that it wasn't entirely a solo record either—Kantner branded it with an appropriately forward-looking touch: The finished product was attributed to Paul Kantner–Jefferson Starship.

With no new Jefferson Airplane album having been released since *Volunteers*, and none on the horizon, RCA took the opportunity in late 1970 to issue its first Airplane compilation, containing highlights from the first six albums. Kantner, ever the wise guy, came up with its title: *The Worst of Jefferson Airplane.* Ironically, the collection ultimately became one of the best-selling pieces in the band's discography, reaching number 12 on the charts and selling a million copies.

It wasn't until they returned from the November East Coast tour that anyone really started to think seriously about making a new Airplane record. It had been more than a year, and the record company and fans were getting antsy. The band knew it had to get cracking, but getting motivated wasn't proving easy now. In just a couple of months, everything had changed.

For one thing, there was no longer an outside producer to mediate, to help give the album direction and cohesion. Al Schmitt was gone, and although the Airplane was determined to make this one on their own, some band members were barely on speaking terms with others: Tempers were still flaring between the Grace/Paul faction and the Jorma/Jack faction, and neither was in any mood to make music with the other. The two teams could even be found, on certain nights, working in separate studios at Heider's, Grace and Paul polishing their songs in one and Jack and Jorma rehearsing Tuna in the other.

Not unlike what had happened to the Beatles in their final throes, the Airplane was no longer a group so much as a collection of competing, bickering singer/songwriter/musicians, each jockeying for position, trying to place his or her compositions on the album.

But the lack of a producer wasn't their greatest problem. Nor, even, was the feud between factions. The major difference this time was that Marty Balin had stopped coming around. He'd finally made good on his threats. No one had even heard from him since Thanksgiving.

25

GOTTA LET GO, YOU KNOW

CHINA WING KANTNER poked her head into this world on January 25, 1971. Despite decades of persistent rumors to the contrary, the seven-pound baby's name at birth was not god. Or was it?

The story that Grace likes to tell is this: She was lying in her bed at French Hospital in San Francisco that first day, cuddling her newborn. Paul had left during her labor and was nowhere to be found. A nurse walked into Grace's room, asking what the baby was to be called.

GRACE SLICK: I said, "god, with a small *g*, because we are humble." I was just fucking with her; but she went out of the room and called [*San Francisco Chronicle* columnist] Herb Caen. I kind of got nailed with that for a while.

The media jumped on the newsworthy story, savoring its shock value, but Grace had indeed been planting the god rumor prior to the child's birth. An article in *Rolling Stone*, published a few weeks before China arrived—and before Grace found out the baby was a girl—said, "Their son, who will be named 'god, just god,' has grown large inside her."

When she left the hospital, Grace shouldn't have been too surprised to find a team of reporters awaiting her. Yes, she told them, god is what she had named her child, and thus another rock and roll urban legend was hatched. But the birth certificate reads China Wing Kantner, the girl's name having been chosen by Paul. He and Grace had become increasingly enamored of certain aspects of Asian culture—Bruce Lee movies, acupuncture, communism—and China seemed an appropriate appellation for their child.

Grace—whose ex-husband Jerry had finally filed for divorce once she'd become pregnant—returned to work just weeks after giving birth, but the mood within the group was becoming more and more somber.

The Airplane had managed to patch together some new basic tracks, but lethargy and apathy were still the prevailing mood. With Marty keeping his distance from the band and his role in its future dubious, the entire meaning of Jefferson Airplane had to be rethought. In April, Marty made it public: he had indeed departed Jefferson Airplane.

> **MARTY BALIN:** People never had any reason to come to work. It was like, "I'll do my thing." And I didn't think doing *my* thing was as important as doing *the* thing. Not one person ever called me.

> **BILL THOMPSON:** That's not true that no one called him. I begged him to come back.

The band bought out Marty's share in Jefferson Airplane, for approximately $30,000. He also relinquished his part ownership of the band's name. Marty Balin no longer had any financial stake in the group he had founded.

> **JORMA KAUKONEN:** Marty really had this thing about "my band," and maybe it started that way. But it really wasn't anybody's band. I don't think Marty's ever gotten over the fact that we didn't just back him up and do what he said. We did drive him nuts, but when he left, the Airplane was pretty much without direction.

There were other important changes going on in Marty's life at the time, which undoubtedly contributed to his withdrawal. In 1970, his longtime girlfriend Janet Trice left him and moved to Boston. She'd made a valiant effort to keep the relationship afloat, but in the end they just couldn't work. Marty began dating Trish Robbins, a music librarian and part-time disc jockey on KSAN.

Marty maintained a low profile for the next few years, relaxing, reading voraciously, going to the movies with Trish. He got involved with a northern California Native American tribe, helping them publicize their fight against fishing companies trying to buy up all their land.

But he never truly dropped out of the music scene. Within months of leaving the Airplane, Marty began working behind the scenes with Grootna, a funk band from Marin County. The septet, managed by Bill Graham, signed a deal with Columbia Records and released its only album the following year, produced by Marty. Then, in 1973, Marty put together a new group of his own, Bodacious D.F.

MARTY BALIN: When we rehearsed, if somebody played something good, somebody would say, "That's bodacious." And when somebody played something stupid, we'd say, "You dopey fuck."

This time Marty took an active role as its lead vocalist. The band recorded one underrated album for RCA, led off by "Drifting," one of the songs Marty had been singing with Hot Tuna and the Airplane toward the end. The album cover, designed by San Francisco poster artist Bob Fried, featured a photo of the extended Bodacious family shot at the Old Mill Tavern in Mill Valley, hosting some very drunk and disheveled hippies—Marty's father is the bartender.

But Marty's name, by his own choice, did not appear on the album cover, much to RCA's chagrin, and the record sold poorly. Bodacious never made another record, and by the summer of 1974, Marty was without a band again, waiting for the muse to return.

Balin wasn't the only ex-Airplane member to find new life after his departure from the group. Spencer Dryden had all but retired from playing music after being sacked from the Airplane—the drums were packed away and he hadn't touched them once. Then Owsley called. The New Riders of the Purple Sage, the Grateful Dead's psychedelic country-rock offshoot, were looking for a helping hand. Spencer had never given much thought to country music as a career path—he was still a jazz guy at heart. But this promised to be much less stressful than the Airplane.

SPENCER DRYDEN: Originally, I thought they were just asking me to produce, which was what I wanted to do. Then Jerry Garcia and [then-current Dead manager] Jon McIntire came over and said, "Okay, the band's going to be in the studio next week, we want you to play." The next thing I knew I was on tour.

Spencer replaced the Dead's Mickey Hart as the New Riders' drummer, opening with them on the East Coast in February 1971. The group landed a record deal with Columbia and Spencer played on part of the first album, whichever tracks Hart was not on. He stayed with them as drummer until 1978, playing on all of their records and touring. Spencer also became the group's manager, an ill-fated arrangement that put him at odds with the others in the band. By early 1980s, Spencer had resigned and gone back into semiretirement.

With both Marty and Spencer now gone, the Airplane—now including just two original members, Paul and Jorma—simply carried on. They knew they needed to make a record before they were forgotten completely, and as 1971 got under way, with no tours planned, they buckled down. Unfortunately, they still didn't have a unified idea as to what the album should be. So the reconstituted group went into Heider's and resorted to their old standby method: they winged it.

JOEY COVINGTON: Everybody got caught with their pants down when Marty quit. Nobody had any songs. It was a totally unprepared album.

Paul and Grace each contributed three songs to the record, none of them collaborative. Paul's "Rock and Roll Island," "When the Earth Moves Again" and "War Movie" formed something of a trilogy thematically, expanding on the *Blows* notion that enlightened humans would some day rise up against their oppressor and seek to live in harmony in a new world. Our small problems would give way to the greater concern of sustaining the race.

Grace's new songs were all radically different, save for the anger inherent in her words. "Crazy Miranda," powered by Grace's muscular piano, mines roughly the same territory as "Greasy Heart," a dig at what the author perceives as the shallowness of women who buy into the manufactured myth of femininity, whose lives follow a script written by men.

Scorching, fuzzed-out Jorma guitar and Grace's rhythmic piano punctuate "Law Man." The song tells of a young police officer who bursts in without an invitation, only to find himself face-to-face with a woman who just isn't the mood to be harassed:

Law man, I'm afraid you just walked in here at the wrong time
My old man's gun has never been fired but there's a first time
And this could be, this could be the first time.

Grace's third song, "Never Argue with a German If You're Tired or European Song" is one of the more bizarre, and subtly humorous, entries in Grace's catalog, sung entirely in Grace's own version of the German language. The lyrics were cobbled together from words and phrases she picked up randomly by listening to German tourists on the street—or that Grace simply made up herself.

Grace had begun recording "Never Argue" in April, but a month later she had cause to add to the song some new lines which, when translated, came out roughly to, "My car drives very fast but it is crashing against walls." She was writing from firsthand experience.

China Kantner was only a few months old at the time and already Grace was up to her old tricks. In the early morning of May 13, she was heading home to Marin after a night of heavy drinking at Heider's. Peeling out onto the empty streets, she was in no condition to drive, but that had never been much of a consideration before. Jorma was right behind her when it happened. He too should not have been behind the wheel, but nonetheless they found themselves drag racing madly, heading toward the Golden Gate Bridge.

Grace and Jorma had always had an odd relationship, cordial and respectful, but not overly warm and close. Despite that, as she had done with Jack, Spencer and Paul, Grace had found herself sharing her bed with Jorma on more than one occasion. Some say their affair—if that's what it could be called in an atmosphere where the very concept of cheating was considered a prehistoric notion—went on for longer than either remembers, with their respective mates, Margareta and Paul, fully aware of it.

JORMA KAUKONEN: It wasn't of major significance, but Grace did, certainly, sleep with me a couple of times. The first time involved Jack Daniel's and Tuinol [sleeping pills], which is not exactly a heightening of perceptions.

Jorma and Grace were not planning to stay together that spring morning—so he says—but they had been in a playful mood before they decided to turn the streets of San Francisco into the Indy 500, heading toward Marin County. Careening wildly, Grace lost control of her car and smashed into a divider, totaling the car and nearly killing herself. Jorma was the first person on the scene.

JORMA KAUKONEN: I was going over 100 miles an hour, she must have been going 150. Fortunately, it was very early in the morning, right before rush hour. She spun all the way across. I got out of the car and I saved her life.

Grace was thrown across the car; her head hitting the passenger side—the driver's seat was crushed. Bloodied, she received multiple concussions and messed up her mouth. Naturally, singing was out for a while, so her sessions were canceled while she recuperated.

Around that time, realizing that successful child rearing required more attention than a pair of party-loving rock stars could give—and obviously not ready to give up their lifestyle—Grace and Paul hired a full-time caretaker and nanny named Pat Dugan, a somewhat older woman who'd been recommended by Judy Thompson. The couple bought Dugan a house in Bolinas near their own, and she moved in with her own kids. Dugan did the family's cooking and shopping, and was often left to watch China for long periods of time while the child's parents were on the road. Dugan became something of a surrogate mother to China during the girl's first years.

BY THE SUMMER OF '71, *Bark* was nearing completion. Like Grace and Paul, Jorma contributed three songs. "Wild Turkey" (named after Papa John's favorite liquid refreshment), an instrumental boogie with a country touch, gave Jorma and Creach an opportunity to duel it out. And "Feel So Good" was basically a Hot Tuna track grafted onto an Airplane record, a blaring uptempo blues enveloping a rare straightforward love lyric from the man who had given Marty so much grief about writing love songs.

But it's Jorma's "Third Week in the Chelsea" that is *Bark*'s most telling track. Set to a gorgeous folky melody, with Will Scarlett adding mournful harp licks and Grace singing harmony, it is, in a nutshell, Jorma's farewell letter to Jefferson Airplane.

> **JORMA KAUKONEN:** The song came to me entirely in a dream, the only time this has ever happened. I used to keep a little tape recorder next to my bed. I woke up, pushed the button, played the song, went back to sleep.

> *All my friends keep telling me that it would be a shame*
> *To break up such a grand success and tear apart a name*
> *But all I know is what I feel whenever I'm not playing*
> *And emptiness ain't where it's at and neither's feeling pain.*

GRACE SLICK: That's him telling the band, "I don't want to do this anymore." We'd play the song and think, Oh well, that's Jorma, he's down again. But a good song came out of the band crumbling, him letting us know that he wants to be free, the feeling of being trapped by that group.

Joey also came up with two songs for the album, one of which was chosen as the first single. Originally a 14-minute late-night jam, the alluring ballad was chopped down to a commercial four-and-a-half minutes and named "Pretty As You Feel." Credited to Covington–Casady–Kaukonen, with Joey singing lead, it featured Carlos Santana and his drummer, Michael Shrieve, sitting in. The record became the Airplane's final chart single, and their fourth biggest, reaching number 60.

Joey's other contribution to *Bark* was no one's idea of a hit single. "Thunk" was unlike anything else in the admittedly esoteric Airplane canon. A bit of sullen piano chording leads to a couple of minutes of a cappella vocals, some of it Joey engaging in dissonant multitracked harmonizing with himself. A touch of Zappa, a pinch of *Smile*-era Beach Boys, some street corner doo-wop attitude and mostly the off-center sensibilities of Joey Covington flesh it out.

With 11 songs in the can, *Bark* was completed. Now the band members could freely concentrate on their other projects. Grace, Paul, Jorma and Jack, throughout the year, had been devoting some of their spare time to teaming up in various configurations with Crosby, Freiberg, Garcia, Lesh and other pals. Some of these laid-back Planet Earth Rock and Roll Orchestra (PERRO) sessions resulted in songs that would turn up in finished form on later records, including Garcia's self-titled solo album and Crosby's *If I Could Only Remember My Name*. One PERRO jam, "The Mountain Song," didn't materialize for another dozen years, when Paul placed a revamped version of it on the album he would call—in tribute to this collaborative era—*Planet Earth Rock and Roll Orchestra*. Many of the early '70s PERRO tapes were filed away in various locations, not to be heard for two decades, when Stephen Barncard uncovered some of them—one of the tape boxes contained a pipe still filled with marijuana.

Jorma and Jack, though, were interested primarily in furthering Hot Tuna. They released their second album, a full-band, all-electric effort, recorded live at a hole in the wall in the Santa Cruz Mountains called the Chateau Liberté.

JORMA KAUKONEN: It was a shit-kicking log cabin bar, an old stage stop in the 1800s. It had very low ceilings and was down a muddy road. The sound was horrendous. We played there a lot and wanted to do this album there.

Tuna booked a series of gigs at the club in April, the band at this time consisting of Jorma and Jack, Sammy Piazza, Will Scarlett and, moonlighting from the Airplane, Papa John Creach, who'd been quickly and easily assimilated into the spinoff group. With Allen Zentz engineering and Maurice in his customary role as "Master of the Machines," Tuna played loudly and furiously, ending up with seven tracks, three of them breaking the eight-minute mark in length.

Leading off the record, which they called *First Pull Up, Then Pull Down*—in honor of the instructions often found on dispensers of paper toilet seat covers in public restrooms—was "John's Other," a galloping instrumental which became Papa John's signature number. Both "Candy Man" and "Keep Your Lamps Trimmed and Burning" were from the Reverend Gary Davis songbook, part of Jorma's repertoire since college. "That'll Never Happen No More" was another that Jorma had picked up from his mentor Ian Buchanan years earlier.

"Been So Long," which stems from the PERRO sessions, is a tender and lachrymose ballad, and the only Kaukonen original on the record. The lyrics were inspired—as were so many of Jorma's songs—by what he calls "the ongoing nonrelationship I had with my wife."

"Want You to Know" comes from a semi-obscure country bluesman, Bo Carter. Jorma heard one of his albums on the Yazoo label and fell for the song. Closing out *First Pull Up . . .* is "Come Back Baby," the Lightnin' Hopkins tune that Jorma had been performing with the Airplane since the band's early days.

Released on RCA, with dizzying cover art from Margareta, *First Pull Up . . .* charted in June of 1971 and reached number 43, giving most Airplane fans outside of the Bay Area their first real taste of what the electrified configuration of Hot Tuna was capable of doing in a live setting. With Tuna's star rising while the Airplane fumbled, it was no accident that Bill Graham chose the adjunct group, rather than the Airplane themselves, to partake in a momentous, if sad, occasion, the closing of Fillmore West.

Graham had lost his enthusiasm. Money had changed everything, he said. Although Graham himself had often been accused of being a "capitalist pig," his intimates knew there was more to him than the bottom line: He was passionate about his work, obsessed with presenting quality entertainment. Now, it seemed, everyone was getting greedy. The bands, the managers, the agents, everyone thought they were God now. The bands didn't want the intimacy of the ballrooms and theaters anymore; now they wanted Yankee Stadium!

The audiences had changed too. They were no longer as gentle and loving and free as before—they didn't come to dance or to share a few hours with peers, they came to be entertained. They demanded to be impressed, insisted on encores. And how dare Graham raise the ticket price a whole dollar? He should let them in for free!

Part of the reason for the shift in attitude was the drugs. Pot and acid were still prevalent, but they'd been augmented by harder, meaner inebriants: downers, speed, heroin, coke and smuggled-in flasks of cheap wine and hard liquor. Graham first closed Fillmore East, on June 27, 1971. Then Fillmore West went out, with a five-night bash lasting from June 30 through July 4, all of it broadcast on KSAN. Graham booked only Bay Area bands for the run, with headliners on the various nights including some of Graham's oldest Bay Area friends: Boz Scaggs, It's a Beautiful Day, the Dead, Quicksilver and, on the final night, a killer triple bill of Santana, Creedence Clearwater Revival and Tower of Power, plus a jam including members of several San Francisco bands.

Hot Tuna played on the penultimate night. One song from their set, "Keep Your Lamps Trimmed and Burning," was released as part of a three-record boxed set on Graham's Fillmore label, *Fillmore: The Last Days*. A film, *Fillmore*, in 1972, documented the closing but contained no Tuna footage.

Bill Graham wasn't the only one to give it up in '71. For Glenn McKay, whose Headlights light show had been such an integral component of Jefferson Airplane shows for four years, the fun had also gone out of the game. After one last tour in late 1971, McKay packed up his gear and left the rock business behind.

• • •

THE AIRPLANE'S FIRST LIVE CONCERTS of 1971 took place on the East Coast, in the middle of August. The band stuck largely to the new *Bark* material, although the album had not yet been released to the public. When it did finally come out, more than a year after they first began working on it, the label on the record did not read RCA but rather Grunt, the Airplane's very own record company, its name suggested by Grace in deference to some juvenile bathroom humor. For some time the Airplane had been thinking about establishing their own imprint, allowing them greater artistic control. The Beatles and several other top bands had launched their own labels, and given the Airplane's dissatisfaction with RCA and its censors, it seemed a natural next move. When their RCA contract ran its course in 1970, Bill Thompson and the others got to work on it.

Thompson held negotiations with several major labels, but despite all of their previous problems with the company, the Airplane ended up signing on with RCA as the manufacturer and distributor of Grunt. This way, a company already familiar with the band and its ways would still handle the marketing, advertising and promotion of the product, but the Airplane would maintain complete creative control.

With the infusion of money from the Grunt deal, Thompson was able to hire more staff. Diane Gardiner, who had already been the Airplane's publicist for a few years while employed by an outside firm, continued to do the same for Grunt. Not long after Grunt began operating, though, Gardiner disappeared, only to finally call the office to say she wouldn't be coming back. She had met a wonderful man, she said, and fallen in love with him. His name was Charles, but most people knew him as Chuck—Chuck Berry. Gardiner's assistant, Heidi Howell, who was married to Grunt's A&R director, Jamie Howell, took over the publicity position. To handle promotions, dealing mainly with radio, Thompson brought in Augie Blume, while his wife, Nancy, was made the director of sales and marketing.

But despite the influx of new help, the workload increased tremendously. Now assigned exclusively to the Airplane and Grunt, Maurice, as production consultant, was responsible for making sure the musicians got to the studio, for the budgeting, for booking the studio time, for managing all of the contracts. He took care of the paperwork involved with securing the song publishing (the band had set up its own publishing firm in the wake of the Matthew Katz debacle, naming it Icebag after a particularly potent strain of marijuana). He hand-delivered the mixed tapes to the mastering lab, sent finished discs to each of the three RCA pressing plants and then flew to those plants himself to check the test pressings. Maurice kept all of the books on recording and rehearsal costs, paid all shipping, telephone bills, instrument rentals and limo bills. Every time a musician sat in to jam with the Airplane, Maurice made sure the guest received the standard union fee—whether he ended up on a record or not.

It was also Maurice's impossible task to attempt to keep frivolous spending down so the band wouldn't have to repay the record company out of their earnings later, a standard industry practice. But that, he says, was a lost cause.

> **PAT "MAURICE" IERACI:** There was no sense of responsibility. They were spoiled. I wasn't so much coordinating, I was a baby-sitter.

Jacky—who by that time was going by her husband Peter's last name, Kaukonen—continued to perform the equivalent tasks at the office at 2400 Fulton.

> **JACKY (WATTS KAUKONEN) SARTI:** I was always working while everybody played around me. We celebrated birthdays and anniversaries, with flowers and presents and champagne and cake and whatever was going on at that time drug-wise. But even at my own birthday party, I was the one that was writing the checks.

Bark was given a catalog number of Grunt FTR-1001, the first release on the new label. Perhaps to make the point that they considered their music only so much product now, the Airplane went with a rather drab-looking plain beige cover, depicting little more than some knotted string and the toothy head of a fish sticking out from a corner. They had become fishmongers.

The word "BARK" was scrawled with a felt-tip pen at the top and the entire package was sold inside of a brown paper bag covered with portraits of the band members and Maurice, all drawn by Grace (except for the one of Grace, which Thompson drew). A "Bark lyric flyer" was inserted inside the album, the words to the songs on one side and, on the other, a poem by Blackman containing several dozen suggestions as to

"What you can do with the bag." Despite its simplicity, the album cover for *Bark* was the only one of the Airplane's ever to be nominated for a Grammy award.

Upon its release, the Airplane backlash went into full swing. Some journalists condemned the changes in the group's personnel—particularly Marty's absence—and overall sound. Some loved the addition of Papa John, but others complained that he turned the Airplane into a pseudo-funk band. Some applauded Covington's harder-edged drumming, others missed Spencer's intricacies.

Bark sold well, reaching number 11 in *Billboard*, the group's third-highest showing. Now Jefferson Airplane had to prove to RCA that they could sell records by others too.

26
REALITY CHECK

RCA'S ORIGINAL PROPOSAL for Grunt Records required the Airplane to come up with five albums, Hot Tuna with three, Paul three and Grace one. But Thompson had managed to cajole the corporate parent into letting them build Grunt into something greater, a vanity label that would showcase the best of San Francisco's most promising new talent. He wangled $10 million out of the company, and convinced RCA to let the Airplane run Grunt themselves, taking care of all recording, design and day-to-day business. Grunt would record what it wanted to, and RCA would sell it to the world.

Grunt got off to a quick and prolific start. Most of the first releases were solo and spinoff recordings by members of the Airplane. But once they started signing their friends to the label and running it as a self-governing business, Grunt, like the Beatles' Apple Records, turned into an unmitigated disaster.

> **PAUL KANTNER:** Grunt was an attempt to try to provide a community base, to encourage local bands as well as our own interests. We thought we could do it, but to be a record company and a musician was just too much.

With *Bark* off and running, the Airplane threw an invitation-only gala at the Friends and Relations Hall, formerly the Family Dog's place on the Great Highway. The band and its fellow Grunt pals celebrated their new venture in style, at a cost of $35,000—more money than the Airplane had received when they first signed to RCA in 1965. Wine and beer flowed freely, cocaine, marijuana and nitrous oxide almost as freely and soul food was brought in by friends of Papa John's. RCA flew in 100 journalists and put them up at the expensive Jack Tar Hotel.

The entertainment was plentiful and reportedly lasted a staggering

10 hours. Most eyes and ears were not even on the Airplane that night, but rather the new artists that would comprise the Grunt Records roster. There was Jack Bonus, a singer, guitarist, pianist, flutist and saxophonist. The Ace of Cups, the female vocal group that had helped out on *Volunteers* (but never did get around to releasing an album on Grunt), performed a set. Black Kangaroo, fronted by Peter Kaukonen, was a highlight of the evening, with their hard-rocking, guitar-heavy sound.

One of the more curious acts was a group called One or, more specifically, 1, acquaintances of Paul's and Grace's from Bolinas. A nine-piece ensemble, they engaged in lengthy, drifting tunes that drew as much from raga as from rock, with touches of jazz and country. The leader of the group was a mysterious man who went by the name Reality D. Blipcrotch. He vocalized in his own unique way, often wordlessly. A former marine (from grunt to Grunt), no one knew anything else about him, not even his original name—he'd had it changed legally, swears Bill Thompson.

The making of One's self-titled album for Grunt, released in 1972, is a tale that defines the nutty, out-of-control tenor of the post-Aquarian times, as well as the Airplane's utter inability to run a serious business.

PAT "MAURICE" IERACI: This guy Reality comes into my office and he's smoking a joint made out of newspaper. "Maurice, I want to do a recording. But I gotta do it on a certain day, and I wanna do it in Bolinas. I'm waiting for this wave to come in."

I said, "Wave?"

"Yeah. At 4:32," on a particular day, "a wave is coming in and I want you to record this wave."

"Record the wave? You want me to set up recording equipment at the ocean? How am I gonna know which wave?"

"And I want you in a rowboat. I want a microphone for the top of the wave and a microphone for the bottom."

I said, "Jacques Cousteau is who you gotta call, not me!"

Ever the trouper, Maurice actually made arrangements to have recording equipment dragged down to the ocean in Bolinas, to record Reality D. Blipcrotch and his perfect wave. But Ieraci's ordeal was far from over even after the wave crashed. Reality was still orbiting high above planet reality.

PAT "MAURICE" IERACI: We get it all mixed down. It sounds like waves. Then I said, "I'm gonna go to Indianapolis and make test pressings. I'll listen to it and then I'll call you."

He says, "Before you go to Indianapolis, I want a couple of special things."

I take out my pen and he says, "On band three, bar 30, I want a marijuana leaf to pop out."

I write down, *Band three, bar 30, marijuana leaf pop out.* Pop out of the record. He's putting me on, right? But I write it down!

"One more thing. At the end of side two, as it rejects, I want the record to self-destruct."

So I write down, *End of side two, self-destruct.* "Why do you want it to self-destruct?"

"Because they'll go out and buy it again and I'll get double sales." He leaves. I take the pad, I throw it out. Two and a half, three weeks later, he calls me up and he's yelling. "You bastard! You cocksucker!" Later he comes in, takes the test pressing and flings it and it cracks! He said, "You lied! You cheated!"

I said, "What are you talking about?! What's wrong with the test pressing?"

"You told me that a marijuana leaf would pop out on the third band, on bar 30! And I played side two until I'm blue in the face and the damn thing never reached its self-destruct!"

Not all of the non-Airplane Grunt recordings generated quite so much grief for the parties involved, but none exactly turned the world of music upside down either. *One*, for all of its faults, was at least deemed listenable enough to be foisted upon the public. Another Grunt album, *Gettin' Plenty*, by Richmond Talbott, really did self-destruct.

Talbott was a blues guitarist and singer who, during the preceding decade, had gone by the name Steve Talbot and was part of Jorma's inner circle—it was Talbot who'd originally given Jorma the moniker Blind Thomas Jefferson Airplane. Jorma signed his old acquaintance to Grunt and Talbott went about making his album. But, according to both Maurice and Jorma, the album was so atrocious that they determined it was in Grunt's best interest to kill it and cut their losses.

The other two albums by non-Airplane members in the first Grunt batch showed some promise. *Black Kangaroo* shared its title with Peter Kaukonen's touring band (Kaukonen, a while later, began calling himself Peter Kangaroo). The album hinted at influences from Delta and

Chicago blues as well as more contemporary artists like Hendrix, Santana and Johnny Winter. The other maiden Grunt release, Jack Bonus's self-titled album, runs the gamut from orchestrated pieces to funky blues.

While the Airplane may have gotten some gratification from scoring their friends deals, the record-buying public shrugged. None of the albums by their pals made the charts or put any money in the Grunt coffers. In the end, it was only the music made by the Airplane members that had any commercial impact.

Those who did sell some records included Papa John, whose debut solo album, simply titled *Papa John Creach*, was released near the end of 1971. Papa John used half of San Francisco to make the record: Jorma, Jack, Grace, Paul, Joey and Sammy Piazza all contributed. John Cipollina of Quicksilver played guitar on one track, Jerry Garcia on one and Carlos Santana on another. Dave Brown and Gregg Rolie of Santana sat in, and Pete Sears, an English musician, put down bass licks on the opening track, "The Janitor Drives a Cadillac," a song Joey penned. At the age of 55, Papa John Creach enjoyed his first charting record when his album landed in *Billboard* on New Year's Day of 1972.

A week earlier, on Christmas day, *Sunfighter*, the second album to be issued on Grunt, began its own brief chart run. Credited to Paul Kantner and Grace Slick, the record featured a chubby, months-old China Kantner on its orange and red cover, the infant being lifted from the sea by a pair of strong arms, one her mother's, the other her father's, a new life springing from the primordial soup that gave birth to all living things.

Sunfighter, unlike *Blows Against the Empire*, was not a concept album, just a collection of new songs. Still, those songs are unified by circumstance: They were all written and recorded during the Bolinas period, when Paul and Grace experimented with domesticity, rural living and child rearing, and found themselves thinking about the ramifications of those changes in their lives. Parenting inspired some of the songwriting on the album.

PAUL KANTNER: I'd never expected to be that involved as a father, but I fell right into the pattern. Your world changes, and it's well worth the effort.

Still, being Daddy and Mommy now didn't mean Paul and Grace were going soft. Grace leads off *Sunfighter* with "Silver Spoon," a song that concerns itself with, on one level at least, what Grace calls in the lyrics "the cannibalism question," in which she proposes that it's acceptable to eat one's friends "with your fingers and your hands."

> **GRACE SLICK:** That comes from being badgered. In Bolinas at that time there were shitloads of hippies: serious, hairy armpits, no-work, bake-your-own-bread and buy-organic hippies. I'm basically saying, don't bother me with that shit because I'm not interested.

Paul's "Diana," the second song on *Sunfighter*, was inspired by Diana Oughton, a member of the revolutionary Weathermen brigade and one of three people killed in the March 1970 explosion of a Greenwich Village apartment where the radicals were building bombs. The album's title track addresses another fight, the one against the stupidity of the planet's most destructive species, homo sapiens. "When I Was a Boy I Watched the Wolves" is a highlight, not only because it is one of Kantner's most perfectly realized compositions, but also for Jerry Garcia's stunning guitar work. Grace's paean to "China" celebrates not only the individual child but the quality of being childlike. The song was dedicated to Edgar Prentagrasst, which Grace confessed was not a real person but actually Paul's pet name for his penis, undoubtedly making "China" the first rock song not only to honor a child but also the organ of the male who sired her. "Earth Mother," an ecology-oriented song, was written by Paul's old friend Jack Traylor, who contributed guitar and vocals to the recording. Teenager Craig Chaquico (pronounced chuh-KEY-so), a student in Traylor's English class and a member of his band, Steelwind, provided the hotshot guitar licks.

Sunfighter is an album about renewal, an appropriate symbol for its times: within the Airplane, the culture, and Grace and Paul's own lives. If *Blows* looked for solutions in worlds beyond, *Sunfighter* trained its lens on matters closer to home.

The last of the initial Grunt releases was *Burgers*, Hot Tuna's third release and first studio album. Now they were down to a quartet—Kaukonen, Casady, Creach and Piazza—with Will Scarlett having exited. Five of the nine songs on the record were Jorma originals.

JORMA KAUKONEN: *Burgers* was one of the most significant Hot Tuna records. It was a relief to be out on our own, but it was also intimidating because now we had to make our own band stand. At the time there was a lot of momentum, a lot of excitement about it.

On *Burgers*, the originals "Sea Child," "Highway Song" (with harmony vocal from David Crosby) and "Ode for Billy Dean," as well as the two instrumentals, the exquisite "Water Song" and the lumbering "Sunny Day Strut," establish a new benchmark for Kaukonen's songwriting. Most of Jorma's trademark lyrical touchstones are present and expanded upon: the naked self-examination; a longing for simple, honest pleasures amidst the harder truths of life, death and love; the search for spiritual redemption and some palpable meaning behind existence on this planet and whatever lies beyond. Each song is a microcosmic example of one of the several facets of Jorma's style, taking in the old-timey country blues of his heroes, the various fingerpicking and electric blues-rock guitar stylings he'd developed as signatures with the Airplane and the intuitiveness of the interactions with Jack.

Burgers serves notice that Jorma Kaukonen has much more to say than he'd ever let on in the Airplane, as a composer and performer. The cover songs, meanwhile, complement Jorma's own material ideally. "Keep on Truckin'" has a particularly fascinating history, notable because it is directly responsible for the origin of the Hot Tuna name. The song is credited to Bob Carleton, who had written a nonsense song in 1918 called "Ja-Da." The song's melody was later coopted by blues singers Tampa Red, for his song "What Is It That Tastes Like Gravy?" and Blind Boy Fuller, whose "Truckin' My Blues Away" and "What's That Smell Like Fish" both contributed to the Tuna version's lyrics. *Burgers* was recorded quickly, and was in the stores by February of 1972. For the cover art, photographer Bruce Steinberg hauled the band down to the beach in Jorma's rare 1934 Buick Victoria.

With Tuna taking off on its own, Jorma and Jack would soon have to make a decision: to devote all of their time to the new venture or continue to attempt splitting their time. In all of 1971, Jefferson Airplane had played fewer live shows than many working bands do in a week. Jorma and Jack wanted to play music.

It was apparent to all that Jefferson Airplane had become a band in name only. Paul and Grace rarely saw Jorma or Jack, Papa John came in only when called and Joey was off doing his own thing. But Joey's days were numbered anyway. If the Airplane was to survive, Jack and Jorma made clear, they wanted him out, and Grace and Paul no longer cared enough one way or the other. Joey was still with the Airplane when they began piecing together their next album, *Long John Silver*, and played drums on sessions for two songs. But in April of 1972 he became the next casualty. Thompson says Joey was fired, Joey says he quit. In any case, he didn't leave the Airplane clan entirely. Changing the spelling of his name temporarily to Joe E. Covington, he remained part of the decaying family as a solo artist, putting together his own band and beginning work on an album, *Joe E. Covington's Fat Fandango*. It was released on Grunt in 1973.

With Joey out of the band, the drum chair was passed along to a seasoned veteran, John Barbata. Born in Passaic, New Jersey, in 1945, Barbata had been the drummer for the Turtles, the enormously successful folk/pop-rock group whose many hits included the classic "Happy Together." Barbata stayed with them for three years, then, in 1970, he joined Crosby, Stills, Nash and Young, appearing on the quartet's live *4 Way Street* album. When CSNY fizzled out, Crosby informed Barbata that the Airplane was in need of a new drummer.

> **JOHN BARBATA:** It was the first time that the Airplane had had a real studio musician in the band. But the sessions for that were tense. Jack and Jorma were pretty wrapped up in Hot Tuna.

Long John Silver, to put it mildly, was not the favorite Airplane album of anyone involved. Still, it had its moments. Produced at Heider's by the band, it's a harder, more consistent album than *Bark*, but less whimsical and adventurous. There's a ferocity to much of it, but little that breaks new ground. The songs, for the most part, feel like outtakes from the various solo and spinoff albums everyone was making at the time.

> **GRACE SLICK:** I'm just drunk as a fart for most of it. I'm not paying attention. Jack and Jorma would much rather be off with Hot Tuna. Paul is having trouble trying to control it. Everybody was so disparate and disassociated, it was kind of pathetic.

Ironically, Grace was the major contributor of song material this time. Two of her songs, "Aerie (Gang of Eagles)" and "Easter?," were self-penned. "Milk Train" was cowritten with Papa John and Roger Spotts, while the title track, "Long John Silver," was a rare collaboration with Jack Casady. "Eat Starch Mom" was a nearly as rare Grace–Jorma composition in which, once again, Grace gets in her digs at the hippie purists who would give up the conveniences of modern life to live off the land.

Although RCA was now contractually forced into taking a hands-off position regarding the lyrical content of the Airplane's music, the label still balked at releasing the recording the Airplane ultimately turned in. RCA's newest president, it seemed, was a devout Catholic who wasn't pleased about his company putting out an album bearing back-to-back songs that criticized the Church and Catholicism. "Easter?" (originally titled "Pope Paul") was offensive enough to the new company head. But it was Paul's "The Bastard Son of Jesus" (which postulated, among other things, that "Jesus had a son by Mary Magdalene") that caused the real flap: RCA refused outright to distribute the record unless the track was removed.

RCA won a small part of the battle this time, but not the war: "The Son of Jesus" did go on the *Long John Silver* album, but the word "bastard" was removed from the title and the song, and a line sung by Paul and Grace, "So you think young Jesus never balled a lady," became instead the ridiculous "smiled a lady," the replacement word grafted from the next line in the song.

Both Paul's and Grace's new songs feel like little more than outtakes from *Sunfighter*. On Paul's "Twilight Double Leader," the usual fire is missing, almost as if he wrote the song because he felt the album needed one like it, not because he had anything new or insightful to impart. His other track, "Alexander the Medium," at least makes the effort to present itself as one of his larger-than-life epics: This time the wooden ships of escape are heading *under* the water, where life will be just as free and easy. Both Paul and Grace deliver their best singing of the record on the track, and the musicians engage in beautiful subtlety together.

Jorma's "Trial by Fire," like most of his recent work, was a song more apropos of Hot Tuna than the Airplane in its structure. Jorma's acoustic and electric guitar playing on the track are rich, and Jack burns as always.

Long John Silver would be the last new Jefferson Airplane studio album for 17 years.

27
JEFFERSON AIRPLANE FLAKES OFF

IT WAS SPEED that killed the Airplane. Speed and ice.

Watching the 1972 Winter Olympics, Jorma and Jack were in awe. It was like seeing Cream or Hendrix for the first time, only this guy was using ice skates, not a guitar. Ard Schenk was his name, he was Dutch, his sport was speed skating and he was electrifying. The next thing they knew, Jack and Jorma found themselves spending as much time speed skating as playing music—they went to Los Angeles for lessons and spent their vacation time in Wisconsin and various European locales, trying out the world-class rinks.

> **JACK CASADY:** At that time, so many people in the music business were dying from abuse or otherwise. The speed skating was mostly to say, "We're alive." I never did any sports as a kid. I had rheumatic fever and I wasn't allowed to. So the first sport that I ever encountered was skating. In a way, it's like playing an instrument: You have to have discipline, but through the discipline you can get grace and beauty.

GRACE AND PAUL HAD DECIDED they'd had enough of the country life and that it was time to get back to the city. Paul had long ago eyed a multistory house on El Camino del Mar in ritzy Sea Cliff, on the northwestern tip of San Francisco. He vowed that if it ever became available he was going to grab it. It offered a breathtaking, unobstructed view of the Golden Gate Bridge and Marin County—any vessel that sailed into San Francisco passed by the house and was plainly visible through its oversized windows. For a San Francisco lover like Paul, it was a dream home.

Just for the hell of it, Jacky Kaukonen wrote to the current occupants of the house to let them know they had a ready buyer should they ever want to sell. As it turned out the couple that owned it was divorcing and planned to put the house on the market. Paul and Grace made a deal on the half-million-dollar residence and in June they moved in, along with China, Pat Dugan and Pat's son Danny. For a while, Paul and Grace's flirtation with a less stressful home life remained the order of the day. But soon enough Grace was keeping herself amused by befriending the black militants who kept the house next door as a headquarters.

Long John Silver was released in the summer of '72—six months after its expected delivery date. The record came in a package that would, only a few years ago, have given the RCA executives a massive coronary but now barely raised an eyebrow: The album cover converted into a marijuana stash box, and just in case the buyer had no dope to place in the assembled container, the inside of the fold-open jacket revealed a full-sized photograph of some mighty fine buds, so at least the box would *look* filled. In August, *Long John Silver* became the Airplane's tenth album to chart in *Billboard*, ultimately peaking at number 20 and earning another gold record for the band.

The critics came forth with their now standard guarded evaluations. Lester Bangs, in *Rolling Stone*, admitted that the record "mostly consists of one churning vat of fury after another," then went on to complain that "the fury has gotten so predictable as to drive you to the heights of frenzied indifference."

When the Airplane went back on tour to support the new album, they not only had new drummer Barbata in tow, but another new member as well. Ever since Marty had left, Grace missed having a strong male voice to bounce off, and she and Paul believed that David Freiberg could fill that hole. Freiberg had left Quicksilver and was coproducing Dead drummer Mickey Hart's solo album, *Rolling Thunder*. Freiberg suggested using Paul and Grace for vocal harmonies on one track, "Blind John," and when the couple came in to record their parts the idea of drafting Freiberg came up. The Airplane became a seven-piece band.

Born in Boston in 1938, David Freiberg later moved with his family to Ohio, where he studied violin and viola. After a few years of college, he asked himself what he was doing there, couldn't come up with a convincing answer, dropped out, got married and, in 1959, moved to California. When his wife ran out on him, the forlorn Freiberg took up the guitar and fell in love with folk music. In the early '60s, he teamed up with a woman named Michaela Cerreti and billing themselves, appropriately enough, as David and Michaela, they never hurt for work. But he was a doper and she was not, and in those days that equaled incompatibility. Freiberg performed solo for a while as David Landau, but after the Beatles arrived Freiberg saw the writing on the coffeehouse wall: his folkie days were numbered.

Throughout the next eight years, Freiberg and Kantner saw each other often, as their respective bands rose to the top of the San Francisco rock pile. But it wasn't until both of those bands were winding down that the two old friends ended up in the same one. The Airplane's 1972 tour began in Hartford, then took them to Long Island's Roosevelt Raceway, for a benefit show called the Festival of Hope. There, when police wearing riot helmets approached the stage near the end of the band's set, Grace went into a boil: "What is this, Auschwitz?!" she screamed as she left the stage.

Next stop was the Bronx. As it began to rain that hot summer afternoon in Gaelic Park, a young woman from the audience found her way to the microphone and implored the other females to remove their tops—maybe they could make the rain stop if they did, she theorized. Grace Slick shrugged, pulled hers off and stood there baring all while sucking on a lollipop, enjoying the impromptu shower and giving the photographers in the audience one of their most saleable shots of the summer.

The next day, the band played another free show in Central Park, attracting at least 50,000 people. But it wasn't until the Rubber Bowl in Akron, Ohio, that the Airplane was reminded of who they used to be. The vital statistics show that 26 people were arrested before it was all over, among them Paul Kantner, Grace Slick and Jack's brother Chick, the Airplane's equipment manager.

The problems began when fans seated on a hill outside of the Bowl threw rocks at police, injuring five officers and damaging seven police cars, according to news reports. The police moved in to make arrests and used tear gas in an attempt to calm things down. The gas wafted into the Bowl itself, affecting the paying audience and, of course, the Airplane and their crew. When word of the police action outside reached the band, Chick Casady was alleged to have urged the audience to attack "the pigs." Approximately eight cops descended upon Casady, charged him with disorderly conduct and abusing the police, and locked him in a basement room, where 15 or 20 of the others who'd been arrested were being held.

When Grace saw her band's quippie being carted off, she went into full Grace mode. According to the arresting officer, she yanked at his whistle, clawed at his face and took a swing at him. The policeman, according to Airplane sources, retaliated by grabbing Grace in a headlock and popping her one in the face. Before the scuffle was over, Grace was also arrested, well on her way toward sporting a new black eye. Amazingly, the Akron incident was Grace's first time in jail. Paul, not one to run in the other direction while his woman was being attacked, tackled the cop who was giving Grace a hard time, and was soon on the floor surrounded by cops as well.

The band canceled the following night's gig in Detroit but made it to the Chicago Auditorium Theatre a few nights later, where they were set to record the shows for a live album. "Show us your chastity belt!" someone else in the audience shouted. "What chastity belt?" Grace retorted. "I don't even wear underpants." She then hiked her skirt up to her chest to prove she wasn't kidding.

The handful of September shows that followed weren't quite as newsworthy as the August run. The shows hadn't been going well, and the band members were becoming increasingly apathetic. Their onstage chemistry was nil and their interpersonal relationships had passed the point of strain. But still, there was no reason at the time to believe that the two nights they played at Winterland, September 21 and 22, would hold any great significance. It was only later that history would note them as the final Jefferson Airplane concerts.

GENESIS

JEFFERSON AIRPLANE NEVER BROKE UP.

There was no farewell tour, no press conference or tear-filled announcement, no vicious mud-slinging in the press. They just went along on their merry way, until one day they noticed they were no more. Following the final Airplane gigs, Jorma and Jack spent the rest of the year touring with Hot Tuna, then took off to Europe to speed skate.

> **JORMA KAUKONEN:** I wasn't really good at closure in those days. I just breathed a sigh of relief and went off with Hot Tuna.

It was time for Jefferson Airplane to touch down. The city that had birthed them had changed—the Haight was a shambles, a ghost town populated by hard-drug burnouts, charlatans and opportunists. Many of the musicians had changed too—not necessarily for the better. The same could be said for the audience, which had once found peers in groups like the Airplane and had now traded in its idealism and activism for apathy, cynicism and defeatism. Many of the young people who had been on the front lines in the '60s lost interest in political involvement and true exploration, while holding on to other trappings of the counterculture—the rock music, the drugs, long hair.

Just a short time ago it seemed that rock's icons would really change the world. Now they were losing their edge, giving up or dying off, one by one: Jim Morrison was gone, found sprawled in a Paris bathtub in July '71, a victim of his own excesses at 27. The Dead's Pigpen, the Allman Brothers' Duane Allman and Berry Oakley, Mama Cass, Gram Parsons and Clarence White of the Byrds, Canned Heat's Al Wilson, Phil Ochs, Keith Moon, Elvis and, of course, Jimi and Janis—all of them died in the '70s, each death another slap in the face of rock and roll.

Some artists who survived were as good as dead to the rock scene, so ineffectual had their music become by the '70s. Meanwhile, although some offshoots of '60s musical styles (southern rock, country rock and progressive rock) took off, other genres like glam and the first rumblings of disco announced that the next generation was rejecting outright what the '60s had offered.

The new, younger fans of popular music were more interested in style and escapism than in intellectual content or a serious commitment to complex musical ideas. The best-seller charts were littered with lightweight confections. Reflective singer-songwriters captivated many shell-shocked rock fans looking for some peace and quiet after years caught up in the frenzy. It was a time for both healing and for moving on. As the '70s dawned, Simon and Garfunkel offered to build a "Bridge Over Troubled Water," but John Lennon put his fist down and mourned, "The dream is over." Only in the area of black popular music did social commentary still sell; some of the greatest of '60s soul artists, Curtis Mayfield, James Brown and Marvin Gaye among them, graduated easily to the new funk styles and spoke their minds openly in their music, finding an audience quite willing to listen.

In the political arena itself, many of the counterculture's leaders lost their platform or became disillusioned; the strength of the movement had undeniably dissipated. Some radicals gave up the fight altogether. Others became less outspoken or compromised, trying now to work within the system rather than bring it down. Those who still had something incendiary to say were often silenced: Abbie Hoffman, busted for drugs, disappeared into the underground; Timothy Leary, also convicted on drug charges, went to jail, then escaped; John Lennon, who had become an outspoken militant, was hounded by the FBI after settling in New York; a number of the Black Panthers were murdered in cold blood by the authorities.

Some '60s refugees took the position that change could take place only within oneself; they went the self-awareness route, setting the scene for the New Age movement (and, taken to extremes, the proliferation of cults). They adhered to various spiritual paths or headed for communes far from the cities, retreating from the chaos of the '60s to seek answers through other means. In some ways, the era of self-expression was yielding to one of self-indulgence.

Then there were those who retreated back into the straight world they'd once fought so hard to escape, taking jobs they once criticized their elders for holding. Many, however, took elements of what they'd learned and experienced during the '60s and integrated them into their communities and personal lives. Some of the ideals and ideas that had staying power—feminism, gay rights, environmental and health concerns, human and civil rights, the antinuclear movement—had their roots in '60s activism and were then absorbed into the mainstream.

With time, some of what had seemed so threatening just a few years earlier was coopted and institutionalized; even some of the cops who'd had such a good time bashing longhairs with billy clubs were now growing their own hair long. And everyone, it seemed, smoked marijuana—even future national leaders.

Most important, though, was that antiwar sentiment remained strong. Being opposed to the Vietnam War had long since ceased being an unpopular position. Rallies continued to draw massive crowds—an estimated 350,000 marched in D.C. and San Francisco in April 1971. Many of the marchers were now themselves Vietnam veterans, protesting the continuation of a conflict they knew firsthand was not only unwinnable but wrong.

Concurrent with the continuing protests, the Nixon administration found itself red-faced and tongue-tied after *The New York Times* published the first installment of what it called the Pentagon Papers, a document that proved the U.S. government had been lying to the public for decades about the extent of its role in Vietnam. But the more celebrated breach of public trust occurred in 1972, when a break-in was discovered at the headquarters of the Democratic National Committee at the Watergate complex in Washington, D.C. Few people in America, Nixon included, could possibly have understood at the time the significance of the burglary. But Richard Nixon's demise began that day.

WHEN JORMA AND JACK FINALLY RETURNED from their skating vacations in early '73, there was an attempt on the part of some of the others to lure them back—David Freiberg even took up speed skating so he'd have something in common with them—but it was halfhearted. Still, despite their withdrawal from the Airplane, both Jorma and Jack were happy to oblige with contributions when Paul and Grace began their next album. The record was credited not just to the two of them this time, but to

Freiberg as well. It took on the mysterious title *Baron von Tollbooth & the Chrome Nun*.

> **GRACE SLICK:** That was David Crosby's name for both of us. The gag name for Paul was Baron von Tollbooth, because of the World War One fighter, Baron von Richtoven. Paul is very German. He stands up very straight and he likes organization. I'm the Chrome Nun. She's modern, she's shiny, she's also very protective of herself—it's like having a suit of armor on. Nuns don't fool around. I don't know where the Tollbooth came from; that's just Crosby.

Less popular sales-wise than *Blows Against the Empire* or *Sunfighter*, *Baron von Tollbooth*, like its two forebears, included an impressive cast of characters, among them the whiz kid from Steelwind, Craig Chaquico. *Baron von Tollbooth* also contained more than its fair share of commendable songs. Kantner's "Your Mind Has Left Your Body," with Garcia on pedal steel guitar, Mickey Hart playing gongs and water phones, Jorma and Jack contributing guitar and bass, John Barbata on drums, Slick and Freiberg handling keyboards and Paul providing the 12-string guitar work, is a masterpiece of this transitional period.

"Across the Board," which features a roaring vocal by Grace, was a song she later performed in concert. One particular stanza of the song stands out:

> *Seven inches of pleasure*
> *Seven inches going home*
> *Somebody must have measured*
> *All the way down the old bone.*

> **GRACE SLICK:** I was trying to gross out the record company or something. It's just an amusing thing on sex. I was being my usual friendly self.

The only other Grunt release of note during 1973 was *Thirty Seconds Over Winterland*, the live Jefferson Airplane album compiled from tracks recorded at the Chicago and Winterland shows at the end of the band's run. Featuring the final lineup of Kantner, Slick, Kaukonen, Casady, Creach, Freiberg and Barbata, it's an unexceptional set in comparison to, say, *Bless Its Pointed Little Head*, four years earlier, but a representative sampling of the highlights of the final Airplane tour.

Jorma and Jack are particularly steaming during the entire 11-minute length of "Feel So Good," and studio creations such as "Have You Seen the Saucers," "Trial by Fire," "When the Earth Moves Again" and "Twilight Double Leader" make the transition easily to the live format. Bruce Steinberg's cover art depicts seven flying toasters, each embedded with a clock showing a different time, apropos for a band whose members no longer gave each other the time of day.

With the Airplane in limbo, Hot Tuna found themselves playing somewhere virtually every month of the year during 1973. The shows were now marathons, often lasting three or more hours, with the full band, or just Jorma and Jack playing acoustically, running through nearly every song from their three albums, extending many of them into double-digit-minute jams.

While in Europe early in the year, Jorma had written prolifically. A few of his new, unrecorded songs, like "Genesis" and "Flying Clouds," began seeping into Hot Tuna's set list. But although the band performed these songs in concert, they ended up not on the next Tuna album but on *Quah*, the first Jorma Kaukonen solo album.

The initial concept for *Quah* was that Jorma would record one side of the album and an old guitar-playing friend, Tom Hobson, the other. A version was actually completed that way in mid-1973 and presented to RCA, which complained that the Hobson tracks were too quirky and not fit for release. Jorma ultimately kept one track that Hobson both wrote and sang, "Sweet Hawaiian Sunshine," and another, Gordon Jenkins's "Blue Prelude," that features a Hobson vocal. But most fans consider *Quah*, which was released in its revised form in 1974, to be pure Jorma.

An all-acoustic album, with surprising, lovely strings garnishing a couple of tracks, it's closest in style and spirit to the first Hot Tuna album. There are a couple of Reverend Gary Davis tracks Jorma hadn't yet recorded, "I am the Light of This World" and "I'll Be All Right," but the bulk of the album consisted of new Kaukonen originals. "Genesis," which leads off the album, remains, as does much of the record, in Jorma's repertoire decades later.

JORMA KAUKONEN: In 1973, I was writing a lot of songs about true love almost gone wrong but saved at the last moment. Some people have suggested that it would be nice if you could write songs like "Genesis" all the time, and I always say, "Yeah, it would be, but it would be great not to have to be in the place I was when I wrote it."

Quah—its title suggested itself when the Dead's Mickey Hart karate-chopped a pile of bricks and made that sound—stands on its own as a shining example of an artist blossoming, a fine showcase for Jorma's superb fingerpicking and mature, soul-stirring vocals. Jack is credited with the album's production (although Mallory Earl was also involved), and the cover art is by Margareta. It is one of the most fully realized and durable recordings in the entire Airplane-related canon.

Between the spring and summer of 1973, during the same general period that Jorma was making *Quah*, Hot Tuna was also working at Wally Heider's on their next album, *The Phosphorescent Rat*. Their second studio recording, it marked the group's genuine emergence as a stand-alone creative unit—Jorma composed nine of the 10 songs on the album this time. The album brought Hot Tuna down to trio size with the departure of Papa John. He had been working overtime, playing not just with Tuna but with his own band, Zulu (which introduced a young guitarist, Kevin Moore, who would later emerge as a major blues star under the name Keb' Mo'). Creach had already recorded a second album on Grunt, *Filthy*, and was starting a third, *Playing My Fiddle for You*—he was still considered very much a part of the extended family but Jorma wanted to take Hot Tuna in a more electrified rock direction.

JORMA KAUKONEN: We're down to the nucleus here. This was when we got so obnoxious nobody else could stand us. We're talking rock and roll here.

Released at the same time as *Rat* was one of the more ambitious records to bear the Grunt logo, Grace Slick's first solo album, *Manhole*. Recorded at Heider's, the record featured the same team that had assembled *Baron von Tollbooth*, Grace, Paul and David Freiberg, with, in the PERRO spirit, a cast of thousands helping out. Keith Grant and Steve Schuster coproduced, and Schuster also created the orchestral arrangements on two of the album's showpiece tracks, Grace's "Theme from the Movie 'Manhole'" and the Kantner-written "Epic (#38)," which also includes some lyrical input from Grace and Traylor.

Grace, who painted a self-portrait for the cover, showing off her new, curly hairstyle, named the album *Manhole*, in her typical fashion, to push some buttons.

GRACE SLICK: Women were badgering me about women's liberation, so I was being very sarcastic and just calling myself a cunt. Manhole. I assumed people would understand it and nobody did. It's not that I don't like myself. This is a comedy.

"Theme from the Movie 'Manhole' " begs the question whether there ever was a movie called *Manhole* to accompany the album. The answer is no, but Grace conceived it as such, a grand work that would combine her two greatest musical loves, Spanish music and orchestration.

Grace went all out for the track, utilizing the talents of Paul, Freiberg and Crosby on vocals, Chaquico on lead guitar, Peter Kaukonen on mandolin, Freiberg on rhythm guitar, bass by both Jack and the great jazz player Ron Carter and her own piano, along with a roomful of violins, cellos, oboes and the rest. When she decided she wanted an orchestra, she flew the production team to England to record the London Symphony Orchestra there. "Better Lying Down," at the other extreme, is just Grace and Pete Sears, who wrote the music and plays a wicked barrelhouse blues piano, the only straight blues Grace ever wrote.

Paul's "Epic (#38)" closes *Manhole*, another extravaganza adding orchestra (and a line of bagpipes!) to the basic lineup. The latest in a long line of Kantner invocations for the world to come together and practice love, the song, which begins with a paraphrase from Rudyard Kipling, winds its way through several tempo and textural changes before fading off into a barrage of Chaquico guitar blasts.

They sounded good together, this group of musicians, and they enjoyed playing with one another. Maybe they didn't need to wait for Jorma and Jack after all.

29
HYPERDRIVE

PAUL KANTNER WAS READY to play live music again. In all of 1973, he had not once stepped out on a stage with guitar in hand. He missed it. Paul didn't get the same satisfaction in the studio that he got playing for an audience.

> **PAUL KANTNER:** The nature of those times was to experiment, and the nature of experiments is that most of them fail. Most of the music that we put on record was an abject failure to us as musicians. The recording was a pale, two-dimensional photograph of a three-dimensional reality.

Grace didn't miss performing, at least not as much as Paul did. Those last few years with the Airplane hadn't been the best of times. But she was ready for a change of scenery.

> **GRACE SLICK:** Paul was moved to have a group. I said, cool, if you want to organize it, I'll do that.

Thompson had been pushing Paul and Grace for some time to start a new band. Grunt was losing money by the bucketful—*Manhole*, which had taken six months and a fortune to record, had only hit a disappointing number 127—and RCA was not pleased. With little fanfare or forethought, a new entity quickly materialized: Paul, Grace and Freiberg would be its core, the singers and writers. Freiberg would play keyboards and sometimes bass, Paul rhythm guitar. John Barbata stayed on as the drummer. Papa John readily agreed to sign up. Paul asked Peter Kaukonen to play bass and occasionally double on guitar with the seventh member of the new team, Craig Chaquico. Bill Thompson, who was already managing Hot Tuna and Creach's Zulu, was retained to keep the business straight.

With the decision now made to regroup, the next order of business was to come up with a name. Paul and Grace initially insisted on something completely unrelated to Jefferson Airplane, hoping to instill in the fans the idea that this was a new start, not a continuation from where the Airplane had left off. But they ultimately agreed with Thompson that maintaining the connection made good business sense, and Paul christened the new band Jefferson Starship, swiped from the album cover of *Blows Against the Empire*. By January of 1974, they were in rehearsals for their first tour.

Nearly 15 years the junior of the band's leaders and almost 40 years younger than Papa John, Craig Clinton Chaquico was originally from Sacramento. Both of his parents were native Californians of Portuguese descent. Bill Chaquico had owned a dairy farm and later his own upholstery business, while Muriel worked for California's Department of Corrections Parole Division. Craig, born in 1954, was their second son, following his brother Howard by a dozen years.

Craig began playing guitar when he was 10, but two years later he was involved in a serious car accident, breaking several bones and falling into a coma for three days. Both of Craig's hands were in casts and his little finger could reach only one string, but when he came to, the first thing he asked for was a guitar. To give his son incentive while undergoing physical therapy, Craig's father told him that the great jazz guitarist and electronics innovator Les Paul had also wrecked his hand and survived professionally. If Craig would hang in there, Bill Chaquico said, he'd buy him a Gibson Les Paul guitar when it was over.

Craig's father kept his word, and the boy practiced constantly. As he got older he discovered rock and roll—Hendrix, Clapton, Jeff Beck, the Stones and the San Francisco bands. Some time after his release from the hospital, Chaquico formed his first band, Duck Soup, and by the time he hit 14 he was proficient enough for Jack Traylor to ask Craig to join his band. Before long Traylor brought his young charge down to San Francisco to meet Kantner. Craig was still in high school when he made his recording debut on *Sunfighter.*

CRAIG CHAQUICO: I thought, Man, I'll be famous. But the record came out and even though my name was on it I still had to ride my bicycle to school. Then one of the reviews came out and it said,

> "Craig Chaquico is obviously a pseudonym for someone like Carlos Santana or Clapton, who can't use his real name."

Traylor's band, which took the name Steelwind, was still going in 1973. Kantner signed them to Grunt, and they released their sole album, *Child of Nature*, produced by the Airplane's former studio mentor, Al Schmitt. Craig, his stick-straight black hair already falling past his shoulders, adolescent peach fuzz trying to become a mustache, is pictured on the back album cover, and also receives credit for cowriting the final track, "Caveat Emptor."

Jefferson Starship rehearsed daily in early 1974, played a dress rehearsal at San Francisco's Kabuki Theater, and on March 19 opened the tour at the Chicago Auditorium—the site of one of the final Airplane gigs. Performing a minimum of Airplane songs, they stuck largely to material from the solo albums. The band went over well, most audiences understanding that this was not the Airplane they were seeing and accepting the new configuration happily.

CRAIG CHAQUICO: The first show we did in Chicago, I stepped in the front of the stage to do a solo, and I hear, "Where's Jorma?!" And this huge bottle of red wine busted on the stage right in front of me. I thought, What have I gotten myself into?

Chaquico was kept especially busy during that first outing, doing double time by opening the shows with Steelwind. To be closer to the center of the action, Craig moved into 2400 Fulton. He was in for the long haul, and a long haul it would be.

To wrap up the first tour, which first hit cities in the Midwest and on the East Coast, the Starship came home to San Francisco in April to play Winterland. It had been a year and a half since Jefferson Airplane's last gig. The *San Francisco Chronicle* treated the homecoming as a major event. Reviewer Joel Selvin praised the band's performance overall and singled Craig out, saying, "Chaquico is easily the best thing about Starship. His guitar sings . . . Chaquico drives and rails his six strings, stylishly shifting tones, colors, shading with electronics. His feeling is unerring and the bountiful solos he provided were by far the most rewarding aspect of the performance."

Media coverage throughout the tour was plentiful. Even mainstream TV jumped at the chance to cover the rock event—Grace was interviewed by television personality Geraldo Rivera, telling him she would have "blonde hair and big boobs" if she could do it all over.

Before the new aggregation entered the studio to cut its first album, though, Paul and Grace needed to make one more change: Peter Kaukonen was out. As the group already had two guitarists, and Freiberg was capable of playing keyboards and bass, the natural replacement for Kaukonen was Pete Sears. He could also play both keyboards and bass, so he could switch off with Freiberg. Plus, he wrote. The offer came at a great time for the British Sears, who had fallen in love with the Bay Area and wanted to stay there.

Peter Roy Sears was born in 1948 in Bromley, Kent, a suburb of London. The second child of Leslie and Jane Sears, he began taking piano lessons at eight and playing guitar at 13. He joined his first semiprofessional bands, the Strangers and the Spitfires, in 1963, playing skiffle music and rock and roll in the styles of Elvis and Britain's Shadows, with a little Beatles thrown in. During that time Pete's brother John turned him on to jazz, R&B and the blues, and Pete scrapped his plans to go to art college. In 1964 he joined his first professional band, the Sons of Fred, playing bass. The group recorded a few singles for the Parlophone and Columbia labels, and appeared on hit British TV programs like *Thank Your Lucky Stars* and *Ready Steady Go!*

Some time in 1966, Sears, back to playing piano, joined Fleur de Lys, a British psychedelic group. Although the band never racked up any commercial hits, some of their recordings are now considered highly collectible because they were produced by soon-to-be rock legend Jimmy Page. They also recorded a cover of the Impressions' song "Amen," with a pre-Experience Jimi Hendrix providing the guitar, but the recording was never released and no copies of the tape appear to remain in existence. Sears next hooked up with Mick Hutchinson, the Sons of Fred's guitarist, and together they went to a new band called the Sam Gopal Dream, Gopal being an Indian tabla player. They played psychedelic Indian music and were a favorite at such trendy London clubs as Happening 44, Alexandra Palace and the Electric Garden.

During the late '60s, Sears played and recorded with several bands, including one in Los Angeles called Silver Metre that also included Leigh Stephens of the San Francisco hard rock outfit Blue Cheer. Sears then settled in San Francisco, where he joined Stoneground, a funk-rock group formed around the vocals of former Beau Brummels singer Sal Valentino. Sears appeared on their first album and quickly began to build his reputation around the Bay Area.

An opportunity to play with Rod Stewart took him back to England, and Sears ultimately appeared on four of Stewart's classic 1970s albums—*Gasoline Alley, Every Picture Tells a Story, Never a Dull Moment* and *Smiler*—virtually commuting between England and San Francisco whenever Stewart summoned him. In 1971 Sears started a new band with ex-Quicksilver guitarist John Cipollina, Copperhead, but Pete had exited by the time they recorded their sole album for Columbia. It was at Cipollina's home during the Copperhead period that Pete met his future wife, Jeannette Louise Dilger. During that period he also learned to fly antique aerobatic open cockpit aircraft, a passion that he held onto for many years.

While Sears was coproducing, arranging and playing on Kathi Mc-Donald's critically acclaimed *Insane Asylum* album, David Freiberg introduced him to Grace Slick. Pete and Grace worked up "Better Lying Down" for her *Manhole* album and he first discussed with her and Paul the possibility of joining the new band they were assembling. He signed on in June of '74.

Now they needed to get some product out. RCA had taken up the slack in early '74 by issuing a collection of previously unreleased Airplane tracks, *Early Flight*. More than half of the material came from 1965–66, leftover studio recordings like "High Flyin' Bird," the uncensored "Runnin' 'Round This World" and Skip Spence's "J.P.P. McStep Blues." The Airplane's recording of Peter Kaukonen's "Up or Down," along with both sides of the "Mexico"/"Have You Seen the Saucers" single, rounded it out. But what fans wanted was the new group. By July, Jefferson Starship had commenced recording their first album, *Dragon Fly*. Back in the familiar setting of Wally Heider's and armed with a handful of new songs, they began the uncertain process of creating a new entity.

To ensure that the band get a fresh start, they brought in independent producer/engineer Larry Cox, a Texan who had worked previously with artists as diverse as Bing Crosby and Tiny Tim and, long before that, had once played drums with Buddy Holly. Cox had been an engineer for Wally Heider and in 1972 had produced the hit single by Climax, "Precious and Few." Maurice suggested using Cox when the Starship went searching for a new producer, but at first Cox was reticent, unimpressed with the band in concert. A friend convinced him to rise to the challenge, but Cox had yet to put his autograph on the contract when Grace confronted him, nearly scaring off their potential new producer.

LARRY COX: She started in on me, "Who the hell do you think you are?!" I was in shock because I'd never had anybody talk to me like that.

Cox soon learned how to play Grace—just walk out of the room when she got like that—and he learned how to contend with Paul's obstinacy. They quickly got down to work, recording "Come to Life," cowritten by Freiberg and Steve Schuster, with words by Grateful Dead lyricist Robert Hunter, and "That's for Sure," with music by Craig and words by Jerry Gallup. As the band and producer became accustomed to one another's ways, they established a rapport in the studio. "Hyperdrive," a Slick–Sears collaboration, followed, one of the album's high points.

From the first sessions, it became apparent that the music they were making was only peripherally like the Airplane's, which was how they wanted it. Although most of the participants were holdovers from the old band, they all made a concerted effort to graduate to something new. There was little attempt to be political or salacious in the lyrics, and nothing overly cryptic.

Musically, the bluesy, improvisational tendencies of Jorma and Jack were replaced by tighter, more accessible pop-oriented arrangements. Chaquico's approach to playing was nothing like Jorma's, more in touch with current developments in '70s rock while avoiding the clichés of the heavy metal and glam guitar styles of the day. Even at his most blistering, Craig never lost sight of the melodic structure, and in the quieter songs he could be endearingly mellifluous. Neither Sears nor Freiberg approached the bass the way Jack did, and keyboards played a much greater role in this band.

"Devil's Den," a joint Creach–Slick effort, and "All Fly Away," an outside contribution by folksinger/songwriter Tom Pacheco, were among the next tracks cut. So was "Be Young You," by Grace. Its title is a tribute to Byong Yu, Grace and Paul's Tae Kwon Do teacher, who also turns up alongside the couple as one of the credited authors of "Ride the Tiger," the album's leadoff track.

"Ride the Tiger" is quintessential early Jefferson Starship, a kinetic rocker that displays some of the most impassioned singing from Paul and Grace in years and explosive guitar work from Chaquico. The Starship opened their shows with it for quite some time.

Wrote Paul in a commentary on the song, "Byong Yu gave us the reflection on the differences between Asian and Western cultures . . . Grace was responsible for the lyrics: 'Black wants out of the streets/ Yellow wants the country/Red wants the country back.' And I added, naturally: 'White wants out of this world.' "

In one of its signature lines, Kantner plays psychic, predicting, "Look to the summer of '75, all the world is gonna come alive."

THERE WAS STILL ONE MORE SONG that Paul wanted to get on the album. He'd had the music for some time, but it needed words. Paul visualized it as a love song, and no one wrote words for love songs like Marty Balin. Paul picked up the phone and called him.

Marty had been hearing from others about Paul and Grace's new band. It wasn't the same without him, people kept telling him. Enough time had passed, Marty felt when Paul Kantner asked him to write some lyrics; maybe things had changed. Sure, he told Paul, he'd help him out with the song. He'd even sing it.

"Caroline," their collaboration, is a gem, a heart-on-your-sleeve, bare-emotions thriller. It dances from one tempo to the next seamlessly, cuddles close and lets you know it cares. But unlike most of the treacle that passes for romantic music, "Caroline," which Marty sang in one of the most heart-wrenching performances of his career, is sincere in the way true love should be:

> *It's like a wind from the other side of the world*
> *Like a far-off pack of hounds*
> *Sound like a whole universe—throbbin' with life*
> *I get so hypnotized in the lights*
> *Just like the gaze of a mantis*

Why even Atlantis sank beneath the waves in a day and a night
Oh, in a day and a night I could write you a symphony
It would be just like a bird and carry my love over the mountains.

When *Dragon Fly* was released in September of 1974, some critics didn't quite know what to make of the album. *Rolling Stone*'s Bud Scoppa called Paul and Grace "unknowing self-parodists" and the album "at worst listenable and at best surprisingly engaging." But the Airplane's old audience welcomed it, as did a new crop of younger fans who'd perhaps become familiar with the legend through records and word of mouth but had never had the opportunity to experience the Airplane firsthand. Marty's participation and an all-out effort by RCA's promotion department turned the album into an event, and it took off to number 11 on the charts, the single of "Ride the Tiger" making it to number 84. "Caroline," strangely, didn't chart at all when it was released as the follow-up single.

Demand was high for more concerts, and in October the Starship headed out for the second time, playing cities like St. Louis, Cleveland and Boston before heading to New York for a triumphant run at Radio City Music Hall. *Rolling Stone* reviewed the October 16 show there positively, writer Ian Dove commenting, "The former rambling incoherencies in performance are now confined only to Slick's Dada-esque introductions to the material. Somebody has seen to it that the Starship is presented properly; individual members are allowed a share of spotlight."

Still performing no more than two or three Airplane songs per show—"Wooden Ships," "Volunteers" and "Somebody to Love," but not even "White Rabbit"—the Starship began tucking in songs from the new album, with Freiberg handling the vocals on "Caroline."

But when they came home to Winterland, there was no need for a substitute. On November 24, much to the surprise and glee of the hometown crowd, following a winning performance of the suite from *Blows Against the Empire*, Marty ambled out onstage. "I'm supposed to do a song called 'Caroline' that Paul and I wrote. And then they'll feed me," he said, proving to San Francisco that he had lost none of his soul or charisma. Marty sang as if he'd never left, following up the new tune by reprising his parts in "Somebody to Love" and "Volunteers." Marty had to admit that the applause felt good. He had missed it.

SAMMY PIAZZA KNEW that his time was coming soon, and maybe it was just as well. Things had been getting weirder. He'd been living at 2400 Fulton with his wife, Annie, throughout much of his tenure in Hot Tuna and it had become a three-ring circus. One time Sammy discovered that an intruder had entered the house by climbing the scaffolding being used by house painters, and was now lying on top of Annie. Sammy kept a gun in the room and he went for it. He pointed it at the man's head, marched him down the stairs and sent him scampering into Golden Gate Park. On another occasion, Annie went downstairs to make some coffee and found a dozen uninvited guests, all naked, sitting on the floor doing yoga. Sammy again went for his firearm and persuaded them to leave.

By the end of 1973, though, Sammy could feel the axe falling. On the eve of a Hot Tuna tour Jorma suddenly stopped returning his calls. Thompson was left with the task of firing the drummer. Sammy went to play with Stoneground after his dismissal. Jorma and Jack, meanwhile, played acoustically the first half of the year, and in the summer began searching for a new drummer. They found him in Bob Steeler, an acquaintance of Jack's younger brother Michael Casady, who'd been working as a roadie with Tuna.

Steeler—previous spelling Stuhler—was originally from Westfield, New Jersey, where he'd once played with a garage band with the intriguing moniker of the Driving Stupid. While working in Manhattan with Sam Andrew of Big Brother and the Holding Company, Steeler was heard by Kathi McDonald, who convinced him to go out to California with her to assemble a band. That didn't work out but by 1974 Jorma got word of Steeler's abilities and thought he might be right for the direction in which he wanted to take Hot Tuna.

Thus began the Tuna era that fans sometimes refer to as the "metal years," or the "rampage years." They became unquestionably harder and louder, playing through stacks of amps cranked up to maximum volume, even more furiously than before—this was not a band for the weak of heart.

BOB STEELER: Jorma would go, "Man, my fingers are killing me. I don't know if I'm going to be able to make it tonight." Then we'd go play for six hours.

Steeler began playing with Hot Tuna in July of 1974. After a series of gigs, they recorded the next Hot Tuna album, *America's Choice*. There were eight songs, produced by the band and Mallory Earl, who also engineered. All of the material was written by Jorma with the exception of "Walking Blues," the Robert Johnson blues standard, and "Funky #7," which Jorma cowrote with Jack. With Hot Tuna now into its fifth year, Jorma had become downright prolific. Some of his songs now confronted darker issues, as a way to come to terms with some of his own fears and weaknesses.

JORMA KAUKONEN: I think I'm happier than some of those songs are, but I like melancholy stuff. I like sniveling, I really do. Sometimes it just feels right to be miserable.

A few of the songs on *America's Choice* have remained crowd pleasers throughout the years. "Hit Single #1" was so named, Jorma recalls, because he honestly believed it had the makings of one, and for a while the TV music program *Don Kirshner's Rock Concert*, which had had Hot Tuna as a guest, used part of the recording as a trailer as the ending credits rolled.

America's Choice was released in the spring of '75 with an RCA-designed pop-art cover that resembles a detergent box. A notation on the front informs, "This album to be played at full volume for maximum effect."

In concert, Tuna continued to play marathon shows, and by the mid-'70s their audience was arguably more rabid than the Airplane's had been. The cry of "Hot fuckin' Tuna!" greeted the band at every stop, where often they would find the same fans they'd seen at the last show.

As 1975 dawned, Jorma decided to take on a second guitarist, Greg Douglass, an East Bay musician who had worked with a number of local bands. Douglass joined Hot Tuna for several months, but ultimately Jorma decided the dueling guitars concept wasn't for him, and Douglass was gone by the time Tuna began their next album, *Yellow Fever*, also released in 1975.

That record retained the same basic team used on *America's Choice*. RCA designed the cover again and even came up with the album's title. Jorma wrote most of the songs, the only exceptions being the two lead-off tracks, Jimmy Reed's "Baby, What You Want Me to Do," which Jorma had been playing since he first picked up an electric guitar, and "Hot Jelly Roll Blues," a song written by Atlantan George Carter circa 1930.

The first half of the record includes a standout track from this period, "Sunrise Dance with the Devil," but the album really comes alive during its second half. "Bar Room Crystal Ball," overrun by ominous, sludgy guitar, is one that Jorma describes as "a great alcoholic moment-of-clarity song."

As impressive as *Yellow Fever* and the other Tuna albums from this era might have been, most of the group's devoted followers did not get their main dose of the band on vinyl, but in concert. In performance a song that is clipped at four or five minutes on a record might go double or triple that length. A set of 20 to 25 songs, each extended by way of lengthy jams, added up, and both audience and band were spent by the end of a show, which might come four or more hours later.

IT WASN'T EASY for Marty to come to the decision to join Jefferson Starship as a permanent member. He knew Grace and Paul all too well, and he was understandably hesitant to go back to that place. He still harbored resentment, and although half of the problem—Jorma and Jack—was gone, the other half was still there. Marty recalled how alienated he had felt when he'd left the Airplane. Did he really want to subject himself to those emotions again?

But maybe, he thought, they could put all that behind them and just make music together now, in a mature manner, minus the barbs and petty bickering. It wasn't the '60s anymore, it was a new world, and it would be great if they could all find their place in it, be as vital to the people as they had been before.

They just had to figure out what that place might be. Certainly, they all knew, the state of the nation was no longer what it had been when the Airplane had flourished—no one wanted to listen to music that ranted and raved anymore, Marty included. So much of what had fueled the Airplane in the '60s was no longer an issue. Nixon's government had brought itself down with his 1974 resignation, without the aid of any violent revolution to push it over the edge. For most young Americans, politics and world events had become a minor, distant concern, and a bore. They'd had enough of that. This was a period of retreat. The big event on campus was no longer the antiwar demonstration but streaking, a fad that involved nothing more than running naked in public. Perhaps there was little else left for the '70s generation to do.

Pop music had, many '60s denizens felt, bottomed out—although there was still plenty of creativity to be found, the radio was now dominated by a mix of post-bubblegum tripe, protodisco, overblown progressive rock, overproduced mainstream rock, macho southern boogie, soppy singer-songwriters and watered-down heavy metal. With the exception of the increasingly popular Grateful Dead, a Crosby, Stills, Nash and Young reunion and Bob Dylan's comeback tour, it was almost as if the '60s had never happened. The success of *Happy Days* on TV and *American Graffiti* at the box office confirmed a nostalgia for a simpler, less stressful time. Americans were trying to forget—they wanted the '70s to be more like the '50s than the '60s.

With the end of the Vietnam War in 1975, many of the reasons for groups like Jefferson Airplane to exist were now set aside. The fight had been real, the emotions genuine. For a brief while, people had come together. Who knew if they ever would again?

> **BILL LAUDNER:** As the '70s matured, more people decided that [other] people shouldn't be allowed to do their own thing. Everybody should be required to do what everybody else does, and the world should be required to cater to the lowest common denominator rather than try to get more people further out there. That came as a shock to me.

About the only remaining high-profile evidence that there was still a radical left in America came when a disorganized, whacked-out group calling itself the Symbionese Liberation Army (SLA) kidnapped the 19-year-old newspaper heiress Patricia Hearst from her Berkeley apartment in February 1974. When Hearst later apparently joined her captors in their revolutionary struggle and took part in a bank robbery, fringe politics was big news again for a while. But most of the SLA managed to get themselves killed and, for the most part, apathy ruled the day.

Grace, for her part, was spending more of her time becoming better acquainted with the bottle and causing trouble. "About once a month there's an explosion," she told Lester Bangs of *Creem* magazine. "It's usually triggered by alcohol. I have a destructive, sarcastic, caustic mouth, and if they had a black belt for that, I've got it." Once Grace became so wild, Paul recalled, that she came after him with an Arabian scimitar. Paul threw a bedspread over her, wrested the blade away and threw it over a balcony, tying Grace up with gaffer's tape for several minutes to keep her from becoming abusive.

> **JULIA (GIRL FREIBERG) BRIGDEN:** When David was first asked to be in the band, Paul and Grace were living together and we went over to their house in the city. Paul was in bed asleep and Grace was really drunk. She starts telling David about the sexual abilities of all the band members. The gist of the whole thing was she wanted David to go to bed with her. In the meantime, she's holding this big butcher knife, and she's accentuating every point by stabbing this knife into the top of this butcher-block tabletop.

Marty had to consider whether he was prepared to deal again with Grace's indulgences. Although he too enjoyed his liquor, he was able to stay in control. If he could function, he reasoned, maybe she could too. Besides, there were other signs that perhaps his old colleagues were tearing down some walls of their own. Marty had been very surprised when Paul actually complimented him on his singing—no one in the Airplane, that he could remember, had ever done that before. Paul was even telling the press that he'd missed Marty since the day he'd left. Marty agreed to give it a try. He could always leave again; they'd always had an open-door relationship. He told Paul to make room for one more.

JEFFERSON STARSHIP BEGAN WORKING on their second album, *Red Octopus*, in February. The title was both a tribute to Communist, or "Red," China and the band's new eight-member configuration. Larry Cox and the band produced it at Heider's, with Cox also engineering. Maurice was still their production coordinator. Frank Mulvey, an artist who'd worked on some of the earlier albums, created the cover, a simple but elegant design of gold lettering on a red background, with a red heart in a gold circle in the middle, another tribute to China.

Lucky for the group that they chose the cover they did—according to Cox, one of the rejected designs had a gatefold cover which, when opened, would reveal a huge penis popping out.

The album firmly established Jefferson Starship as its own entity—there is little about its music, other than the familiar vocal blend, that suggests Jefferson Airplane.

> **PAUL KANTNER:** *Red Octopus* was one of those times where all of the elements came together. The band was charming and hot, the record company was moving and working, the PR department locked in, the single caught on, the album caught on, everybody was playing good and we were playing great places.

One of the first songs recorded for the album was a tune that Marty had been laboring over for some time, "Miracles." Inspired in part by "a girl I was in love with then" (probably Trish Robbins) and the Indian guru Satya Sai Baba, said by many of his devotees to be a man who performed miracles regularly, Marty slowly but deliberately crafted the song that many believe is his masterwork. When he presented the finished song to the band, though, Marty says, he received the same reaction he'd gotten in the past when he wrote an unabashed love song.

> **MARTY BALIN:** Everybody went, "I don't know about that, that's pretty weird, man." I was really worried; nobody liked it. But I told myself, after about five days, Maybe they're wrong.

"Miracles," with its laid-back pace and rounded-off edges, was as perfectly suited to 1975 as "Somebody to Love" had been to 1967. Cox nailed the production—there isn't a wasted, out-of-place note. Strings glisten, the keyboard sound is contemporary and Grace and Paul's harmonies are relatively traditional. Freiberg came up with the memorable signature organ riff that begins the song and Craig with a fresh supply of delicious guitar sounds. Marty is at his most open, crooning his words of love like he hasn't in years—without a hint of irony or awkwardness he uses the word "baby" at least 25 times, something for which the others would have crucified him in the old band.

> **PAUL KANTNER:** Marty has the ability to express really simple emotions that most people might be embarrassed expressing. He's able to get away with singing, "Oooh, baby," and meaning "Oooh, baby."

LARRY COX: There was an aura about Marty. Grace was in such awe of him. There was an electricity that happened between Marty and Grace. Once they start singing together, there's just something there that you don't teach or rehearse. You're just damn lucky to capture it on tape.

After *Red Octopus* was released in June, the album version of "Miracles" was edited down by Maurice and Cox from its seven-minute length to a more radio-friendly 3:25. Some of the more contentious lyrics, like "I had a taste of the real world when I went down on you, girl," were removed to protect the innocent. It rose to number 3 on the *Billboard* singles chart, out-polling everything the Airplane had ever released as a single, and helped drive the album itself to number 1, the first time the Jefferson name made it to the top. Marty's voice was finally all over the radio, just as he'd always wanted during the Airplane years.

GRACE SLICK: That was Marty's era, the Starship thing. We were coming out of the screwball topics for lyrics that were going around in the '60s and getting more into dance music and romantic love, which is Marty's forte. So he got his chance to shine.

Twenty-five years later, at the end of the twentieth century, "Miracles" still enjoyed frequent radio play, and was a recipient of BMI's (Broadcast Music Inc.) Million-Airs award, with more than two million documented airings to its credit. But, according to Marty, he still couldn't catch a break.

MARTY BALIN: It felt good that they played it. But every time they played it, they were still saying, "That's Grace Slick and Jefferson Starship." Never once did they mention my name. So, no matter what I do . . .

Although "Miracles" certainly dominated the record, *Red Octopus* boasted several other strong entries. Grace took part in composing four tracks, including the rocking album opener "Fast Buck Freddie" and the well-crafted "Play on Love," which she cowrote with Sears. Grace's songs on *Red Octopus* eschewed her usual obtuseness and evasiveness. They neither rambled in several directions nor attempted grandiosity. Like most of the other tracks on the album, hers, with the exception of "Fast Buck Freddie," are forthright ruminations on the subject of love.

And they came from the heart. Because Grace Slick had fallen in love.

30

TUNA MELT

FIRST THEY WERE DRINKING BUDDIES. Skip Johnson was only 22, a fresh face in from the East Coast and having the time of his life. He worked as a lighting man for rock bands, and he loved the job and the lifestyle. Now he was sleeping with Grace Slick, who was pushing 35.

Grace had first noticed him in a St. Louis hotel during the first Jefferson Starship tour. She saw how the groupies gravitated toward Skip and wondered why they chose him over the others on the crew. Certainly, he was good-looking, tall with long dark hair and a thick mustache. He appeared sure of himself, and didn't seem to gloat each time he made a conquest. She made a mental note to keep an eye on that one.

Philadelphian Edward Johnson had acquired his nickname as a child and it stuck; he later changed it legally. He'd worked all sorts of odd jobs and gravitated toward the concert business, working for Larry Magid, Philly's largest concert promoter. Skip soon became the stage manager at the Spectrum, and while still in his teens he worked lights for major names like Stephen Stills, the Who and Jethro Tull. In 1974, for their first tour, Jefferson Starship hired the lighting company Skip worked for. Although he'd never been a big Airplane fan, he enjoyed working with the new group.

At first, Grace and Skip were just two business associates who shared an instinct for finding their way to the nearest bar. They hit it off and looked forward to hanging out, but although she was the fantasy of millions of young men, Skip didn't idolize Grace in that way.

SKIP JOHNSON: She just seemed to have that same energy that I did. When everybody else was leaving the bar or going to bed for the night, she was just getting up. When I met her she was just somebody who seemed to want to have as much fun as I did.

It wasn't long before Skip and Grace got to know each other intimately. And because Paul and Grace kept separate hotel rooms while on the road—Grace always maintained her own space regardless of who she was with—it took quite some time before Paul even became aware that Grace and Skip had been spending their nights together. Paul's custom was to retire to his room after a show, get high, watch TV and play music. He knew Grace would be off drinking with anyone who cared to join her, but by the time she returned to her room he was fast asleep. It seemed that everyone but Paul knew of the trysts.

It was John Barbata who finally told him, seeing it as a preemptive strike—if Paul found out on his own, he might get livid and break up the band. This way, they would all talk it over like mature adults. Since everyone involved believed in open relationships, particularly Paul, it wouldn't be a big deal.

But it was. According to Barbara Rowes's Grace biography, Paul fought with Grace, shouting at her and driving her to tears. She stormed out and headed to the lounge of the hotel where they were staying, but a short while later Paul, angrier than ever, came down and dragged her by the hair, shoving her into his room. According to Grace's account, he pushed her to the floor and picked up a gun, the two of them screaming at each other, getting out all of their pent-up hostilities. Paul eventually called Thompson and told him he'd better intervene before something awful happened.

After the ruckus, Paul had Johnson kicked off the Starship's crew, and Skip went back to working with other bands. He joined a Stephen Stills tour and Grace went back to living with Paul in Sea Cliff, staying in her room during the day, rethinking her life and career and going out to bars into the wee hours of the morning.

In June of 1975, both Skip and Grace were guests when Pete Sears married his girlfriend Jeannette in a beautiful ceremony in Mill Valley. At the reception, Grace realized how much she liked Skip, not just as a drinking companion but also for his good humor and company. A few days later, Grace and Sally Mann, who had by then left Spencer Dryden and was now lusting after Stills, decided to make a spur-of-the-moment trip to Alaska to seek their intended companions, who were on tour there. Sally didn't end up with Stills, but Grace and Skip began a more serious relationship, seeing each other whenever their respective schedules allowed.

> **SKIP JOHNSON:** I'd be out on the road and Grace would come out to see me. It certainly bothered Paul a lot, but I didn't really care what anybody else thought. There wasn't really anything left there anyway; it wasn't like she was torn.

Although Skip and Grace partied heavily when they were together, she seemed to drink even more when they were apart.

> **CRAIG CHAQUICO:** One time we were playing in Madison, Wisconsin. There was this big storm. John and I were looking out the window and we heard some kind of singing. We couldn't figure out what it was. Then the lightning flashed and there was Grace, hanging out of her window, totally naked, singing to the storm. "Hey, that's our lead singer! Grace! Go back in your room!"

It hadn't taken long for Grace to find her way back to her pre-Starship state of mind. But now the stakes were higher. If Grace acted up, it was no longer just a matter of pissing off a few stoned hippies in the front rows of Fillmore East. Now that they were a bona fide hit machine, the Starship had begun playing larger and larger shows, sometimes attended by as many as 50,000 or more paying customers, high-profile concerts where it was essential that they behave as professionals. Hundreds of thousands of dollars could be lost if something went wrong and a gig had to be canceled.

Business had never been a top priority for the Airplane, and in those couple of years between bands, financial disaster always lurked around the corner. After Grunt Records was formed, the band, following an initial burst of enthusiasm, had shown little interest in running the label, leaving the day-to-day business to Thompson. The label ultimately failed miserably—none of the artists signed by the group had sold any records and RCA dropped them all, even Papa John—and Grunt now existed solely as the RCA-distributed logo on which Jefferson Starship and Hot Tuna albums appeared.

But those dark days of losing their shirts were over and RCA was in a forgiving mood: The Starship was a bankable commodity now, and as long as the revenue kept flowing in, the company would smile on them.

Perhaps, RCA's executives felt, the group was ready to play the game now: Their next recordings would follow in the footsteps of the hits, and they would shoot for the largest possible concert audiences, thereby selling even more records.

But Paul hated playing the huge stadium extravaganzas, and finally he and Marty decreed that the Starship no longer would—they went so far as to withdraw the band from a Bill Graham–booked, multi-act megashow in Oakland, causing the promoter, not surprisingly, to blow up.

More to Paul's liking were the gigs that served as reminders of the altruism of yore. In March '75, the Starship took part in a Graham-presented benefit concert at Kezar Stadium in San Francisco to raise money for the needs of the city's students—also appearing at the show were the Dead, Bob Dylan, Neil Young, Santana and others. And in the spring there were free concerts in Golden Gate Park—the first large-scale show there in years—and New York's Central Park, drawing thousands. In the fall, the Starship played yet another freebie in Golden Gate Park, this time with the Dead.

For Grace, Paul and Marty, the return of the free shows was welcomed. It put the musicians back in touch with the spirit that had sparked the Airplane a full decade earlier, and took them away, even if just for a short while, from the uneasy feeling that their band was now perceived by many as little more than a cash cow, a hungry cow that needed to be fed constantly.

Of everyone in the band, it was Marty who was feeling the most pressure. Critical reaction to *Red Octopus* had basically added up to one thing: they were lucky to have him. Although some reviewers found favor in the others' contributions, it was generally agreed that "Miracles" was the real miracle. *Rolling Stone*'s Ed Ward went so far as to say, "If it weren't for Balin, *Red Octopus* would be completely unlistenable."

But even now, as he was regaining his leadership role and garnering some long-coveted respect, Marty still seemed as dissatisfied as he'd been when his fellow musicians were picking on him for writing mushy songs. He still griped about the band, but now the cause of his unhappiness was not only Grace's continued domination of the media but his new role as breadwinner. When he agreed to come back, he hadn't done so expecting to have to hold up the entire band.

As he'd done on *Red Octopus*, Marty cowrote and sang the only real hit on the next album, *Spitfire*. The track, "With Your Love," also gives authorship credit to Vic Smith, with whom Marty had worked in Grootna and Bodacious and, returning for one final moment of glory, Joey Covington, who was still friendly with Marty. Sessions for the album began in March 1976, in the wake of the Paul–Grace breakup, and all of the band members contributed to the writing, even drummer Barbata.

For *Spitfire*, producer Larry Cox returned for his third project with Jefferson Starship and the rest of the crew remained roughly the same. They were minus one band member though: Papa John had left to again pursue a solo career. He played clubs and concerts with his own bands and made a few more records over the next several years, always retaining a modest audience based on his role in the Airplane/Starship/Tuna story. But Creach never again enjoyed the level of exposure he had in the early '70s.

Spitfire, although it is often viewed as being too similar—and somewhat inferior—to *Red Octopus*, certainly boasts some excellent material. "St. Charles," in particular, is one of the most underrated songs in the Starship's entire catalog, a masterpiece of production and performance, every element of the track—vocals, playing, arrangement—rendered perfectly. There are five credited writers: Paul, Craig, Marty, his friend Jesse Barish and Thunderhawk, an Oglala Sioux Indian Marty had befriended.

Spitfire reached number 3 in the Bicentennial summer of 1976, hardly a number to scoff at. But for most of the participants, it is an album that barely invokes memories or is dismissed as transitional.

By the time *Spitfire* was released in June, Grace was already gone from the Sea Cliff house she'd shared with Paul and China and living again in Sausalito. China, just entering kindergarten, split her time between Grace's place and Paul's, a difficult period for all involved.

CHINA KANTNER: I went to a private school in Marin County, and a lot of my friends' parents would say things to their kids like, "Don't hang around China, she's probably on drugs because her parents are on drugs." Really ignorant comments. I'd spend time at their houses, and think, My parents don't blend in with this.

• • •

SHORTLY AFTER THE STARSHIP FINISHED RECORDING *Spitfire*, the band's publicist Heidi Howell, who was nine months pregnant, left her job. To fill the slot, Thompson enlisted Cynthia Bowman. The newest employee's job duties, like Howell's, included entertaining journalists, setting up interviews and arranging parties. But Cynthia's role went beyond that: She was also responsible for providing Grace with female companionship, a rare commodity within that male-dominated organization.

Originally from Cleveland, Bowman had first arrived in the city at the tail end of the Summer of Love. A nasty fall a few years later left her with a mangled leg, and Cynthia took a job at the office of one of the orthopedic surgeons who had treated her. Later, she worked for an internist, whose clients included Jack Casady and Jorma Kaukonen.

> **CYNTHIA BOWMAN:** I was the unfortunate individual who used to give them shots for the clap.

Her next job was at *Rolling Stone* magazine, as an editorial assistant, where she stayed until 1976. She ran into Thompson one night in a club, the Boarding House, and although Cynthia had never worked in public relations before, Thompson, who knew her from the magazine, hired her on the spot. Not long after her arrival, Cynthia became the new object of affection for Paul.

> **CYNTHIA BOWMAN:** Everyone was relieved when I showed up because they were hoping Paul would find someone else to be infatuated with, to take his mind off of Grace.

For one of their first dates, Paul took Cynthia to see Paul McCartney and his band Wings. Afterward, the couple got a chance to spend time with McCartney and his wife, Linda, who, in her groupie days several years earlier, had been among the young women who'd found her way into Kantner's bed. Linda remained friendly with Kantner, and McCartney had always been fond of the Airplane.

Cynthia began spending time at Kantner's house, which complicated the existing relationships between Paul, China and caretaker Pat Dugan. Paul found himself trying to juggle all of his relationships: with Cynthia, the band, Grace and Skip and with his daughter. But regardless of what else was going on in his life, he always gave China his full attention.

PAUL KANTNER: I had nothing in my life that I would throw myself on the tracks to die for, until I had a child. That was a very educational thing.

CYNTHIA BOWMAN: China was really a daddy's girl. When he was home he spent a lot of time with her. He went to all the school functions. And when he was gone, he would send postcards every day.

Still, as a little girl, all China knew was that Mommy and Daddy were always leaving her behind.

CHINA KANTNER: I understood why they had to go away so much, but it still hurt. It's what they had to do. I wouldn't have had the schooling I had, the life that I had, had they not done that.

Tension between Paul and Grace remained strong even after Paul took up with Cynthia. But he relented when it was suggested that the band rehire Johnson as lighting director, if only because they could find no one else who was as proficient at the job. Then, on November 29, 1976, Grace Slick became Grace Slick Johnson. She and Skip were married in Maui, with China serving as the flower girl and Cynthia as Grace's maid of honor. Grace's parents flew in for the occasion, as did most of the band members and the crew. Only two of the invited guests stayed at home, Paul Kantner and Marty Balin. One had a grudge with his ex. The other just had a grudge.

HOT TUNA RELEASED THEIR NEXT ALBUM, *Hoppkorv*, in the fall of '76. Another studio effort, it featured the same Kaukonen–Casady–Steeler lineup as the previous two, with Nick Buck, a keyboardist they'd met in New Orleans and who'd helped out on *Yellow Fever*, returning to do the same. They enlisted a new producer/engineer, Harry Maslin, best known at the time for his work with David Bowie.

The album's unusual title had its origin, as did so much of Jorma's inspiration during this time, in an incident that occurred during a speed skating trip, this time to Sweden. Another skater, it seemed, had dropped a messy sausage all over his new white sweater, causing him to blurt out "*hopp korv*," Swedish for jumping sausage. Jorma found it funny at the time.

Like the two albums before it, perhaps even more so, *Hoppkorv* is nearly all raging guitars, fat bass and merciless drums. The exception is "Watch the North Wind Rise," a folky acoustic piece featuring double-tracked acoustic guitars, heavy on the effects. It is among Jorma's most melodic and durable compositions. The other three Jorma-penned tracks—"Santa Claus Retreat," "Extrication Love Song" and "Song from the Stainless Cymbal"—are all very much of their time, well-suited to the marathon, ear-splitting shows the band was performing in the mid-'70s. The cover songs on the album included a crisp, nearly minimal pop-rock take on Buddy Holly's "It's So Easy," the Muddy Waters classic "I Can't Be Satisfied" and Chuck Berry's "I'm Talkin' 'Bout You."

Both Hot Tuna and Jefferson Starship toured fairly extensively during 1976, Tuna including a short European run in their summer schedule. But while Tuna continued to work straight through 1977, slotting in some new songs along the way and adding Buck to the official lineup, the Starship took a sabbatical from live performance for virtually all of 1977, using Marty's reluctance to commit himself to the band as their public excuse. Both bands worked on new recording projects, however. For Tuna, that meant another live album, a two-record set (one side acoustic, three electric) called *Double Dose*, taped in August at San Francisco's Theatre 1839, the former synagogue located next door to the original Fillmore and on the same block as the People's Temple, whose spiritual leader, Reverend Jim Jones, would lead more than 900 followers in a mass suicide the following year.

To produce, Tuna called on Felix Pappalardi, who had produced all of the legendary Cream albums and had been both bassist and producer of Mountain, one of the hardest-rocking bands of the late '60s and '70s. *Double Dose* became the last Hot Tuna album ever to make the *Billboard* chart. It also captured some of their final gigs for quite a while. By the time the album was released in the spring of 1978, Hot Tuna had broken up, their final show having taken place the previous November at the Palladium in New York.

Hot Tuna didn't know they were packing it in. Like the Airplane before them, they just sort of stopped being. Jorma attributes the band's parting primarily to his wife Margareta's worsening physical and mental condition. She'd attempted suicide and developed a thyroid disorder, and Jorma's preoccupation with his domestic situation precluded any interest in making music with Jack. Besides, the Hot Tuna mainstays had experienced something of a falling out. After nearly two decades of close friendship, Jorma Kaukonen and Jack Casady had stopped speaking to each other.

JEFFERSON STARSHIP'S FOURTH ALBUM, *Earth*, was begun in the summer of 1977 and took the better part of the remainder of the year to complete. Earlier in '77, RCA had released *Flight Log*, a two-record compilation intended to document the progress of the Airplane and the various spin-offs through their first decade of recording. In addition to select tracks from each Airplane album (except *Thirty Seconds Over Winterland*), the anthology included cuts from various albums involving Paul, Grace, Jorma, Tuna and combinations thereof. To entice those who already owned the other records, RCA tossed in an unreleased Jefferson Starship version of "Please Come Back," a song written by San Francisco artist Ron Nagle, recorded at Winterland in '76.

Earth would wrap up the next phase of Jefferson Starship, although the band wasn't aware of that until months after the album's release. Still, it seemed that they were almost sealing their own fate just by choosing *Earth* as the name of the album. Each of the Starship's first four album titles correlated with one of the so-called four elements the ancients believed comprised the universe, and which formed the basis of astrology: *Dragon Fly* represented air, *Red Octopus* suggested water, *Spitfire* obviously was fire and now *Earth*. By acknowledging that they'd completed this cycle, Jefferson Starship was putting closure on something, even if they didn't know what that something was.

The album continued musically along the lines of *Spitfire*, with Cox again producing—his final record for the band. But *Earth* was the most complicated production the band had ever undertaken—among other extras, string and horn arrangements by Gene Page, one of the best in the business, were incorporated into several tracks.

The songwriting credits were spread fairly thin, Marty and Paul contributing very little. Grace was the most prolific, sharing one credit with Craig, one with Pete ("Take Your Time," supposedly directed at Marty), and writing "Show Yourself"—a return to the Grace Slick venom of old that targets American governmental and corporate hypocrisies—on her own. Craig was responsible for the music on the record's first cut, the jazzy "Love Too Good," with words by an old friend of his named Gabriel Robles. "Skateboard," Craig's other major contribution to *Earth*, was inspired by a film on the subject in which Craig also appeared; the song features his music and words he cowrote with Grace.

Earth, which charted at number 5 in *Billboard*, produced two Marty-sung hit singles, "Count on Me," which made it to number 8, and "Runaway," with a number 12 placing. The latter came from Nicholas Dewey, formerly known as Dewey Dagreaze when he was a member of Marty's band Bodacious, while "Count on Me" was solely the work of Jesse Barish, a songwriter who had been introduced to Marty in the early '70s. Marty had produced a demo record of Barish singing "Count on Me," which RCA deemed commercial enough that the company offered Barish his own recording deal. Then the song made its way to Kantner, who felt, with its soft-rock lilt and lyrics in the vein of "Miracles" and "Caroline," that "Count on Me" would make a perfect vehicle for Marty and the Starship. Barish, who now had his own album to think about, wasn't sure at first that he wanted to give it up, but made the right choice, guaranteeing himself hefty royalties for years to come.

GRACE RANG IN THE NEW YEAR of 1978 in style, with a drunk driving arrest in Marin County. She was booked on January 19 after the police saw her pulled over on a bridge and discovered what they called "a liquid substance" in her presence. She had begun her reign of terror hours earlier at the Boarding House club in San Francisco, where she was a special guest judge at a rock and roll takeoff on TV's *Gong Show*. Some in attendance reported her pushing amateur contestants around the stage, insulting everyone near her with foul language and breaking two microphones before being dragged off the stage.

She had actually been sober for several months, between the making of *Spitfire* and her wedding. Skip had insisted on Grace checking herself in to a rehab clinic, and while she was at it, he mentioned, she could stand to lose some weight. Grace did: She gave up drinking, lost 30 pounds and also abstained from dope for a while. Everyone agreed she looked better and acted more pleasantly than she had in years. But that didn't last long.

Meanwhile, Marty was getting more and more fed up with his situation, and venting his anger in more public ways. He had walked away from fame once, and now it was chasing him again. When a *Rolling Stone* reporter badgered him with questions about whether the new, younger audience he'd picked up with his Jefferson Starship hits bothered him, and if he felt he was getting too respectable to rock, Marty kicked him out of the room. Another time he dubbed the band "Jefferson Wheelchair."

And when writer Mitchell Glazer from *Crawdaddy!* interviewed Marty at length, Marty spent much of the time alternately pumping himself up and tearing down those close to him. "The Starship isn't big enough to keep me busy," he told the magazine. "I refuse to work for imbeciles anymore." He took the opportunity to lash out at Grace at every turn. "She reminds me of my mother—she's not sexy," Marty said at one point (probably offending his mother, as well as Grace). He claimed that Grace used to pound on his door in the middle of the night, demanding sex with him—"Balin, let me in, motherfucker, let me in your room," he quoted her as saying—and that he took pride in his refusal to give in to her.

"I never even kissed her," he said. And then Marty spit out the line that others quoted for years: "I wouldn't let Grace Slick blow me."

> **MARTY BALIN:** I think I was the one she wanted the whole time. Onstage, I would burn her down. I mean, we made love. She'd walk off that stage, and at night, she'd come to my hotel room, take one of those axes out of the hall and be chopping down my door. It was outrageous, some of the things that she'd do. It was hilarious. I'd try to talk to her, and all she'd ever say to me was, "Why won't you fuck me? Why won't you fuck me?"

> **GRACE SLICK:** Maybe he just thinks I'm disgusting.

Marty later complained that his quotes to the *Crawdaddy!* reporter were taken out of context, but according to Cynthia Bowman, Marty's lack of tolerance for journalists didn't help them get the facts straight.

> **CYNTHIA BOWMAN:** Once we were in Los Angeles at a restaurant with some very important writers, and Marty got tired of the conversation and said, "Excuse me, I'm going to the men's room," and never came back.

As the band's publicist, Bowman would soon have her work cut out for her. Jefferson Starship's tour in support of *Earth* began in May of 1978, with gigs in the Midwest and on the East Coast. On June 9 and 10 there were shows at the Nassau Coliseum on Long Island, which were recorded for a live album that never came to be. Then it was off to Europe.

> **BILL THOMPSON:** That summer we had all kinds of huge shows that would gross for us a million-some dollars through August. We were making all kinds of money playing in Europe. And then came the thing with Grace.

31
DIS-GRACE

GRACE SLICK WAS IN HAMBURG, and she was drunk, taking the entire German populace to task, reminding them of World War II and poised to start the next.

There had been an omen even before Jefferson Starship had departed the United States. One of their limousines had caught fire, adding to a feeling of dread that had been mounting for some time, a notion that something monumentally creepy was about to happen. Then they arrived in Europe. Grace spent much of her time in Amsterdam drinking, but the concert there went ahead without incident. By the time they crossed into Germany, however, she had mutated into her evil twin.

The Starship was booked to perform at the Lorelei Amphitheatre, near Saint Goarshausen. The venue took its name from an ancient local legend—the Lorelei, a ravishing but troubled woman, whiled away the hours sitting on the cliffs above the Rhine, singing an unearthly tune that caused sailors below to lose their bearings and crash their wooden ships into the rocks. But on this night, in June 1978, there would be no rock in Lorelei, not from the enchantress named Grace.

By the time the Starship reached their hotel in Wiesbaden, once a favorite of Hitler's, she was in a pathetic state. But it wasn't the alcohol this time, Grace assured her husband. She was really sick. Food poisoning, she guessed. Whatever it was, she wasn't getting out of bed.

This wasn't like her at all, Skip thought; she must be telling the truth—alcohol usually placed Grace at the center of the party, not shirking away from it. He called in a local doctor, who pronounced her fit while neglecting to mention that he worked for the concert promoter. That was all Paul needed to hear, that Grace could sing. He wanted to see that old fighting spirit. Grace had always been able to prop herself up onstage and do her job. He would haul her ass out to the venue himself if he had to. You didn't miss a concert because your tummy hurt and you certainly didn't miss one because you were too high. Paul insisted that Grace get ready for the show, and stop her crabbing. But once again Grace sent word that she wasn't coming out of her room and they could all go to hell.

The opening acts at Lorelei completed their sets. The promoter, practically in tears, was pacing nervously, knowing what a disappointed German audience was capable of. Ten thousand fans were waiting for Jefferson Starship, growing more anxious by the minute.

Paul was through reasoning. He had already graduated to shouting and swearing and now he was ready for another method of persuasion. He jumped Skip, grabbing him by the throat and throwing him down a short flight of stairs, shocking even those who'd seen Kantner's Teutonic temper at its most virulent.

> **PAUL KANTNER:** I went up to Grace's room and Skip was protecting her: "No, you can't come in the room." So I just sort of picked him up and threw him out the doorway.

Bill Thompson pounced, grabbing at the two men playing at being Popeye and Bluto, trying to break up the brawl. "Are you crazy?" he shouted, although he already knew the answer.

Finally, it became plain to all that Grace was not going to change her mind. Some suggested the band play the show without her, but Paul wouldn't have any of that. He announced that there would be no show.

> **PAUL KANTNER:** It would be like the Rolling Stones playing without Mick Jagger. It seemed to be the right decision at the time. I'm not justifying what I did. It wasn't made out of any malice or lack of forethought.

When word reached the promoter he pleaded. The fans could riot, he explained.

> **MARTY BALIN:** I'll never forget what Paul said: "My people will never riot."

At the amphitheater, it fell to Bill Laudner and David Freiberg to explain to the audience what was going on back at the hotel, that the band would not play because Grace Slick was ill. Laudner and Freiberg, along with Chaquico, Barbata and Sears, had gone ahead to the venue ahead of the others.

At first, the fans seemed to understand. But when the promoter followed the musicians to the stage, speaking in rapid-fire German, the mood turned. The crowd began shouting and booing. Then Laudner heard glass. First, it was just one bottle, thrown from the audience, shattering against the concrete stage. Then another, and another. Those who didn't have bottles threw rocks, metal, anything they could get their hands on. A Starship crew member, Paul Dowell, was hit and taken to a local hospital. Others, trying to salvage the group's equipment, quickly gave up, deciding that keeping their heads and bodies intact took precedence over saving an amplifier. A piano was thrown off the stage. Guitars were stolen.

Then the fires began: lighting towers, trash piles, the stage. What they couldn't burn, they chopped up.

PETE SEARS: Somebody got an axe and started smashing the drum kit and then they poured gasoline over it, burned everything. It was a blazing inferno. The two big compressed-air cylinders holding up the lighting trusses exploded. It's amazing nobody was killed. The firemen showed up and got bricks thrown at them and just left. The police never showed up.

Some of the touring party hid in equipment boxes until the carnage was finished, for what seemed like an eternity. Others managed to escape. Freiberg, a Jew, said there was no way he was hiding in a box in Germany—he would take his chances. He made himself inconspicuous and quickly found a way out.

In the '60s and early '70s, Jefferson Airplane had been no stranger to unruly audiences. But now the band—not the police, not the government—was the intended target of the raging mob. Paul Kantner, Grace Slick, Marty Balin and their fellow musicians had become the pigs.

The Starship left the next morning for the 17-hour drive to Hamburg, piled into a bus driven at an agonizingly slow speed by a driver who couldn't stand Americans and who insisted on first taking them past the concert site so the group could see what it had caused.

PETE SEARS: It looked like a bomb had dropped, literally.

Grace and Skip weren't on that bus though—they had flown ahead, Grace greeting the others with a wide, beaming smile when they met up a couple of days later. She was feeling much better now, she told them all, rested and ready to work.

Laudner, Thompson and the others charged with the responsibility of making things happen scrambled to borrow equipment. The band had left Wiesbaden with nothing. By the time of the show, somehow, they had managed to find what they required. Returning to the band to tell them the good news, Laudner took one look at Grace and knew she was as drunk as he had ever seen her.

CYNTHIA BOWMAN: Thompson sent me up to her room and she was just fucked-up. Dealing with her was impossible. I was trying to get her to put her pants on and she was throwing bottles around the room and screaming. She was kicking me.

Ultimately, when it came time to play, Grace, not wanting a rerun of Lorelei, did stumble to the stage. But no one who witnessed the events of that evening has ever forgotten the Hamburg concert. "You could just see all the life drain out of the group," Cynthia Bowman later said. "It was just a horrible, empty, bad, dark night."

The band's set had been videotaped for later broadcast on the German *Rockpalast* TV program, but—for good reasons—it never aired. One thing German citizens did not need coming into their homes was a sloshed, taunting American rock singer calling them Nazis, sticking her fingers up fans' noses, giving the "Heil Hitler" salute. They took this sort of behavior as a personal affront. Thompson had Grace's microphone turned off before she could spark another riot.

GRACE SLICK: I'm in Germany and I'm gonna get back at them for Dachau or some dumb, drunken decision. That's what that night was about, dumb, drunken decisions.

Grace had finally become not only an embarrassment to the band but a liability. The others had put up with it for years because she was Grace Slick, the one bona fide legend among them. But now here she was, not only insulting an audience justifiably touchy about its nation's past, but making it impossible for the other musicians to concentrate. Onstage, she fondled Craig as he played his solo, and she needled Marty. But Marty knew how to handle her. When Grace moved close to him to sing in harmony, Marty grabbed her tightly in what seemed like an embrace but was in actuality a hammerlock. He held her by the hair and didn't let go. Grace, unable to move, smiled as Marty kept her there. He smiled too. She was enjoying it. They all were. Freiberg says it was his favorite Marty moment ever.

MARTY BALIN: I'm holding her up through all the songs and she's going, "How many more?" Then she got into it and started yelling things at these people. At first everybody got up and just started to walk away, to leave this disgusting thing. But then a lot of people came back and sat down and just watched her do her swan song.

JOHN BARBATA: Paul was crying after the show because he knew it was over. I knew it was over.

After Hamburg it was on to England, for the Knebworth Festival. The band put on a sensational show. Marty pulled out all the stops. But they did it without Grace. A decision had been made to send her home, to give her an opportunity to dry out and consider whether she still wanted to be a part of this soap opera.

She didn't. It was time for her to get out of the game. She'd done the rock band thing, now it was time for a change.

BILL THOMPSON: She quit that night in Hamburg. She just said, "Fuck the band," and went back to San Francisco with Skip.

Returning from Europe, Marty kept his thoughts to himself. After that night in Hamburg, he had become withdrawn once again. He felt the same way he had almost eight years earlier with the Airplane, when he first realized that the dream was over. Once again, Marty didn't bother explaining his feelings to the others; they'd heard it all too many times before.

Instead, on his way to rehearsal one day in San Francisco, Marty Balin rolled down the car window, sucked in the fresh California air, turned around and drove to the beach. It would be nearly a decade before he'd speak to any of them again.

32

THOMAS' JEFFERSON

PUNK ROCK WAS THE BIG MUSIC NEWS NOW, as the end of the '70s drew near. It had been bubbling under for a while, this assault led by bands like the Ramones, the Dictators and Richard Hell and the Voidoids in New York and the Sex Pistols, the Damned and the Clash in England. Punk was about taking rock back to the basics, stripping it of its excesses, disposing of all those guitar and drum solos, the half-hour jams, the fatuous lyrics, the strutting lead singers.

Punk said anyone can do this; you shouldn't have to spend years learning how to play an instrument. Rock and roll should speak directly to the audience in real language, and each song should make its point in a few minutes and then go away. It should be fast and simple and sweaty and angry; it should happen not in a stadium but in some grimy hole-in-the-wall club. Three chords is enough; who needs more, anyway? And it should not be made by aging hippie relics, with their flannel shirts and beards. Spiky, short, brightly colored hair, pierced body parts, leather and ripped jeans, safety pins, the Dracula look—that's what the new rock attitude was all about.

All of which meant that, to the new breed, groups like Jefferson Starship and Hot Tuna were just so yesterday. Once cutting edge, now they were dinosaurs.

San Francisco didn't jump on the punk rock bandwagon immediately, but once it did, punk swept through the city. Clubs sprang up—the Mabuhay Gardens became to San Francisco's punk community what the Fillmores had been to the previous generation of rockers. All of the major bands from New York and England passed through town—the Sex Pistols played their chaotic final concert at Winterland in January of 1978, Elvis Costello played his first American gig at the Old Waldorf. KSAN radio began blaring every punk record it could find, practically forgetting it had ever been the voice of San Francisco rock. And of course, San Francisco sprouted its own punk bands, dozens of them: the Dead Kennedys, the Nuns, the Avengers, Pearl Harbor and the Explosions.

SVT was another. An exciting, raw four-piece new wave/punk group, they had an unlimited supply of pop hooks, well-constructed, intelligent, melodic songs, a loud and fierce attack and an intense bass player named Jack Casady.

That Jack Casady.

This development, needless to say, did not sit well with some fans of Hot Tuna and the Airplane. What was going on here? Why was the master who had virtually reinvented the role of the bass guitar in rock, the musician who had conjured up some of the most mind-bending sounds ever, playing punk rock?

For Jack, it was about trying something different, getting back to the simpler style of playing he had engaged in before Jorma had even invited him to fly out to San Francisco in 1965. After the Hot Tuna split, Jack felt the need to move in a radically different direction, and that's what he did. SVT began as the Jack Casady Band. Managed by Thompson, they debuted at the Old Waldorf in July of '78. Nick Buck played keyboards, Bill Gibson played drums and Brian Marnell, a talented young singer-songwriter-guitarist, was their frontman.

JACK CASADY: Brian was 10 years younger than me and had heard all the Grateful Dead and Jefferson Airplane that he ever wanted to hear. He grew up with that and you tend to not want to play what your parents played.

Jack had heard a tape of Marnell and called him about working together. Marnell recommended Gibson, formerly with the group Clover. Jack brought Buck in from Tuna and they began playing live shortly thereafter. By 1979, they had recorded their first couple of singles, the independently released "Wanna See You Cry" on their own SVT label and "Heart of Stone," for the local 415 Records.

Jack made no secret of the reasons for his surprising musical move when he spoke with the press.

JACK CASADY: I got to be very paranoid about the number of notes I was playing. I wanted to reaffirm my bass playing from a simpler approach. I love melodies, I love good song construction, I love word context, and that's what inspires me to play. When I listen back to SVT, it still sounds like me.

SVT lasted for roughly three years, recording a seven-song EP, appropriately called *Extended Play*, for 415 (with Paul Zahl replacing Gibson) and, as a trio sans Buck, a full-length album, *No Regrets*, for MSI Records in 1981. Brian Marnell died in 1983, soon after SVT split, from complications related to overcoming a heroin habit.

While some of Jack's devotees loved his new direction, many longtime Tuna fans were confused and felt betrayed by the music he was playing. They walked out of gigs; they shook their heads in disappointment; they shouted in vain for Jorma.

But when they saw what Jorma himself was up to, they really gasped. The bright orange hair, combed back into a '50s duck's-ass style, was the first shock. Both Jorma and Jack had shorn their long hair when they got into speed skating, but Jorma's newest look was truly alarming to some of his old fans—they felt dismayed, took it personally. Those who also got a look at his back, now completely covered with tattoos, surely sensed that something was up. But when he began touring with a new band, and they called themselves White Gland, and they too were playing what amounted to a modified take on punk rock, some of the old crowd just had to throw their hands up in exasperation.

Here was the Airplane and Tuna guitar hero—the legendary Jorma Kaukonen, who'd practically invented the all-night jam, the keeper of the blues flame—virtually abandoning the repertoire and style he had cultivated for more than 15 years, performing all new songs peppered with an eclectic choice of covers. Here was one of the great hippie icons, his long hair now gone, looking like he'd dipped his head in a vat of paint for a Halloween party, with a gold tooth up front adding to the bizarre sight.

Jorma's detour, like Jack's, had snuck up on his fans. Beginning in mid-1978, when Hot Tuna was floundering, Jorma began playing a series of solo gigs, drawing material from the various Tuna albums and *Quah*. Those shows got a little stranger when Jorma began following his opening acoustic set with an electric one, backed only by Bob Steeler on drums, no bassist. Performing material entirely unfamiliar to the audience, including one song called "Happy Go Lucky Space Rats on Parade," and jamming in a free-form style, the sound was as out-there as anything Jorma had ever undertaken before.

For a while, Jorma returned to a more standard solo format, playing his usual material, and in the spring of 1979 he recorded his second solo album, simply titled *Jorma*. Coproduced by Jorma and David Kahne, the album featured Jorma playing virtually every instrument, with the exception of keyboards, which Kahne handled. There is some electric guitar, but it is largely acoustic. Jorma wrote nearly all of the record, except for "Vampire Woman," another early twentieth-century blues song, and M. A. Numminen's "Da-Ga-Da-Ga," a minute and a half of improvised guitar weirdness broken up by short bursts of surreal poetry.

Come summer, White Gland arrived, a trio with a decidedly punk flair. They played almost no Hot Tuna–era material, although the occasional "Uncle Sam Blues" and "Rock Me Baby" worked their way into the sets, as did Jorma's own take on "Volunteers." Jorma concentrated mostly on the music from his new solo album and one he was working on, as well as a wide array of cover songs, including Johnny Cash's "Folsom Prison Blues."

By early 1980, White Gland had been transformed into the like-minded Vital Parts. This band also preferred to keep the material new, but threw in some well-chosen oldies. Jorma went into the studio with this aggregation early in 1980 to cut an album. Produced again by Kahne, *Barbeque King* was actually quite a diverse effort. While the opening track, "Runnin' with the Fast Crowd," is as close as Jorma ever came to recording a pure pop song—it would have blended in nicely with any of the era's new wave—there is also plenty of blues and straight-ahead rock.

Jorma's band changed personnel often during the early '80s and he slowly began to reinject the electric portion of his shows with some of the old Hot Tuna material. Then, following yet another band name change, to Spare Parts, he gave up on bands altogether, going it alone, performing a mix of Tuna and solo material.

SVT, meanwhile, had split up. But by that time many fans of both Jack and Jorma had lost track of them, or had, at the least, given up hope of ever hearing them play the kind of music they had played in the heyday of the Airplane and Tuna. Then, finally, in late 1983, came the announcement so many had hoped for: Hot Tuna was back.

JUST WEEKS AFTER RETURNING from Europe to get her life together, Grace Slick was arrested again for drunk driving. Police in Corte Madera, California, said that on July 25, 1978, they received reports of a woman driving a black pickup truck erratically through a shopping center parking lot. Police found the truck parked on the side of a highway with a door opened into the traffic lane. Grace was taken into custody and brought to the Marin County jail. Along the way, she tried to kick out the windows of the patrol car and insisted that she was too important a person to be arrested.

Grace made her exit from the Starship official in the fall of 1978, telling *Rolling Stone*'s Ben Fong-Torres that her drinking had nothing to do with her decision, that the events in Europe and her father's recent heart attack (from which he recovered) had made her "berserk," leading to the July binge resulting in her arrest. She told the magazine that, in fact, she had given up drinking after that night. "I do have an alcohol problem in that I'm an alcoholic," she said, "a nonpracticing alcoholic."

While the Starship hoped that Grace would soon return, she was already thinking beyond the band, and told the magazine that if she made music again at all, it might be in the area of TV and film scores. Shortly after giving that interview she had herself checked in to a rehab center to combat her alcoholism.

Around the same time the Slick article hit the newsstands, Jefferson Starship drummer John Barbata crashed his truck near his Mendocino, California, home. His passenger died, and Barbata suffered multiple injuries, breaking his jaw and an arm and receiving head lacerations, leaving him incapacitated for several months.

With Grace and John out of commission, Jefferson Starship was in flux. Then Marty dropped the bomb: he too was quitting. He had told them he would stay for three albums and had kept his word. When he had first returned to the fold in 1975, he agreed to do so only if he could sign no contracts, freeing him to get out at will. Now he was exercising his option, disgusted by the European calamity and the rampant egotism he thought he'd left behind when the Airplane had split.

The Starship had just lost three of their seven members in the same year, including their two lead singers. Any other group would have packed up its tent and gone home. But not this one. Jefferson Starship—with Paul Kantner now the only remaining link to the Airplane—just continued, business as usual.

That meant that the partying continued unabated; for example, one legendary bash hosted by the Starship at 2400 Fulton following the 1978–79 New Year's Eve concert at Winterland. The show had not even featured the Starship, but rather the Dead, the New Riders of the Purple Sage and the Blues Brothers, a half-parody/half-tribute soul-rock group led by *Saturday Night Live* comics John Belushi and Dan Aykroyd.

> **BILL THOMPSON:** Laudner had a map, probably two feet by three feet or something like that. One of my friends put down a line of cocaine from Seattle to Miami. I think that Belushi probably got to Missouri.

WHEN THE BAND STARTED TO LOOK for replacements for Grace and Marty, it was naturally assumed that the group would hire another male and another female to replace the two singers. But in the end only one person was chosen, a singer whose voice was already known to millions of record buyers, but whose name may have drawn a blank nonetheless.

"Fooled Around and Fell in Love" had been one of the biggest hits of 1976, making the Top 5, credited to the Elvin Bishop Group, led by the former guitarist of the Paul Butterfield Blues Band. Bishop was not the band's singer, however, so few who heard and bought the record probably ever knew that it was the superinflated lungs of Mickey Thomas they were actually hearing.

John Michael Thomas was a southerner, born in 1949 in the small town of Cairo, Georgia. Mickey, as he was always called, was the middle child of Joe, a pool hall owner, and Loki Thomas, joined by a brother named Chuck and a sister, Shane. Growing up, Mickey wasn't nearly as interested in music as he was in the movies but, as it did for millions of other teenagers, that all changed in 1964 when he heard the Beatles for the first time. He played in high school and college bands while developing a strong interest in rhythm and blues.

By 1971, Mickey was out of school, unemployed and living with a girlfriend. Sitting around watching Sonny and Cher's TV show one night, a gospel singer named Gideon Daniels awed him. Two weeks later, Mickey's phone rang and it was Daniels—the singer had heard about Mickey's vocal abilities and invited him to join his band as a background vocalist. Three days later Mickey was on his way to San Francisco.

Thomas worked with Daniels for about a year. When the group fell apart Mickey returned to Georgia, where he stayed into 1974, starting a group called the Jets and returning to school. Then, in late 1974, he received the call from Bishop. The guitarist had just signed a new record deal with the Macon, Georgia–based Capricorn label and was looking for background singers to work on his album. Bishop and Thomas hit it off and Mickey was asked to join the band. They toured through most of 1975 and in the fall of that year went to Miami to record an album with producer Bill Szymczyk, *Struttin' My Stuff*, which included "Fooled Around and Fell in Love."

In 1977, Szymczyk produced Thomas's first solo album, *As Long As You Love Me*, for MCA Records, which featured some of the hottest studio musicians available, including members of Booker T. and the MG's. The album didn't sell especially well, but it did include a funky cover of the Airplane's "Somebody to Love." Ironically, it was not Mickey's choice to put the song on his album, but rather the producer's. Mickey, in fact, was not even a fan of the Airplane or most of the music that had come out of the San Francisco scene.

Because of that, when Thomas received an invitation to try out for Jefferson Starship—he'd been recommended to Thompson by Jeff Pollack, proprietor of the Old Waldorf—he wasn't sure if he wanted to. The Starship, he felt, was a dinosaur band. Still, Mickey decided he couldn't turn down such an offer. He met the band at Paul's Sea Cliff house, and hit it off with most of them immediately.

MICKEY THOMAS: They wanted to look at it as a completely new band. We weren't going to do "Volunteers" or "Miracles" or "White Rabbit" or anything like that. Then we started jamming and it was kind of like a hard-rock band, with my sort of gospel vocals on top of it. I thought, This sounds fresh, kind of different.

Mickey signed with the band in April 1979, agreeing to stay on for two albums to see how things went. He was being placed in the unenviable position of replacing not one but two legendary singers, Grace Slick and Marty Balin, and if audiences didn't accept him, he wanted the opportunity to back out.

Meanwhile, the band was also breaking in another new addition, drummer Aynsley Dunbar. Like Pete Sears, Dunbar was a Brit who came with a high pedigree. Sears had worked with him before on the Kathi McDonald project, but Dunbar had long since established himself as one of rock's great drummers by the time that gig came about.

Dunbar was from Liverpool, and at one time had played with Rory Storm and the Hurricanes, whose original drummer, Ringo Starr, had gone on to bigger things. Dunbar formed his first band at 15, and by 1966 he was proficient enough to be hired by British blues great John Mayall as one of his Bluesbreakers. A brief stay with the Jeff Beck Group followed, which gave way to the Aynsley Dunbar Retaliation, a band that gained popularity both in the U.K. and in the United States. In 1970, Dunbar took a job as Frank Zappa's drummer, then left along with singers Howard Kaylan and Mark Volman, who were reborn as Flo and Eddie, and worked with them for a couple of years. A slew of session drumming dates followed, then Dunbar joined an early incarnation of the new San Francisco band Journey, formed by refugees from Santana. He stayed with Journey through their first four albums, but in late 1978 he was fired, perfect timing for him to get the call to join Jefferson Starship. Like Mickey Thomas, Dunbar had been a fan of neither the Airplane nor the Starship, but he also believed in the new hard-rock direction the band was taking, and in January 1979 he came aboard.

It would still be some time before the new group could put together enough material for an album, so RCA filled the void with *Gold*, a collection of the 10 biggest hits from the Marty–Grace era of Jefferson Starship. The album was released both as a standard-issue black vinyl record and as a special picture disc, a format popular with collectors at the time. As a bonus for those who chose the black LP, RCA threw in a single of Craig's "Light the Sky on Fire," a song that had never appeared on a Jefferson Starship album before.

Freedom at Point Zero was the ideal name for the next Jefferson Starship album. That was precisely how the band members felt, free to start anew, without any of the baggage of the past. Free from Marty's wimpy ballads and from Grace's esoteric ramblings. Free to rock out.

Of course, losing those two characters also meant that they were giving up much of their personality. Mickey Thomas, technically proficient singer though he might be, possessed little of Marty's commanding, charismatic stage presence or Grace's ability to keep an audience on the edge of its seat wondering what might happen next. And although Mickey, like Marty, was steeped in soul music, Mickey's penetrating vocals had more in common with the over-the-top singing style associated with bands like Journey and Foreigner than with anything coming out of Memphis.

To produce *Freedom at Point Zero*, the band called in Ron Nevison, who had worked as an engineer on albums by the Who, Bad Company, Led Zeppelin and others, and whose production credits included Dave Mason, UFO and the Babys. With his experience in the hard-rock arena, Nevison was prepared to give the Starship what they wanted, a clean break, a contemporary sound for the '80s.

By the time Nevison met the Starship, they had already put together the material for the album—something the Airplane could not even have conceived of doing—and were ready to go. Nevison booked them into the Record Plant in Sausalito and began work. "Jane," a song written primarily by Freiberg about his wife Girl, was the first song cut. It became the leadoff track on the album and the first single as well, eventually lodging at number 14.

Kantner provided four of the album's nine songs, still managing to inject poignancy and poetry into his writing, even while aiming his music at a wider audience. "Lightning Rose," a character Paul calls "one of my iconic female Joan of Arc figures," was at least partially inspired by Grace. Paul told *BAM* magazine that the song was "basically about people in an outlaw camp outside a domed city with nuclear reactors they control, and the people inside control other things," but it also includes outright declarations of love that might have made the Paul Kantner of the '60s blanch:

Rose—I need you
Rose—can't go without your love

Rose—I need you
I can't go without you
I won't go without your love.

Craig had cowriting credits on three songs, but the other major contributors of material here were Pete and his wife Jeannette, who wrote two songs together, the album's sole ballad, "Fading Lady Light," and "Awakening." Both songs reflected the couple's budding spiritual alignment with Christianity. At first, no one in the band, even Paul, gave them any grief over that, although that would change.

> **PETE SEARS:** We were never into that TV evangelist-type thing. Those themes that Paul might think are syrupy are actually salvation, compassion. It's really very narrow-minded to assume a Christian theme as being one thing.

Freedom at Point Zero—with Thompson's son Tyrone pictured on front—rose to number 10, and the band and RCA breathed a huge sigh of relief. Reviews were genuinely glowing. Even without Grace and Marty, Jefferson Starship was still a hot brand name. They had already proven themselves as a live act months before the album's release, playing warm-up gigs at local clubs. For Mickey, especially, it was a testy time, having to win over the staunch Marty and Grace fans. But he came through unscathed.

In May of 1979, the Starship put on a surprise free show in Golden Gate Park and received raves from the press. Paul had been battling city officials for a few years trying to secure permits to play a concert in the park, but the city no longer wanted to allow such gatherings, its excuse being that the crowds would damage the flora and leave a mess. Finally, the band decided to bypass the officials and hooked up with another event that was scheduled for the park, appearing as the "incidental music" its sponsors had contracted for. The Starship's stage was built under cover of night and by the time the city knew what had been pulled off, it was all over.

Both Grace and Marty were seen hanging out backstage at that show, but neither took the initiative to step onstage, nor did they approach the band about rejoining. For one thing, Marty was busy, making good on a promise to write and direct a rock musical, *Rock Justice*, in which the lead singer of a band is put on trial for not being able to come up with a hit.

Grace wasn't just sitting around either. Having kept a relatively low profile since leaving the Starship in 1978, she bounced back into the news in early 1980 with the publication of *Grace Slick: The Biography*, written by Barbara Rowes with the full cooperation of Grace and published by Doubleday. Grace disowned the effort shortly after its publication, however, telling *BAM*'s Blair Jackson, "I don't like the book at all."

There was also the release of the second Grace Slick album, *Dreams*. Unlike 1973's *Manhole*, which utilized the talents of many musicians from within the Starship's clique, the team behind *Dreams* was assembled completely from outside of the usual pool. Most of the album was recorded in New York, produced by Ron Frangipane, who'd worked with John Lennon and Yoko Ono, among others.

> **GRACE SLICK:** *Dreams* is more orchestral and the lyrics are concerned with the business of getting sober and how's that gonna be and what does it require to be there?

Dreams became the most successful solo album of Grace's career, climbing to number 32. No sooner did it drop off the chart than Grace began work on the follow-up. This time, she went in the opposite direction. The cool, deep purples and pinks of the *Dreams* album cover, depicting Grace Slick as a magician levitating another Grace Slick, gave way to explosions and shock on *Welcome to the Wrecking Ball*. The album's cover photos—with Grace decked out as an insane and angry punk priestess—were all shot by Roger Ressmeyer, the Starship's official photographer. The shots were all taken outside of the soon-to-be-leveled Winterland, home of so many great Airplane and Starship concerts.

The tone of the music matched the cover—this time, Grace and producer Frangipane went for the gut, unleashing a quasi-heavy metal record. As on *Dreams*, Grace's guitarist Scott Zito is clearly the motivator behind the music, having written all but three songs himself—and those three he cowrote with Grace.

Grace was in New York recording *Wrecking Ball* when she received a startling phone call: Paul Kantner was in intensive care in a Los Angeles hospital, and his prognosis was not good.

33

WE DO WHAT WE WANT!

PAUL'S HEAD HAD FINALLY EXPLODED. Grace, for one, wasn't surprised. She'd been expecting it for some time.

> **GRACE SLICK:** When I first went with him, we were getting into something sexual and he had bangs, so I never saw his forehead. But I was gently going across it and I felt something sticking out. So I pulled the bangs away and I said, "Paul, you have a hole in your head with a wire sticking out of it."
>
> He said, "Yeah, I know, I have to get that fixed. I had a motorcycle accident and they put mesh in my head but it's kind of coming apart."

It had occurred to Grace at the time, if just for a moment, that Paul might actually be from one of those other worlds he longed so much to visit. But he was so matter-of-fact about the bizarre sight she had just pointed out that she shrugged it off.

The accident had occurred in the early '60s, when Paul's bike hit a car; he flew about 40 feet and crashed into a tree. His skull, on the left side, was fractured. Doctors inserted the mesh to literally keep his head together. Now it was a couple of decades later, October 1980. Paul had been in Los Angeles with the band for about a month, working on the next Jefferson Starship album. He and Cynthia returned to their room at the Chateau Marmont one night and went to bed. Then Paul felt ill. "I think I've had a cerebral hemorrhage," he told her.

"You are fucked-up!" Cynthia told him and rolled over.

> **CYNTHIA BOWMAN:** I was completely irritated that he was bugging me in the middle of the night over what I thought was nothing. Paul is the worst patient in America. If he's got a hangnail it's time to call an ambulance. But he got up and went to the bathroom and he

didn't come out. He was obviously really sick. He could not move; he was white as a ghost, sweaty, very, very ill.

Paul told Cynthia to call an ambulance but she hesitated. "If I call an ambulance it will be on the front page of the *L.A. Times* tomorrow and you'll look like an asshole," she told him. But as it became more obvious that something was truly wrong, Cynthia did call and Paul was taken to Cedars-Sinai Medical Center. After spending a number of hours in the emergency room while Cynthia tried to locate Thompson—he was the only one who knew anything about Paul's medical insurance—Paul was taken in for a series of tests.

> **CYNTHIA BOWMAN:** He had a bleed in his brain. They were basically saying he's going to die, he's not going to survive this, and if he does he's never going to play music again, he's never going to talk again. It was a real disaster.

While the doctors worked on Paul, Jeannette Sears organized a prayer vigil in the hospital chapel. Grace was located and informed of the news. Everyone prepared for the worst. But just hours before the surgeons were to cut Paul's head open, the bleeding stopped suddenly. The doctors were astounded—only one in a million had that kind of luck. Paul Kantner had defied the odds once again.

In the days that followed, as Paul recuperated, his hospital room became a party zone. David Crosby brought a guitar for Paul to play. Cynthia ordered lobster and Dom Perignon champagne. And soon Paul started acting like Paul again.

> **CYNTHIA BOWMAN:** He was bitching and moaning because he wanted to rent a Lear Jet to go home in. The doctor said, "Mr. Kantner, you've just had a brain hemorrhage. You can't get in a Lear Jet and fly home." Then we all knew he was gonna be fine because he was screaming and yelling and telling everyone he could do whatever the hell he wanted, goddammit, he was Paul Kantner! So at that point we all stopped praying. We knew our prayers had been answered.

> **PAUL KANTNER:** I was smoking big joints in my room in about three days.

Paul never lost consciousness throughout his ordeal, or his wicked sense of humor. Craig told *Circus* magazine's Philip Bashe that he was sure

Paul had suffered brain damage. "I called him up and didn't know what to expect," Chaquico said. "I only knew he was conscious. So I said, 'Paul, how ya doin', man, how ya feelin'?' And he goes, 'Ughathorp-switz.' I didn't know he was kidding!"

> **DAVID CROSBY:** He had a lucky circumstance. He had a soft place in his cranium from the motorcycle accident that gave the brain room to expand without crushing itself. So it saved his life.

AFTER WRAPPING UP *Wrecking Ball*, Grace was ready for some action. She'd been sidelined too long; she was bored. Now a member of Alcoholics Anonymous—temporarily, at least—she'd toned down her behavior enough to be able to function in public, and she wanted to be back out there. She dismissed the idea of touring as a solo artist, saying she would not have felt comfortable. Too much responsibility. What she liked was being just another band member, and she missed the band of which she'd been a part for so long.

Perhaps fans should have been more surprised when she announced her intentions, but given the revolving-door nature of the organization, few were truly taken aback when Grace Slick turned up in Jefferson Starship again.

> **BILL THOMPSON:** Around Christmas of '80, I get a call. It's Grace. She says, "Bill, I've been talking to Paul and he suggested that I call you. I'm looking for a job."
> I said, "Can you type?"

Grace eased her way back, first making cameo appearances on the next Jefferson Starship album, 1981's *Modern Times*, singing background vocals and a duet with Mickey on Pete and Jeannette Sears's "Stranger." That song didn't fare especially well on the charts, nor had the preceding single, "Find Your Way Back," written by Craig and his friend Thomas Borsdorf. The album itself, produced again by Nevison, also stopped at a relatively disappointing number 26, despite a number of other strong tracks, among them the Searses' "Save Your Love," one of the better Starship tunes of this era, and "Alien."

What the records' relatively poor performance meant in the larger scope wasn't really a matter of worry yet, but people in and around the band were starting to get a little edgy, trying to figure out what had gone wrong. Had they veered too far from the group's roots, or not far enough? Were they making the "right" kind of music for the current market? Maybe they really were too old to rock and roll. Perhaps they needed a different image.

These were not issues with which the Airplane would have grappled—they had gone out of their way at times to make recordings that were not commercial. But, as the Starship constantly reminded themselves—and their audience—they were not the Airplane, and this was not the 1960s. They were into the Ronald Reagan era now, the 1980s, and very little was the same as it had been 10 or 15 years ago. For starters, the holy trinity of sex and drugs and rock and roll was being put through the wringer, and along with it, the core '60s value system represented by groups such as the Airplane. Jefferson Starship was born of a different time, and now, if they didn't care to become just another oldies band capitalizing on nostalgia, they had to get a tune-up.

From the start of the new decade, it was apparent that another cultural and political shift was in motion and, as has always happened, the arts adjusted accordingly. In 1981, the AIDS virus was officially recognized by the U.S. government. The epidemic of unknown origin had been claiming lives for some time, but President Ronald Reagan had all but ignored it until the death count rose among nongays and the drug-free, previously thought by many to be immune to the ravages of the disease. The concept of free love, which had so defined the '60s, was now seen as foolhardy and suicidal.

Simultaneously, drug use underwent a radical change in its public image, with young Americans targeted specifically for education on the subject. While millions from within all age groups and classes still indulged, many of the older veterans of the '60s drug scene had long since had second thoughts, now doing their utmost to try to dissuade their own children from getting started. Nancy Reagan, the first lady, received a great deal of media mileage from her misinformed "Just Say No" campaign, which implored curious youngsters not to try drugs, but fell short of giving them good reasons why.

GRACE SLICK: [By the '80s] you couldn't go screw everybody, unless of course you're brain-dead and you want to die. And you can't go around taking a lot of drugs; it's not considered cool. People think you're a jerk. And both of those things are a lot of fun to do. I'm glad I had that opportunity. I enjoyed it thoroughly.

The '80s was, in its own way, an extraordinary decade, particularly on the global scale. The Soviet Union collapsed and European communism with it, thus extinguishing the so-called Cold War threat. In China's Tiananmen Square, at the end of the decade, students demonstrated for reform and were rebuffed by those in power. That same year, the Berlin wall came down. And in South Africa, the genocidal decades-long program of apartheid began its retreat.

But at home there was a feeling among many veterans of the '60s that the '80s was becoming the inverse of that decade. Reagan, who had been loathed by California's left during his term as the state's governor, was now an extremely popular president with a staunchly conservative agenda. The religious right was also on the ascent. And where so many of the youth of the '60s had shunned material gain in favor of quests for new freedoms and spiritual growth, the new generation, with its neatly trimmed hair and expensive, conservative "power" clothing, lusted openly after money. "Make love, not war" was traded in for "Greed is good," and the hippies and Yippies of the past gave way to the yuppies—young urban professionals—who prided themselves on their acquisition of wealth and goods.

Rock and roll, or what was left of it, was also going through another major upheaval. Image had largely replaced substance, as videogenic stars like Michael Jackson, Cyndi Lauper, Madonna and Boy George dominated the charts. Heavy metal loomed largely, as did overproduced love ballads and urbanized country.

But it was hip-hop, or rap, with its tough street talk and beat-heavy backdrop, that was setting the course for the future. Much rap relied not on original instrumentation but instead on a studio technique called sampling, which involved remixing snippets of existing recordings into a new whole. Hip-hop often eschewed melody and harmony for stripped-down rhythm and replaced singing with aggressive chanting.

As Jefferson Starship eased into the '80s, it was imperative that they find their place within all of that impending tumult, and reinvent themselves to survive in this alien environment. Considered by many to be an anachronism, nothing more than the remnants of a '60s hippie band that was no longer relevant, the Starship was caught between worlds.

They chose the future. As Craig told *Rolling Stone*, the band was making a concerted effort to extinguish its image as "a laid-back older San Francisco band that played slow songs like 'Miracles.' I don't mind when critics put down our new music by saying it sounds like Styx or Journey or Boston or Aerosmith. Those are my favorite bands, so I'm flattered," he said. Still, they had to wonder. Perhaps in this new rock and roll world, Jefferson Starship would have no place, no meaning. *Modern Times* did reflect, among other things, a shift toward a more mainstream, less cumbersome pop sound. The Starship had been swept up in the less-is-more current. But was that what their audience really wanted? Who was their audience? They didn't even know anymore.

Although one might imagine that Jefferson Starship would condemn punk music, some of the musicians were actually quite enamored of the movement, both for its loud energy and finger-pointing content. Was the Clash singing about wanting a "White Riot" really that far removed from the Airplane proclaiming themselves "Volunteers" of America? The Damned, one of England's first punk bands, had even covered "White Rabbit."

Marty, before he'd vacated three years earlier, had claimed that he wanted to steer the Starship in a rawer direction, and now Paul's most noteworthy contribution to *Modern Times* took its musical cues from new wave. But apropos of Paul Kantner, the song had a self-destruct mechanism built in. Paul's deliberate insertion of an X-rated tag line ensured that the record would receive little airplay and stay clear of the Top 40. It was a line that in fact Paul had included in a letter he'd written to *Rolling Stone* after *Freedom at Point Zero* received a negative review. It had been a particularly vicious piece, calling the Starship "a hulk of a band, desperately in need of material," sparing no one in the band from derision.

Paul's response: "Fuck you! We do what we want!"

In deference to Led Zeppelin's classic "Stairway to Heaven," Paul titled his song "Stairway to Cleveland (We Do What We Want)." It's an autobiographical, comedic rant against those who gave the new band little hope of making it after the departure of Marty and Grace, and a defiant commentary on all of the phonies and little annoyances a popular veteran band encounters—as well as a handful of other topics Paul felt like dropping in:

> *Old singer's gone away*
> *Whatcha gonna do about it*
> *Gold records rock 'n' rollin'*
> *Why dontcha sound like you*
> *Used to in '65 '69 '75*
> *Everybody stand up they got to*
> *Make a comment*
> *Critics said they'll never*
> *Make it never make it*
> *Never never never never never*
> *Never never never never*
> *Fuck you, we do what we want!*

PAUL KANTNER: That's one of my favorite songs, one of the few songs that I've ever done humor.

With Grace back in the band—the credits on the album cover say "Introducing Grace Slick"—the personal dynamic within shifted immediately. Although she was walking into an existing situation, she *was* Grace Slick, and that was all there was to that. Just when Mickey was starting to be accepted by the public, and feel comfortable, he was suddenly overshadowed, although he was personally in favor of the new band member.

MICKEY THOMAS: I got to sing with Grace Slick. Come on! How many guys' dream would that be?

But now, no longer a boys' club, Jefferson Starship couldn't help but turn into something else yet again.

CYNTHIA BOWMAN: As soon as Grace got on the stage Mickey was blown off, and that caused problems. Grace is a powerful person, onstage, offstage, in a band, out of a band.

Maybe Grace hadn't come back with the intention of taking over, but she loved working with the band again, loved the music they were making and she wanted to be a part of it. "Now everyone is playing for the music rather than 'me, me, me, me,' " she told David Zimmer in *Music and Sound Output* magazine. "Right now the band simply wants to make good music together instead of jerking off."

When the Starship took to the road in the summer of '81, Grace's role was kept in check. She sang mostly harmonies, and lead on "Somebody to Love," "White Rabbit" and "Fast Buck Freddie," but she certainly did not attempt to steal Mickey's thunder. Inevitably, though, as had happened with the Airplane and the first Starship configuration, conflicts began to arise. There were more outbursts, more petty bickering.

Around the same time Grace was working her way back into the band, Mickey Thomas released his second solo album, *Alive Alone*, for Elektra Records. If Mickey was counting on the album to boost his own star power, he must have been frustrated by the record's failure to reach the *Billboard* chart at all. Meanwhile, Marty's first solo album, a no-frills effort simply titled *Balin*, produced by John Hug and featuring on its cover two appropriately stark black-and-white portraits of Marty taken by the famed photographer Richard Avedon, was also released. It not only rose to number 35 but produced a number 8 single in "Hearts" and a number 27, "Atlanta Lady," both Jesse Barish compositions.

While the Starship was spending months making expensive, overproduced albums, arguing over whose songs would make the final cut and how they should be recorded, and while Mickey Thomas was wondering why his album had tanked, Marty Balin had gone into the studio with a bunch of unknown guys, played some songs and cut a hit record. Following its release, Marty began an extensive tour with his own band, comprised of friends from Mill Valley.

But Marty's revived solo career took its toll on his 10-year relationship with Trish Robbins. Trish, who had started her own new wave band called the Mirrors, fell in love with a guitar player and left Marty.

By the time Jefferson Starship reconvened to work on their next album in 1982, the tight-knit group that had gotten on so well was beginning to unravel. There were tiffs over songwriting, among other things. In Grace's absence, Pete had begun to collaborate prolifically with his wife, and together they had created some of the band's most undeniably appealing and commercial songs. But now that Grace was back, she too wanted to write again with Pete. Only problem was, he was no longer interested.

> **PETE SEARS:** I didn't want to write with Grace anymore because, although I really respected her, we didn't necessarily see eye-to-eye philosophically. She's a good person, but Grace can be very narrow-minded, and very one-track. She's got a rap, and it's the same rap, if you look very carefully, every time. There's a real vulnerability in Grace which is very carefully covered up.

For 1982's *Winds of Change*, the group changed producers again, using Kevin Beamish, a hot name in the business who had just come off of the megaplatinum-selling REO Speedwagon album *Hi Infidelity*. Although Grace had enjoyed working with Ron Nevison, not everyone else had. But despite the new producer and the return of Grace as a full-time member, *Winds of Change* was another comparative stiff, reaching the same number 26 position that *Modern Times* had. And again, there were no hit singles. To make things worse, most of the band members agreed they'd released a dog.

Perhaps one reason for the album's lackadaisical performance was that a potent new force had come into play that completely altered the business of promoting and selling music. MTV—Music Television—was launched in 1981 and became significant quickly both in breaking new acts and keeping established ones alive. MTV was instrumental in pushing young and/or extremely photogenic bands to the top, but many older, established artists didn't benefit much from the phenomenon and were lucky to have their videos played at all. Many of them resented the very idea of having to make videos, feeling that musicians should just play music, not act it out, and that a song's meaning should be up to each listener to interpret, not spelled out in a snappy little vignette.

But the game was changing, and if Jefferson Starship had any hope of survival, they were going to have to change with it. Again. Some wanted to, some didn't. Like Pete, and Freiberg as well, Paul was beginning to feel out of sorts. He was a quirky songwriter, but that had always been his strength, not a liability. Now some of the others felt he was dragging them down with his esoteric material.

> **PAUL KANTNER:** I think we would be terrible failures trying to write pop songs all the time.

Needless to say, Paul didn't take kindly to the escalating ostracism. Paul had founded the band, he was its heart and soul, and its figurehead—and he was stubborn. Now the others were trying to tell *him* what kind of music the Starship should play? Fuck them, he did what he wanted!

One thing Paul wanted was to get rid of Aynsley Dunbar. Like just about every Airplane and Starship drummer preceding him, Aynsley annoyed certain people in the organization. There had been accusations lodged by some band members and associates regarding some of the drummer's alleged personal predilections. "He was sort of asked to leave," Paul told *Rolling Stone*. "He went over the line."

In September 1982, the Starship welcomed Donny Baldwin, the newest successor to the throne formerly occupied by Messrs. Peloquin, Spence, Dryden, Covington, Barbata and Dunbar. Baldwin was, like Mickey, a veteran of the Elvin Bishop Group, drumming with that band from 1973 to '78. But by the time this latest personnel adjustment was solidified, the music press had long ago taken to routinely savaging Jefferson Starship. *Rolling Stone*, in particular, seemed to have it out for them. Writer Tom Carson had demolished *Modern Times*, saying the group "hasn't had so much as a vague whim in its collective noggin in ten years," and practically crucified Paul. A year later, reviewer Stephen Holden compared Grace to the then-homely comedienne Phyllis Diller in both sound and appearance.

As if the critical drubbing weren't enough, now there was the Church to deal with. It seemed inevitable that some clergy person somewhere during that heyday of the Christian right would decide that the devil inhabited this music. With all of Paul and Grace's lyrics condemning the Church and proposing that Jesus had fathered a child and whatnot, it was only surprising it had taken so long.

There had been one incident, when a bunch of anti–rock and roll religious zealots had picked up on "A Child Is Coming" from *Blows Against the Empire*, claiming that if the record was played backward, a devilish message could clearly be heard.

PAUL KANTNER: They heard, "The child is Satan, the child is Satan." They were hoping the child was Jesus until they played it backwards to find out the child was Satan. So I, of course, ran my record backwards to find what they were talking about but I couldn't find anything.

But it wasn't until October 1982, when the Starship was in Illinois, that all hell broke loose. Reverend Wesley Ates of the First Pentecostal Church in Bloomington had stated publicly prior to the group's local appearance that he hoped to debate Grace about her songs that "mock and blaspheme" the name of Jesus. Ates wanted her to apologize and he called for a boycott of the group's concert.

Ates and members of his congregation held a press conference, singing—what else—"Amazing Grace," and then proceeded to burn rock albums on the church's steps. The preacher said that the Starship was "anti-God, anti-Christ, anti-establishment and anti everything else that makes America great," and called on Grace and "lead guitarist" [sic] Kantner to "get down on their knees" and repent.

Cynthia Bowman, entrusted with defending the group to the press, pointed out that Pete Sears was an active, practicing Christian and that some of the others came from Christian homes, that Paul had even attended Catholic school and been an altar boy. But the reverend wasn't swayed. He wanted to save them.

Grace didn't want to get involved, but Paul couldn't resist. At the university where the show was to be held, Kantner met with Reverend Ates for two hours before the concert to discuss the issues. An audience of about 75 listened, and the debate was carried over two local radio stations. Rock and roll, claimed Ates, alienates youth from their parents, advocates drug use and causes sexually transmitted disease. Ates, declaring he was "representing Jesus Christ and the Bible," urged his audience to attend a prayer meeting instead of the concert.

Kantner retorted, "I just don't believe in believing." He had talked to God, but God had never talked back. "What kind of father is it that won't talk to you when you talk to him?" Paul asked. Jesus, he proclaimed, was "the last true Christian. Since then, everybody else has been making money on his name." That night, about 40 people attended the prayer meeting at Ates's church. Thousands went to see Jefferson Starship.

On Paul's next solo album, in progress at that time, he made sure to give a little reward to those religious fanatics who delighted in spinning records backward to find hidden satanic messages. Paul buried about five phrases in the mix: "devil's food cake," "deviled eggs," etc.

Kantner's new record was—to no one's great surprise—a concept album dealing with a rock and roll band that leaves Earth to escape political oppression. Maybe the Starship wasn't interested in his space operas anymore, but on his own album, no one was going to tell Paul Kantner what he could and couldn't do. For the title of the 1983 release—the first to bear only his name since *Blows Against the Empire*—Paul revisited another old theme: He called it *Planet Earth Rock and Roll Orchestra*. *PERRO*, he said, was an accompaniment to an unpublished novel of the same title that he'd written, which explored similar motifs, sort of a sci-fi/political/rock and roll/spy theme. Scott Mathews and Ron Nagle of the local band Durocs, along with Paul, produced the album. In the '60s Nagle had been a member of the San Francisco band the Mystery Trend. Mathews had been yet another member of Elvin Bishop's group.

The basic story behind the album, as told on its inner sleeve, is that this band, Planet Earth Rock and Roll Orchestra, "develops a computer-assisted telepathic amplification technology. . . . They attract the attention of various government and police agencies and right-wing religious forces. Eventually they are forced to flee an increasingly repressive American society for the safety of . . ." Australia?

Yes. According to Paul, somewhere deep in the Australian outback, "over fifteen hundred people have formed a settlement that is nearly totally self-sufficient. . . . The U.S. government agents eventually discover the settlement and launch an attack to recover the extrasensory technology for Cold War use. The children of the settlement are led to construct a telepathic shield around the colony and they escape into space." A tale for the Reagan era if ever there was one.

One track, "Declaration of Independence," has a lead vocal sung by China Kantner and a chorus comprised of kids of the band and their friends. Another, "The Mountain Song," had its origin in the original Planet Earth Rock and Roll Orchestra jams of the early '70s. It's dedicated to "David C., Jerry G., Graham N., Grace S., Billy K. and Mickey H., and to one summer when all of our schedules almost didn't conflict."

Like the early '70s trilogy of *Blows, Sunfighter* and *Baron von Tollbooth*, *PERRO* was a team effort. Paul brought in a large cast of cohorts to add their voices and instrumentation. The Starship members are all present, Jack Casady stops in, guitarist Ronnie Montrose makes an appearance and so do Flo and Eddie. And making his debut on record is one Alexander Bowman Kantner, the son born to Paul Kantner and Cynthia Bowman. One of two positive things stemming from Paul's hemorrhage—the other being that he gave up smoking tobacco for a few years—Alex arrived on New Year's Day 1982.

Cynthia had by that time actually moved out on Paul. And back in. Several times, in fact, she'd left him and returned. One night, after an awards ceremony, she spent the night with him. Alexander was the result.

CYNTHIA BOWMAN: That was going to be the last time. And now I was pregnant. I wasn't really sure what to do, but Paul was so clear that no matter what I wanted to do, I had to have the baby. If I didn't raise the baby, he would raise the baby. If I wanted to raise the baby we could get married. We could do anything I wanted to do as long as I had the baby.

Cynthia agreed to bear the child. As Alexander made his initial appearance, she recalls, the doctor asked Paul, "Do you want to cut the cord?"

"What am I paying *you* for?" Paul asked.

The situation at *casa* Kantner had changed by the time of Alexander's birth. Pat Dugan, who had taken care of China practically since her birth nearly 11 years earlier, had moved out of the Sea Cliff house. She had decided when Cynthia first moved in that it was time to do something else with her life.

Meanwhile, in the busier-than-ever Jefferson Starship office, the staff had grown by one with the hiring of Nadine Condon to handle radio promotions. When Cynthia finally bailed out for good, to raise her son and start her own public relations firm, Nadine took over the Starship's publicity duties as well.

GRACE BEGAN WORK on her next solo album in 1983, using Ron Nevison as producer. Virtually the entire album save for one song was coauthored by Grace and Peter Wolf, a classically trained Austrian who had played keyboards with Frank Zappa (and is not the same Peter Wolf who sang with the East Coast–based J. Geils Band). Nevison had heard Wolf and brought him in to work on Grace's album. Wolf's touch is all over the record *Software*, which is as different from *Welcome to the Wrecking Ball* as that record had been from *Dreams*.

Software, as its name suggests, put Grace in line with the popular, contemporary techno-pop sound of the mid-'80s. Although guitar is used, the album is overshadowed by Wolf's synthesized keyboards and bass, and electronic drums. Grace had become enamored of the synthesizer technology of the time, and decided to jump in all the way. Her singing here avoids her trademark free-form wails in favor of precise, short bursts, learned parts rather than improvisations.

Software, which was released in 1984, did not chart at all, and was the last solo album Grace Slick made. Meanwhile, Marty Balin's follow-up to his successful solo debut had also bombed out—*Lucky* turned out not to be so, topping out at number 156. It was his last solo album to find its way to that chart at all, and Marty was subsequently dropped from the label's roster.

While Grace, Paul and Marty were all issuing albums that the public wasn't buying, another colleague from the peak years of Jefferson Airplane was busy making music that recalled that classic era without concerning himself with charts or even record companies.

Spencer Dryden had ridden out his long stint with the New Riders and taken a hiatus, working as a bartender and getting involved with the arts and film community in Marin. Then he had an interesting conversation one night in 1982 with Barry Melton, the former guitarist of Country Joe and the Fish. Melton had been playing with Peter Albin, the former bassist of Big Brother and the Holding Company. Why not, suggested Melton, get a bunch of the San Francisco '60s musicians together and play a gig? They could bring in a light show and try to re-create the atmosphere of the old ballrooms. Being ancient now, they could even self-deprecatingly call themselves the Dinosaurs. Spencer agreed. Alton Kelley drew a poster, Glenn McKay revived his light show and it was a success. John Cipollina and Robert Hunter joined up and the band—featuring one member each from the Airplane, Quicksilver, Big Brother, the Dead and the Fish—took off, lasting several years, with a revolving cast of characters.

• • •

JORMA AND JACK HAD BARELY SPOKEN to each other in the five years since Hot Tuna had split. But if there had been any truly bad blood between them, by 1983 time itself had resolved most lingering issues. They'd both kept busy working on their own projects and simply hadn't much of a reason to keep in touch.

But when they were approached about the possibility of a Hot Tuna reunion tour, neither one could think of a good reason to say no. It was to be a one-shot deal, a few months out on the road satisfying fan demand and hopefully bringing home a few dollars. Jack dropped by Jorma's studio one day to hash out the details.

The first question was, Who would Hot Tuna be this time around? Jorma didn't bother to call any of the previous members. He had been playing casually for the past several years with his friend Michael Falzarano, a guitarist who'd moved to San Francisco from New York, and Jorma thought he would be a good person to start with. Once Falzarano recovered from the shock, he signed on.

Jorma and Michael bought a small studio together, recording what Falzarano describes as "bizarre tapes, wild stuff." The two guitarists had plans to make an album together when the idea of the Hot Tuna reformation came up. Michael suggested a drummer named Shigemi Komiyama, and Jorma signed him on. When it came time to rehearse, though, Jorma decided Hot Tuna needed a whole new sound. He and Jack had both played different musical styles since the band had broken up, and they'd learned a lot, particularly about simplifying. Jorma and Michael had also investigated other musical realms. Going back to where they had left off in 1977 was not an option for the revamped Tuna. Their audience was an accepting one, they reasoned, and would be open to anything the band had to offer. Big mistake.

JORMA KAUKONEN: This is classic Jorma thinking: We're going to put the band together, people are very excited about it, and I decide we're not playing any classic Hot Tuna songs, we're going to play all new songs. If they really love us, they're going to love it. And of course, it was an error in judgment. Because this is the music business and that's not what it's about. It was a disaster.

34
HIJACK THE STARSHIP

JEFFERSON STARSHIP WAS 10 YEARS OLD. They had now lived three years longer than the Airplane. Four members—Paul, Craig, Pete and David—had been onboard since the first album, and Grace for most of the run. Mickey Thomas, who had extended his initial two-album commitment, was celebrating his fifth year, coming up on tying Marty's tenure with the original Airplane. Jefferson Starship had evolved considerably since their inception. But now, to borrow a concept from their next album, they had reached critical mass.

For the album, *Nuclear Furniture*, they brought back Ron Nevison to produce. Pete and Jeannette Sears contributed material to the final product, as did Craig and Mickey. Peter Wolf, who had piloted Grace's *Software* album, was retained to supply arrangements and some keyboards and also cowrote a song with Grace. Another, the so-called power ballad "No Way Out," the first single from the album, was penned by Wolf with his wife, Ina. Paul landed three songs on the album, one cowritten with Mickey and the others with one of his all-time musical idols, Ronnie Gilbert of the Weavers, who had initially inspired Paul to seek out a woman for the Airplane.

Those tracks, "Rose Goes to Yale" and "Champion," boasted Paul's most biting lyrics since "Stairway to Cleveland," topical songs bookending the album's second side with stark commentary on nuclear war, its aftermath—what's gone (California, Bruce Springsteen) and what's left (Cleveland, assholes)—and what might be done to avoid that scenario. But soon into the proceedings, Paul became dissatisfied with the way the sessions were going, and he was not pleased that when the album was running too long, the others voted to eliminate one of his songs. So Paul stole the master tapes.

PAUL KANTNER: I thought the tapes were being mixed improperly. I just took them home one night.

BILL THOMPSON: He drove around for about three days. Nobody knew where he was. He had all the material that we'd been working on for months. When Paul finally came back he held them for ransom, and the only way he would come back would be if he could edit all of the songs so he could create enough room to get his song on.

Like the two albums preceding it, *Nuclear Furniture* managed a respectable but hardly cork-popping chart placement, number 28, and it did, like all four of the post-Marty Jefferson Starship albums, manage to earn a gold record, indicating several million dollars in sales. By this time, Jefferson Starship was firmly entrenched in the video age, more attuned to MTV than LSD, shooting the promotional clips that every rock band had to make if they expected even a modicum of commercial success. Some of the band members enjoyed—or at least didn't mind—making videos, others detested it, but they had no real choice.

Unfortunately, the video exposure did little to help them; the Starship seemed stuck in a holding pattern. As one song of the period proclaimed, video had killed the radio star, and wordy diatribes about nuclear holocaust were not exactly going into heavy rotation. Les Garland, one of the prime movers behind MTV and a close friend of Thompson's, had always been supportive of the Starship, but there was only so much that even someone in his position could do to get an oddball band like Jefferson Starship across to a generation that considered Duran Duran the hottest thing around. RCA/Columbia Pictures even tried to market a home video release of the band performing live, *The Definitive Concert*, but compared to the high-budget, high-tech fare being shown daily on MTV, that too was a hopelessly hackneyed, misguided affair.

Naturally, the critics, if they paid the group any mind at all, ate them alive. Jefferson Starship was now considered a sellout. Writing for *Rolling Stone*, future MTV news anchor Kurt Loder awarded *Nuclear Furniture* only two stars and called the group "middle-of-the-road heavy-metal mongers." Grace might be walking around now with a punkish hairdo and space-alien outfits, but Jefferson Starship's attempts to go modern were being lost on the record-buying, video-viewing public.

> **PETER WOLF:** You can't say, "Young people don't exist," because it doesn't work, especially in pop music where you're always appealing to a young audience. It's hard to expect people to buy the same old shit, because they also are growing. It ends up that you are the only guy that is not growing.

Clearly, they were stuck in rock and roll limbo. They could go two ways: Either make music that might endear them to the young audience, or roll back the clock and try to regain their appeal to the aging Baby Boomers who had grown up on the Airplane and early Starship. Mickey, Craig and Donny were all for keeping up the contemporary direction. Paul, Pete and David felt ridiculous playing the newer, more synthesized and calculated music, and longed to get back to the organic music-making process of their past—Paul remembers Craig, who had become enamored of Eddie Van Halen's pyrotechnical style of guitar playing and wanted to take the group in a hard-rock direction, belittling him, saying that his songs stunk and that he couldn't play guitar.

But the division wasn't that cut and dried either. Paul also despised the songs Jeannette Sears was writing for the Starship—he likened the situation to a scene in the then-new satirical rock and roll film *This Is Spinal Tap*, wherein the girlfriend of one of the musicians begins to exert an undue influence over the band's creative process.

Grace was the wild card. When push came to shove, there was no telling which direction she'd go. But then she turned against Paul too, encouraging him to "write better songs." Soon it was all-out war between Paul, who admitted being "Führer-like," and the rest of the band. They came close to fist fights at times.

Amidst all of this infighting, an embattled Jefferson Starship began their tour in support of *Nuclear Furniture*. One of the first bookings was a cruise on San Francisco Bay, for winners of an MTV contest. The band played on the lower deck while those above watched on closed-circuit TV. "This was the strangest gig I've ever played," commented Mickey Thomas at the time. Though not as strange as the one on June 23, 1984, at Marriott's Great America, an amusement park in San Jose.

MICKEY THOMAS: Paul had quit the band, but then he agreed to do one more show. We said, "Okay, but we want to make this show special, so we're going to bring in some background singers to enhance the vocals."

So Kantner's like, "If there are background singers at the gig, I'll get a machine gun out."

I said, "Paul, your daughter's one of the background singers. You might want to rethink this."

There were no automatic weapons, but after those two shows Paul stormed off, never to return. Nearly 19 years after the formation of Jefferson Airplane, the sole remaining link to the original 1965 band was gone. He had finally had enough. What drove him over the edge was the band sending Mickey to tell him they would not be using one of his songs on the album. Paul's response: "I'm German, I like war. And World War Three starts here."

Mickey's reply: "Just because you *like* war, doesn't mean you always win the war, Paul."

Paul called a band meeting and, according to Mickey, "issued a bunch of demands," informing the others that from then on he was going to have so many songs on each album, he would decide which videos they would make and where they would tour. Paul's version is that he suggested only that they make one more album together as Jefferson Starship, then go their separate ways and retire the band's name. But whatever his propositions might have been, the others nixed them all. That's when Paul knew it was time to go.

NADINE CONDON: What really put Paul over the edge was Grace siding against him. He just couldn't believe it, because she had always supported him.

CRAIG CHAQUICO: It *was* his band, but it was always set up on the premise of being a democracy, and that's why it worked so great, because it really was that way. But the joke was, "It's a democracy until you don't do what Paul wants to do." Then it becomes a dictatorship.

BILL THOMPSON: Before Grace had come back, we got an offer to open up for Journey at the Rose Bowl, $100,000 to be the special guest star. At this time we're making something like $15,000, $12,500. And Paul turns this down. Calls up the agency, "No, we're not going to do it." Without me even knowing about it.

Mickey calls up Paul: "What are you doing? We could have used that money."

Paul says, "It's bad for my image to be opening up for any band."

And Mickey goes, "Paul, it's bad for my image to be spotted sleeping on a park bench."

Paul says, "I could sell cocaine and make that much money."

Mickey goes, "But, Paul, I don't want to sell cocaine!"

PAUL KANTNER: The band became more mundane and not quite as challenging and not quite as much of a thing to be proud of. It wasn't a *total* failure though. A number of great moments came out of it.

Even after leaving the band, though, Paul didn't just walk away and forget about it. Admittedly "traumatized," his natural, warriorlike response was to strike back.

GRACE SLICK: At hotels they have little boxes with the room numbers on them in case you get mail. We'd walk off the bus or the plane and they'd have a manila envelope and it'd have nasty comments in it, and jokes, and bad reviews, for each one of us. He was annoyed.

BILL THOMPSON: Paul called up Skip's mother or someone, and left a message that Skip had been killed in a car wreck — he did shit like that. He just went off the deep end.

Once Paul was out of the picture, there was no need to keep his girlfriend on the payroll.

CYNTHIA BOWMAN: I officially quit and was fired from the band at the same time. I told Grace her husband was full of shit.

And as long as the Starship organization was cleaning house, Maurice decided to take his retirement. He had been with the group for 17 years, no longer felt that he was wanted and felt that Paul's treatment at the hands of the others had been unfair.

PAT "MAURICE" IERACI: Mickey, Grace and Craig started to rebel, and they didn't want Kantner in the band anymore. It got to be very, very cold. I said, "Paul, I'm gonna bow out when you leave." A lot of people didn't get along with Paul, didn't like him. I loved him. He's the man responsible for the band.

The Airplane waits backstage for their turn to play the legendary Woodstock festival in August 1969. Sitting left to right: Jack Casady, Grace Slick, Sally Mann (Spencer Dryden's future wife), roadie Michael Casady (Jack's brother), and Spencer. Standing at right are singer/songwriter Country Joe McDonald and renowned concert promoter and one-time Airplane manager Bill Graham. *Photo by Henry Diltz/Corbis*

ABOVE: Paul onstage at Woodstock
Photo by Michael E. Frankel © 2003

LEFT: Grace onstage at Woodstock
Photo by Michael E. Frankel © 2003

Marty Balin at the ill-fated
Altamont concert in December
1969, moments before being
pummeled by Hell's Angels.
Photo by Robert Altman © 2003

Grace Slick at Filmore West.
Behind her is Jorma Kaukonen
and onscreen is Glenn McKay's
Headlights light show.
Photo by Robert Altman © 2003

ABOVE: Joey Covington, Airplane drummer 1970–1971 *Photo by LarsMan © 2003*

RIGHT: Craig Chaquico, Jefferson Starship lead guitarist 1974–1990 *© 2003 Ed Perlstein/ musicimages.com*

BELOW: Jefferson Starship recording their *Earth* album in 1977. Back row (left to right: John Barbata, Grace Slick, Pete Sears, and David Freiberg) and front row (left to right: Craig Chaquico, China Kantner, Marty Balin, and Paul Kantner). *Photo by Roger Ressmeyer/Corbis*

Papa John Creach
Photo by LarsMan © 2003

ABOVE: Hot Tuna, 1972 (left to right: Jack Casady, Papa John Creach, Jorma Kaukonen, and Sammy Piazza) *Photo by Bruce Steinberg © 2003*

BELOW: Hot Tuna, 1977 (left to right: Jack Casady, Bob Steeler, and Jorma Kaukonen)
Photo by Roger Ressmeyer/Corbis

Bill Thompson, manager of Jefferson Airplane/Starship and Hot Tuna *Photo by Roger Ressmeyer/Corbis*

Jacky Watts Kaukonen Sarti, longtime office manager *Photo by Roger Ressmeyer/Corbis*

Bill Laudner, road manager for Airplane and Starship
Photo by Roger Ressmeyer/Corbis

Pat "Maurice" Ieraci, production coordinator from 1967–1984
Photo by Roger Ressmeyer/Corbis

ABOVE: Grace with Jefferson Starship, still packing them in. *Photo courtesy of London Features © 2003*

LEFT: Mickey Thomas, Jefferson Starship vocalist 1979–1990 *© 2003 Ed Perlstein/ musicimages.com*

RIGHT: Jefferson Airplane reunite, 1989 (top: Jorma Kaukonen and Paul Kantner; bottom: Marty Balin, Grace Slick, and Jack Casady).
Photo by Lynn Goldsmith/Corbis

The never predictable Grace Slick as a nun, 1982 . . .
Photo by Larry Hulst © 2003

. . . in blackface makeup on
The Smothers Brothers Show,
1968 . . . *Photo by Chuck*
Boyd/Redferns © 2003

. and as '80s heavy metal shock-rocker.
to by Roger Ressmeyer/Corbis

LEFT: Grace Slick finger salute, 2002 *Photo by Robert Knight © 2003*
RIGHT: Marty Balin finger salute, 1998 *Photo by Jeff Tamarkin © 2003*

The Airplane is inducted into the BAMMIES Walk of Fame at San Francisco's Bill Graham Civic Auditorium in 1999. (left to right: Paul Kantner, Jorma Kaukonen, Spencer Dryden, and Jack Casady). Smiling at far left is former Airplane office manager Jacky Kaukonen Sarti. In shades between Paul and Jorma is former Airplane manager Bill Thompson. *Photo by J.C. Juanis © 2003*

Taking Maurice's job as production coordinator: Grace's husband, Skip Johnson.

IF PAUL THOUGHT THE OTHERS would consider his departure the end of the world, he was wrong. They soldiered on, attaining a level of commercial success they had never been able to achieve with Paul in the band. Still calling themselves Jefferson Starship, one of the first things the band did following Paul's exit was to tape a video for the next single, "Layin' It on the Line," a Chaquico–Thomas song on *Nuclear Furniture*. Capitalizing on the fact that 1984 was a presidential election year, the theme of the video was a political convention for the "Mick and Slick" ticket, as in Thomas and Grace. The video included cameos by Bill Graham, Country Joe McDonald, San Francisco Assembly Speaker (and future Mayor) Willie Brown, comedian Pat Paulsen and the San Francisco avant-garde group the Residents.

In October, the feud between Paul and the group culminated with Paul taking them to court, suing over money he said he was owed and their continued usage of the name Jefferson Starship. He claimed that he had created the group and the name and therefore the remaining musicians had no right to use it. In his claim, filed in San Francisco Superior Court, Paul argued that he was owed $90,000 in loans and nearly $100,000 in earnings from recordings and touring. The suit contended that a 1982 agreement stipulated that the group was to share its money equally. At that time, the Starship had re-signed with RCA for four albums. Kantner said that by the group shutting him out of participating in the two yet-to-be-made albums that would fulfill that contract, he was losing $70,000 in advances. In addition, he claimed, by being barred from the group's current tour, expected to gross $1.4 million, he would lose out on his share.

Further, Paul charged, as a co-owner of the name Jefferson Starship, along with Bill Thompson and Grace Slick, he had the right to hire and fire anyone but those two and, if he deemed it necessary, to retire the group's name. According to Thompson, Paul's attorney seized the Starship's financial accounts, leaving them no operating capital. According to Paul, Thompson attempted to stop all payments he was to receive. Shades of the Matthew Katz debacle, 20 years later.

The lawsuit was settled in March 1985. Kantner ended up with a cash settlement, and the name Jefferson Starship became the legal property of Grace Slick and Bill Thompson—Grace, with 51 percent of the corporate stock, actually had controlling interest. The ownership of the name immediately became a moot point, however, because all of the parties also agreed to drop the usage of the word "Jefferson" in any future endeavors. For a short while the Mickey-led group continued to perform defiantly as Starship Jefferson, but by the time they were ready to record their next album, they had shortened the name simply to Starship.

Although David Freiberg was named in the lawsuit and had stayed on after Paul left, it was time for him to get his walking papers too. Like Paul, Freiberg was an old-schooler. For him it wasn't about making videos or playing the stadiums or finding the most commercial formula in the studio. He just wanted to play music. Freiberg had already noticed the change in outlook back in 1979—as soon as his song "Jane" had become a hit, there was pressure on him to write another just like it. Not a prolific writer to begin with, there was no way he was even going to attempt to copy himself just because he'd written a hit. By the mid-'80s, Freiberg was considered dead weight by the others.

BILL THOMPSON: Grace said, "Let's kick out Freiberg. He doesn't contribute. Why are we paying him?"

Freiberg was gone before the next album was recorded, but Paul never forgave him for not quitting the same time he did. They've rarely spoken to each other since they left the Starship.

DAVID FREIBERG: I should have agreed with Paul and gone with him. But everybody was acting like a spoiled brat. I guess I betrayed him, by not taking his side. Everybody was kind of right, that was the problem.

After leaving the Starship, Paul wasn't about to sit around moping. In October of '84, he turned up onstage in Golden Gate Park with Marty Balin's band and sang "It's No Secret," the first Jefferson Airplane single. Afterward, they talked. "Why don't you come play with us for a while?" Marty suggested.

Paul took him up on his offer, and by the spring of 1985 the reunion of the two founding members of the Airplane had become something more serious. With Hot Tuna temporarily in limbo again, Jack, who had no pending beefs with Marty or Paul from the Airplane days, was happy to join their project. The KBC Band, as they called it—Kantner, Balin, Casady—also included someone named Slick, but not that one; this was Mark "Slick" Aguilar, who had been serving as the guitarist in Marty's band, having worked previously with David Crosby. The group began gigging around the Bay Area, performing a mix of Airplane/Starship favorites and newly written tunes.

One early gig took place in November 1985 at the newly resurrected Fillmore, the legendary venue where it had all begun some two decades earlier. Bill Graham turned the reopening into a San Francisco extravaganza, a grand celebration of the '60s featuring Country Joe and the Fish, the Sons of Champlin, KBC and others. During their set, KBC was joined by Spencer Dryden, who was still going strong with the Dinosaurs, and Signe Anderson, whose voice hadn't graced that stage since 1966. At another gig soon thereafter, KBC found itself sharing the bill with another old colleague, Jorma Kaukonen. Jorma sat in with KBC, the first time since 1972 that he, Jack, Paul and Marty had shared a stage. While there was no talk that night about any possible future collaborations, the ice was broken.

Neither Jorma's career nor his private life were in great shape at the time. Having been dropped by RCA Records after the last two records sputtered, he had recently hooked up with a new independent record label based in Brooklyn, Relix Records, an offshoot of the same-named fanzine that covered the San Francisco music scene. Relix first released *Splashdown*, culled from tapes of a radio broadcast of acoustic Tuna from 1975, then *Magic*, eight tracks taken from a Jorma solo show. The label also released *Historic Hot Tuna*, from a 1971 KSAN broadcast, and *Too Hot to Handle*, an acoustic Jorma album recorded in 1984, half new songs and half old favorites.

That album was dedicated "with love and respect" to Margareta Kaukonen, and while the sentiments were sincere, it was during that same year that Jorma finally extricated himself from the prickly, two-decade-long relationship. He had finally walked out the door for good after she cracked his head open with a wooden shoe.

JORMA KAUKONEN: I was, in the recovery parlance, codependent with her. I started doing heroin in the mid-'80s and I was pretty much strung out during those years. I was drinking, doing a lot of drugs and continued to do so until '93, and it affected my judgment and my playing. There's this TV ad where this guy says, "Nobody says, 'I want to be a junkie when I grow up.'" Well, I always wanted to be a junkie. Absolutely. It looked like the coolest thing you could be. It took me a long time to get into it, fortunately.

Beginning in early 1985, in yet another surprising turn, Jorma started playing shows with Jaco Pastorius, one of the most renowned jazz bassists in the world, a pioneer whose work with the 1970s fusion band Weather Report is some of the most highly respected and influential of its time. Jorma had never played jazz to any serious extent. It was a bizarre coupling, save for the fact that these were two extraordinary musicians with a shared penchant for exploration and heavy drug use. Before long, the Jorma–Jaco experiment accommodated a larger group of players, among them Rashied Ali, the intense jazz drummer who had followed the great Elvin Jones in John Coltrane's mid-'60s ensemble. Pastorius soon vacated, but the group continued for several months. By early '86, though, Jorma and Jack found themselves drawn toward each other once again and Hot Tuna was back on a part-time basis, in acoustic form, just the two of them. The familiar repertoire was back too, giving the faithful a reason to feel relieved.

Jorma now spent some of his time with Jack, some performing solo and some with Falzarano, while Jack split his time between Tuna and KBC. That band now had a record deal with Arista, the label helmed by Clive Davis, who had once signed the likes of Janis Joplin and Santana to Columbia Records. The self-titled *KBC Band*, released in the fall of 1986, fared moderately well, reaching number 75.

Two of the new Kantner–Balin songs on the album were particularly powerful compositions. "Mariel," which opens the record, was, Paul wrote, "To the memory and spirit of Victor Jara and to the future of Nora Astorga." Paul had become infatuated with the dicey political situation in Nicaragua, where the Sandinista revolutionaries had taken control of the country in 1979. Astorga, Paul later wrote in a published commentary, "had been a corporate lawyer . . . in Nicaragua prior to the revolution. But she'd secretly supported and worked for the Sandinistas from inside the "belly of the beast."

Eventually, Astorga became Nicaragua's representative to the United States. Paul met her in San Francisco and wrote the song in her honor. She invited Paul to come to Nicaragua with KBC, but the band was reluctant to perform in a war-torn nation, so Paul went down by himself, traveling with the American singer-songwriter Kris Kristofferson and playing music for the Nicaraguan people. Paul had, he said, "the most marvelous time, met some truly inspiring people—poets, soldiers, musicians, comandantes and priests."

He recounted the experience in a book he wrote in 1987, *Paul Kantner's Nicaragua Diary*, subtitled "How I Spent My Summer Vacation or I Was a Commie Dupe for the Sandinistas." Self-published in a small quantity by Paul's own Little Dragon Press, it was sold only in independent San Francisco bookstores. The book consists of just over 100 pages of pure Kantner. It includes the Nicaragua saga and other stories, some jokes, some cartoons and a handful of lyrics.

Among those were the unexpurgated lyrics of "America," Paul's epic song-poem about a girl who had lost her father in Vietnam and now her husband in Lebanon. On her way to Washington to pick up a medal from the president, she sees sights she'd never seen, "hungry people in the streets, young mothers who could not eat," and starts thinking about the so-called American dream. The version in the book is about twice as long as the one on *KBC Band*, which was edited down by Marty to a reasonable six-minute tour de force.

KBC continued throughout most of 1987. There were plans for a second album, but the band lost the support of Arista when Marty, once again feeling the urge to move on, refused to tape a video and left for a vacation in Hawaii. Abruptly after that, Paul decided to leave the band, signaling its demise.

WHILE PAUL HAD BEEN INVOLVED WITH KBC, the band that he'd left behind became one of the most successful in the country. In 1985, Starship released their first album under that name, *Knee Deep in the Hoopla*, its title, grafted from a line in one of its songs, a less-than-subtle commentary on the tribulations of the recent past. Peter Wolf was promoted to the position of producer, and his first move was to reject the idea of Starship contributing their own material—only one track here, Craig and Mickey's "Private Room," comes from within the band. All of the other eight songs were chosen from a pool submitted to Wolf and Starship for consideration, and Wolf made undeniably smart choices. Self-expression was never much the point for this version of the band. Having hits was.

> **GRACE SLICK:** This was a working commercial, professional, older band—it's not a kids' band. We've been around for a while, we know the ropes, we go on tour, we do the shit. We get pimple cream sponsorship. It got boring after a while, but it didn't bother me.

Knee Deep in the Hoopla opens with "We Built This City," a song cowritten by Elton John's lyricist, Bernie Taupin, along with Martin Page, Dennis Lambert and Wolf himself. Entering the *Billboard* Hot 100 at number 73 on the chart dated September 7, 1985, it climbed steadily until November 16, when it dislodged Jan Hammer's "Miami Vice Theme" from the top spot. Starship, on their first time out, accomplished what Jefferson Airplane and Jefferson Starship had never been able to, a number 1 single.

Many fans of those earlier groups were appalled by the highly polished new sound and offended by Starship's claim to have "built this city on rock and roll." But according to Grace, the song was never intended to suggest that this band was in any way responsible for the San Francisco rock and roll explosion. As she explained it, it was actually about Los Angeles clubs being closed down.

> **MICKEY THOMAS:** "We Built This City" is not really about any particular city; it's not a geographical thing. It's a "city" of people all over the world, all over the planet, who have an idealism that is attached to music, who believe that rock and roll can change the world, and music can make you feel good, music can keep you young, music can save you in times of desperation. To me, it was a musical "city."

> **PETER WOLF:** I didn't feel this was a smash right out of the box. I thought that it was a novelty song. But then the president of the record company called me and said that it is the most amazing thing he's ever heard, and it's gonna be huge. "Can you finish this thing immediately?"

Wolf came up with the idea of using Thompson's well-connected MTV friend, Les Garland, to supply a brief spoken interlude over the song's bridge, playing the part of a San Francisco disc jockey, a role he'd held for many years. The bit gave the song a unique characteristic and helped send the sales skyward.

> **LES GARLAND:** Peter Wolf said, "Garland, just say something so we can get a feel for what it might sound like with a voice on there." They rolled it, and what you hear on that record is the first take.

> **MICKEY THOMAS:** When it went to number 1, the vindication and the validation that I felt was really special. It was like, we were right. It was worth it. We made the right move.

As for Paul Kantner, he humbly accepted the ascent of the group to the top.

> **PAUL KANTNER:** I figured it was some learning irony that I was supposed to absorb. A little stretch of humility.

Starship was finally garnering the commercial success they had craved, but now they had to survive strictly on their own merits. They were past the point of coasting on the long, twisted history of the Jeffersons—the present rock audience either didn't know or didn't care where they had been before. But any jitters were quickly purged: With music written by Peter Wolf and words by his wife, Ina, "Sara," the next single, entered the chart during Christmas week and followed "We Built This City" straight to number 1.

Knee Deep in the Hoopla itself peaked at number 7 on the album chart, the group's best showing since *Earth* in 1978. When they gathered to make the follow-up album, 1987's *No Protection*, Starship was lighter one member: Pete Sears had been ousted. Now they were four, half the size of the group that had made *Red Octopus* a dozen years earlier. Like David Freiberg before him, Sears had begun to feel useless in the band. Besides, Pete was embarrassed.

> **PETE SEARS:** One day, I'm standing onstage, and I'm playing this keyboard around my neck, which I hate. I'm looking at Mickey, who's lying down on a park bench onstage, with a lamppost as a prop, like Las Vegas or something. I thought, What in the hell am I doing here?

Starship almost lost one other member after the success of *Knee Deep*. Mickey Thomas had received a call in 1985 inquiring whether he might be interested in joining the hugely successful Chicago, whose lead singer, Peter Cetera, had left. According to some in the Starship organization, Mickey used the offer as ammunition to get a raise, but ultimately the negotiations fell through and Thomas stayed with Starship.

> **SKIP JOHNSON:** We found out, a year or so later, from Chicago's manager, that, "Yeah, we talked to Mickey, but we didn't like him. He wasn't a team player." So the whole thing was a bluff to begin with.

No Protection, the number 12-charting album released in the summer of 1987, was a more scattered affair than *Hoopla* had been. Wolf returned to produce six of the album's 10 tracks, but three others were credited to Keith Olsen. Although he had produced records by the Dead and Santana, Olsen was best known for his work with Fleetwood Mac. One last track, "Nothing's Gonna Stop Us Now," was produced and arranged by Narada Michael Walden, whose credits included mostly R&B singers like Aretha Franklin and the then-new sensation Whitney Houston.

"Nothing's Gonna Stop Us Now," like "We Built This City" and "Sara," an eminently catchy if sterile tune, was used in the soundtrack of a film called *Mannequin*, a dismal trifle of a movie whose success with the teen date crowd managed to boost the single to number 1. It was also top of the pops in Britain, the first time any recording by an Airplane/Starship affiliate managed that feat—the Airplane, in fact, had never had a chart single there at all.

The song was written by Diane Warren and Albert Hammond, and sung as a duet between Mickey and Grace. "Nothing's Gonna Stop Us Now," which *Billboard* lists as the best-performing single of any ever associated with the Airplane or either Starship incarnation, was nominated for an Academy Award for Best Original Song and a Grammy for Best Song Written Specifically for a Motion Picture or Television. At the time, Grace raved about the song. Later she too reconsidered its value.

> **GRACE SLICK:** I was damn near 50, and I'm singing "nothing's gonna stop us now." I know goddamn well how fast a relationship

can come apart. It's distracting and disconcerting to me to be singing lyrics I don't believe.

What bothered Grace even more was what happened in the studio during the recording of the album's other Diane Warren song, "Set the Night to Music." Originally arranged as another duet between Grace and Mickey, Grace arrived to find out that Thomas had decided to record it without her.

MICKEY THOMAS: I just felt it was a very personal song that would have been better done in a single voice than singing it to someone. More of an intimacy that way.

Meanwhile, on the same track, Craig's role was called into question when Wolf sampled his guitar rather than let Craig create his own guitar parts. Grace remembers walking into the studio, hearing what she thought was Craig's guitar down the hall, and entering the room to find that it was actually Wolf toodling on the keyboard.

CRAIG CHAQUICO: I did see the place of the guitar getting smaller in the band. I was going, "Jeez, somebody must like it. It's selling lots of records," so I wasn't too bummed out about it yet. But I started to get bummed when people started leaving the band.

Which is what Grace Slick did in early 1988, quitting after a gig at a private corporate party for a semiconductor company on the Peninsula, by then better known as Silicon Valley. Grace had finally come to the realization that this band was no longer her home. She felt she was being squeezed out, much as Paul and the others had been, and she was tired of playing second banana to Mickey Thomas. She had nearly quit once, not long before, but Craig had talked her out of it.

CRAIG CHAQUICO: There had been some animosity developing [between Mickey and Grace]. Those were the ugliest times in the band. I was a lot more aware of the conflicts and I was starting to get involved, emotionally. I'm totally digging both performers, and respecting what they do, and being tortured by the fact that they're not able to do it together.

Grace's decision to leave might have come as a great shock even a year or two earlier. But for nearly everyone who was still involved, it was becoming obvious that the end was near and just as obvious that few cared anymore whether the band lived or died. Grace's departure was almost anticlimactic.

GRACE SLICK: There's no use beating a dead horse. And it was a dead horse as far as I was concerned.

SKIP JOHNSON: When Paul Kantner was still around, he always insisted on creativity and spontaneity, experimentation. Once he was gone, they went the opposite way.

MICKEY THOMAS: The only thing that Grace really wanted was for me to look at her more onstage. But once we started to have hits, maybe I developed a tendency to be more intimidated by Grace's presence onstage, and sometimes when we would sing some of the duets, I would be more into playing to the audience than playing to Grace. That might have hurt her feelings a little bit.

And then there were none. With Grace out, Starship, now a band consisting of three people—Craig Chaquico, Mickey Thomas and Donny Baldwin—no longer had a single remaining link to what was once Jefferson Airplane.

Not that that stopped them. Mickey hired two new musicians, bassist Brett Bloomfield, who had played before with Baldwin and on Grace's *Software* album, and Mark Morgan, a keyboardist who had toured as a sideman with Starship. Together they made a new album, *Love Among the Cannibals*, its title a deliberate dig at those who'd abandoned ship or been thrown overboard.

MICKEY THOMAS: The love generation was really a bunch of cannibals to me, so that's where I came up with the idea of a bone through the heart for the cover art.

There was one hit single from the album, the number 12 "It's Not Enough," in the summer of '89, but the album itself—which Mickey calls his favorite of the group's recordings—snuffed out at number 64.

The very week that *Love Among the Cannibals* entered the chart, Jefferson Airplane began their comeback tour.

35
PEACE AND WAR

JACK CASADY REFERRED TO IT as "getting together with all of your ex-wives in one room and having to create." In 1989, for the first time in 17 years—not including court appearances—Jefferson Airplane was together again. It was Jack who provided the final nudge that turned the fantasy into a reality.

KBC had taken them halfway there—three of the principals proved you could go home again. But Paul, Marty and Jack did not the Airplane make. Grace had made it clear that she was not interested in going backward, and Jorma had been saying for years that he'd never play with any of those people again (other than Jack, of course). Then, Jorma had a change of heart.

In May 1987, at the Great American Music Hall in San Francisco, Paul, at Jorma's invitation, sat in with Hot Tuna. Afterward, Paul and Jorma spoke and agreed to go on the road together and see what happened. The Tuna/Kantner tour began that December in Chicago, Paul and the boys pooling their talents for a set that included the usual Hot Tuna fare, some KBC material, plus old favorites like "Martha," "Wooden Ships" and "The Other Side of This Life."

The tour snaked its way around the Northeast through December, Papa John Creach performing with them in New Jersey and New York. They broke for the new year and Tuna resumed on their own for a while, then Paul returned for the West Coast leg in February, starting in Seattle. At the next stop, Portland's Starry Night, local resident Signe Anderson made her way to the stage to sing "High Flyin' Bird" and "Chauffeur Blues."

On March 4, 1988, they were back in San Francisco to play the Fillmore. It was Jack's idea to call Grace. She had just walked away from Starship the month before. Her motivation in doing so was certainly not to jump from one dysfunctional family to another; she was going to give it all up and retire. But, Jack mentioned, it would be a goof to surprise Paul. And Grace was always up for a goof.

She turned up at the soundcheck, surprising Paul as planned, and then again at the show that night. For the audience it was an amazing treat to see Grace Slick, Paul Kantner, Jorma Kaukonen and Jack Casady making music together again. She sang her parts on "Wooden Ships," joined Jorma for "Third Week in the Chelsea" and "Good Shepherd" and returned at the end for "Volunteers."

There still was no talk of an Airplane reunion at that point. Tuna went back to doing what they usually did, without Paul—they performed one New York show in early 1989 billed as Jack Casady and the Degenerates, joined by Jack's old friend from D.C., the guitar whiz Danny Gatton. But everyone seemed restless, as if they knew that the inevitable was coming. They just didn't know when or how it would happen.

It was some time late in 1988, a year after RCA released its latest collection of tunes recycled from the Airplane albums, *2400 Fulton Street,* that the idea of a Jefferson Airplane tour and album was first discussed seriously. Jorma was still hesitant—going on the road with Paul Kantner doing Hot Tuna songs and the occasional Airplane number was one thing, but did he really want to be out there day after day rehashing "White Rabbit"?

Then he thought about it in real-world terms. He'd recently moved from San Francisco to Key West, Florida. He also had a home in Woodstock, New York. He was in bad shape financially, and strung out on junk. He'd met a woman named Vanessa Lillian and married her. A Jefferson Airplane reunion might not be optimum musically, but it could help him turn things around.

Grace was going to be a harder sell. Her feud with Paul had been bitter. Even after the lawsuit over the Starship name had been settled, the carping had continued. In 1985, Grace sued Paul over her half of the Sea Cliff house. The following year Paul sued Grace, saying that she and Skip had illegally taped private phone conversations and played them for people in the entertainment industry. The battle became so fierce that even China was so fed up with Paul's shenanigans she wanted nothing more to do with him; Paul said at the time that China thought of him as "the devil incarnate."

But after Grace left the Starship, she and Paul began a slow reconciliation. Grace sat in with Paul at a few other shows, but she still wasn't convinced that a full-blown revival of Jefferson Airplane would make the best possible use of her time. The '80s had been a stressful period for her—not as crazy as the '70s, but taxing nonetheless. Her parents had both died; she and Skip had both struggled to regain their sobriety, not always successfully; she'd dealt with problems affecting China, some of the normal teenage variety, others directly stemming from the girl's own mishandling of alcohol. And, of course, there was the split from Starship, which left her neither bitter nor angry but simply exhausted, wanting to spend some time away from the rock and roll world.

Besides, Grace had developed other interests. In 1985, after watching a TV special, she had fallen in love with the panda and, upon learning that the beautiful Asian species was nearing extinction, Grace threw herself into the animal rights movement. She joined PETA (People for the Ethical Treatment of Animals), one of the leading animal rights groups, and became appalled when she learned about the brutal testing carried out on animals by cosmetic companies. She read everything she could find on the subject and studied biomedical research intently. She began speaking out on the subject, appeared in ads, on TV and radio talk shows, anyplace that would have her. She fought the killing of animals for fur and became a vegetarian. She once found herself in a debate on the subject where one of the other guests sharing her views was G. Gordon Liddy, one of Nixon's favorite henchmen—that was a first.

There was also another reason that Grace wanted to keep to herself for a while: her marriage to Skip Johnson had been unraveling for some time. The couple had often been apart—she was on the road with her band, he was working with various others—and so it came as no great shock to Grace when Skip confessed that he had been seeing another woman, half Grace's age. The affair was over, he told Grace, and he wanted to give their marriage another go. Grace agreed but in spite of her own romantic history, she was hurt by the revelation. She took the news calmly, but she and Skip grew further apart, spending less time together.

Grace was pondering where she was in her life in the post-Starship era when Paul called to ask her about doing the Airplane. She told him she'd need a lot of convincing. So just as they'd done in 1966 when they tried to persuade her to join the band the first time around, the others sent Jack over to lay his charms on her.

> **PAUL KANTNER:** Casady is the quiet interlocutor between all of our warring forces. He got me and Grace back together. He got me and China back together. He got me and Jorma together.

It was a major accomplishment that they were all even standing in the same room without pulling out weapons. These were people who had been calling each other nasty names for years, not to mention taking each other to court. At one point near the end of her Starship tenure, Grace was involved in so many lawsuits she didn't even know what some of them were. Considering that the 21-year series of cases involving the Airplane's first manager, Matthew Katz, had only just wrapped up in 1987, it was perplexing that any of the former Airplane members would voluntarily choose to visit the inside of a courthouse again.

> **BILL THOMPSON:** Paul sued the band, then Grace sued Paul, then Joey sued the band [for back royalties he felt he was owed], then Paul and Grace sued us. She sued everybody in the Starship.

Finally, Grace agreed to the reunion. An announcement was made. Only problem was, they'd forgotten Marty—and a drummer. Technically, Marty did not have to be included for the Airplane to use the name legally—he was not one of its owners, whereas Jack, Jorma, Grace and Paul were. But they knew in their hearts it wouldn't be right without him.

> **PAUL KANTNER:** Grace insisted that Marty be part of it, to her credit. Marty was difficult at the end of KBC—he is difficult at the ends. He's sort of a pain in the ass, the way we all are to each other at those times. To do a project with me, Jack, Grace and Jorma is not at all out of the question, and it could have made for a very good project. But we wouldn't have called it Jefferson Airplane. We'd have called it Airplane Parts or something.

Marty was busy working with his newest group, the Wolfpack, when he got the call. He had already heard that the others were planning a reunion, but he wasn't about to beg his way in. He was content doing what he was doing. He'd just met a woman named Karen Deal, a musician and singer, in Florida, and they were about to be married. Life was good; Marty wasn't wanting for anything. If the Airplane wanted him to join, they knew his number. They dialed it in March of '89 and Marty signed on as an independent contractor, a hired hand. And it didn't take long, he recalled, for the old hostilities to resurface, for the factions to recongeal.

MARTY BALIN: At first they weren't even talking to each other, the four of them. Then we'd go to rehearsals and Jorma and Paul were like two children, yelling. One time they got so ridiculous at each other, ready to draw swords, that they began laughing. And that broke the ice.

Spencer Dryden was still playing with the Dinosaurs in 1989 when he heard that Jefferson Airplane was going to reunite. Assuming they were reassembling the entire band from the classic 1966–70 lineup, he waited for his call, but it never came. Exasperated, he took matters into his own hands, phoning Brian Rohan, the band's lawyer. Rohan didn't call him back, but Paul did. "Very honestly, man, it's that thing about Graham," Paul explained. Kantner was still holding a grudge against the drummer for his part in having Bill Graham fired as manager, more than 20 years earlier. Besides, added Paul, they needed a younger, more energetic drummer for this reunion tour, and the others felt he wouldn't be able to cut it.

Instead, the reconstructed Airplane chose Kenny Aronoff, a mighty, precise drummer who was best known for his work with mainstream midwestern rocker John Mellencamp. It was Ron Nevison, hired at Grace's insistence to produce the Airplane reunion album, who asked Aronoff if he would be interested in the gig. Aronoff, who'd been an Airplane fan while growing up in Indiana, gladly took the job.

The reconstituted band would also need a manager. Bill Thompson was still working with what was left of Starship and declined an offer to switch camps, so at Grace's insistence, the Airplane instead chose Trudy Green, who had guided the careers of top acts like Janet Jackson and Heart. Green's first act was to secure a deal for the album with Epic Records and to begin lining up tour dates, starting in August.

Nevison made certain before agreeing to the album project that he would get to call the shots. He felt that Peter Wolf, a man he had first brought into the picture, had wrested Starship away from him and re-made that band in his own image. Nevison had worked long enough with Jefferson Starship to know they were a contentious lot, but he had no real hint of what he was coming up against with the Airplane.

His first problem was Jorma and Jack. Nevison must have known about the factions, but he must also have thought he could get around that. It was worse than he thought. Nevison's ideas for the album went directly against theirs, and to make things worse, Jorma was still taking heroin and Jack had developed a drinking problem. Both he and Paul, once the band's most active dopers, had begun adding substantial quantities of alcohol to their menu in recent years—each of the members of the prime-era Airplane, the one-time poster group for LSD and "recreational" drugs, had now gone through a period of regular alcohol indulgence.

Although the acid-taking days were over and piles of coke no longer sat in ashtrays in dressing rooms, no one in the band had quite found a substance-free existence yet. And Paul, of course, was still Paul.

BILL THOMPSON: Paul would smoke dope anywhere, in front of anybody, at any time. On an airplane, in a restaurant, a limousine. It didn't matter where it was. And he always had the greatest stuff.

WAVY GRAVY: Paul would smoke in police stations, he's so bad.

Titled simply *Jefferson Airplane*, the album was coproduced by Nevison with Greg Edward and the group. In addition to the basic lineup, a team of outside musicians was brought in to flesh out the sound. Aronoff was on drums and old friend Nicky Hopkins on keyboards, while Peter Kaukonen and Michael Landau were used on guitars. Charles Judge played keyboards, Flo and Eddie sang background vocals, Efrain Toro handled percussion and Mike and Steve Porcaro and David Paich—three members of Toto, the quintessential bland, '80s studio-rock outfit—took on various bass and keyboard duties.

Fans weren't the only ones questioning why a band that included Jorma Kaukonen and Jack Casady, and Grace Slick for that matter, needed help with the guitar, bass and piano chores.

JACK CASADY: That was difficult for us to swallow because that didn't seem to be using the talents that were there. And of course the talents that were there weren't really ready to work hand-in-hand with Ron Nevison and that attitude, which was, "Make 'em get a pop song so we can sell some records." Ron would leave the studio and leave it to the second engineer whenever Jorma would do a solo, he had such a low opinion of him. Then they had a keyboard player play what he thought was a modern '89 bass part for me. Everybody would go off in their little corner—I'd go off in my own little alcohol corner, Jorma goes off in his corner . . .

KENNY ARONOFF: I think what Nevison was saying was, "Let's get this fucking record done. I want a good record."

Ultimately, no one involved in the project was overjoyed with it, although some believe there were aspects of the music itself that were commendable.

PAUL KANTNER: It didn't work as successfully as I would have liked. But we moved people. We had good shows. We made a pretty good record, with interesting stuff on it, though there was no scene around it to weave within, like there was before.

RON NEVISON: I expected the band to just get back together, naively, and just be the old band. So we brought in other people. We probably should have just stayed with it, as bad as it was because, technically, the Airplane was never a great band. I think that if I had paid more attention to it, it could have been better.

The album was recorded in Los Angeles at the Record Plant. Some 13 songs were squeezed in, all but two ("True Love," penned by two of the Toto guys, and "Solidarity," a poem by Bertolt Brecht set to music by Marty) written by members of the group, either alone or in various combinations.

Paul started things off with the gleeful "Planes (Experimental Aircraft)," an appropriately soaring tune about a boy who dreamed of flying and who, as he grows up, holds on to his desire to "touch the stars again." The dense, rather murky production is wrong for the song but typical of the album and of the times—Jorma is so completely overpowered by the other guitarists that one wonders why he's there at all. Paul also contributed "Madeleine Street" and "The Wheel," both part (along with KBC's "Mariel") of what he calls his Nicaragua trilogy. "The

Wheel" was inspired by the poetry of Central American revolutionaries, particularly a piece called "For the Good of All," by a young, deceased Guatemalan named Otto Rene Castillo.

Jorma gets the spotlight for "Ice Age," a song he'd been playing with Hot Tuna. Written from the perspective of a dying man, what might have been a potentially gnashing tune onstage with Tuna is drained of most of its life here, covered up with gloss and rendered largely powerless.

Marty's "Summer of Love" took a major critical drubbing when the album was released. A sentimental, wistful ballad, it is admittedly naked in its naivete, its lyrics so simplistic some must have wondered if it was a put-on.

> **MARTY BALIN:** I went down to the office and they had the head of the record company, Ron Nevison and a few other people. They said, "Wow, that's a great song!"
>
> I said, "Paul and Grace really liked that one too. We ought to do that one as a single."
>
> And they'd say, "That's a hit song but it's not an Airplane song!"
>
> I got really mad and I said, "What the hell are you telling me what an Airplane song is? If I write it, and we sing it, it's an Airplane song, you jerks."

The powers that be decided to go with "Planes" as the single instead.

Grace's "Common Market Madrigal" is beautifully sung, but its tender true-love lyrics are the kind that would have made the Grace Slick of 20 years earlier gag. An instrumental by Jorma, "Upfront Blues," is, in its own way, the purest piece on the record, a Delta-style Tuna jam, finally giving Jorma, Jack and Aronoff an opportunity to show what they're capable of when left alone. Jorma's "Too Many Years" is another highlight, a candid commentary on the failure of his marriage, placed in a warm acoustic guitar setting that belies the hostile feeling generated by so much of the rest of the album.

Grace's "Panda" closes the reunion album, both a love song to the endangered animal and a plea for the cessation of its poaching by shortsighted, money-hungry traders. Like Marty's "Summer of Love," the song was criticized as being mawkish, but there is no denying the sincere affection behind it.

The record finished, the revamped Jefferson Airplane buckled down to rehearse for the tour, which would begin at the Riverside Theater in Milwaukee on August 18. More than 25 dates were scheduled initially, taking the band to the East Coast first, then to the Midwest, a handful of dates in the South and finally back to California and a Golden Gate Park free show on September 30. As the tour got under way, several dates were canceled, but a pair of shows was scheduled for the prestigious Radio City Music Hall in New York and several at the Fillmore in San Francisco.

One major difference between this Airplane tour and those of old was that the set list was standardized—no more winging it as they went along. Every night, the same songs were to be played in the same order, with the exception of a flexible mini-acoustic Hot Tuna set—included at Paul's suggestion—that would take place between the two Airplane segments.

Another difference: Just as they'd used additional musicians on the album, the Airplane decided to augment the basic band onstage. Joining them were Aronoff on drums, Tim Gorman of KBC on keyboards and two guitarists: Randy Jackson, who'd played with a New Orleans band called Zebra (and who doubled on keyboards): and Peter Kaukonen, the latter finally getting the opportunity to be in Jefferson Airplane some 24 years after his father made him refuse Jorma's initial offer.

PETER KAUKONEN: This seemed to be quite a beautiful way of closing circles, although in retrospect it seems like [Jorma] needed somebody to keep his chair warm while he dealt with his drug use and his own insecurities about playing "White Rabbit."

Although many fans were disappointed with the expanded lineup—they would have preferred having the six-person band of yore—Jorma was, in fact, unwilling to play some of the material chosen for the show, particularly the Jefferson Starship hit "Miracles." As the tour proceeded, Jorma sat out that tune and some others, with Peter taking over the guitar duties.

JORMA KAUKONEN: That isn't why I brought my brother in, but it did ultimately work out that way. I had never anticipated having to play "Miracles." Looking back at that tour, I didn't really realize what was required in a reunion. You can't burst on the scene like a new band, because you're not a new band. And you've got to play songs that are recognizable.

In the portrait that adorns the front cover of the *Jefferson Airplane* album, Jorma is seen sniffing an embarrassed-looking Jack's hair (or maybe whispering sweet nothings in his ear). Looking equally uncomfortable is Grace, who's got Paul falling asleep on her left shoulder and Marty, eyes closed, giving her a loving embrace on the other side.

For Marty, though, some things never changed: Despite the faux display of affection, he still felt that Grace was stealing the spotlight.

MARTY BALIN: I sang my ass off. I had Grace dancing and singing. But they would turn me off. I was really struggling to sing. I'd go to the sound guy and say, "Are you turning my mike down?"

"Oh, no, no, no. I wouldn't do that to you, Marty."

Later on, in an electronics magazine, I read an article by the sound guy and he said, "Yeah, I was turning down Marty's mike." Jesus, people never tell you the truth. But that was my karma.

JACK CASADY: Marty is no more of a victim than the rest of us. The others may perceive that because Jorma and I know each other that therefore we're off cackling in a corner together, when we're actually as miserable as everybody else.

MEANWHILE, BACK IN THE PARALLEL UNIVERSE, Starship's *Love Among the Cannibals* had been released a month before the Airplane reunion album, and based on the group's high profile in recent years, they had every reason to expect their audience to still be there for them. Starship's album did outpace the Airplane's on the charts by better than 20 points, but compared to their past performance, it was barely limping along. And while the Airplane reunion tour did fairly brisk business, putting bodies in most if not all of the seats at their shows, the other group was suddenly lucky to draw a thousand paying customers to a club gig.

Then, when the chips were already down, along came something Mickey Thomas needed even less than an empty arena: a broken face. Starship was in Scranton, Pennsylvania, for a gig when the incident occurred during the early morning of September 24, 1989. After the show was canceled due to inclement weather, the band retired to a local club where it planned to celebrate Craig Chaquico's thirty-fifth birthday. According to initial news reports in the area, the jealous boyfriend of a fan punched Mickey several times during an autograph session at the Hilton Hotel, where the band was staying. But the story was changed in a press release put out by RCA a few days later, wherein it was claimed that he was really beaten when he attempted to defend the honor of one of the band's female backup singers.

At first, Mickey claimed he had no idea who hit him. Bill Thompson, who was not in Scranton when it happened, backed up that story when he spoke with the press. "It happened outside his hotel room," he told Michael Snyder of the *San Francisco Chronicle*. "He was pretty drunk. He doesn't remember much." Scranton police said at the time that neither Mickey nor the Starship crew was very cooperative and that no witnesses had come forward.

Whoever hit him, hit him hard. Mickey's injuries were so severe that he required three titanium plates inserted into his face. He also suffered broken ribs and cracked bones around the eye.

Mickey managed to call Bill Laudner's room following the attack and the road manager took Thomas to the emergency room of the local Mercy Hospital. Naturally, all upcoming dates for Starship were canceled.

So was their drummer. Rumors began spreading only days after the beating that the assailant was not a stranger at all, but Donny Baldwin. Although he had been a close friend of Mickey's since their days in the Elvin Bishop Group, and Thomas had brought him into Starship, they had been at odds recently. Although he refused to comment on any possible involvement of Baldwin at the time, Thompson admitted that the drummer and the singer had been in a shoving match in Colorado during the same tour. Even when Baldwin's departure from the group was announced just weeks after the beating, attributed to the usual "creative differences," the group and RCA still refused to reveal what had really happened.

Then, finally, it was confirmed: Mickey and others involved with the group admitted that Baldwin had been responsible for Mickey's beating. No charges were ever filed, but Baldwin's days with the organization were over.

MICKEY THOMAS: Donny was a great drummer, and a funny, good-looking guy. He just had that little dark side. He went to a place that I really wish he had not gone to, because I lost a friend in the process, as well as a piece of my face.

A couple of weeks before the actual beating, Mickey recalled, Donny had hit him on the head with one of his drumsticks. The following night they had an emotional discussion and seemingly worked everything out. Then came Scranton, and a night of drinking. Mickey remembers a glass shattering against his hotel room door, a fight ensuing and being punched and kicked. He went to bed, but woke up in pain three hours later. His ribs hurt terribly, and his face was swollen, black and blue.

At the hospital in Scranton, a CAT scan was taken and Mickey was told that he had massive facial fractures and needed reconstructive surgery. Doctors back in San Francisco performed a cranial facial entry, which, as Mickey described it, "basically means that they took my face off and then reattached it, with 60 staples in the top of my head."

Mickey never saw Baldwin again.

MICKEY THOMAS: From that day on, whenever I look in the mirror it's a different face looking back at me than the face I previously knew. So it's pretty hard to forget. I'm just afraid that if we were to see each other and try to be friends again, something would happen that would open the old wound and we'd be at it again, and I just don't want that. But, boy, I do miss him.

In 1990 Craig Chaquico, the sole remaining link to the original Jefferson Starship of 1974, decided to call it quits. He was the only musician who had been on all of the group's albums during its 16-year history, and he was ready to move on. He'd weathered all of the musical changes well and supported most of them. But from *Love Among the Cannibals* onward, it had started to feel like something he no longer wanted to be a part of.

CRAIG CHAQUICO: I could see the sun setting on the trip. Everyone I had enjoyed playing and writing with over the many years with Starship had left the band, except for Mickey. It became like Mickey Thomas is our star and everything is going to be about him. He's going to write all the songs and choose all the material. That left a lot of my roots in the dust.

Mickey still attempted to keep the band alive, with a Starship that included Peter Wolf. But in 1991, after one more charting single called "Good Heart," it was finally over for the group that had sung "It's Not Over ('Til It's Over)."

BILL THOMPSON: I essentially fired the band. There had been the incident with Mickey's face, plus we weren't selling tickets. I told RCA that we were done.

Before long, RCA dropped Starship from its active roster, severing a relationship of more than 25 years that had begun with *Jefferson Airplane Takes Off* in 1966 and encompassed more than 50 album releases.

The Starship name didn't stay dormant for long: In early 1992, around the same time Paul Kantner emerged with a new lineup that revived the name Jefferson Starship, Mickey also debuted a new band, consisting of no one associated with the old group. He called his group Mickey Thomas's Starship.

Neither had the legal right to use the name—it was still owned by Grace and Thompson—but no action has ever been taken to stop either party from calling his band Starship.

GENERALLY, CRITICS BLASTED the Airplane reunion record but agreed the band sounded better in concert than they had expected it to, and that Hot Tuna's miniset was a highlight. But they also carped that the new songs were far inferior to the old favorites that turned up, among them "She Has Funny Cars," "Plastic Fantastic Lover," "Won't You Try/Saturday Afternoon," "Today," "Miracles," "Good Shepherd," "Lather," "3/5 of a Mile in 10 Seconds," "Crown of Creation," "Wooden Ships" and the obligatory "Volunteers," "Somebody to Love" and "White Rabbit."

One critic, the *Boston Globe*'s Steve Morse, complained that Marty's vocal microphone was turned up too high, which must have exasperated the singer to no end.

The tour ended officially on September 30 in Golden Gate Park, as appropriate a finale as could be. The band then traveled to Washington, D.C., to perform five songs at the March for the Homeless on October 7. And that was it. A planned tour of Japan was canceled, and although there was talk about picking it up again, they all knew it wasn't going to happen.

Jefferson Airplane never played for the general public again.

At the end of 1989, *Rolling Stone* magazine's critics voted the Airplane the "most unwelcome comeback of the year." But several years later, in 1996, some of those same critics, apparently having seen the light, were among hundreds of music industry insiders who voted Jefferson Airplane into the Rock and Roll Hall of Fame. Paul, Marty, Jorma, Jack and Spencer attended the ceremony inducting them, held at the ritzy Waldorf-Astoria Hotel in New York. There they played a few songs for the formally attired heavies who'd paid over a thousand dollars a plate for the privilege of being in the same room as the Airplane and other inductees.

Grace stayed home because her feet hurt.

Six months into the year 2000, Paul and his current manager were sued by Jefferson Airplane Inc., the corporate entity that retained rights to the usage of the band's name, image, likenesses, merchandising, etc. The corporation claimed that Paul had infringed on the Jefferson Airplane trademark by wrongly using the band's name to promote a tour in which he was involved.

Jefferson Airplane Inc., in addition to Jorma, Jack, Grace and Thompson, included Paul Kantner. In essence, Paul was suing himself. Even he had to laugh.

Despite the never-ending saga, Paul was still hoping to get the Airplane back together again. He wasn't having much luck, but if time has proven anything, it's that there are never endings when Jefferson Airplane is involved, only new dawns.

WHATEVER HAPPENED TO WISHES WISHED ON A STAR?

IF THERE IS a theme that runs through the post-reunion lives of the former members of Jefferson Airplane, Jefferson Starship and Hot Tuna, as well as those who were closest to them, it might just be the Starship's hit "Find Your Way Back." Virtually all of the musicians have spent the '90s and beyond being true to themselves and their art, giving up the show business trappings and sticking with those things that bring them satisfaction and inner peace. Most are sober these days, older and perhaps a bit wiser, but still dreamers.

The Classic 1966–1970 Jefferson Airplane Lineup

MARTY BALIN—Following the 1989 reunion, Marty went back to his solo career, working with his band the Wolfpack. In early 1990, Rhino Records released Marty's first greatest hits anthology, *Balince: A Collection*. In 1991, he released his next album of new recordings, *Better Generation*.

Beginning in 1993, Marty found himself back in the familiar company of Paul Kantner and Jack Casady in the newest incarnation of Jefferson Starship. Marty has toured with Paul on a semiregular basis since then, and has appeared on the group's recordings.

In 1997, Marty released another solo album, *Freedom Flight*, and, two years later, a two-CD *Greatest Hits* compilation featuring newly re-recorded studio versions of his signature songs on one disc and an interview on the other.

Marty has a room full of unreleased master tapes, but he isn't actively pursuing a record deal. "I'll probably never get a contract again," he said. "When you get to be my age, nobody wants you. But I've got too much to do to worry about it. I've always been a little ahead of the game, too busy to be bothered. I feel I'm very fortunate."

In 1999, Marty called attention to one of his other passions, painting, in his first-ever art show. A number of his works were displayed at galleries in Tampa, Florida, and in New York. He also wrote his autobiography, *Full Flight: A Tale of Airplanes & Starships*, which was scheduled for publication in early 2003.

Marty lives in Tampa with his wife, Karen, and their daughter, Delaney Mariah Skye, who was born in 1995. He is also the grandfather of a girl named Victoria, born to his daughter Jennifer, from his first marriage.

Still looking toward the future, there is one project Marty says he'd like to see happen before it's all over: "I would love to take Grace in a studio, just her and me, and sing together and make an album. She doesn't have to go out on the road or anything, just sing."

JACK CASADY—For Jack, the focus remains the same as it's ever been: the music. He has continued working with Jorma in Hot Tuna on a regular basis (for a while, he also played in the revived Jefferson Starship), and when he's not busy doing that, Jack often teaches bass at Jorma Kaukonen's Fur Peace Ranch guitar camp in Ohio.

"Teaching clarifies your own approach to your music, and it forces you to explain what you do and hopefully encourage them to learn on their own," he said.

Jack also helped design and endorses a signature model bass manufactured by the Epiphone company, and he has an instructional videotape available from Homespun Tapes. He was planning on releasing his first "solo" album in mid-2003, using various musicians he admires, and he recorded a film score with Jorma, for the Brad Silberling–directed *Moonlight Mile*.

Jack continues to inspire in his fans a near-cultlike awe. Some casually refer to the master bassist as "God," and they discuss among themselves not only his playing technique and the equipment he uses, but such intricacies as Jack's habit of moving his eyebrows in time to the music. Casady, while humbled, laughs it off: "It's weird. I try to keep it all in perspective. I'm a working musician and deep down inside I'm as insecure as anybody, if not a lot more so. All I can do is try to play well."

Being sober for more than 10 years has helped Jack keep sight of what is really important in his life. "I don't like to preach about anything," he said, "but I feel better, my life is in better shape and I play better."

Jack lives in Los Angeles with his wife, Diana Balfour Quine.

SPENCER DRYDEN—Following his run with the Dinosaurs and their spin-off Fish and Chips in the '80s, Spencer Dryden retired from music. Spencer last saw any of the others in 1999 when the Airplane was honored by the California Music Awards with a brass San Francisco Walk of Fame plaque at the Bill Graham Civic Auditorium. Spencer, who has had some health problems, lives with the youngest of his three sons, Jackson, in Sonoma County, California.

"I've said my piece already," Spencer said about hanging up his drumsticks. "I don't feel I need to keep saying it. I'm enjoying my retirement."

PAUL KANTNER—"Let there be travelers who venture far from the beaten path/And let one of them be me," Paul Kantner once wrote. That has always been a fitting slogan for his life and career, and Paul has continued along his journey.

A number of fine musicians and singers have come and gone from Paul's post-Airplane reunion aggregations. In an early version there was Darby Gould, a woman who had previously sung with a San Francisco band called World Entertainment War. Another young female singer, Diana Mangano, has been with the group since the mid-'90s, and keyboardist Chris Smith has been a regular member. Jack Casady, the late Papa John Creach, former Tubes drummer Prairie Prince, Slick Aguilar and of course Marty Balin have all been part of the ongoing enterprise at various times. Signe Anderson even came out of semiretirement to do some shows in the early '90s.

As unpredictable as the membership on any given night is the band's name: Acoustic Warriors, Acoustic Shuttlecraft, Acoustic Explorer, Native Son and Jefferson Cybership were all tried out for a tour or two. Usually it was just Jefferson Starship. Paul began using the name again, despite his earlier agreement not to, because, he said, he wanted to rescue it from its sullied reputation. Trading on his love of sci-fi, Paul has also taken a cue from *Star Trek* and called the band Jefferson Starship—The Next Generation.

He has written new songs, some of his finest in years, songs that the '80s Jefferson Starship would never have let him get away with: There was "Shadowlands," about a woman serial killer who specializes in Republicans; "Millennium Beyond," which, Paul said, "talks about future, science fiction, fucking in space and children in space, as an evolutionary moment as well as just passionate embrace." And "The Light," which he describes as "more intellectual, just pursuit of where ideas come from, and how they affect us." Some of these songs have made it to new CDs. One was *Deep Space/Virgin Sky*, recorded live at the House of Blues in Hollywood at a benefit concert for the widow of Papa John. Grace Slick came out of seclusion for the occasion.

In 1996, Paul released a two-CD spoken word album, *A Guide Through the Chaos*, on which he told tales of the Airplane, the Starship, Bill Graham, Monterey, Woodstock and Altamont, Grace, Papa John, Nicaragua, Jerry Garcia, punk rock, radio "shock jock" Howard Stern, the Internet and more. That same year, Jefferson Starship began recording *Windows of Heaven*, a new studio album. One Kantner tune, "I'm on Fire," features a guest vocal, recorded years earlier, by Grace. Another, "Let Me Fly," has guitar lines by the teenage Alexander Kantner. *Windows of Heaven* features some of the most poignant, poetic Kantner music of his career, heavy on the philosophy and state-of-the-world proclamations, as well as fine new songs from Marty and Jesse Barish.

More recently, Jefferson Starship has been releasing its recent live concerts on CD and selling them via its official website (see Sources and Resources). One of those, *Across the Sea of Suns*, includes selections from a 2000 tour during which they performed, for the first time ever, most of the Airplane's classic *Volunteers* album. The following year they did the same with *Surrealistic Pillow*.

Paul, who, of course, still lives in San Francisco, is not giving up on getting the Airplane back together one more time. "There's always a chance," he said, "until we die."

JORMA KAUKONEN—When the Airplane drifted apart following the 1989 reunion, Jorma reconvened Hot Tuna and was back on the road just a couple of months later. In 1990, the band recorded a new studio album, *Pair a Dice Found*, for Epic Records, the same label that had released the

Airplane reunion album. The album consisted of a trio of new Jorma songs and five tracks by Michael Falzarano, who had by then become an integral part of the band. Also joining the Tuna fold was drummer Harvey Sorgen. Originally a second engineer on the project, he remained Tuna's drummer throughout the decade.

Tuna and Jorma then returned to the Relix label. *Live at Sweetwater* was an acoustic set recorded at the tiny Marin County club of the same name in January 1992. Those shows introduced a new member of Hot Tuna, pianist Pete Sears, who had bolted from Starship several years earlier.

Hot Tuna continued to tour throughout the '90s, playing everywhere from the smallest clubs to huge festivals such as Woodstock '94 and Furthur, the latter organized around former Grateful Dead members. (Jorma also put in a few appearances with an ad hoc group pulled together by former Dead bassist Phil Lesh; one show was released on CD by the Dead's label.)

A second volume from the Sweetwater shows was issued in 1993, followed in 1995 by *Magic Two,* an expanded version of the 1985 *Magic* live acoustic album. That same year brought *Embryonic Journey,* a most unusual collection that consisted of 11 different takes of Jorma's signature instrumental composition, most of them duets with Tom Constanten, an early Grateful Dead keyboardist.

Jorma's next album, *The Land of Heroes,* was another 1995 release. Recorded in Nashville, the album includes a couple of Reverend Gary Davis numbers, a track called "Re-Enlistment Blues" that Jorma heard played by guitarist Merle Travis, a remake of the Airplane-era "Trial by Fire" and a handful of new originals." It was the first album that I ever made sober," Jorma said. Another unusual Jorma solo record, *Christmas,* was released in 1996, 10 songs, some spiritual in nature, others more festive, celebrating the holiday and its true meaning.

Several other Relix releases followed, among them *Live in Japan,* recorded at a tiny club in Yokohama, and *Too Many Years.* Featuring the acoustic Jorma–Michael–Pete group that toured when Jack was off playing with Jefferson Starship, that album is a mix of blues covers, country tracks, an interpretation of the Dead's "Friend of the Devil," a remake of Jorma's own "Man for All Seasons" (aka "Junkies on Angel Dust") and several new Kaukonen and/or Falzarano tracks.

Jorma dedicated the album to his mother, who, in a brilliant posed photo (taken circa 1949) on the inside sleeve, can be seen persuading the young Jorma to finish his piano lesson—by pointing a gun at his head! ("The Kaukonen family does not promote pointing firearms at people," Jorma notes in a caption.)

RCA/BMG stepped back into the picture in 1998 with the two-CD *The Best of Hot Tuna* (its cover painted by Grace Slick), and 1999 saw *And Furthurmore . . .* , another live Tuna set, recorded with the full electric band during their shows at the Furthur Festivals of 1996 and '98.

In late 2001 Jorma signed a new record deal with Columbia—his first for a major label in more than a decade—and recorded an album, *Blue Country Heart*, with bluegrass mandolinist Sam Bush, Dobro player Jerry Douglas and standup bassist Byron House, performing the music of white country-blues artists of the 1930s and '40s. The following summer, Jorma toured extensively behind the Columbia album, playing both clubs and festivals, and made plans for a follow-up in the same vein. The album was nominated for a Grammy in 2003, in the Traditional Folk category.

As if Jorma weren't being kept busy enough, he returned to teaching, a passion that preceded his involvement with Jefferson Airplane in the early '60s. Purchasing a 119-acre plot of land in 1989, in rural Meigs County in the Appalachian foothills of southeastern Ohio, Jorma and his wife, Vanessa Lillian Kaukonen, founded Fur Peace Ranch (as in "It's a fur peace from anywhere"—a bit of local yokel humor). Every February through November, Jorma, Jack and various guest instructors (among them Arlo Guthrie, John Hammond and Chris Smither) gather with small groups of students in the homey atmosphere to share what they know about making music. Most of the classes, which are given at entry, intermediate and advanced levels, are guitar-oriented, but workshops in percussion, keyboards, voice and other instruments are also offered.

Vanessa and her sister Ginger Lee are largely responsible for maintaining the camp's comfortable, low-key atmosphere. Jorma, who has been sober for many years, allows no drugs or alcohol. "You just play guitar," he said.

Which, in the end, is what it's always been about for Jorma.

GRACE SLICK—Grace retired from the music business following the 1989 Airplane reunion. Although she still sings and composes for her own enjoyment, she refuses to return to public music making on a full-scale basis. No longer feeling pressured to look and behave a certain way, she started taking a new attitude toward herself, rising early, dressing casually, hanging out with close friends and feeding the raccoons around her house.

Grace has never been far from the public consciousness, however, and has, despite her proclamations to the contrary, poked her head back into the world of music on a few occasions. In 1991, Grace and China appeared at a Festival for the Animals in San Francisco, where Grace sat at the piano to play a half-hour set that included some new songs as well as "Panda" and an impromptu version of "White Rabbit."

Grace received a lot more media coverage, however, when, on September 16, 1993, the house in Mill Valley that she'd shared for 17 years with Skip Johnson burned to the ground. All of Grace's memorabilia from her days with the Airplane and Starship—gold records, personal photographs, an extensive doll collection, musical instruments—was destroyed. Grace was not home at the time. It later transpired that a county work crew had accidentally started the blaze. Grace and Skip sued and collected nearly $900,000. By then, however, the couple had already separated.

Grace's next big news splash came on March 5, 1994 when she found herself in the midst of the very saga depicted in her own '70s song, "Law Man." Police received a call saying that shots had been fired at Grace's new home. When they arrived, Grace, in an obvious drunken state, pointed a gun at the officers, imploring them to leave her property. After a standoff, Grace was tackled and arrested. She pleaded guilty to a misdemeanor charge and received a six-month suspended sentence. She was also ordered to attend Alcoholics Anonymous four days a week, perform 200 hours of community service and submit to random drug testing. As part of her probation, Grace was told not to drink for six months, nor to possess any firearms for 10 years.

Grace's next move, in 1994, was south, to a dream house in Malibu, where she lives by herself. Sober for several years, Grace spends much of her time painting, drawing, sewing, writing and creating in various other ways. She rarely gives interviews about the old days, saying she is "bored talking about the '60s." She listens to classical and orchestral soundtrack music, and still loves all things Spanish, including flamenco music.

If she ever records again, she has said, it would be for a film soundtrack. Her recorded musical contributions since 1989 have been sparse: Grace lent her voice as a harmony singer to *In Flight*, a 1996 album by Linda Perry of the group 4 Non Blondes, and to a song on Jefferson Starship's *Windows of Heaven* album. RCA recounted her career with a *Best of Grace Slick* compilation, which included one previously unreleased track from her Starship days. Her only major public appearances as a singer were at Jefferson Starship's 1995 benefit concert for Papa John's widow, released as the album *Deep Space/Virgin Sky*, and at a 2001 free concert by the band in L.A., in the wake of the September 11 terrorist attacks, where she performed in a makeshift *burqa*, the full-length robe worn by Muslim women under Taliban rule in Afghanistan. Removing that garment, she revealed another surprise: a bath towel emblazoned with the words "FUCK FEAR."

For the majority of her fans, the only way to see Grace Slick in person after her retirement was to attend one of her book signings. Her autobiography, *Somebody to Love?*, cowritten with Andrea Cagan, was published in 1998 by Warner Books. Grace, who reportedly was paid a million dollars for the memoir, made a handful of promotional appearances in selected major markets, doing both signings and lectures. She appeared on a number of radio and TV programs, including one hosted by former '70s bubblegum sensations Donny and Marie Osmond. Also, Grace has displayed her artwork at several galleries, and has appeared at the openings.

As she entered her sixties, Grace, who had been dyeing her hair since the Airplane days, went au naturel, revealing a whitish gray. Her beauty was still undeniable.

The Supporting Cast (in alphabetical order)

MARK "SLICK" AGUILAR—When KBC disbanded in 1987, guitarist Aguilar formed the nine-piece Slick-Hurley Band with Tim Gorman, Donny Baldwin, guitarist Kevin Hurley and others. They stayed together until the early '90s, when Aguilar went back to work with Kantner. He has remained with him since, playing lead guitar in the many variations of Jefferson Starship. Aguilar lives in New Jersey.

SIGNE (TOLY ANDERSON) ETTLIN—The Airplane's first female singer returned home to Oregon after leaving the band in 1966. She and her husband Jerry Anderson raised their two daughters, Lilith and Onateska, both of whom now have children of their own. The couple split in 1974 (Jerry later died of cancer) and Signe married Michael Ettlin, a building contractor, in 1977. She has held a number of jobs since leaving the Airplane, and continued to sing for a while, including a long stint with a 10-piece Portland-based band, Carl Smith Natural Gas Company. Signe has withstood a broken neck, a bout with cancer, bypass surgery and a serious financial crisis, but she maintains a positive attitude and defines the word "survivor." "I learned when I was a very small child that the only one who's going to take care of me is me. I raised my children the same way. I don't believe you can point fingers at somebody else. It's nobody's fault one way or the other. The money, the things I didn't get, don't matter anymore."

DONNY BALDWIN—In 1994, Donny Baldwin joined the Jerry Garcia Band. He remained with them until Garcia's 1995 death and then continued on with other musicians from the band, calling themselves JGB.

JOHN BARBATA—Since his convalescence from a near-fatal accident in 1978, John Barbata has kept a low public profile. He played for some time with singer Rita Coolidge, and later became a born-again Christian, got married and moved to Oklahoma. He still drums and holds drum clinics.

CYNTHIA BOWMAN—After leaving the employ of Jefferson Starship in 1984, Cynthia Bowman started her own public relations firm and began working with non–rock and roll clients, including the San Francisco Symphony Orchestra and the *San Francisco Examiner*. She still does PR work for some of the individual band members on occasion, however. As the mother of Alexander Kantner, Cynthia is still very much in Paul's life. "That's the one thing that Paul and I managed to do pretty seamlessly was raise our kid," she said.

JOE AND JEAN BUCHWALD—Marty's parents still reside in Haight-Ashbury, where their gorgeous home is a shrine to Marty and Jefferson Airplane. In his mid-eighties, Joe still counsels his son on business matters and tries to get out and see Marty perform whenever possible, occasionally traveling with him.

CRAIG CHAQUICO—After leaving Starship, instead of getting deeper into rock, Craig went in the opposite direction. In 1991, while his wife Kimberly was pregnant with their son Kyle, Craig began recording tapes of acoustic music to soothe the baby. Someone suggested sending them to a label and that resulted in Craig's first solo album, *Acoustic Highway*. Released on the Higher Octave label in 1993, it was a huge success, reaching number 1 on *Billboard*'s New Age/Adult Alternative chart.

Craig has since continued in this direction. In 1994 he released *Acoustic Planet*, which also reached the top of the New Age chart and received a Grammy nomination for Best New Age Album. That was followed in 1996 by *A Thousand Pictures* and *Once in a Blue Universe* in '97.

The following year, Craig recorded *From the Redwoods to the Rockies* with Russ Freeman of the contemporary jazz group the Rippingtons, for the Windham Hill Jazz label. *Four Corners*, another acoustic gem, came in 2000, followed later that year by *Panorama: The Best of Craig Chaquico*. The track "Café Carnival" from that album went to number 1 at many smooth jazz stations in the U.S. *Shadow and Light*, Craig's next album, was released in 2002. He has been named Best Pop Instrumental Guitarist by *Guitar Player* magazine.

Craig also designed the appropriately named Craig Chaquico Model Washburn EA-26 guitar and worked out an arrangement with several environmental organizations to plant a tree for every guitar made. He later made a similar arrangement with Carvin Guitars.

Craig headlines his own national tours, playing clubs, theaters and jazz festivals. But he never forgot what the guitar did for his life when he was 12 and was laid up with a few broken limbs, so Craig spends a good deal of his time volunteering for the American Music Therapy Association. "I play for geriatric patients, pediatric patients, psychiatric, autistic children, Alzheimer's patients and chemo kids," he said. "It's a chance to get back in touch with that energy of music before it was a business."

NADINE CONDON—Named by *BAM* magazine as one of the top 100 Californians in the music business, the former Jefferson Starship publicist runs her own artist development and mentoring company. Her clients have included Steve Miller, John Mayall, Travis Tritt and several record companies. She is the mastermind behind Nadine's Wild Weekend, an annual three-day festival of local music in the Bay Area.

JOEY COVINGTON—In 1978, Joey assembled the first of several San Francisco All-Stars bands. The initial lineup included Quicksilver's John Cipollina, his brother Mario on bass and Buddy Cage and Steve Love of the New Riders. Other musicians, including Papa John Creach, Merl Saunders and John "Marmaduke" Dawson of the New Riders, fell in and out as the band carried on. They played club dates and headlined a fair on Haight Street in 1986, which drew 10,000 people.

In 1980, Joey played on an album by Nick Gravenites, *Blue Star.* Joey continues to play drums, working with Willy Chambers (of the Chambers Brothers) and others. Following the September 11 terrorist attacks he put together a benefit performance for the New York Fire Department Widows' and Children's Fund.

LARRY COX—The producer/engineer behind the first four Jefferson Starship albums returned home to Texas. He has continued to work behind the boards, but has not kept a high profile in recent years.

PAPA JOHN CREACH—The violinist who'd played with the Airplane, the Starship and Hot Tuna recorded a number of albums for labels such as DJM and Buddah, and toured with his own bands, as well as with the San Francisco All-Stars and the Dinosaurs.

In 1987, Creach was the subject of a one-hour documentary film, *Setting the Record Straight*, made by Stevenson J. Palfi of New Orleans. In the film, which seeks to make viewers aware that Papa John was a versatile musician who was comfortable playing many genres, he performs not only with Jorma but with New Age pianist George Winston, singer/saxist Eddie "Cleanhead" Vinson and jazz bassist Red Callender.

In 1992, Creach joined the newly minted Jefferson Starship—The Next Generation and remained a regular member of the band.

Papa John suffered a heart attack during the major Los Angeles earthquake of January 1994 and died on February 22, at age 76. The following year, a tribute concert was held at the House of Blues in Los Angeles, featuring the latest incarnation of Jefferson Starship and several guests. Among the new songs on the album culled from the show was Marty Balin's "Papa John." The opening line: "They don't make 'em like that anymore."

PAT DUGAN—The former caretaker of China Kantner and housekeeper for Paul and Grace lived in Hawaii for several years. She then returned to San Francisco and worked at the Cliff House, a city landmark, for more than a decade.

AYNSLEY DUNBAR—Since his 1982 firing from Jefferson Starship, Aynsley Dunbar has continued to play drums for a number of different bands. He joined the heavy metal outfit Whitesnake in 1985 and appeared on their best-selling, self-titled album of 1987. In the late '90s, Dunbar joined up with former Animals lead singer Eric Burdon and toured with him.

MICHAEL FALZARANO—With the exception of Jack Casady, Michael Falzarano has played with Jorma Kaukonen longer than anyone, for more than two decades. Falzarano remains a core member of the electric configuration of Hot Tuna and the Jorma Kaukonen Trio, and has also toured with Jorma as a duo. Michael and Tuna drummer Harvey Sorgen also have another band on the side, the Memphis Pilgrims. They released an album, *Mecca*, on Relix in 1996, which includes guest appearances by Jorma and Pete Sears.

DAVID FREIBERG—After being asked to leave the Starship, David Freiberg largely stayed out of the spotlight. He and his wife, Linda Imperial, appeared as background vocalists on a couple of latter-day Quicksilver albums, *Peace by Piece* in 1986 and *Shape Shifter* 10 years later.

Freiberg spends most of his time now running FreeMountain Studio out of his Marin County home, recording dance music, computer game sound tracks, voice-overs and his wife's own dance-pop music.

David describes himself now as a "computer geek," a passion that seems to run in the family: his two children, Polly and Jessica, both work in the computer industry. David and Linda are practicing Buddhists. David, who is now a grandfather, is still close to his ex-wife, Julia (Girl Freiberg) Brigden.

BILL GRAHAM—Rock's most prominent and volatile promoter remained at the top of the game long after closing the Fillmores and Winterland. He owned and/or operated a number of other venues, helped organize major benefit shows and continued to promote concerts and tours by the biggest bands of the era.

On October 25, 1991, Graham and his fiancée, Melissa Gold, were returning from a concert he had promoted in Concord, California, when their rented helicopter crashed into an electrical transmission tower, killing Graham, Gold and pilot Steve Kahn instantly. Paul Kantner was one of many who spoke at Graham's funeral.

In honor of the late entertainment giant, the San Francisco Civic Auditorium was renamed the Bill Graham Civic Auditorium, and in New York, the street corner closest to the former Fillmore East was named Bill Graham's Way.

BOB HARVEY—After getting booted from the Airplane in 1965, bassist Bob Harvey joined a folk-rock group called Holy Mackerel, featuring actor/singer-songwriter Paul Williams. Eventually, he gave up music in favor of a journalism career, becoming the entertainment editor for a magazine called *Mother Trucker News.* In the '80s he joined the Naval Reserves and soon found himself in Kuwait in the midst of the Desert Storm conflict, serving as a photojournalist.

In the late '90s, now a great-grandfather living in Georgia, he resumed playing music and writing songs. His band San Francisco Blue recorded an album, *Idiot's Vision,* in 2000. In early 2002, Bob played a show in Maryland for which original Airplane drummer Jerry Peloquin, who he hadn't seen since 1965, joined him.

PAT "MAURICE" IERACI—The production coordinator for the vast majority of Airplane-related recordings retired in 1984, although he threw himself back into the fray briefly to work on the 1992 boxed set, *Jefferson Airplane Loves You*. A grandfather, Maurice lives in the Los Angeles area with his wife, Cecelia.

SKIP JOHNSON—The band's lighting director left Starship around the same time that his wife, Grace Slick, did. After their split, Skip lived in Minnesota for a while, working with Prince, then moved back to his home state of Pennsylvania, where he took a job as production manager for a local concert venue. In 2001 Johnson made the news for suing a web company and an advertising agency for using an early '70s photo of him with long hair without his permission—the ad made light of Skip's appearance during the heyday of the Starship and Johnson claimed invasion of privacy. Johnson maintains a cordial relationship with Grace.

ALEXANDER BOWMAN KANTNER—The son of Paul Kantner and Cynthia Bowman appreciates his father's music and calls Paul a "phenomenal songwriter," but Alexander's personal choice leans more toward the blues, and he is an accomplished guitarist in that area. He has, however, performed with Jefferson Starship on occasion. Despite being around musicians who were known for their prodigious chemical intake, Alex has never indulged in drug or alcohol use: "The house I grew up in wasn't some decadent palace of drugs and sex," he said. Alexander was a college student at the time this update was being compiled.

CHINA KANTNER—In July of 1986, the 15-year-old daughter of Paul Kantner and Grace Slick became the youngest MTV VJ—video jockey—in the station's five-year history. She turned out to be a natural with her exuberance and feisty personality, and was a hit with viewers. China loved it and returned for the next few years during her summer breaks. The down side came when she returned to school. "There were jealousy trips. People would say, 'Oh, I'm mowing the lawn this summer, and you go to New York . . . ' I felt bad. But then I thought, I have a great job! Why do I have to feel bad about this?"

China became an actress after her stint with MTV. She appeared in the TV series *Home Improvement* and the films *The Stoned Age*, *Airheads* and *The Evening Star*. Then, disillusioned with Hollywood, she gave up her acting aspirations to return to school, with plans to teach. "I have no desire to make a *business* out of my talent," she said. "I've seen people go down, either by death or drugs or isolation or loneliness, too often to want to be involved in it. Fame is a monster to me. I saw what it did to my parents."

China describes herself as "basically a carbon copy mix of both my parents with a little of myself thrown in there." She married a dentist, Dr. Jamie Azdair, in 1999 and lives with him and his son in the Los Angeles area. As a sober Christian, she's had some heated debates with her parents, particularly Paul. "It's like speaking Chinese and French to each other," she said.

MATTHEW KATZ—Since the '60s, the original Airplane manager has remained on the periphery of the music business, releasing recordings on his San Francisco Sound label by the various groups with which he worked. Matthew has continued to serve as either plaintiff or defendant in a number of lawsuits stemming from his management of San Francisco bands in the '60s, particularly Moby Grape and It's a Beautiful Day. A new case initiated by Katz in 1999, in which he charged defamation, emotional distress and other complaints, included as defendants Grace Slick, members of Moby Grape, their attorneys, Sony Music, the Geocities and Yahoo! web companies and several other parties. He also sued the Napster file-sharing website *and* its millions of users. Katz resides in Malibu, California.

MARGARETA KAUKONEN—After Jorma and his wife divorced in 1984, she became increasingly self-destructive. "She set about dismantling her life and did a credible job of it," Jorma said. "The last time I saw her was on the street in 1989 and I barely recognized her." Margareta died of liver failure in 1997, in San Francisco.

PETER KAUKONEN—Peter hasn't performed music often in public in recent years. For a while he worked as a clinical psychologist in mental health, which he describes as "a fitting coda to my erstwhile musical associations." He is now retired from that field and spends a great deal of time bicycling and writing and recording his own music. Following the deaths of his parents, Peter composed a number of songs dedicated to their memory, collectively titled *Going Home*, which he hopes to release on CD and to perform live.

BILL LAUDNER—The road manager stayed onboard all the way until 1990, then retired. He is now a rancher in central California.

GLENN MCKAY—Although he continued to work with the medium of light into the '80s, Glenn McKay eventually came to a realization: "I want to do light shows as fine art or I don't want to do light shows." That decision led to an exhibition at the San Francisco Museum of Modern Art, "Glenn McKay: Altered States—Light Projections 1966–1999." The show featured one light installation each from the '60s, '70s, '80s and '90s, illustrating how the art form—and the technology used to create it over the years—evolved, with computers and video playing a larger role in the later works. He later had an installation at the Experience Music Project, the rock and roll museum in Seattle, and a live performance at the Brooklyn Academy of Music in New York. McKay is also involved in the arts of photography and painting. He lives in Marin County and is working on a book called *Backstage Rock and Roll*, about his adventures on the road.

RON NEVISON—The Jefferson Starship/Airplane producer/engineer has remained active. His clients have included Chicago, Heart, Ozzy Osbourne, UFO, Europe and others.

JERRY PELOQUIN—The Airplane's first drummer remained in the music business for about 10 years, working with a group called the New York Electric String Ensemble and with stars such as José Feliciano, Tim Buckley and Chad Mitchell. A resident of Maryland, he later became a management consultant in the field of organizational psychology. In 2002 he and original JA bassist Bob Harvey were considering forming a new musical act together.

SAMMY PIAZZA—After leaving Stoneground, Sammy and his wife, Annie, played with their church band and choir. He worked for a while with Gary Duncan in Quicksilver and still plays drums, usually with local bands in Sonoma County, California. Sammy has worked a number of non-music jobs. While involved in television advertising, he lost sight in one eye in a freak, work-related accident. Since the mid-'90s, Sammy and Annie, who have two daughters, Tina and Mia, have owned their own business, Alpha Omega USA, which performs criminal background checks on a national scale for employers. In 2000 he and a couple of ex-cops formed a private investigation service. In an ironic twist of fate, one of Piazza's partners once arrested Grace Slick for drunk driving.

TRISH ROBBINS—Marty Balin's '70s girlfriend went back to radio in the '80s. She spent eight years at San Francisco radio station KFOG, and then went to KGO as an executive producer.

SALLY (MANN) ROMANO—After four years of marriage and a child named Jesse James, Sally Mann left Spencer Dryden in 1974. She next took up with Richard Manuel of the Band and moved to Malibu. She later worked for the Grateful Dead's booking agency. Sally has kept in touch with some of the Airplane people, but not on a regular basis. "I could go for 20 years without seeing Grace and I would still say that she's my best friend," she said.

In the '80s, Sally married musician Rock Romano and moved to Houston, where they own a recording studio. Sally also returned to school, and became an attorney in 1996, working in the areas of First Amendment defense law and entertainment law. Her firm represents print media and journalists.

JACKY (WATTS KAUKONEN) SARTI—After her divorce from Peter Kaukonen in 1980, Jacky married the Starship's travel agent, Randy Sarti, and they had a daughter, Gina, in 1983. Jacky left her job as assistant to Bill Thompson in 1985 and went to work for Ultra Sound, a high-tech sound company that provided audio systems for the Starship and Hot Tuna, as well as the Grateful Dead, the Dave Matthews Band, Primus and others. She stayed there until 1998 and now runs her own company, Room Service Theatre. She is also president of the board of trustees of a local Montessori school and works for a holistic publishing company, City Spirit Publications. Jacky lives with her family in Marin County.

WILL SCARLETT—After leaving Hot Tuna the harmonica man went back to playing acoustic music. He recorded with Rosalie Sorrels, David Bromberg and others, worked with bluesman Brownie McGhee and, more recently, blues guitarists Freddie Roulette and Roy Rogers. Still living in Berkeley, Scarlett is a single father who works with kids, teaching them how to play the blues.

AL SCHMITT—The producer of the most significant Jefferson Airplane albums remains one of the top names in the music business. He has won 10 Grammys and has worked as either producer or engineer with such giants as Frank Sinatra, Steely Dan, Dolly Parton, Toto, Barbra Streisand, Diana Krall, George Benson, Natalie Cole and many others.

GINGER (JACKSON) SCHUSTER—The former girlfriend of both Paul and Jack, and later the wife of Steve Schuster, is a family nurse practitioner, working at Bay Area Addiction Research and Treatment.

PETE SEARS—After leaving Starship, Pete returned to the rootsier music he preferred, and to what he considered a more meaningful lifestyle. He played blues piano in clubs and began doing human rights work along with his wife, Jeannette. In 1988, he went into the studio to record his first solo album, *Watchfire*. The album included a host of fine local musicians, among them Jerry Garcia, David Grisman, Mickey Hart, Mimi Farina, Holly Near, John Cipollina and others. Sears later wrote the soundtrack for a documentary film on Cesar Chavez and the Farm Workers Union, aired on PBS. Since 1992, Pete has been a member of both Hot Tuna and the Jorma Kaukonen Trio. "I had this sense that I'd come home," he said.

In 1997, Sears released a second solo album on a Japanese label, a collection of improvisational piano music called *Millennium*, re-released in the U.S. as *A Time to Remember*. He has also played music with artists such as Los Lobos, Leftover Salmon, Taj Mahal and Alvin Youngblood Hart, and in 2000 he released a new blues CD, *The Long Haul*, with special guests including John Lee Hooker, Charlie Musselwhite, Jorma Kaukonen and Levon Helm.

DARBY SLICK—Following his return from India and the Airplane's success with his "Somebody to Love," Grace's brother-in-law, in his own words, became "an addict, an alcoholic." After several years, Slick's annual royalties from the song's airplay and usage in various films, TV shows, compilation albums, etc., began to pay enough so that Darby never had to work again if he didn't care to. He spent time raising his disabled son and getting back into playing guitar. Darby became sober in the '80s and in 1991 wrote a book, *Don't You Want Somebody to Love*, his recollections of the San Francisco music heyday. Darby has made two albums with his oldest son, Jor, a bassist: *Sandoland* and *King of the Fretless Guitar*.

SKIP SPENCE—The saga of Alexander "Skip" Spence is one of rock and roll's saddest. The drummer on the first Airplane album, and later cofounder of Moby Grape, Spence became violent and schizophrenic in the late '60s. Following an incident in New York when he tried to knock down the hotel door of one of his Moby Grape bandmates with an axe, Skip was hospitalized for treatment. Upon his release in 1969 he went to Nashville to record his only solo album, the eccentric *Oar*, which sold very little at the time, but has since become a treasured cult favorite.

Spence spent most of the rest of his life institutionalized or homeless and, due in good part to contractual machinations beyond his comprehension, destitute. He rarely played music in public again but his legend continued to grow. In 1999, a tribute album, *More Oar*, featuring artists such as Robert Plant and Beck interpreting the songs from *Oar*, was released. But Skip didn't live long enough to see its release: He died April 16 of that year in Santa Cruz, California, age 52, a victim of numerous ailments and a system that could not turn him around or give him justice.

BOB STEELER—After Hot Tuna broke up in the late '70s, their drummer became involved with the punk rock scene, playing with the San Francisco band the Offs. He later moved to Colorado, where he is a graphic artist and painter. Steeler still plays drums with local bands.

JANET (TRICE) SWINBURNE—After leaving Marty, his '60s girlfriend Janet returned to the East Coast and became a registered nurse. She married and had three sons.

MICKEY THOMAS—Following the dissolution of Starship in 1991, Mickey attempted unsuccessfully to form a band with Jeff Baxter of the Doobie Brothers and John Entwistle of the Who. Mickey then put together his own group, which he called alternately Mickey Thomas's Starship or Starship Featuring Mickey Thomas. They play state fairs, casinos and clubs, but one of their more memorable gigs was at a nudist colony in Michigan. Mickey's Starship, although having undergone numerous personnel changes, was still together by 2002, but had yet to record.

Mickey was also involved in singing and doing voice-overs for a PBS children's program called *Adventures with KangaRoddy*, about a teenage kangaroo martial arts expert.

BILL THOMPSON—The former manager of Jefferson Airplane, Jefferson Starship and Hot Tuna continues to oversee many of the business interests of those bands. Thompson serves as a liaison and consultant to BMG Music (formerly RCA Records), helping to determine which of the bands' recordings are reissued, and which previously unreleased music sees the light of day. He also administers the publishing for the Airplane's Icebag Corp. song catalog, and works out licensing deals with record labels and film and TV producers interested in using the band's recordings in soundtracks, films, commercials, etc.

Bill Thompson Management continues to function as an ongoing concern, representing contemporary artists. Thompson has also served as a consultant to record labels and for a while booked concerts in the Far East. Bill and his wife, Stephani, whom he married in 1990, live in Marin County. Tyrone, Bill's son from his previous marriage to Judy Thompson (who passed away in 1983), is a computer graphic artist in Los Angeles.

The Legacy of Jefferson Airplane

Fort Zumwalt North High School in O'Fallon, Missouri, found itself in the glare of the national media spotlight in 1998. The reason for the commotion was that the school's marching band and color guard had chosen to play "White Rabbit" as part of a "Salute to the Late '60s" medley to be performed at football games. A concerned parent, it seems, objected, because it was felt that the song's lyrics glorified the use of drugs.

Regardless of the fact that the kids did not plan to sing the lyrics—they were performing an instrumental version—the school's principal announced that "White Rabbit" was an "anthem of the drug culture" and demanded that the band delete the song from its repertoire.

Fifteen students sued, calling it a free speech issue and thus drawing reporters and TV crews to the otherwise un-newsworthy midwestern hamlet. The American Civil Liberties Union became involved, defending the students in federal court, but the judge sided with the authorities, saying that the school had the right to determine just what constitutes allowable speech within its confines, and the song was dropped.

Nonetheless, the fuss over the ban ultimately had another, more lasting effect. As the vast majority of the high school's students had been unaware of "White Rabbit" or Jefferson Airplane before the furor overtook their town, they flocked to the Internet to see just what those contentious lyrics could possibly be.

"Now I have two Jefferson Airplane CDs," one 16-year-old student told the *St. Louis Post-Dispatch*. "And I listen to them all the time."

SOURCES AND RESOURCES

Selected Websites

THIS BOOK AND ITS AUTHOR

Got a Revolution! (www.gotarevolution.com)

Jeff Tamarkin (www.jefftamarkin.com)

E-mail: JeffAirplane@aol.com

THE BANDS

Jefferson Airplane

Jefferson Airplane Official Website (www.jeffersonairplane.com)

Fly Jefferson Airplane
(grove.ufl.edu/~number6/Jefferson.Airplane/airplane.html)

Jefferson Airplane Base
(www.mv.com/ipusers/owsley/airplane/jabase.txt)

The Garden (www.thebigj.demon.co.uk/garden/index.htm)

Journal of Trionic Physics
(www.geocities.com/SunsetStrip/Palms/2424)

A New Continent of Earth and Fire
(www.airplane.freeserve.co.uk/airplane.htm)

To join the Jefferson Airplane mailing list 2400 Fulton Street, go to:
http://lists.netspace.org/cgi-bin/wa?SUBED1=2400fulton&A=1

Jefferson Starship
  Official Jefferson Starship Website (www.jeffersonstarshipsf.com)

  A Jefferson Starship/Airplane Website (www.starship.pp.se)

  Jefferson Starship (members.tripod.com/JeffersonStarship)

  Jefferson Starship Base
    (members.tripod.com/JeffersonStarship/jsbase.htm)

  Unofficial Jefferson Starship Page
    (www.geocities.com/starshipper.geo)

Hot Tuna
  Official Hot Tuna Website (www.hottuna.com)

  Tuna Base (www.tunabase.com)

INDIVIDUAL BAND MEMBERS AND RELATED

Marty Balin
  Marty Balin (www.martybalin.com)

  Miracles—The Unofficial Marty Balin Website
    (www.geocities.com/balinmiracles)

Jack Casady
  Jack Casady's Equipment Club (www.casadybass.com)

Craig Chaquico
  Craig Chaquico Official Website (www.craigchaquico.com)

Joey Covington
  Official Joey Covington Home Page
    (members.aol.com/bandinusa/j/home.htm)

Papa John Creach
  Papa John (members.aol.com/bandinusa/j/papa.htm)

China Kantner
  China Kantner Homepage
    (www.airplane.freeserve.co.uk/china.htm)

Jorma Kaukonen

Jorma Kaukonen's Website (www.jormakaukonen.com)

Fur Peace Ranch (www.furpeaceranch.com)

Peter Kaukonen

Peter Kaukonen (www.peterkaukonen.com)

Pete Sears

Pete Sears—The Long Haul (www.petesears.com)

Grace Slick

Unofficial Grace Slick Website (www.geocities.com/gslicktrip)

White Rabbits
(www.geocities.com/SunsetStrip/Lounge/1395/whiterabbits.html)

DISCOGRAPHY

Following is a basic U.S. albums discography of Jefferson Airplane and related artists, including spinoff groups and solo releases. It does not include singles, EPs, cassettes, samplers or items such as promotional releases, radio programs, audiophile recordings, Quadraphonic, budget compilations, bootlegs, unreleased music, guest appearances on others' recordings, collectible variations (picture discs, etc.) or any foreign releases. This discography does not distinguish between vinyl albums or CDs—most of the major recordings listed here have been released on CD at some time, somewhere in the world, but as CDs tend to go in and out of print, any attempt at an accurate survey of currently in-print CDs would be futile. Due to space limitations, the discography also does not include label or catalog number. A more comprehensive discography, including many releases and other features not included here (plus a filmography/videography), can be found at this book's website, http://www.gotarevolution.com.

JEFFERSON AIRPLANE

Original Albums

   Jefferson Airplane Takes Off (1966)

   Surrealistic Pillow (1967)

   After Bathing at Baxter's (1967)

   Crown of Creation (1968)

   Bless Its Pointed Little Head (1969)

   Volunteers (1969)

   Bark (1971)

Long John Silver (1972)

Thirty Seconds Over Winterland (1973)

Jefferson Airplane (1989)

Compilations and Other Posthumous Releases
  The Worst of Jefferson Airplane (1970)

  Early Flight (1974)

  Flight Log (1977)

  2400 Fulton Street (1987)

  White Rabbit and Other Hits (1990)

  Jefferson Airplane Loves You (1992)

  The Best of Jefferson Airplane (1993)

  Live at the Fillmore East (1998)

  The Roar of Jefferson Airplane (2001)

  Ignition (2001)

JEFFERSON STARSHIP

Original Albums
  Dragon Fly (1974)

  Red Octopus (1975)

  Spitfire (1976)

  Earth (1978)

  Freedom at Point Zero (1979)

  Modern Times (1981)

  Winds of Change (1982)

  Nuclear Furniture (1984)

  Deep Space/Virgin Sky (1995)

  Windows of Heaven (1999)

Greatest Hits Live at the Fillmore (1999)

Across the Sea of Suns (2001)

B. B. King's Blues Club 10-31-00 (2001)

Vinoy Park, St. Petersburg, FL 11-11-00 (2001)

Compilations
  Gold (1979)

  At Their Best (1992)

  Extended Versions (2000)

STARSHIP

Original Albums
  Knee Deep in the Hoopla (1985)

  No Protection (1987)

  Love Among the Cannibals (1989)

Compilations
  Greatest Hits (Ten Years and Change 1979–1991) (1991)

Jefferson Airplane/Jefferson Starship

Compilation
  36 All-Time Greatest Hits (1999)

Jefferson Airplane/Jefferson Starship/Starship

Compilations
  Hits (1998)

  Love Songs (2000)

  VH-1 Behind the Music: The Jefferson Airplane/Jefferson Starship/Starship Collection (2000)

HOT TUNA

Original Albums
  Hot Tuna (1970)

  First Pull Up, Then Pull Down (1971)

Burgers (1972)

The Phosphorescent Rat (1973)

America's Choice (1975)

Yellow Fever (1975)

Hoppkorv (1976)

Double Dose (1978)

Splashdown (1984)

Historic Hot Tuna (1985)

Pair a Dice Found (1990)

Live at Sweetwater (1992)

Live at Sweetwater Two (1993)

Classic Hot Tuna Acoustic (1996)

Classic Hot Tuna Electric (1996)

Splashdown Two (1997)

Live in Japan (1997)

And Furthurmore . . . (1999)

Compilations
    Final Vinyl (1979)

    Hot Tuna in a Can (1996)

    The Best of Hot Tuna (1998)

KBC Band
    KBC Band (1986)

SOLO ALBUMS

Marty Balin—Original Albums
w/ Bodacious D.F.
    Bodacious D.F. (1973)

Solo

    Balin (1981)

    Lucky (1983)

    Better Generation (1991)

    Freedom Flight (1997)

Compilations

    Balince (1990)

    Greatest Hits (1999)

    Marty Balin (2000)

Jack Casady w/ SVT

    No Regrets (1981)

Joey Covington

    Joe E. Covington's Fat Fandango (1973)

Craig Chaquico—Original Albums

    Acoustic Highway (1993)

    Acoustic Planet (1994)

    A Thousand Pictures (1996)

    Once in a Blue Universe (1997)

    Four Corners (1998)

    From the Redwoods to the Rockies (w/ Russ Freeman) (1998)

    Shadow and Light (2002)

Compilation

    Panorama: The Best of Craig Chaquico (2000)

Papa John Creach

    Papa John Creach (1971)

    Filthy (1972)

    Playing My Fiddle for You (w/ Zulu) (1974)

I'm the Fiddle Man (1975)

Rock Father (1976)

The Cat and the Fiddle (1977)

Inphasion (1978)

Papa Blues (1992)

Compilation
  The Best of Papa John Creach (1994)

Spencer Dryden w/ The Dinosaurs
  Dinosaurs (1988)

Bob Harvey w/ San Francisco Blue
  Idiot's Vision (2000)

Paul Kantner
  Planet Earth Rock and Roll Orchestra (1983)

  A Guide Through the Chaos (A Road to the Passion) (1996)

Paul Kantner/Jefferson Starship
  Blows Against the Empire (1970)

Paul Kantner and Grace Slick
  Sunfighter (1971)

Paul Kantner, Grace Slick and David Freiberg
  Baron Von Tollbooth & the Chrome Nun (1973)

Jorma Kaukonen
  Quah (w/ Tom Hobson) (1974)

  Jorma (1979)

  Barbeque King (w/ Vital Parts) (1980)

  Too Hot to Handle (1985)

  Magic (1985)

  Magic Two (1995)

  The Land of Heroes (1995)

  Embryonic Journey (with Tom Constanten) (1995)

Christmas (1996)

Too Many Years . . . (1998)

Blue Country Heart (2002)

W/ the Jorma Kaukonen Trio
Jorma Kaukonen Trio Live (2000)

Pete Sears
Watchfire (1988)

Millennium (1997)

The Long Haul (2001)

Grace Slick—Original Albums
Manhole (1973)

Dreams (1980)

Welcome to the Wrecking Ball (1981)

Software (1984)

Compilation
The Best of Grace Slick (1999)

The Great Society with Grace Slick
Conspicuous Only in Its Absence (1968)

How It Was (1968)

Collector's Item (1971)

Born to Be Burned (1995)

Alexander "Skip" Spence
Oar (1969)

Mickey Thomas
As Long As You Love Me (1977)

Alive Alone (1981)

GRUNT RECORDS RELEASES BY NON-AIRPLANE MEMBERS

Jack Bonus
　Jack Bonus (1972)

Peter Kaukonen
　Black Kangaroo (1972)

One
　One (1972)

Jack Traylor and Steelwind
　Child of Nature (1973)

SELECTED MISCELLANEOUS COLLECTIONS FEATURING JEFFERSON AIRPLANE MATERIAL UNAVAILABLE ELSEWHERE

　Monterey International Pop Festival (1997)

　Woodstock (1970)

　Woodstock Two (1971)

BIBLIOGRAPHY

Books – General

Amburn, Ellis. *Pearl: The Obsessions and Passions of Janis Joplin*. New York: Warner Books, 1992.

Anson, Robert Sam. *Gone Crazy and Back Again: The Rise and Fall of the Rolling Stone Generation*. Garden City, NY: Doubleday, 1981.

Anthony, Gene. *The Summer of Love: Haight-Ashbury at Its Highest*. Millbrae, CA: Celestial Arts, 1980.

Belz, Carl. *The Story of Rock*. New York: Oxford University Press, 1969.

Beran, Michael Knox. *The Last Patrician: Bobby Kennedy and the End of American Aristocracy*. New York: St. Martin's Press, 1998.

Brightman, Carol. *Sweet Chaos: The Grateful Dead's American Adventure*. New York: Clarkson Potter Publishers, 1998.

Bromell, Nick. *Tomorrow Never Knows: Rock and Psychedelics in the 1960s*. Chicago: The University of Chicago Press, 2000.

Brook, James, Carlsson, Chris and Peters, Nancy J. (editors). *Reclaiming San Francisco: History, Politics, Culture*. San Francisco: City Lights Books, 1998.

Burks, John and Hopkins, Jerry. *Groupies and Other Girls*. New York: Bantam Books, 1970.

Burt, Rob and North, Patsy. *West Coast Story*. Secaucus, NJ: Chartwell Books, 1977.

Buskin, Richard. *Inside Tracks: A First-Hand History of Popular Music from the World's Greatest Record Producers*. New York: Spike Books, 1999.

Casale, Anthony M. and Lerman, Philip. *Where Have All the Flowers Gone? The Fall and Rise of the Woodstock Generation*. Kansas City: Andrews and McMeel, 1989.

Chalmers, David. *And the Crooked Places Made Straight: The Struggle for Social Change in the 1960s*. Baltimore: The Johns Hopkins University Press, 1991.

Christgau, Robert. *Any Old Way You Choose It: Rock and Other Pop Music, 1967–1973*. Baltimore: Penguin Books, 1973.

Collier, Peter and Horowitz, David. *Destructive Generation: Second Thoughts About the '60s*. New York: Free Press Paperbacks, 1996.

Crosby, David and Bender, David. *Stand and Be Counted: Making Music, Making History*. San Francisco: HarperSanFrancisco, 2000.

Crosby, David and Gottlieb, Carl. *Long Time Gone: The Autobiography of David Crosby*. New York: Doubleday, 1988.

Curry, Jack. *Woodstock: The Summer of Our Lives*. New York: Weidenfeld & Nicolson, 1989.

Dachs, David. *Inside Pop 2*. New York: Scholastic Book Services, 1970.

Dalton, David. *Piece of My Heart: The Life, Times and Legend of Janis Joplin*. New York: St. Martin's Press, 1986.

Denselow, Robin. *When the Music's Over: The Story of Political Pop*. Winchester, MA: Faber and Faber, 1989.

DeRogatis, Jim. *Kaleidoscope Eyes: Psychedelic Rock from the '60s to the '90s*. Secaucus, NJ: Citadel Press, 1996.

Dickstein, Morris. *Gates of Eden: American Culture in the Sixties*. Cambridge, MA: Harvard University Press, 1997.

Doukas, James N. *Electric Tibet: The Rise and Fall of the San Francisco Rock Scene*. N. Hollywood: Dominion Publishing, 1969.

Draper, Robert. *Rolling Stone Magazine: The Uncensored History*. New York: Doubleday, 1990.

Echols, Alice. *Scars of Sweet Paradise: The Life and Times of Janis Joplin*. New York: Metropolitan Books, 1999.

Eisen, Jonathan, ed. *The Age of Rock: Sounds of the American Cultural Revolution*. New York: Vintage Books, 1969.

Engelhardt, Tom. *The End of Victory Culture: Cold War America and the Disillusioning of a Generation*. Amherst, MA: University of Massachusetts Press, 1995.

Farber, David, ed. *The Sixties: From Memory to History*. Chapel Hill, NC: University of North Carolina Press, 1994.

Fong-Torres, Ben. *Not Fade Away: A Backstage Pass to 20 Years of Rock & Roll*. San Francisco: Miller Freeman, 1999.

———, ed. *The Rolling Stone Rock 'n' Roll Reader*. New York: Bantam Books, 1974.

Fornatale, Peter and Mills, Joshua E. *Radio in the Television Age*. Woodstock, NY: The Overlook Press, 1980.

Frame, Pete. *Rock Family Trees*. New York: Omnibus Press, 1993.

Friedman, Myra. *Buried Alive: The Biography of Janis Joplin*. New York: William Morrow & Co., 1973.

Frum, David. *How We Got Here: The 70's—The Decade That Brought You Modern Life—For Better or Worse*. New York: Basic Books, 2000.

Gaskin, Stephen. *Amazing Dope Tales & Haight Street Flashbacks*. Summertown, TN: The Book Publishing Company, 1980.

Gitlin, Todd. *The Sixties: Years of Hope, Days of Rage*. New York: Bantam Books, 1987.

Glatt, John. *Rage & Roll: Bill Graham and the Selling of Rock.* New York: Birch Lane Press, 1993.

Gleason, Ralph J. *The Jefferson Airplane and the San Francisco Sound.* New York: Ballantine Books, 1969.

Goerner, Fred. *The Search for Amelia Earhart.* Garden City, NY, Doubleday, 1966.

Goldstein, Richard. *The Poetry of Rock.* New York: Bantam Books, 1969.

Gottlieb, Annie. *Do You Believe in Magic? The Second Coming of the 60's Generation.* New York: Times Books, 1987.

Graham, Bill and Greenfield, Robert. *Bill Graham Presents: My Life Inside Rock and Out.* New York: Doubleday, 1992.

Grogan, Emmett. *Ringolevio: A Life Played for Keeps.* New York: Citadel Underground, 1990.

Gross, Michael. *My Generation.* New York: Cliff Street Books, 2000.

Harrison, Hank. *The Dead.* Millbrae, CA: Celestial Arts, 1980.

Heinlein, Robert A. *Stranger in a Strange Land.* New York: Putnam Books, 1961.

Hicks, Michael. *Sixties Rock: Garage, Psychedelic, and Other Satisfactions.* Urbana and Chicago, IL: University of Illinois Press, 1999.

Hill, Debora. *Cuts: From a San Francisco Rock Journal.* South Bend, IN: and books, 1979.

Hoffman, Abbie. *Soon to Be a Major Motion Picture.* New York: Perigee Books, 1980.

Hofmann, Albert. *LSD, My Problem Child: Reflections on Sacred Drugs, Mysticism and Science.* Los Angeles: J. P. Tarcher, 1983.

Holzman, Jac and Daws, Gavan. *Follow the Music: The Life and High Times of Elektra Records in the Great Years of American Pop Culture.* Santa Monica, CA: FirstMedia Books, 1998.

Hopkins, Jerry, ed. *The Hippie Papers.* New York: Signet Books, 1968.

———. *The Rock Story.* New York: Signet Books, 1970.

———. *Festival!* New York: Collier Books, 1970.

Hoskyns, Barney. *Waiting for the Sun: Strange Days, Weird Scenes, and The Sound of Los Angeles.* New York: St. Martin's Press, 1996.

Isserman, Maurice and Kazin, Michael. *America Divided: The Civil War of the 1960s.* New York: Oxford University Press, 2000.

Jackson, Blair. *Garcia: An American Life.* New York: Viking, 1999.

Jones, Dylan, ed. *Meaty Beaty Big & Bouncy! Classic Rock & Pop Writing from Elvis to Oasis.* London: Hodder and Stoughton, 1996.

Kaiser, Charles. *1968 in America: Music, Politics, Chaos, Counterculture and the Shaping of a Generation.* New York: Grove Press, 1988.

Kantner, Paul. *Paul Kantner's Nicaragua Diary.* San Francisco: Little Dragon Press, 1987.

Keith, Michael C. *Voices in the Purple Haze: Underground Radio in the Sixties.* Westport, CT: Praeger Publishers, 1997.

Kostelanetz, Richard. *The Fillmore East: Reflections of Rock Theater.* New York: Schirmer Books, 1995.

Leary, Timothy. *Flashbacks: An Autobiography.* New York: G. P. Putnam's Sons, 1983.

Lee, Martin A., and Shlain, Bruce. *Acid Dreams: The Complete Social History of LSD: The CIA, the Sixties, and Beyond.* New York: Grove Press, 1985.

Mailer, Norman. *Miami and the Siege of Chicago.* New York: Signet Books, 1968.

Makower, Joel. *Woodstock: The Oral History.* New York: Dolphin/Doubleday, 1989.

Manzarek, Ray. *Light My Fire: My Life with the Doors.* New York: Putnam, 1998.

Marwick, Arthur. *The Sixties.* New York: Oxford University Press, 1998.

McDonough, Jack. *San Francisco Rock: The Illustrated History of San Francisco Rock Music.* San Francisco: Chronicle Books, 1985.

McNally, Dennis. *A Long Strange Trip: The Inside History of the Grateful Dead.* New York: Broadway Books, 2002.

Meltzer, Richard. *The Aesthetics of Rock.* New York: Something Else Press, 1970.

———. *A Whore Just Like the Rest: The Music Writings of Richard Meltzer.* New York: DaCapo, 2000.

Miller, John and Koral, Randall, eds. *White Rabbit: A Psychedelic Reader.* San Francisco: Chronicle Books, 1995.

Milton, Joyce: *Tramp: The Life of Charlie Chaplin.* New York: DaCapo Press, 1996.

Mitchell, Mitch. *Jimi Hendrix: Inside the Experience.* New York: Harmony Books, 1990.

Morrison, Joan and Morrison, Robert K. *From Camelot to Kent State.* New York: Times Books, 1987.

Moseley, Willie G. *Guitar People.* Bismarck, ND: Vintage Guitar Books, 1997.

Neer, Richard. *FM: The Rise and Fall of Rock Radio.* New York: Villard, 2001.

Newfield, Jack. *Robert Kennedy: A Memoir.* New York: E. P. Dutton & Co., 1969.

Norman, Philip. *Symphony for the Devil: The Rolling Stones Story.* New York: Linden Press, 1984.

Obst, David. *Too Good to Be Forgotten: Changing America in the '60s and '70s.* New York: John Wiley & Sons. 1998.

Opsasnick, Mark. *Capitol Rock.* Riverdale, MD: Fort Center Books, 1997.

Orloff, Katherine. *Rock 'n' Roll Woman.* Los Angeles: Nash Publishing, 1974.

Owen, Ted and Dickson, Denise. *High Art: A History of the Psychedelic Poster.* London: Sanctuary Publishing, 1999.

Palmer, Laura. *Shrapnel in the Heart: Letters and Remembrances from the Vietnam Veterans Memorial.* New York: Vintage Books, 1988.

Passman, Arnold. *The Deejays.* New York: Macmillan, 1971.

Payne, J. Gregory. *Mayday: Kent State.* Dubuque, IA: Kendall/Hunt, 1981.

Peck, Abe. *Uncovering the Sixties: The Life & Times of the Underground Press.* New York: Pantheon Books, 1985.

Perry, Charles. *The Haight-Ashbury: A History.* New York: Vintage Books, 1985.

Perry, Charles and Miles, Barry, Henke, James with Puterbaugh, Parke, eds. in *I Want to Take You Higher: The Psychedelic Era 1965–1969.* San Francisco: Chronicle Books, 1997.

Pierce, J. Kingston. *San Francisco, You're History!* Seattle: Sasquatch Books, 1995.

Riordan, James and Prochnicky, Jerry. *Break on Through: The Life and Death of Jim Morrison.* New York: William Morrow and Co., 1991.

Robinson, Richard. *Pop, Rock, and Soul.* New York: Pyramid Books, 1972.

Rocco, John, ed. *Dead Reckonings: The Life and Times of the Grateful Dead.* New York: Schirmer Books, 1999.

Rolling Stone, The Editors of, *The Rolling Stone Interviews 1967–1980.* New York: Rolling Stone Press/St. Martin's Press, 1981.

Rosenman, Joel, Roberts, John and Pilpel, Robert. *Young Men with Unlimited Capital.* New York: Bantam, 1989.

Roszak, Theodore. *The Making of a Counterculture.* Berkeley and Los Angeles: University of California Press, 1995.

Rothschild, Amalie R. *Live at the Fillmore East: A Photographic Memoir.* New York: Thunder's Mouth Press, 1999.

Rowes, Barbara. *Grace Slick: The Biography.* Garden City, NY: Doubleday, 1980.

Sander, Ellen. *Trips: Rock Life in the Sixties.* New York: Charles Scribner's Sons, 1973.

Santelli, Robert. *Aquarius Rising: The Rock Festival Years.* New York: Dell Publishing Co., 1980.

Sayre, Nora. *Sixties Going on Seventies.* New Brunswick, NJ: Rutgers University Press, 1996.

Sculatti, Gene and Seay, Davin. *San Francisco Nights: The Psychedelic Music Trip 1965–1968.* New York: St. Martin's Press, 1985.

Selvin, Joel. *Monterey Pop.* San Francisco: Chronicle Books, 1992.

———. *Summer of Love: The Inside Story of LSD, Rock & Roll, Free Love and High Times in the Wild West.* New York: Dutton, 1994.

Shapiro, Harry and Glebbeek, Caesar. *Jimi Hendrix: Electric Gypsy.* New York: St. Martin's Press, 1990.

Shaw, Greg. *The Doors on the Road.* New York: Omnibus Press, 1997.

Slaven, Neil. *Zappa: Electric Don Quixote.* London: Omnibus Press, 1996.

Slick, Darby. *Don't You Want Somebody to Love: Reflections on the San Francisco Sound.* Berkeley: SLG Books, 1991.

Slick, Grace and Cagan, Andrea. *Somebody to Love?* New York: Warner Books, 1998.

Sloman, Larry. *Steal This Dream: Abbie Hoffman and the Countercultural Revolution in America.* New York: Doubleday, 1998.

Smith, Joe. *Off the Record: An Oral History of Popular Music.* New York: Warner Books, 1988.

Spitz, Robert Stephen. *Barefoot in Babylon: The Creation of the Woodstock Music Festival, 1969*. New York: The Viking Press, 1979.

Stern, Jane and Michael. *Sixties People*. New York: Alfred A. Knopf, 1990.

Street-Porter, Tim (photographer). *Musical Houses: Homes and Secret Retreats of Music Stars*. Philadelphia: Running Press, 1980.

Szatmary, David. *A Time to Rock: A Social History of Rock 'n' Roll*. New York: Schirmer Books, 1996.

Taylor, Derek. *It Was Twenty Years Ago Today*. New York: Fireside Books, 1987.

Walley, David: *Teenage Nervous Breakdown: Music and Politics in the Post-Elvis Age*. New York: Plenum Press, 1998.

Wenner, Jann S., ed. *Twenty Years of* Rolling Stone: *What a Long, Strange Trip It's Been*. New York: Friendly Press, 1987.

Williams, Paul. *Outlaw Blues*. New York: Pocket Books, 1970.

Wolfe, Tom. *The Electric Kool-Aid Acid Test*. New York: Farrar, Straus and Giroux, 1968.

Wyndham, John. *The Chrysalids*. New York: Carroll & Graf, 1955.

Zimmer, Dave. *Crosby, Stills & Nash: The Authorized Biography*. New York: St. Martin's Press, 1984.

Books–Reference

Brooks, Tim and Marsh, Earle. *The Complete Directory to Prime Time Network and Cable TV Shows 1946–Present*, sixth edition. New York: Ballantine Books, 1995.

Ehrenstein, David and Reed, Bill. *Rock on Film*. New York: Delilah Books, 1982.

Fein, Art. *The L.A. Musical History Tour*, second edition. Los Angeles: 2-13-61 Publications, 1998.

George-Warren, Holly, ed. *The Rolling Stone Encyclopedia of Rock & Roll*, third edition. New York: Fireside, 2001.

Getz, Michael and Dwork, John R. *The Deadhead's Taping Compendium, Volume 1, 1959–1974*. New York: Owl Books, 1998.

Grushkin, Paul D. *The Art of Rock*. New York: Abbeville Press, 1987.

Hansen, Gladys. *San Francisco Almanac: Everything You Want to Know About Everyone's Favorite City*. San Francisco: Chronicle Books, 1995.

Katz, Ephraim. *The Film Encyclopedia*. New York: Perigee Books, 1979.

King, Eric. *The Collector's Guide to Psychedelic Rock Concert Posters, Postcards and Handbills 1965–1973, Volume. 1*. Berkeley: Svaha Press, 1996.

Lemke, Gary. *The Art of the Fillmore 1966–1971*. Petaluma, CA: Acid Test Productions, 1997.

MacLean, Hugh and Joynson, Vernon. *An American Rock History Part One: California—The Golden State*. Telford, England: Borderline Productions, 1987.

Maltin, Leonard. *Movie & Video Guide, 2000 Edition.* New York: Signet Books, 2000.

Muirhead, Bert. *The Record Producers File: A Directory of Rock Album Producers, 1962–1984.* Dorset, UK: Blandford Press, 1984.

Olsen, Eric, Verna, Paul and Wolff, Carlo. *The Encyclopedia of Record Producers.* New York: Billboard Books, 1999.

Scott, John W., Dolgushkin, Mike and Nixon, Stu. *DeadBase XI: The Complete Guide to Grateful Dead Song Lists.* Cornish, NH: DeadBase, 1999.

Selvin, Joel. *San Francisco: The Musical History Tour.* San Francisco: Chronicle Books, 1996.

Umphred, Neal. *Goldmine's Price Guide to Collectible Record Albums,* fourth edition. Iola, WI: Krause Publications, 1994.

———. *Goldmine's Rock'n Roll 45 RPM Record Price Guide,* third edition. Iola, WI: Krause Publications, 1994.

Whitburn, Joel. *Billboard Hot 100 Charts: The Sixties.* Menomonee Falls, WI: Record Research Inc., 1990.

———. *Billboard Hot 100 Charts: The Seventies.* Menomonee Falls, WI: Record Research Inc., 1990.

———. *Billboard Hot 100 Charts: The Eighties.* Menomonee Falls, WI: Record Research Inc., 1991.

———. *Billboard Pop Album Charts: 1965–1969.* Menomonee Falls, WI: Record Research Inc., 1993.

———. *Top Pop Albums: 1955–2001.* Menomonee Falls, WI: Record Research Inc., 2001.

———. *Top Pop Singles: 1955–1999.* Menomonee Falls, WI: Record Research Inc., 2000.

Williams, Fred. *The 1996 Rock Poster Price Guide,* second edition. Salt Lake City: Dallas Design Group, 1995.

Magazines/Newspapers

Selected issues of:

After Dark, BAM, Bay Guardian, Beat, Beetle, Berkeley Barb, Billboard, Boston Globe, Cavalier, Circus, CMJ, Crawdaddy!, Cream Puff War, Creem, Dark Star, Discoveries, Down Beat, East Village Other, Eye, Go, Goldmine, Good Times, Grinnell College Scarlet & Black, Guitar Player, Guitar World, Hit Parader, Holding Together, Hullabaloo, International Music and Recording World, Jazz & Pop, Life, Living Blues, Look, Los Angeles Daily News, Los Angeles Free Press, Los Angeles Times, Melody Maker, Modern Drummer, Modern Recording & Music, Mojo, Mojo Navigator Rock & Roll News, Music

& Sound Output, New Musical Express, New York Daily News, New York Times, New York Times Magazine, Newsweek, Oui, Philadelphia Inquirer, Pop/Rock Music, Ramparts, Record Collector, Relix, Rock, Rolling Stone, San Francisco Chronicle, San Francisco Examiner, San Francisco Oracle, Sing Out, Song Hits, Songwriter's Review, Sounds, Spin, Stereo Review, Teenset, Time, Toronto Star, Trouser Press, Vancouver Sun, Village Voice, Vintage Guitar, Zoo World

Miscellaneous

Blasi, Gianluigi (Johnny). *Jefferson Airplane: We Are All One.* Italy: Sonic Book 3, 1996 (CD insert).

INDEX

7/09   10   10/07